Production Planning and Control with SAP®

 PRESS

SAP PRESS is a joint initiative of SAP and Galileo Press. The know-how offered by SAP specialists combined with the expertise of the publishing house Galileo Press offers the reader expert books in the field. SAP PRESS features first-hand information and expert advice, and provides useful skills for professional decision-making.

SAP PRESS offers a variety of books on technical and business related topics for the SAP user. For further information, please visit our website: *www.sap-press.com.*

Jochen Balla, Frank Layer
Production Planning with SAP APO-PP/DS
2007, 336 pp., ISBN 978-1-59229-113-7

Marc Hoppe
Sales and Inventory Planning with SAP APO
2007, 440 pp., ISBN 978-1-59229-123-6

Marc Hoppe
Inventory Optimization with SAP
2006, 483 pp., ISBN 978-1-59229-097-0

Martin Murray
Understanding the SAP Logistics Information System
2007, 328 pp., ISBN 978-1-59229-108-3

D. Rajen Iyer
Effective SAP SD
2007, 365 pp., ISBN 978-1-59229-101-4

Sachin Sethi
Enhancing Supplier Relationship Management Using SAP SRM
2007, 695 pp., ISBN 978-1-59229-068-0

Jörg Thomas Dickersbach, Gerhard Keller, Klaus Weihrauch

Production Planning and Control with SAP®

Galileo Press

Bonn • Boston

ISBN   978-1-59229-106-9

1st edition 2007
1st reprint, with corrections 2008

Editor Frank Paschen
Translation Lemoine International, Inc., Salt Lake City, UT
Copy Editor John Parker, UCG, Inc., Boston, MA
Cover Design Silke Braun
Layout Design Vera Brauner
Production Steffi Ehrentraut
Typesetting SatzPro, Krefeld
Printed and bound in Germany

Contents at a Glance

Contents

11 Capacity Requirements Planning 337

12 Production Execution 379

Foreword to the Second Edition

Just over five years have passed since the first edition of this book was published. Far-reaching changes have taken place since then, both within SAP and in the markets. New technological developments in the area of service-oriented architecture will continue to increase the flexibility and, thus, the freedom that enterprises enjoy.

At the same time, the hype surrounding the "New Economy," which was triggered by the rise of the Internet, has settled down to more realistic levels; the main issue now is how enterprises can successfully maintain their position in ever-changing global markets. Germany, in particular, is traditionally a production center and is still intensively involved in this area. An increasingly important requirement now is to use intelligent services to expand this strength and maintain competitiveness.

Another challenge is to successfully manage the agility bred by today's market and the potential flexibility enabled by technology, such as Web services. The many functions required and the parameterization made possible by SAP systems do not make this management task an easy one. The goal here is to structure business administration in a way that supports and enhances its function as a stabilizing entity.

For this reason, we have re-designed the structure of this book in its second edition, orienting it to the processes of production planning and production control. In doing so, we hope to make it easier for the reader to understand the progression from the business administration tasks to the processes in the SAP system and their configuration. The process modules are intended to help the reader analyze and manage complex enterprise structures from top to bottom. It is to be hoped that future developments will also be geared towards these structures, and that enterprises will thus benefit from a stabilizing entity in an ever-changing environment.

There is no limit to the complexity of production planning and production control, especially when it comes to illustrating difficult production processes. Therefore, in this book, we have purposely restricted ourselves in our illustrations to a straightforward (hypothetical) example based on the production of air-conditioning systems. Although this example of discrete manufacturing is a straightforward one, this edition presents it in detail, including its customizing. We explain the functions of production planning and production control in SAP ERP much more comprehensively and in greater detail than we did the first edition.

Dr. Jörg Thomas Dickersbach and **Dr. Gerhard Keller**

This introduction provides an overview of the goals, target readership, structure, and necessary restrictions of this book.

1 Introduction

1.1 Goal

The goal of this book is to present and explain the basic processes of production planning and production control with SAP ERP. These processes are presented to the reader on the following three levels:

- **Business administration**
  Our explanations of the business administration background are not limited to an overview of the production planning and production control processes. Process overview diagrams and document flow diagrams for each individual process are used to show the steps in the process, how the steps are related to each other and to adjacent processes, and the reasons for taking the steps. We provide only explanations here; recommendations for modeling and parameterizing the processes are beyond the scope of this book.

- **Application**
  Screenshots are used widely throughout to illustrate the processes step by step. SAP ERP 6.0 is the system release used for the screenshots. The parameters and transactions in question are specified.

- **Configuration**
  In cases where a configuration is required for a process step, or where a configuration triggers a process change, the most common options are explained using screenshots and customizing transactions or customizing paths.

This book focuses on the most straightforward scenario in discrete manufacturing, where the process steps are taken in the usual order and where there are no special cases, such as production steps requiring complex modeling or special forms of procurement (see

Section 1.4). We believe that an understanding of the straightforward case is a good basis for using and implementing the SAP Production Planning (PP) module.

1.2 Target Audience

This book is intended for all readers who use production planning and production control with SAP ERP, whether they are project leaders or project team members in an implementation, or work on the operational level in industry as production planners or production controllers. Because the book comprises the three levels mentioned above—business administration, application, and configuration—it is suitable for all the following groups: beginners; students of industrial management, industrial engineering, or information management specializing in business administration; users of other PPS systems, and consultants and advanced users.

1.3 Structure and Content

This book provides a thorough overview of the fundamentals of production planning and production control with the SAP ERP system. **Chapter 2**, *Tasks in Industrial Operations*, presents in detail the business administration basis of production planning and production control in the context of industrial operations. **Chapter 3**, *Production Planning and Control in SAP ERP*, describes how the SAP *Production Planning (PP)* module fits into the SAP ERP system, and gives an overview of the processes in production planning and production control in SAP PP.

Chapter 4, *Organizational Structures*, and **Chapter 5**, *Master Data*, describe the basic requirements for mapping production planning and production control in SAP ERP.

In the subsequent chapters, a sample scenario—the production of air-conditioning systems—is used to illustrate a straightforward case. Each of these chapters describes a specific process, as follows:

▸ Sales and Operations Planning (**Chapter 6**)

▸ Demand Management (**Chapter 7**)

- Material Requirements Planning (**Chapter 8**)

- Long-Term Planning (**Chapter 9**)

- Production Order Creation (**Chapter 10**)

- Capacity Requirements Planning (**Chapter 11**)

- Production Execution (**Chapter 12**)

Chapter 13, *Supply Chain Management and Integration with SAP APO*, outlines the potential for using supply chain management and integrating it with SAP Advanced Planner and Optimizer (APO), and presents a number of different integration scenarios.

The book concludes with a comprehensive **Glossary** containing production planning and production control terms, and lists of **Transactions** and **Abbreviations**.

1.4   Restrictions

In this book, we concentrate on the core processes of production planning and production control. We purposely do not cover the entire scope of the powerful and complex SAP ERP production planning and production control functions. The following list provides an overview of the functions that we do not deal with, or deal with only briefly.

- **Special forms of procurement**
  Special business requirements are handled by means of special forms of procurement, which enable planning that is different from the norm. The following are examples of special forms of procurement.

  - **Direct production**
    When an order for a saleable product is created, orders are also created directly for the components. These orders are clearly assigned to each other and together represent an order network.

  - **Production in another plant**
    Planning and production take place in different plants. Thus, planning for multiple plants can be carried out in a single planning plant.

▶ **Withdrawal from another plant**
A component is withdrawn from another plant without the need for transportation processing between the plants.

▶ **Phantom assemblies**
A group of materials can represent a logical assembly without actually being assembled on a daily basis. A set of car tires or a spoiler with fixing elements are examples of phantom assemblies.

▶ **MRP areas**
MRP (material requirements planning) areas can be used to carry out separate material requirements planning within a plant (for example, for spare parts).

▶ **Change management**
A change-management system is intended for frequent technical changes that in some cases will not occur until some point in the future, both for the *bill of material* and *routing* master data, and for production orders.

▶ **Variant configuration**
In make-to-order production, saleable products are often configured to the customer's individual requirements. Examples are cars, specialized machines, and computers. The whole area of variant configuration, which also has a significant effect on sales, is not dealt with in this book. For further information on this subject, see Dickersbach 2005a.

▶ **Shop floor information system**
The *logistics information system* (LIS) enables you to create comprehensive reports relating to production. In this book, we provide only a rough outline of these functions.

▶ **Integration with quality assurance and warehouse management**
Some aspects of the production planning functions are related to quality assurance (inspection lots, for example) and warehouse management.

▶ **Distribution resource planning**
SAP PP contains very restricted functions for cross-plant planning.

Section 3.3 describes production types other than discrete manufacturing (albeit in less detail): repetitive manufacturing, process manufacturing, kanban, and engineer-to-order.

Production planning and production control do not take place in a vacuum; they are based on real, specific tasks that are completed in industrial operations contexts. This chapter presents in detail the business administration basis of production planning and production control.

2 Tasks in Industrial Operations

2.1 Technical Tasks

2.1.1 Development and Design

When a product comes into existence, it does so on the basis of the needs of an individual or a group of persons. The starting-point of the development of a new product is to determine the functions that the product will have. These functions are derived from the requirements that the product is intended to fulfill. After the general principles of the new product are worked out, the product-design process begins, during which the first creative designs are drawn up, and the drawings are created. A large part of the data volume required for the whole process chain (geometry data, for example) is defined at this point.

Design process

While the focus in classic CAD (Computer Aided Design) systems is mainly on creating drawings, modern CAD systems also support integration requirements, incorporating production planning systems (PPS) and databases as well as the whole design process. In the design process, the design documents are created step by step on the basis of a pre-defined task set. These documents then form the basis of the subsequent production process. The design process is defined in accordance with Association of German Engineers (VDI) guideline 2223, as follows: "Design is the process of conceiving technical products, identifying their functional and structural composition, and creating production-level documents. This process is a chiefly creative one, is based on knowledge and experience, and strives to achieve optimal solutions." (see Kühn, 1980)

The design process is made up of an irregular series of heuristic and algorithmic activities; in other words, some of the tasks in question are mainly creative ones, while others are based on conventional logic and thus can be represented in a schema.

Product design The key orientation point is the progress of the work. The most important phases are planning, conception, design, and finalizing. While the conception, design, and finalizing phases are usually executed exclusively in the product design or design department, the planning phase is often taken on by other departments. Which department triggers the product design process depends on various factors, such as the type of order placement. If a customer places the development order directly with the enterprise, the planning phase is very often executed in the sales department. If, on the other hand, the enterprise is developing the product for an intended market, the initiative usually comes from the market-research team.

Product specification When the planning phase ends and the order is approved, the conception phase begins. In this phase, the task set is first clarified and documented in the form of the requirements list, also known as the product specification. This list contains fixed and minimum technical requirements, requests, budget, and deadlines. Next, the overall function is divided up and formulated on the abstract level. The process of working out the general principles is another component of the conception phase. In this process, alternative working principles, which are intended to support the completion of tasks, are defined for the various functional principles that are defined in the functional phase. Then, a special solution principle is defined on the basis of technical and financial criteria.

An initial full-scale design is then created on the basis of this solution principle. The working principles are fleshed out using established design and calculation procedures and a value analysis. At the same time, any technical and financial weaknesses that may have originated in the conception phase are removed at this point. For example, if the cost aspects of the product creation process are a major concern, cost-relevant product issues will be examined. The result—that is, the "cleaned-up" design—contains all the solution components required for problem-solving.

Once the optimal design has been created, the next step is to work out detailed design documents, both for the whole product and the individual components. These documents include design drawings, design bills of material, and design-specific instructions for production. In many companies, a prototype very close to the production solution is often created before these documents are released. This prototype then can be used to test the technical functionality and financial feasibility of the product (see Pahl/Beitz, 1986, pp. 47–56).

Design

The individual design phases do not follow along strictly from one to the next. Depending on the circumstances of the individual design process, it often may be necessary to re-visit previous phases. We can therefore regard the design process as a series of iterative loops in which the degree of circularity depends on external conditions, such as how clear the customer is about its product requirements.

Design phases

In many design processes, it is not necessary to complete all the standard design phases. It is often possible to simply refer to existing documents. To restrict the scope of the existing information used, and thus to be able to estimate as accurately as possible the work required to create the design documents, it has become common practice in the industry to classify design projects according to design types.

DIN guideline VDI 2210 specifies the following design types:

▸ Original design
▸ Adaptive design
▸ Variant design
▸ Design with clear principle

Original design refers to designs in which the components are not based on any existing models or templates; the design is developed gradually during the process. In principle, original designs are concerned only with the functions specified in the requirements list. In this case, all four phases of the design process must be completed.

Original design

Adaptive design can be regarded as an intermediary phase between original design and variant design. An adaptive design is often derived from a predecessor, which it resembles in certain respects. With this kind of design, geometric changes generally apply to both the dimensions and the structure of the geometric characteristics.

Adaptive design

Individual elements are modified in accordance with their form and function while the underlying configuration of the elements remains the same. Another way of describing the adaptive type of design is as a known solution principle that is adapted to suit a modified set of tasks.

Variant design A characteristic feature of *variant design* is that the solution principle for certain variants stays the same; that is, the geometry elements of the variants contain the same structure. With this kind of design, the structural phase and the detail phase are mandatory. Depending on the complexity and degree of detail of the standard parts, variant construction is also known as assembly-menu technology for relatively complex parts, and as geometry parameterization for relatively simple parts.

Design with clear principle The VDI gives the following definition of *design with clear principle* (VDI, 1975, p. 12): "A design is considered to be a design with clear principle if the functional structure, order, and form of all elements are fixed and only the dimension of all or individual elements are modified." It is thus different from variant design in that the form is not modified. Because variant design does not necessarily modify the form, design with clear principle can be regarded as an extreme, special case of variant design. The main task in the case of design with clear principle is to set dimensions for the individual parts.

Establishing functions In the development and design phases, the main tasks, besides establishing the functions and carrying out the relevant physical calculations, are describing the objects, creating the drawings and bills of material, carrying out the administration tasks necessary for development and design, and gathering information. The time and effort involved in these tasks depend heavily on the complexity of the product and the degree of product standardization. The results of the development and design activities are the drawing(s) and their technical descriptions (product specifications), and the design bill of material (BOM). The production BOM and the routing are created on the basis of this data. Figure 2.1 shows the central tasks of the development and design phases.

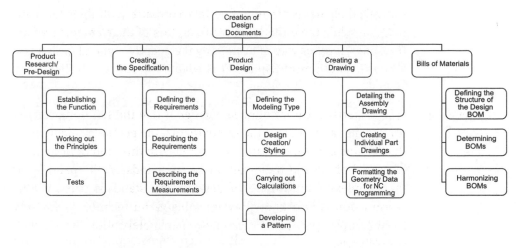

Figure 2.1 Tasks in the Development and Design Phases

2.1.2 Work Scheduling

The *routing* describes the transformation of a component from its raw to its finished state. The aim is to convert the product information specified in the development and design phase into instructions for the production and assembly phases. The basis of the routing can be materials or, in the case of assembly-based activities, previously produced assemblies or individual components. The routing specifies the steps in the work process and the order in which they are taken to produce the component. Also, production procedures, operating resources, and capacity requirements are assigned to the process steps. The process of creating a routing includes the completion of the following tasks (see Eversheim 1989, pp. 30–55):

Routing

▸ Determining the original component

▸ Determining the order of steps in the work process

▸ Selecting machines

▸ Assigning production resources and tools (PRTs)

▸ Determining standard times

Similarly to the planning phases in the development and design phases, the task of creating the routing from the scheduling viewpoint can be subdivided as follows:.

Creating the routing

▸ Regenerative planning

▸ Adaptive planning

- ▶ Variant planning

- ▶ Repeat planning

The degree to which existing documents can be used is a characteristic of these types. The support provided by efficient routing management plays an important role here. Depending on the type and scope of the tasks, follow-on tasks can be generated that involve a considerable amount of document-creation work.

Repeat planning can be used in cases where the component is identical to an existing component. With *variant planning*, the planned component has similarities with an existing component. In this case, a routing that largely corresponds to the standards can be generated and parameterized (if the task is to create component families, for example). In the case of *adaptive planning*, a core routing determines the logical structure of the overall routing. In *regenerative planning*, the result of the PRT determination process is often that new functions have to be developed and built, and thus routings have to be created and produced. For this reason, the resources department is often its own production department within an enterprise.

As already mentioned, there are differences between creating a production routing and an assembly routing. The primary goal of a *production routing* is to modify the form of a component so that it fulfills its future function. *Assembly routing*, on the other hand, is concerned with combining individual components to form assemblies (pre-assembly) and/or to combine assemblies to form complex end-products (final assembly). Thus, the degree of complexity of an assembly routing is determined by the level of standardization of the end product.

Resources planning

Resources planning is of special significance in the creation of production documents. This process includes all the resources that are required to create the product, such as machines, tools, and equipment. A key issue is whether the enterprise has its own internal resources department where tools and equipment are produced and maintained, or whether the resources are procured externally on the market. In the former case, there is a close relationship between the planning and production departments and the resources department, and in the latter case, between the enterprise and the supplier. The complexity of these interrelationships depends on the degree of complexity and standardization of the product—and, in this case, of the tools and equipment in particular—and is the same for both internal and external procurement. In all cases, the main thing is that the company has the expertise in producing tools and equipment, or that the business partner (supplier) has this expertise.

Machinery is usually procured on the market. The level of interaction with the supplier in this case depends very much on whether the machine in question is a standard product or an individually commissioned, customer-specific machine. In all cases, the complexity of the product is high.

Regardless of the procurement type used to procure resources—that is, internally within the company or externally on the market—the value of the resources means that the tasks of requirements planning, procurement, and administration have to be carried out for all resources. While tasks that relate to tools and equipment objects are short-term or mid-term planning and procurement tasks, the planning and procurement of machinery tends to be a mid-term to long-term task. Administration functions should always be included in your planning, as archived resources are an important basis for creating production documents in daily operations. Figure 2.2 shows the tasks involved in work scheduling.

Procurement type

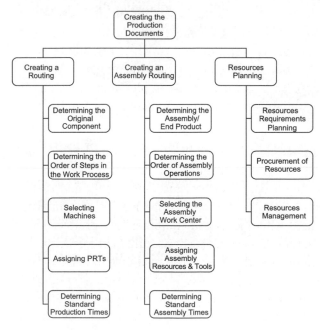

Figure 2.2 Work Scheduling Tasks

2.1.3   Programming

NC programming   Some authors include programming in their work scheduling. The increasing number of companies with Numeric Control (NC) machine tools is resulting in differences between this kind of work scheduling and conventional work scheduling, and changed requirements for both humans and machines. For these reasons, we will dedicate a special section to this subject.

In conventional production, production equipment is controlled by human beings. In computer-controlled systems, NC machines and robots are created by programs, which in turn are created by human beings. These programs contain instructions for the movement and operating functions. The tool paths are controlled using the contours and surfaces of the components. This results in differences in comparison with conventional routing creation, both in terms of the type of data preparation and data transfer.

The documents that are created in the development and design phases are the basis for the creation of an NC program. The first decision to be made is whether the programs will be created manually or with the aid of computers, taking into account the available machine facilities. The production procedure and the machine tool to be used are also determined at this point. The following three main tasks have to be completed for all types of programming:

▸ Calculating geometric quantities

▸ Defining technical data (defining process sequence, choosing tools, calculating tool path)

▸ Encrypting information and creating control program

Manual programming   With *manual programming*, the data that is relevant for the NC program is calculated, encrypted, and transferred to lists on the basis of the documents that are available in conventional form. For example, the component geometry of the design drawing has to be enlarged in accordance with the scale used to determine tangent intersection points for the NC program. The data of the control program that is created in list form is then input to the control function, either manually or by means of an external data carrier, such as floppy disk or magnetic tape.

Computer Aided Programming can reduce the work required in creating an NC program, because the program carries out the geometric calculations and the NC control data is thus generated automatically. The goal is to create the program so that it is as independent as possible of any specific machine tool.

Unlike conventional work scheduling, computer aided systems allow you to make available to the NC program the data created in the CAD system without the need to re-input this data. However, in many cases, the format of the geometric data generated in the CAD system cannot be used directly in the NC program. Thus, the sectional drawings, for example, have to be specially prepared for use in the NC program. Besides the geometric data of the component, the description of the component and the technical data required for creating the NC program are also very important. Also, different types of interfaces have emerged in practice, which depend on the geometrical complexity and production procedures. The interface, in turn, affects the ways in which the program can be structured organizationally.

Precisely calculating the work and time involved requires more than consideration of the similarities between geometries; that is, the similarities between components and tools. The calculation also must include the geometric complexity—what can be described analytically vs. what cannot be described analytically—and the available work procedures. Because the functionality of NC programming very often depends on the production machines, the machine facilities have to be regarded as a restricting factor in this type of programming.

The work steps in robot programming are similar to those in NC programming, as the same control principle is used in both cases. Before creating the program itself, we first need to determine the programming type. With online programming, the control program is created at the robot itself, with the result that the robot cannot function during programming. With offline programming, the control program is created on a computer that is separate from the robot. Next, the motion sequence of the robot needs to be determined and the work process synchronized.

Computer Aided Programming

Programming robots

The main difference between online and offline programming—
other than the different locations of the programming work—is that
with online programming the processes of creating and testing the
program are carried out step by step. The program is then checked in
a test run using the robot. Once collisions have been re-programmed
and time-coordination problems removed, the final control program
is complete. A frequently used procedure in online programming is
called the *teach-in procedure*. In this procedure, the propulsive force
of the machines is used to calculate the track systems of the robot
from interpolation points entered via manual control. The temporal
motion sequence is fixed by manually entering speed and motion
parameters. Once the motion is defined, the kinetic data is stored in
the accumulator control. In the *playback procedure*, the robot arm is
manually moved to the required interpolation points, the points are
stored, and the motion path is then calculated from the individual
points. The temporal motion path is determined by the manually
controlled movement of the robot arm (see Kief, 1989, pp. 351–356;
Rembold, 1990, pp. 143–145).

Offline programming supports the programmer more effectively, as
textual programming languages and interactive graphical programming can be used. This means that many tests that originally had to
be carried out directly at the robot can now be run in advance, which
significantly reduces the amount of work involved.

As with NC programming, geometry and production technology are
significant influencing factors in robot programming. Along with the
actual product geometry, the motion geometry of the robot, which is
affected by the product geometry, is an important consideration in
the type of programming. Online programming makes financial
sense if the level of product complexity is not very high. If the complexity level is high, on the other hand, online programming
involves a lot of work and thus means that the robot cannot function
for long periods. Likewise, online programming is not recommended if many different products are produced, as the constant set-
ups again mean that the robot is frequently out of action. Figure 2.3
shows the main programming tasks.

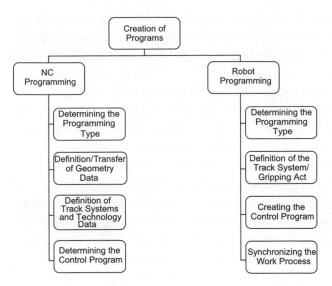

Figure 2.3 Programming Tasks

2.1.4 Quality Management

Quality management increasingly involves more than simply checking the product after it is produced; it is now a planning-oriented and forecasting-oriented quality assurance concept that applies to the whole production process. It is also concerned with ensuring the technical safety of the product and its suitability for use by the customer. The goal of quality assurance is to define quality requirements in conjunction with the customer, and then to ensure that these requirements are met in the process of creating the product.

Section 11 of the DIN 55350 standard divides the tasks of quality assurance into the areas of quality planning, quality control, and quality inspection. *Quality planning* includes all tasks having to do with selecting, classifying, and weighting quality characteristics, and determining the relevant inspection characteristics for measuring the degree of fulfillment of customer requirements or product requirements. *Quality control* uses the results of the quality inspection to monitor the degree of compliance with quality standards and, if necessary, to implement appropriate corrective measures.

Quality planning and control

This section focuses on the operational tasks of quality management; in other words, *quality inspection*. The quality inspection process should plan and execute the inspection of the product, record the

Quality inspection

results of the inspection, and analyze the results in light of the original requirements. DIN Special Report 15 (see DIN 1987) divides the quality inspection process into the following tasks: inspection planning, inspection execution, inspection data analysis, and inspection order control. The tasks of inspection planning are particularly important when it comes to preparing the relevant documents for quality inspection in production and assembly. The initial data required for creating an inspection plan are the product specification, the drawing, and the routing. Thus, the development team is involved in determining the maximum quality requirements; the design team specifies the dimension data for the inspections, and the work scheduling team defines the requirements in terms of PRTs and inspection processes. Quality inspection thus represents the link between quality requirements and quality compliance.

We will now explain the inspection plan creation, inspection equipment planning, and inspection plan execution sub-tasks.

Inspection plan creation

First, we have to define the inspection characteristics. Starting with the documents that are already available, such as specification, design drawings, BOMs, production plan, and order documents, the required documents are extracted and checked for correctness. Characteristics that need to be inspected are the physical and geometric properties, completeness, appearance, and product functionality. In the process of creating the inspection specification we will define the inspection characteristics and their nominal values, as well as the procedure that will be used in the inspection. The inspection instructions describe the inspection procedure for every inspection characteristic. Besides the type of procedure, this description also details the quantity of samples, the permitted share of defects per sample, and the interval between two inspections, among other things. The inspection drawing marks the points to be inspected on the object. The process of creating the drawing allows you to establish—prior to the production start—such factors as whether the geometric elements of the inspection object will hinder the inspection. The inspection schedule creation process also aims to optimize the temporal and logical sequence of inspection steps for every inspection characteristic, and thus defines the individual inspection times. The last step is to assign the inspection to a central auditing department or a production work center. The standard times for the inspection will need to be defined for this purpose, in accordance with the location and type of the inspection.

Because the product specification, drawings, and routing are prerequisites for creating the inspection plans, the process of creating an order-specific inspection plan also can be divided into the regenerative, adaptive, variant, and repeat inspection-plan classes. In other words, it can also be described in terms of the degree of product standardization.

Planning and inspecting the product are not the only methods of assuring product quality. The trends toward stricter standards and increased guarantee requirements, manufacturer liability, and inspection costs mean that besides creating inspection instructions and executing the inspection, planning the inspection equipment has become a central task. Because the quality of the inspection equipment changes due to wear and tear, and this quality can affect the accuracy of the quality measurements, it is necessary to also monitor the quality of the inspection equipment. Also, in the inspection planning stage, you have to ensure that the planned inspection equipment is available at the time of the inspection. The goal of planning inspection equipment requirements is therefore to ensure that the required inspection equipment, and the right type and quantity of this equipment, are available for any production inspections, goods receipt inspections, and goods issue inspections that are to be carried out.

Inspection equipment planning

One thing that is required for this planning process is an overview of the available inspection equipment; another is up-to-date inspection plans for the products to be inspected. The requirements in terms of quality suitability and inspection equipment precision are also specified in the inspection equipment requirements-planning process. The inspection equipment procurement process then ensures that the required inspection equipment is available in time for the inspection. This process is thus responsible for procuring new inspection equipment and for providing replacement inspection equipment without affecting the timing of the inspection. If new inspection tasks are to be carried out, design drawings may have to be created for these tasks.

Like the object to be inspected, the quality of the inspection equipment also has to be ensured and monitored. The first step in *inspection equipment monitoring* with new inspection equipment is the *suit-*

Inspection equipment monitoring

31

ability test. This test defines whether the equipment in question meets the requirements. If necessary, the measuring equipment is calibrated and adjusted at this point, and an acceptance findings report is created for every piece of inspection equipment submitted for testing. Next, the inspection equipment is labeled so that it can be identified, and the inspection result is uniquely assigned to the inspection equipment. Besides analyzing the inspection equipment at a specific point in time, the performance of the equipment also needs to be monitored over the duration of the inspection. To do this, an inspection history is generated for the inspection equipment. This history documents the life cycle of the equipment to date, and records the times and results of suitability tests, changes and repairs, and the storage data and sample removal data in each case. The data stored in the inspection history is also used as a central information resource for inspection equipment requirements planning and procurement, and for creating inspection plans. Figure 2.4 shows the tasks involved in quality inspection.

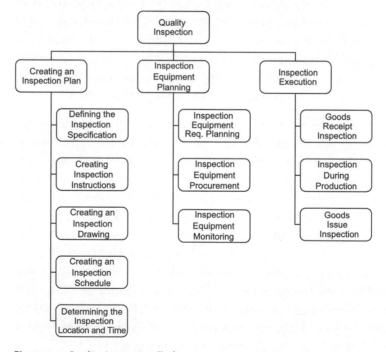

Figure 2.4 Quality Inspection Tasks

2.1.5 Production Execution

In production, two things happen. The technical information (see Section 2.1) and the business information (see Section 2.2) of the industrial operations are combined, and the flows of information and material within the physical product creation process merge.

The areas that precede production focus mainly on structuring the information flow of sales, purchasing, materials management, development, work scheduling, production planning, and so on, and making the most consistent and low-redundancy use possible of shared basic data, such as bills of material, routings, production resources, and work centers (see Chapter 5, *Master Data*). In contrast, the main concerns in the capital-intensive production area are optimizing the machine facilities (machines for production, assembly, quality inspection, maintenance, and so on) and structuring the material flow in an integrated manner.

Optimizing material flow

From the IT viewpoint, the control instructions for the production facilities are closely linked to the temporal and spatial control functions for sales and production orders and to the completion confirmation function within the plant data-collection system. Production facilities in this context include machine tools, industrial robots, transport, and storage systems, flexible production cells, and transfer lines.

Developments in the production area cannot be regarded separately from developments in the global market and the latest technology. With the increasing penetration of IT and the development of ever-more powerful processors, production machines such as industrial robots can carry out increasingly complex processes. Up to the 1960s, the market was dominated largely by standardized products and standardized products with manufacturer-specific variations for a mainly generalized customer base. The demand today is more for customer-specific products. The emphasis in production has thus moved from efficiency and economy to customization and the fulfillment of individual customer requirements. This customer orientation can be seen in the absolute necessity of meeting delivery deadlines while maintaining the required minimum quality.

Customer-specific products

Flexible production
machines Increasing customer requirements and companies' need to react as quickly as possible to changes in these requirements are reflected in the growing complexity of products and production machines in manufacturing companies and industrial companies with mechanical production. It is for these reasons that programs and machine systems for computer aided, flexible, automated production processes are becoming more and more common. Machine facilities in the production area can be classified as follows, in accordance with the degree of flexibility and the production tasks at hand (see Venitz, 1990, pp. 65–89).

▸ **Flexible production facilities**
NC machines, processing centers, flexible production cells, flexible manufacturing centers, flexible production systems, and transfer lines

▸ **Flexible handling, transport and storage facilities**
Industrial robots, automatic transport and storage systems

▸ **Flexible assembly facilities**
Assembly cells and assembly systems

2.2   Business Tasks

Sales order
processing The *order processing* process in its widest sense comprises all the tasks required to handle an order. This includes order receipt, preliminary costing, materials management, time and capacity management, order release, production control covering production and assembly, plant data collection, delivering the product to the customer, and issuing the invoice.

2.2.1   Sales and Distribution

Sales and distribution activities are often the starting-point for sales-processing tasks. Supplying the customer with the goods that the company manufactures can be regarded as the defining task of sales and distribution in manufacturing companies. For a company to be able to market its products realistically, there has to be demand, or demand has to be created. The type of service or product that is offered in the market and the resulting type of order placement are the main influencing factors that trigger the creation of a sales order.

If the product is produced for a market, rather than for a specific customer, the initiative for a new order usually comes from the market-research department. On the other hand, if the company has received an order from an individual customer, the initiative generally comes from the sales department. There are also differences in the types of sales tasks required for short-term consumer goods and those required for long-term consumer and investment goods. In the case of short-term consumer goods, a central sales task is to sell the product to a distributor, who then will sell the product to the consumer. Long-term consumer goods, on the other hand, with their greater technical complexity, usually require personal consulting, among other things.

Personal consulting, especially technical consulting, is even more important in the investment-goods industry, in which the goods produced are used to improve the future output of other goods and services. In this case, the customer is usually a company that has specific requirements in terms of product functionality. The high complexity of the products and the technical requirements require an advanced level of technical knowledge, both on the part of the customer and the provider. This is why technical consulting is so important when it comes to order processing for investment goods.

Besides general customer care, the tasks of *quote processing* and *inquiry evaluation* are also regarded as primary sales tasks. A quote-processing phase is usually necessary if a company sells its products mainly by means of sales orders, and a quote is usually preceded by a customer inquiry. Depending on the frequency of inquiries, an inquiry evaluation system may be used to decide how to handle each inquiry. Quote processing can include some or all of the following tasks, depending on the individual company.

▶ Evaluating the technical feasibility of the customer inquiry
▶ Pricing (determining production costs and sales price)
▶ Deciding on delivery deadline
▶ Reservation

Sales market

Quote processing

As you can see from this list of tasks, *quote processing* involves accessing data in other areas, and this can trigger an extensive range of activities throughout the company. Therefore, when creating quotes for customer-specific production, it is important to work out preliminary costs. Having access to basic production data (bills of material, routings, PRTs) is a prerequisite for these cost figures (see Section 2.2.2), The scope of the quote—which, we must remember, can lead to order placement and order processing—depends on the degree of standardization of the product, the corresponding degree of input that the customer will have during order processing, and the structure of the product. Thus, in customer-specific production, which involves non-standardized or only partially-standardized products, the order data recorded in the sales department has to be passed on to the development and design departments, where the required design documents are created using the technical specification. The amount of work involved in this depends on the design type.

As we have noted previously, if the company creates products for a general market or markets, the initiative for planning the sales program does not come from specific sales orders. Thus, when the company rolls out a new product, it has to forecast sales on the basis of market analyses. If the products in question are standard products that have already been selling for a certain period of time, the historical data can be used in conjunction with expected future developments to forecast demand. Because of the mid-term to long-term nature of this planning process, this demand forecast is carried out on the basis of product groups.

Order processing type
Once an order is placed, the type of order processing then has to be defined. If the target market is a non-specific one, order processing comprises only shipping processing and ex stock, delivery-note creation, and invoicing. If the company is producing customer-specific products, on the other hand, internal production and administration steps have to be defined and monitored. Thus, besides the order placement type, the degree of standardization of the products has a significant effect on the tasks involved in order processing. Figure 2.5 shows the tasks involved in sales and distribution.

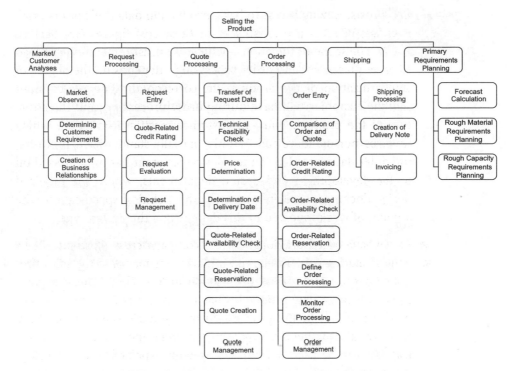

Figure 2.5 Sales and Distribution Tasks

2.2.2 Product Cost Planning

Cost planning involves calculating as accurately as possible the cost of goods manufactured and the cost of goods sold. To calculate the cost of goods manufactured, you will need to know the materials costs and production costs. There are two types of costs: direct costs and overhead costs. Direct costs can be individually assigned to the produced goods without the need for any cost allocations, while overhead costs are determined by overhead charges. However, even with direct costs, you can never be sure that all the required documents are available at the time of calculation. For this reason, the costing process is divided into the following types, based on the time of the costing (that is, before, during, or after the product is produced).

Cost planning

▶ Preliminary costing

▶ Final costing

▶ Interim costing

▶ Standard costing

Preliminary costing is carried out before production. It is based on a specific order or a customer inquiry for an individual product. One characteristic of preliminary costing is that it is carried out on the basis of incomplete data (because it takes place before production), which means that the result is necessarily subject to some uncertainty. It is usually carried out in the context of quote processing as part of order processing. Kilger differentiates between preliminary costing for quotes and preliminary costing for orders (see Kilger, 1988, pp. 605–655).

Preliminary costing for quotes takes place before the order is placed. Its results are used in pricing negotiations and to eliminate competitors. *Preliminary costing for orders*, on the other hand, takes place after the order is placed—after the work- scheduling phase, to be precise—and calculates more exact planning data on the basis of concrete quantity data. Again, the amount of work involved in the costing calculations depends on the degree of product standardization. Some exact data from the final costing can be used for standardized and partially standardized products. The supplier's planned prices can be used for externally procured components; that is, those that are not produced internally from scratch.

Components that are developed, designed, and produced internally pose a problem for preliminary costing. As mentioned previously, these components originate in the development and design departments. Because the design created in these departments has a major influence on the production materials, BOMs, and production procedures, it is important that the cost-related consequences of the development and design phases are recognized as early as possible. There are various quick costing procedures for this purpose, which can be used as part of the design process. The aim is to extract cost information as early as possible in the case of order-based production. Thus, the actual preliminary costing for the order is moved forward in time in the product-creation process.

The *final costing* is carried out after the product is produced. It is based on the actual data from the production process and is used for unit-based cost and results control.

Interim costs are used mainly for longer-term projects in order to control and monitor the production process in various phases. One thing that the three costing procedures mentioned above have in common is that they are unit-based or order-based. With *standard costing*, on the other hand, costs are calculated in advance for a specific period. Before the planning period starts, all costing-relevant data has to be available in the appropriate format. As this is only the case with uniform production and assembly, standard calculation is used only for the production of standardized products. Figure 2.6 provides an overview of the tasks involved in cost planning.

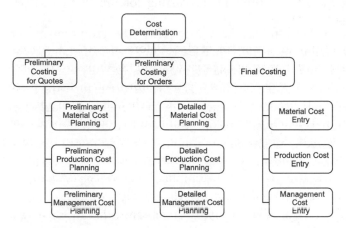

Figure 2.6 Cost Planning Tasks

2.2.3 Materials Management

The tasks involved in *materials management* are not clearly explained in the available literature. The significance of materials in the production process can be assessed on the basis of their role in value creation. Also, materials management creates and manages information that is important for the entire production process. In general, we can say that the job of materials management is to provide the materials required to create the products, in the right quantity and quality, at the right time, in the right place. Materials management here refers mainly to the tasks involved in material requirements planning. Tasks that have to do with procuring third-party components are dealt with in Section 2.2.4.

Materials requirements planning comprises all tasks involved in fulfilling material requirements in terms of type, quantity and time. The aim is to use the planned independent requirements (of sales and distribution, or market research) calculated in the demand program to establish the dependent requirements; that is, requirements in

Material requirements planning

terms of subordinate components. The BOM is the data structure used for this purpose. It describes how the components are assembled to form the end product. The following are the sub-tasks of material requirements planning:

▶ Requirements planning

▶ Stock management

▶ Requirement split

The requirements-planning phase determines the requirements in terms of the assemblies, individual parts, and raw materials necessary to fulfill the agreed demand program. It also defines the required quantity and the deadline. The product structure, the type of order placement, and the value of the components available for material requirements planning purposes are key characteristics of the work involved in requirements planning and add to its complexity. Calculations for planning requirements have to take into account the materials, components and assemblies in stock. Planned stock also has to be taken into account; that is, materials, individual components, and assemblies that are not available at the present time but will be available when required. To calculate this information, the requirements planner has to have access to data on stock movement, production statuses, and planned orders. If the calculated requirements cannot be matched up with an economical lot size, the optimal lot size of the production orders is calculated for the components that will be produced in-house. The production orders are then transferred to the order-planning phase (time management, capacity management, and order release). The requirements of third-party components are then sent to the purchasing department.

Planning independent requirements

If the independent requirements-planning process combines multiple sales orders of a planning period, this destroys the relationship between sales orders and production-relevant period-related secondary requirements. Similarly, in requirements planning (requirements breakdown), the factors of lot formation, and the transfer of secondary requirements to other periods cause the information relationships between requirements and the order to be lost. Thus, a variety of requirements-tracking processes are used to ensure that the requirement source can be uniquely identified at all times. This is mandatory in customer-specific production. Figure 2.7 shows the main tasks involved in materials management.

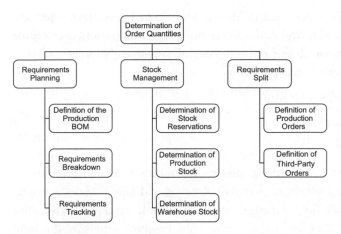

Figure 2.7 Materials Management Tasks

2.2.4 Purchasing

Purchasing involves all the tasks connected with the external procurement of materials, components, end products, and PRTs. The order procedure can be adapted as needed to the market situation, in the same manner as the sales and distribution tasks. The main difference between ordering and sales and distribution is that the company in this case operates in the market as the customer rather than as the provider.

Normally, before placing the order, the company obtains a quotation. To do this, it must first make an inquiry. The starting-point of the order process is the existence of a requirement (such as a particular component) that will be supplied by a third party. Purchase requisition can take place in response to a demand breakdown within the requirements-planning process, a specific request from a user department, or a notification from the warehouse or another part of the production chain. If there is an existing supplier for the component in question that can fulfill the technical requirements, the company makes a request for a quotation as soon as the purchase requisition has been created and checked. Assuming that the technical and qualitative aspects of the component are unchanged, the main issues to be queried in the request are price, delivery date, and quantity. On the other hand, if there is no existing supplier for the specific component required, the company has to identify potential suppliers from its supplier network. Once it has done this, a process of vendor evaluation is used to select the most reliable ones. This process iden-

Procurement

Order process

tifies the suppliers to whom the inquiry will be sent. Naturally, the company should also establish at this stage whether it needs new suppliers, and evaluate external sources accordingly. Note also that the process of obtaining a quotation can serve purposes other than fulfilling a specific requirement; companies can also carry out this process in order to update their purchasing information.

Selecting a quotation Once quotations are received from the suppliers, the selection procedure begins. Each quotation is formally checked to establish the degree to which it corresponds to the request, and how complete and clear it is. Material factors such as price, delivery date, delivery conditions, quality, and payment terms are also analyzed. The company selects the most suitable quotation, and thus the supplier, and places the order. The contract is legally binding once the supplier sends back confirmation of the order, and the delivery terms specified in the order are then considered to be accepted by both parties.

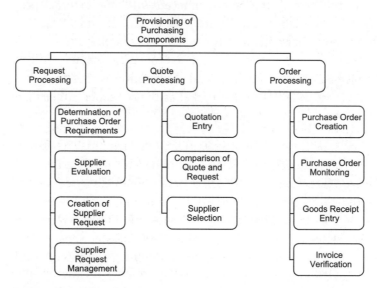

Figure 2.8 Purchasing Tasks

The interval between order placement and goods receipt is usually quite long, and so this procedure needs to be monitored. Deadlines have to be checked, open partial stocks identified, and any required corrective measures taken. When the goods are delivered, entry of goods receipt and invoice verification is carried out. The scope of work involved in the procurement process depends very much on the scope of the external procurement process and any additional agreements between supplier and customer. The quantity, value, and complexity of the product can be used as measurement points when calculating these values. Figure 2.8 shows the tasks involved in purchasing.

2.2.5 Production Planning

One of the tasks of materials management is to calculate the quantity of components needed to create the product, regardless of the available resources. *Production order planning* aligns these requirements with the capacities of the production department. It does this by assigning the production orders identified in the materials management process and the corresponding completion dates defined in the order planning phase to the required capacities.

Production order planning

In accordance with the approach of Glaser (see Glaser, 1986, p. 69), lead-time scheduling and lead-time minimizing should be carried out before the actual finite scheduling, which can be represented in load overviews. To do this, the start times and end times of the process steps pertaining to a production order are first defined without regard to capacity restrictions, in order to test the feasibility of the finish date of the production order that was specified in the materials management process. Forward scheduling, backward scheduling, and bottleneck scheduling are the procedures used for this purpose. Finite scheduling is carried out individually for each order here; that is, any interdependencies that may exist between various orders are not taken into account. If the deadline is not feasible, you can try to minimize the lead time by overlapping, splitting, compressing, or reducing the transition times. The tasks involved in finite scheduling and its reduction depend partly on the production department; because of the high wait times, lead-time reduction measures are particularly relevant in workshop production.

The purpose of *finite scheduling* is to create a load overview in graphic or tabular form that depicts capacity demand and capacity supply. If the company works to customer-specific orders, a pegged requirements display is required. *Capacity leveling* corrects any disparities between supply and demand in order to balance the load as much as possible. This leveling process can run fully automatically, or in a dialog. The latter method has the advantage that the company's staff can add their knowledge and experience to the process

Finite scheduling

to get the best possible result. If capacity demand exceeds supply, full orders or parts of orders can be moved to free periods. If this changes the sequence of steps in the process, you will need to ensure the integrity of the order using a network. This is necessary for contract manufacturers who produce multi-component products. However, it is possible to change the sequence only if the company does not have a linked-flow manufacturing process. Alternatively, organizational measures such as overtime or extra shifts can be used. Before the production orders are passed on to the production department, you need to check whether the resources required for the order—such as materials, PRTs, tools, and NC programs—are available at the right time. Once you are satisfied that this is the case, the order can be released. Figure 2.9 shows an overview of the tasks involved in production order planning.

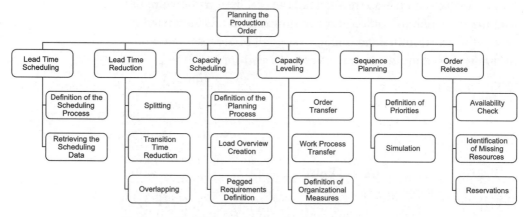

Figure 2.9 Production Order Planning Tasks

2.3 The Production Area in Industrial Operations

2.3.1 Production in Computer Integrated Manufacturing

CIM *Computer integrated manufacturing* (CIM) is the term given to a concept that has arisen from practice and that deals with integrated information processing for business and technical tasks in industrial operations. Discussion of this topic was begun by J. Harrington in the early 1970s (see Harrington, 1973). Harrington defined the basic elements of CIM as follows:

- *Computer Aided Design*
- *Computer Aided Manufacturing*
- *Computer Aided Quality Assurance*
- *Production planning*

The first German-language works in this area were published by the authors Maier-Rothe and Lederer, both of whom focused on using modern computer technologies in a coordinated way (see Maier-Rothe et al., 1983; and Lederer, 1984). In his studies of CIM, Grabowski likewise emphasized the technical aspects of computer aided design and production (see Grabowski, 1983). In terms of the former, he focused on geometric processing; that is, creating design drafts and drawings. In terms of the latter, he concentrated on production processing; that is, physically modifying materials by means of production procedures such as milling, drilling, and turning (see Grabowski, 1983). In 1984, Spur narrowed down this understanding of CIM to the technical production aspects of industrial operations: computer aided production (see Spur, 1984).

While this discussion was going on, Scheer published a CIM model in 1983 (see Scheer, 1983) that included both the business aspects (sales, materials management, time and capacity management, production control, and dispatch control) and the technical aspects of product creation (design, work scheduling, machine programming, production execution, maintenance, and quality assurance). Scheer also re-focused attention from the primarily technological aspects to the logical structure of the information flow. He stated that cross-application data organization and small control cycles should be used to support a logically oriented information flow based on transaction chains (see Scheer, 1990, pp. 14–16).

Information flow

Based on the views outlined above, we can establish the following main points on the subject of CIM (see Figure 2.10).

- The use of IT is of central importance.
- Enterprise data should be stored with low redundancy in order to avoid inconsistent datasets.
- The information flow should be structured in a process-oriented manner in order to minimize the number of process interfaces.

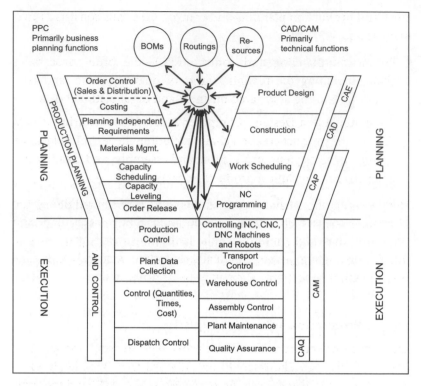

Figure 2.10 "Y" Model for Computer Integrated Manufacturing (from Scheer 1990, p. 2)

- ▶ It is essential to use integrated information processing for the various applications in order to minimize the number of information interfaces.

- ▶ It is necessary to have logically and technically balanced enterprise architecture in order to make information available quickly.

Integrated IT use In 1985, the German Committee for Industrial Production (*Ausschuss für wirtschaftliche Fertigung, AWF*) made a recommendation (see AWF, 1985) that was similar to Scheer's findings. The committee's aim in doing so was to provide a common basis and an orientation point for the various approaches to CIM. The AWF described CIM as the integrated use of IT in all areas of production. The technical and organizational functions of product creation could be integrated by the use of a common, universal data basis. The CIM concept comprises applications for computer aided design, computer aided planning, computer aided manufacturing, computer aided quality assurance, and production planning and control. CIM thus consists of two main areas:

- ▶ Production planning and control (PPC)—the order processing chain, including the planning tasks of quantity, time, and cost planning, and the associated business and organizational data
- ▶ Computer Aided Design / Computer Aided Manufacturing (CAD/CAM)—the product creation chain, including the technical tasks of product development, production, and assembly, and creating the geometric and technical production data

The various authors have expanded this industry-oriented definition to include terms such as computer-integrated business, computer-aided industry, and computer-integrated enterprise, but its core is still based on the interpretation of Scheer and the AWF (see Bullinger et al., 1987; Venitz, 1990, p. 57; Scheer, 1990, p. 17).

2.3.2 Production as Part of Logistics

Logistics is derived from the Greek roots *logos* (reason) and *logistike* (art of calculating). The related English word *logic* is understood to mean *consequential and consistent thinking*. Only in 1780 did the term *logistics* take on a specific meaning in the military world, and has since been used in that context to mean *activities necessary for military provisioning*. These activities are: planning, providing, and using the resources and services required for military purposes to support the forces (see Bartels, 1980).

At the beginning of the 1960s, the logistical experience and know-how of the military in the United States was applied in the business area. Both areas have one thing in common: goods transport. Of course, military logistics also covers troop transport, while business logistics is concerned with goods only. Another difference is that military logistics decision-making has to take into account political and military goals, while business logistics is based on economic goals (see Pfohl, 1996). In the 1970s, Bowersox described logistics as "the process of managing all activities required to strategically move raw materials, parts, and finished inventory from vendors, between enterprise facilities, and to customers" (Bowersox, 1974, p. 1).

Goods transport

The study of business administration in Germany began to critically analyze this approach in the late 1960s and early 1970s. The field of

Enterprise processes

47

logistics was widened to include all time-independent and space-independent enterprise processes having to do with materials. Logistics was discussed within the decision-oriented and system-oriented approaches of business administration. Academics in this area began to look at enterprises and their environments as complex systems, and to analyze decisions for structuring, controlling, and regulating business systems (see Kirsch, 1971, and Pfohl, 1996).

Business logistics The discipline of *business logistics* is similar to the other business disciplines of distributive trade, finance, and production management. It is a sub-discipline of business administration studies and aims to describe, explain, and structure the processes within social systems. The range of the logistical systems that it analyzes depends on the type and number of parties involved. It is therefore subdivided into the following areas (see Bäck 1984, Kirsch 1971, and Pfohl 1996).

▸ **Macro logistics**
Macro-logistical systems comprise subsections of the study of economics, such as traffic system planning (road networks, rail networks, air transport networks) and site planning of community and social facilities (schools, day-care facilities, hospitals).

▸ **Micro logistics**
Micro-logistical systems are examined from the viewpoint of individual companies. Micro-logistical systems are restricted by law and by market relationships to customers and suppliers, among other things. The focus here is on analyzing companies' internal organizational relationships. Examples of micro- logistical issues would be planning the vehicle fleet of a company or a public body, route planning for a waste-management company, and patient handling in a hospital.

▸ **Meta logistics**
Meta-logistical systems analyze the internal organizational relationships of a number of economic entities. These relationships involve cooperation between organizations that are linked by the flow of goods. An example of this would be a company that outsources its entire delivery system for safety components to a transportation service provider that specializes in this area.

Material and information flow The goal of business logistics is to structure, control, and regulate from the economic viewpoint the flow of material and information in a company. The relationships between supplier, company, and

48

customer are the scope of this goal. The job of logistics in the wider sense is to ensure the availability of goods at a specific place, at a specific time, in the right quantity, while its purpose in a narrower sense is to transport, store, and sort materials (see Bloech 1984, p. 6).

In the 1970s, logistics was first applied in companies in order to supply the production line with materials. Today, the term logistics refers to the regulation of the product-creation process, and includes the coordination of the flow of materials, information, and production across department boundaries. In general, logistics structures the following:

▶ Delivery relationships with customers

▶ Procurement relationships with suppliers and the associated put-away of raw materials and supplies

▶ The production process, including planning transport routes and storing intermediate products and finished products

Classically, logistics is subdivided into the areas of procurement and production logistics (or intra-enterprise logistics) on the one hand, and sales logistics (or distribution logistics) on the other (see Pfohl, 1996, pp. 71–215). The goal of sales logistics is to structure, control, and monitor a company's flow of goods within or to the sales market (see Figure 2.11). The aim is to deliver the requested goods to the customer in time and to minimize the associated storage and transport costs. Sales logistics comprises the following activities: inquiry and quotation processing; order processing and management; shipping and invoicing; and financial accounting, which checks that payment is made in the proper manner. Sales logistics may take any of the following forms, depending on the type of company.

Sales logistics

▶ It may be separate from procurement and production logistics, as in the case of a producer of mass-market goods (washing machines, televisions).

▶ It may be directly linked to the production logistics chain, as in the case of a supplier who manufactures order-specific products from stored raw materials.

▶ It may be directly linked to the procurement and production logistics chain, as in the case of an automobile manufacturer that individually configures its vehicles for each customer and to whom procured parts are delivered using a just-in-time procedure.

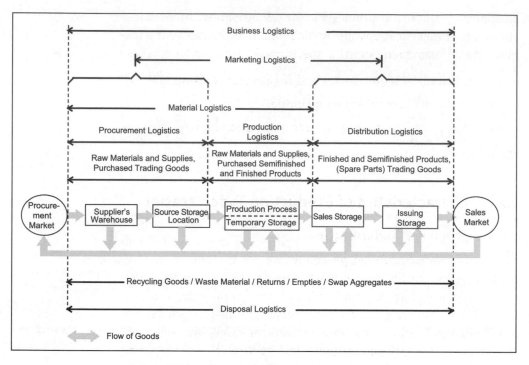

Figure 2.11 Flow of Goods in Enterprise Logistics (from Pfohl, 1996, p. 18)

Production logistics

The purpose of production logistics is to ensure that the semi-finished products are made available in an optimal fashion in the individual stages of the production process. The focus here is on physically structuring the flow of materials. Besides the actual production and assembly of components and assemblies to create saleable products, this process also includes the following steps (as well as the transport and storage steps mentioned above):

▸ Production planning, including capacities, quantities, and resources

▸ Production control; that is, controlling the logistical process between machines and of individual machines

The greater the degree of production automation in a company, the greater the interconnection between company logistics and production.

Procurement logistics

The purpose of procurement logistics in manufacturing companies is to ensure that the raw materials and supplies required for production are provided at the right time and in the right quantities. In trade companies, its job is to provide the products required by potential customers as quickly as possible while minimizing storage and transport costs. Procurement logistics' specific tasks are as follows:

▶ Determination of requirements and requirements planning

▶ Monitoring delivery dates and quantities

▶ Monitoring quality, packaging, transport, and shipping requirements

2.4 Characteristics of Production Type Creation

2.4.1 Product Standardization

The *product standardization* process expresses the degree of standardization of the finished product. This degree of standardization can affect the geometric, structural, and procedural aspects of production. Thus, the degree of standardization influences geometrical and procedural tasks at the order-placement stage, and sales and costing tasks. The influence of individual customers on the type and structure of the product is also relevant to product standardization. While the type of product process is primarily based on the external relationship between the company and the customer, the degree of product standardization is primarily based on the internal relationships within the company. It thus expresses the degree to which certain internal standardizations are possible.

Degree of standardization

With *standardized products*, the individual customer has no influence at all on how the product is developed, designed, and produced. Therefore, the business processes are very much oriented around internal company factors. The company itself defines the product requirements within the scope of market conditions. If the company receives an order, no technical or planning work is required, as all the relevant documents already exist before production begins.

Customer influence

With *partially standardized products*, the company can still use some existing documents. A product that uses an adaptive or a variant design is an example of geometric partial standardization. Structural partial standardization is the case if the company can standardize sub-components of the finished product. Typical examples of the use of structural partial standardization are general mechanical engineering companies that use assembly systems. However, the customer's influence on partially standardized products at the order placement stage is so high that a large part of the order lead time in the order-processing phase has to be devoted to planning tasks, especially technical planning tasks.

As the name suggests, *non-standardized products* are produced on the basis of the requirements and requests of a specific customer. This means that the information for the individual task parts has to be newly generated for each order. Each non-standardized sales order necessitates a very high degree of input into the various tasks in the order-processing and product-creation chain. Close cooperation and contact between the company and the customer is a defining characteristic of this situation. Also, problems often occur with the execution of pre-production tasks. The order lead time depends heavily on the areas upstream of production. Typical examples of producers of non-standardized products are heavy machine construction and special machine construction companies.

2.4.2 Product Structure

Structure of finished product

The *product structure* describes the structure of the finished product that's made up of sub-components. This reflected in three ways. The first of these is the product structure; that is, the structure of the design-based BOM. Schomburg sub-divides the product structure into the following characteristics classes: *single-component products*, *multi-component products with simple structure*, and *multi-component products with complex structure* (see Schomburg 1980, pp. 44–47).

The existence of BOMs, and the scope of these, are criteria for evaluating the product structure.

Bill of material

The second way in which the product structure is reflected and can thus be analyzed is the connection between the design-based BOM and the production-based BOM. The latter is the basis for MRP and work scheduling. While the design-based product structure describes from the design viewpoint how the finished product is created from assemblies and components, the production-based product structure describes from the production viewpoint how the finished product is created and expressed in the production drawings and BOMs for production and assembly. When checking for consistency, you should make sure that there is *congruency* between these two viewpoints.

The third characteristic aspect of product structure is the *production structure*. Unlike the product structure, it is based not on the product tree, but on the routing. The production structure is determined by the number of production levels (machine reservations) and the number of process steps per routing. The number of machine reservations indicates how many machines are processing components, the number of process steps, and the total number of process steps required to produce the finished product.

Schomburg subdivides the production structure as follows: *production with low depth*, *production with medium depth*, and *production with high depth*. However, he also points out that the production structure should be regarded as a consequence of the product structure, among other things. Thus, the depth of the production structure correlates to that of the product structure, for example, although the production depth can be reduced by external procurement. If we disregard external procurement, we see that a deeper product structure usually also leads to a higher production depth. Correspondingly, the transparency of production decreases, and the order-planning and production-control requirements increase. These effects are subsumed under the *product structure* characteristic in the forms of *simple structure*, *medium structure*, and *complex structure*.

Typical instances of the *simple structure* form are the production of cast parts or screws, single-level production, and single-level assembly. Small electric motors belong to the second group, and large machines to the third.

2.4.3 Production Type

One typical characteristic that describes the production type is the frequency of creation of the same product in the production process; that is, the degree of replication in a certain period and the degree of certainty that the same product will be created again. The problem of precise differentiation between mass production, large-lot production, medium-lot production, small-lot production, and make-to-order production is referred to by Schäfer (see Schäfer, 1969, pp. 59–79) in his work *Der Industriebetrieb* (*The Manufacturing Company*).

Using this work as a reference, mass production can be described as follows (referred to by Schäfer as "mixed/differentiated mass production" or "type production").

Production structure

Product creation in production

Mass production

In mass production, different products are produced over a longer period of time. These use the same source material and processing procedures, and so are closely related from the production viewpoint. Schäfer gives the examples of a screw factory, and the production of files, pliers, and so on. However, contrary to Schäfer, we will not restrict our definition of mass production to the production of simple, uncomplicated products; we will include the production of complex products, if the customer does not have the option of choosing between different variants of a production line.

Repetitive manufacturing

Repetitive manufacturing includes the aspect of change and is closely related to mass production. Thus, in large-lot repetitive manufacturing, closely related products are created in the same way. Schäfer describes this as the "uninterrupted production of product types over several years" and mentions automobile and typewriter production as examples. Again deviating from Schäfer, we include under repetitive manufacturing product types that are produced in large quantities but where the customer basically has the option of choosing between different variants of the type. Thus, besides automobile manufacturers, we also classify manufacturers of provider-specific machine tools under repetitive manufacturing. It should be noted at this point that both these company types operate in different markets. Supplier companies can also count as large-lot manufacturers. In this case, the customer determines the lot type and its possible variants. The main difference is that in the case of the first two types, it is mainly the assembly process that is affected, while in the case of suppliers, production itself is also affected.

Small-lot production

Small-lot production is the term used when different products are produced in small production runs within a period of time. Unlike make-to-order production, all order-related technical documents for production and assembly have to be fully available in order to replicate the product in small quantities. A typical example is machine tool production with customer-specific customization. Pilot series production in supplier companies is another example of small-lot production.

Make-to-order production

The central characteristic of *make-to-order production* is that the product is tailored to the customer's individual requirements, and thus its production run is always 1. Schäfer calls this "made-to-measure production" (see Schäfer, 1969, p. 71). Large machine production, special machine production, and ship production are examples of make-to-order production.

2.4.4 Production Organization

The literature frequently treats *production and assembly* as a single topic under the headings of production organization types, production process types, or production systems. However, closer examination reveals fundamental differences between production and assembly. While the object and the order of individual production procedures are the important thing in production, the flow of objects is the central factor in assembly processes. Another difference is that in production, input materials are converted into output materials, while assembly processes are about combining various components to form an assembly or a finished product. In practice, there are companies that do production only or assembly only. Based on Schäfer, in our analysis of the various organizational types, we will consider only the artificial, purposely conceived types.

Production and assembly

The *workshop principle* is based on the spatial proximity of machines and work centers that have related functions or tasks. Similar production procedures are used for machines with similar functions. The production organization concept is indicated in terms such as turning shop, milling shop, and drill shop.

Workshop principle

The concept of organizing production according to same or similar objects can be regarded as the opposite of organizing processing stations based on related tasks. Thus, with the concepts of manufacturing center and flow manufacturing, processing stations are organized according to object characteristics. With the *flow principle*, PRTs are strictly organized according to the flow and the machines are interlinked as much as possible. An example of this is the processing of an engine block on a transfer line. This procedure has advantages and disadvantages: on the one hand, it has quick turnaround and total transparency, but on the other, it is not very flexible and is very error-prone. The *production center* concept is object-oriented and allows for flexible handling in determining the sequence of process steps. Thus, the production process is not fixed, as it is in flow manufacturing; the production center staff can set it in accordance with

Flow principle

the specific situation. Unlike the other organizational types, this type enables a certain degree of flexibility and decision-making competence on the part of staff.

Building-site principle As mentioned above, assembly is characterized mainly by orienting the people who work with it and the machines towards the object being processed. Its most extreme form is known as the *building-site principle*, under which the required PRTs and people are moved to the object. Typical examples of this are large machine production and plant construction. The *assembly center* is the same as the production center, except that it is used for assembly processes. In the ideal case, a production station can consist of production and assembly processes, depending on the product spectrum, which amounts to a *production center*. The flow principle is implemented more intensively in the assembly area than in the production processes of manufacturing companies with mechanical production. The spectrum ranges from automated, clocked assembly lines in the automobile and electronics industries, to the assembly halls of aircraft and railway construction, in which the speed of the transport line depends on the staff. Another important difference is that where the flow principle is implemented with time pressure, the degree of specialization is considerably higher than in cases where it is implemented without time pressure.

The production planning and control functions of SAP ERP are contained in the PP module. The most important PP processes are sales and operations planning, demand management, material requirements planning, long-term planning, production order creation, production order execution, and capacity requirements planning.

3 Production Planning and Control in SAP ERP

3.1 SAP PP in the Context of SAP ERP

The main features of SAP ERP are as follows: an extensive range of business functions; a high level of modularity alongside close integration of individual modules, support for international requirements in the form of country-specific functions (such as Payroll, which is available in various country versions with the relevant statutory conditions and tax requirements), multi-lingualism, and the ability to run on a range of platforms.

SAP ERP is based on a three-tier client-server architecture and can be subdivided into two main work areas: the basis and the application. The purpose of the basis layer is to keep the business applications separate from the system interfaces of the operating system and the database and communications systems, and to ensure that business transactions are executed quickly and efficiently. The application layer contains the implemented solutions that support the enterprise's business requirements.

SAP ERP consists of business application modules that can be used both individually and in combination with each other. SAP's delivery strategy is to deliver the complete system to the customer and then to activate and customize the required functions and business processes on-site at the customer's premises. The disadvantage of this strategy is that the individual customer requires an over-dimensioned computer configuration at the start of the implementation process. The advantage is that it is easier to activate functionalities in production operations from the existing range of solutions than it is to deliver them retroactively.

SAP ERP can be roughly subdivided into three main areas: *Accounting*, *Human Resources Management*, and *Logistics*.

Accounting

Accounting maps business transactions in accordance with their financial value and is responsible for planning, controlling, and monitoring the value flow within the enterprise. It is subdivided into financial accounting and managerial accounting, in accordance with the addressee group. Managerial accounting consists of cost accounting and activity accounting, and its purpose is to provide the decision makers in the enterprise with quantitative information. Financial accounting is structured in accordance with statutory regulations; enterprises use it to comply with requirements for disclosure with regard to external parties, in particular tax authorities and investors. The main components that support the tasks of accounting are: Financial Accounting (FI), Investment Management (IM), and Controlling (CO). These modules are further subdivided into corresponding sub-modules.

Human resources management

Human Resources Management (HR) is divided into the areas of personnel planning and development, and personnel administration and payroll. Personnel planning and development supports the strategic utilization of staff by providing functionality that enables the enterprise to systematically and qualitatively manage its staff. Personnel administration and payroll comprises all administrative and operational human resources activities.

Logistics

Logistics in the business context structures the flow of materials, information, and production from the supplier through production to the customer. The SAP ERP logistics application modules enable enterprises to plan, control, and coordinate their logistical processes on the basis of existing integrated data and functions across department boundaries. The integration of the individual application modules in SAP ERP prevents unnecessary and time-consuming multiple entries on the part of the staff who process business logistics transactions. Likewise, the integration of quantity-based processing steps includes the value-based side of the business transaction and thus fulfils the requirements of accounting. Logistics contains the following individual application modules: *Sales & Distribution* (SD), *Materi-*

als Management (MM), *Production Planning and Control* (PP), *Quality Management* (QM), *Project System* (PS), and *Plant Maintenance* (PM).

The PP link in this chain deals with quantity-based and time-based product planning and controls the production process. Besides its master-data maintenance functions, the PP module supports all quantity-based and capacity-based production planning and control steps. Production planning and control comprises various planning concepts, such as MRP II and kanban, and various production types, such as production by lot size, make-to-order production, variant production, repetitive manufacturing, and process manufacturing.

The various modules are closely interconnected due to integrated data retention, the internal flow of documents, and the functional integration of the modules. This enables many possible scenarios: a production planning process can be triggered by Sales and Distribution; Production Planning can create a purchase requisition; or a production confirmation within the plant data collection process can trigger a value-based update in Controlling and Human Resources Management in order to calculate salaries. Likewise, the high degree of integration between the modules means that the recording of goods movements in the execution of a production order can be based on quantity and values (see Keller, 1999, pp. 67–115).

The several thousands of customers in the different industries and countries have different requirements of production planning. These requirements are reflected in the customer's system by parameterizing the relevant functions in a process known as Customizing. In this process, the required functions are set in accordance with the requirements of the industry, the product range, the production procedure, the product structure, and organizational and legal requirements. Chapters 6 to 12 use process modules to describe the most important settings.

It is absolutely essential for the proper functioning of the system that you set and maintain the required basic data correctly. Chapter 5 describes in detail the basic data required for production planning. The focus there is on describing the basic data for production planning execution in companies with discrete manufacturing.

3.2 Processes in Production Planning and Control

Processes in production planning and production control comprise the following main areas:

▶ *Sales and operations planning* for determining the quantities to be produced

▶ *Material requirements planning* to calculate net requirements and component requirements, taking into account scrap and lot sizes

▶ *Capacity requirements planning* for detailed production planning, taking into account available capacities

▶ *Production control* to control and record the production process (create production documents, record confirmations)

These four areas represent the scope of the process only roughly. Figure 3.1 shows a detailed overview that explicitly illustrates the process modules that we will deal with in detail in subsequent chapters, along with their most important input and output values.

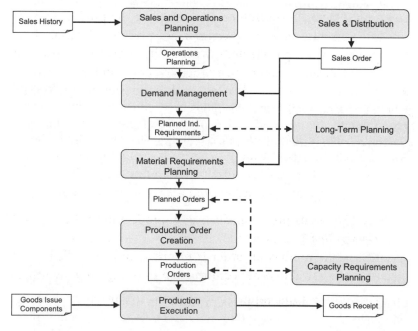

Figure 3.1 Process Overview

Sales planning plans future requirements without considering stocks and available capacities. The sales history often serves as a basis for sales planning. *Operations planning* uses the results of the sales planning process to plan the production quantities, and takes initial stocks and capacities into account on a general level.

Sales and operations planning

Demand management aligns sales planning with the customer requirements in accordance with the planning strategy, and thus calculates the independent requirements for production.

Demand management

Material requirements planning is the central function of production planning. It calculates requirement coverage elements for all MRP levels, based on the demand program, and taking into account lead times, lot sizes, and scrap quantities.

Material requirements planning

Long-term planning is basically a simulation of material requirements planning. It can examine how a change in planned independent requirements would affect capacity utilization, stocks, and external procurement. Long-term planning is also suitable for short-term simulations.

Long-term planning

The central factor in controlling and recording the production process is the production order. *Production order creation* describes how the production order is created—whether by converting a planned order or by means of interactive order creation—and the functions that are executed in this process, such as master-data selection, scheduling, and availability checking.

Production order creation

Capacity requirements planning schedules in detail the worklist, which usually consists of the processes for created or released production orders. The result of capacity requirements planning is a production sequence that is feasible from the capacity viewpoint.

Capacity requirements planning

While the previous processes dealt with production planning, *production execution* is concerned with how the actual production as specified in the production order is recorded and controlled, from material withdrawal to order confirmation to storage and invoicing.

Production execution

Chapters 6 to 12 deal with these processes in detail.

3.3 Production Types

3.3.1 Overview of Production Types

The *production type* characterizes the frequency with which a product is produced in the production process. The frequency with which production of identical or similar products is repeated and the production quantity of production orders are typical characteristics that determine the production type. Production organization is closely related to production type, as the production type often significantly affects the structure of the production process. Thus, the *flow manufacturing* production type, for example, implies the production of large quantities of identical product types or products. At the same time, flow manufacturing ensures that the production equipment is arranged in accordance with the organizational form of flow manufacturing. A typical example is the assembly of cars in the automobile industry. The degree of product standardization and the depth of the product structure also often affect the actual production type used. Therefore, various forms of production types, implicitly including production organization, have arisen from the basic theoretical types (mass production, repetitive manufacturing, small-lot production, make-to-order production). The following are important production types (see Keller/Curran, 1999, pp. 137–154):

- Discrete manufacturing
- Repetitive manufacturing
- Process manufacturing
- Kanban
- Engineer-to-order production

These types are briefly explained in the following sections. In this book, we restrict ourselves to discrete manufacturing, as this is the most common type of production.

3.3.2 Discrete Manufacturing

Discrete manufacturing (also called shop floor production) describes the production of a product on the basis of production orders. Discrete manufacturing is used if the products in question change frequently, if the pattern of demand is very irregular, and if production is workshop-oriented in character. A range of master data is required for discrete manufacturing; the most important of these are material, bill of material (BOM), work center, and routing (see Chapter 5).

Discrete manufacturing starts when a production order is created and processed. A production order is created either manually or when a planned order that was created in the production and procurement planning process is converted. A production order is a request to the production department to produce or provide products or services at a specific time and in a specific quantity. It specifies the work center and material components that are to be used for production. The creation of a production order automatically creates reservations for the required material components. Purchase requisitions are created for externally procured material components and services, and capacity requirements are created for the work centers at which the order will be executed.

Production orders are released on the release date, provided that the required materials and capacity are available. The relevant documents in the production order can be printed in order to prepare for the execution of the production order. The capacity situation can be evaluated and any required capacity leveling can be carried out in any phase of production order processing, although this is usually done before production starts. The components required to produce the products are read out from the production order, and the goods issue is posted. The product is then produced on the basis of the production order. The finished quantity and the services provided are then confirmed back to the production order. The product is put into storage and the goods receipt is posted. Finally, the production order is settled.

3.3.3 Repetitive Manufacturing

Repetitive manufacturing is characterized by the interval-based and quantity-based creation and processing of production plans (in contrast to single-lot and order-based processing). With repetitive manufacturing, a certain quantity of a stable product is produced over a certain period of time. The product moves through the machines and work centers in a continual flow, and intermediate products are not put into intermediate storage. Figure 3.2 illustrates this concept using the example of motherboard production.

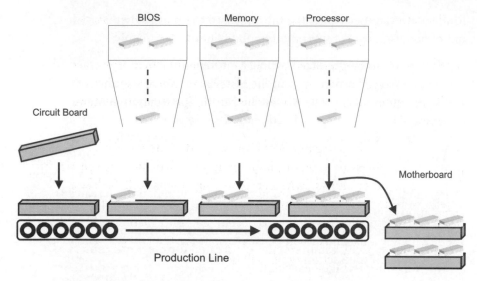

Figure 3.2 Producing a Motherboard on a Production Line

The work required for production control with repetitive manufacturing is significantly reduced compared to single-lot and order-based production control, and the entry of actual data is simplified.

Repetitive manufacturing is suitable for a variety of industries, such as branded items, electronics, semiconductors, and packaging. Repetitive manufacturing also can be used for pure make-to-stock production. Production in this case has no direct connection to a sales order. The requirements are created in the demand management process, and the sales orders are supplied from stocks. Sales order-based production—for example, in the automobile industry (see Geiger/Kerle, 2001, pp. 69–95)—can also be implemented using the methods of repetitive manufacturing. In this case, production is directly related to the sales order or is triggered directly from the sales order.

The most important forms of master data in repetitive manufacturing are as follows:

▸ Material
▸ Production version
▸ BOM
▸ Production line
▸ Rate routing

The main differences between this data and the master data for discrete manufacturing are briefly described later.

If a material is to be produced by means of repetitive manufacturing, it has to be flagged accordingly in the material master. This is done in the SAP system in the **MRP 4** view by setting the **Repetitive Manufacturing** flag.

A *repetitive manufacturing profile* is also assigned to the material. This profile determines the type of planning and confirmation. It specifies, among other things, whether reporting points will be used, whether production activities will be posted to the cost collector for material confirmations, whether a decoupled confirmation will be used, whether a backflush will be carried out for the entry of actual data, and which transaction types will be used.

Repetitive manufacturing profile

Because there are different BOMs and routings for a material, depending on the production process, a *production version* is used to specify which BOM and which routing are to be used to produce the material. The alternative BOM for the BOM explosion, the plan category, the task list group, and the group counter for assignment to the plans also are specified in the production version. The production version also specifies the lot size for which the production version is valid. It is important to set the **Repetitive manufacturing allowed** flag. There can be one or many production versions for a material, and there has to be at least one production version in repetitive manufacturing. The **MRP 4** view is used to create the production version for a material, as before.

Production version

The costs that are incurred in repetitive manufacturing are posted to a *product cost controller*. In the process of entering actual data, the material costs and production costs are added to the product cost controller. Costs are subtracted from the product cost controller when a goods receipt, for example, is posted. The product cost controller is created for a material within a plant in a specific production version.

Product cost collector

The BOM for the material to be produced specifies what quantities of which components are required for production. In repetitive manufacturing, not every goods issue is recorded at the same time as the physical withdrawal of the material from stock. Usually, component usage is automatically posted only when the finished product is

Backflush

received (*backflush*). To do this, a storage location is specified in every BOM item, and the backflush is carried out from this location.

Production lines
Work centers in repetitive manufacturing are called *production lines* (see Section 5.4) because the product moves through the machines in a continuous flow, and the machines are usually spatially arranged in a line. These can be simple production lines, which often consist of just one work center, or complex production lines, which consist of several work centers. The individual processing stations are set up as individual production lines and are grouped into a line hierarchy. A production line determines the available capacity of the processing station and is assigned to a single cost center.

Rate routings
In repetitive manufacturing, routings are known as *rate routings*. A rate routing contains the processes that are required to produce the material. Because the same product is produced over a long period of time in repetitive manufacturing, very simple routings can be used, often containing just one process. This kind of process specifies the production rate, which in turn specifies the quantity per time unit that is produced on the line (for example, 100 items per hour).

In repetitive manufacturing, the planned orders for a material that result from the production and procurement planning process are managed in a planning table. In these tables, the planner can schedule the production quantities on the assembly lines. In repetitive manufacturing, we use the term *run schedule quantity* instead of planned orders (see Figure 3.3).

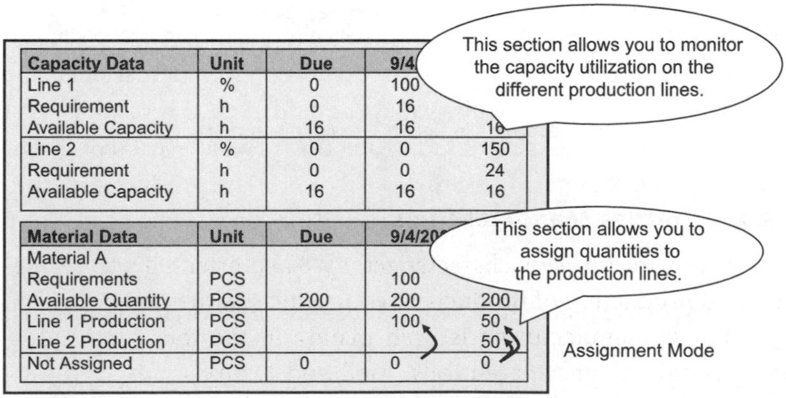

Capacity Data	Unit	Due	9/4
Line 1	%	0	100
Requirement	h	0	16
Available Capacity	h	16	16
Line 2	%	0	0
Requirement	h	0	0
Available Capacity	h	16	16

This section allows you to monitor the capacity utilization on the different production lines.

Material Data	Unit	Due	9/4/20
Material A			
Requirements	PCS		100
Available Quantity	PCS	200	200
Line 1 Production	PCS		100
Line 2 Production	PCS		
Not Assigned	PCS	0	0

This section allows you to assign quantities to the production lines.

Assignment Mode

Figure 3.3 Planning Table in Repetitive Manufacturing

In repetitive manufacturing, the components are supplied anonymously to the production line. This can be done very easily using the pull list. The components required on a production line for a specific period can be calculated in the pull list. The missing quantities that are detected can be replaced by means of direct stock transfers; for example from the central warehouse to the production location.

The production of the product usually takes place in a continuous flow along the production line. Entry of actual data is carried out at regular intervals for each finished production quantity. Component use and production activities are automatically posted when the finished product is received. In the case of longer production lead times, actual data can also be recorded along with reporting points within the production line, in order to post consumption data more promptly (see Figure 3.4).

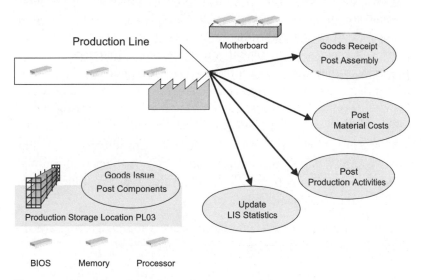

Figure 3.4 Actual Data Recording in Repetitive Manufacturing

3.3.4   Process Manufacturing

Process manufacturing is characterized by batch-oriented and recipe-oriented production of products or co-products in the process industry. Process manufacturing is used mainly in the following industries: chemicals, pharmaceuticals, food and luxury foods, and process-based electronics (see Datta, 2001, pp. 145–172). A number of processes can be used in process manufacturing. These are described as follows:

Continuous production

Continuous production is the name given to a process in which production runs within a specific period in an ongoing procedure. Material components are continuously supplied to the production line, and the finished product is continuously produced. The plant and machinery are continuously and fully in use, with the result that partial orders and partial allocations cannot be handled.

Discontinuous production

In *discontinuous production*, as the name suggests, the products are not produced in a continuous process. Instead, the material components are provided and weighed out as required for each step of the procedure. The same line can be used to produce multiple products.

Regulated production

Regulated production is used if the product quality requirements are very specific, or if legal regulations apply, such as the Good Manufacturing Practices (GMP) overseen by the U.S. Food and Drug Administration (FDA). Examples of this process can be found in the pharmaceuticals industry, and certain parts of the food and cosmetics industries. In regulated production, orders can be created only with approved recipes. If changes need to be made to master recipes, these are subject to change administration procedures. Filling processes that are separate from and take place after the actual production process can also be handled in process manufacturing. Loose goods (bulk) are moved from production and held in intermediate storage containers until they are filled. This production type supports complex filling procedures and simple manual filling procedures. Process orders that are created on the basis of a filling recipe are a prerequisite for the filling process.

The central master data elements in process manufacturing are the *material*, the *BOM*, the *resource*, and the *master recipe*.

Process order

Process manufacturing starts when a *process order* is created and processed in accordance with a master recipe. A production order is created either manually or when a planned order that was created in the production planning process is converted. A production order is a request to the production department to produce or provide products or services at a specific time and in a specific quantity. It specifies the resource and material components that are to be used for production. The creation of a production order automatically creates reservations for the required material components. Purchase requisitions are created for externally procured material components and services, and capacity requirements are created for the resources at which the order will be executed. Production orders are released on the release date, provided that the required materials and capacity are available. At the time of release, an automatic batch-determination process can be run for components that are subject to a batch management requirement. The relevant documents in the production order can be printed in order to prepare for the execution of the production order.

The capacity situation can be evaluated and any required capacity leveling carried out in any phase of the production order-processing process, although this is usually done before production starts. Production can now begin, with or without the use of process management. If process management is used to execute a process order, this serves as the interface between the SAP system and process control. The flexible structure of this interface makes it possible to connect automated, semi-automated, and manually controlled plant and equipment to the production process.

Once the process order or the relevant phases of the process order is released for production, control recipes are generated from the process instructions in the process order. *Control recipes* contain all the information required for the process- control function to execute a process order. Next, either the control recipes for the process control system themselves, or the control recipes in the form of process instruction (PI) sheets, are sent to the relevant process operator. In the latter case, the process instructions are expressed in natural language, so that the process operator can display them on-screen and process them.

Control recipes and process instruction sheets

The process data that results from the execution of the process order is sent back to the SAP system or is transferred to external function modules for further processing, or both. This data is transferred from the process control function to the various recipients by means of the process-coordination interface with the help of process messages. A material consumption message, for example, causes a goods issue to be posted for a component.

If a process order is executed without process coordination, the material components required to produce the finished product are withdrawn for the process order, and the goods issue is posted in the inventory management menu. The required finished product is then produced in accordance with the process order. The quantities created and the products produced are then confirmed to the process order, the finished product is put into storage, and the goods receipt is posted.

In the invoicing process for a process order, the actual costs incurred for the order are assigned to one or more recipient objects (such as the finished material or a sales order). The process data documentation process creates lists of production-relevant and quality-relevant data that can be optically archived. We draw a distinction here between order logs and batch logs. Order logs contain all the quality-relevant SAP data that is created for a process order, while batch logs contain all the quality-relevant data having to do with producing a batch. The structure, content, and processing of batch logs comply with the international standards defined in the GMP guidelines for the pharmaceuticals and food industries.

3.3.5 Kanban

Kanban is a procedure for production control and material flow control that avoids any time-consuming requirements planning and implements requirements-oriented production control. With kanban, a material is produced or procured only when it is actually required. A specific quantity of the components required to produce a material are stored on-site in containers. Once a container is empty, this component is replenished in accordance with a predefined strategy (in-house production, external procurement, or stock transfer). In the interval between the request for replenishment and the delivery of the re-filled container, the other containers simply do the work of the empty one. Figure 3.5 illustrates the basic principle of kanban.

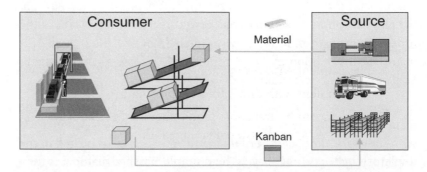

Figure 3.5 Basic Principle of Kanban

The replenishment process is largely automatic in the kanban process, which greatly reduces the amount of manual posting work required. Also, the kanban process reduces stock levels, as only components are produced that are genuinely required. The material is not pushed through the production process in accordance with an overall plan; rather, it is requested by one production level (consumer) from the previous production level (source) as needed.

With kanban processing, the plant is divided into *production supply areas* (PSAs). The components required for production are stored in these PSAs and various work centers can take what they need from the PSAs. A kanban control cycle is defined in order to specify how a material should be obtained within a PSA. The control cycle defines a replenishment strategy for the material that specifies whether the required material is to be produced in-house or procured externally, for example. The control cycle also specifies the number of containers in circulation between consumer and source and the quantity per container.

Production supply areas

Replenishment strategies specify how a material component should be replenished and which of the following replenishment elements are created for this purpose:

Replenishment strategies

▸ In-house production
  ▹ Manual kanban
  ▹ Replenishment with run-schedule quantity
  ▹ Replenishment with production order
▸ External procurement
  ▹ Replenishment by order
  ▹ Replenishment with schedule agreement
  ▹ Replenishment with summarized just-in-time (JIT) call
▸ Stock transfer
  ▹ Replenishment with reservation
  ▹ Replenishment with direct transfer posting
  ▹ Replenishment by transport requirements of warehouse-management (WM) administered storage location

Replenishment with kanban is very simple. First, a material is produced at a machine. The components required to produce it are available on-site in containers, ready for withdrawal. If one of these containers is empty, the source that is responsible for its replenishment has to be informed accordingly. If kanban processing without SAP system support is being used, the consumer sends a card (by courier, for example) to the work center (source). The card contains the information about which material is required, in what quantity, and where it should be delivered to. The process gets its name from the Japanese word for these cards (kanban). The source can now produce or procure the material and then re-fill the container (see Figure 3.6).

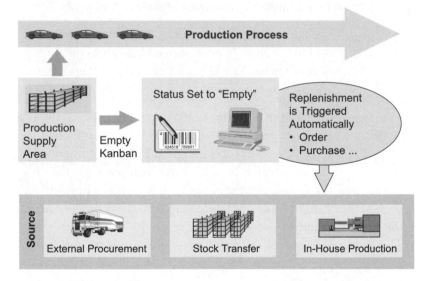

Figure 3.6 Kanban Signal

If kanban processing with SAP ERP system support is being used, the containers are managed in the system and have a specific status. Once the last component is withdrawn from a container, the status of that container is simply changed from "full" to "empty." This status change is the kanban signal and can be set by passing a barcode reader over the card that is attached to the container. It is also possible to have the system display the containers in a production area in the form of a kanban table and to make the status change there. The kanban signal now triggers the replenishment process and creates—for example—a production order in accordance with the replenishment strategy. The source then processes the production order and the finished material is transported back to the container. The status of the container is set to "full" again (barcode or kanban table), and the goods receipt for the material is posted with reference to the procurement element.

The SAP system also supports other kinds of kanban procedures besides the classic procedure described above. While in classic kanban the user sets the container to "empty" using a barcode or a kanban table, thus triggering the kanban signal, in kanban with a quantity signal the user or a plant data-collection system enters the relevant withdrawn quantities into the system. As soon as the quantity in the container equals zero or drops below a specific threshold value, the system automatically changes the status.

Unlike classic kanban, where the number of containers and their quantities are fixed in advance, in event-driven kanban a container is created only when required. The required quantity is then entered directly. Once the replenishment has been made, the container is deleted.

Kanban can also be used for production supply with the use of anticipatory material requirements planning. The replenishment elements in this case are created by a material requirements planning run. However, the replenishment elements function as a preview for the source; they do not directly trigger production or procurement. Now, the setting of the kanban to full or empty controls only the flow of material itself and the actual production process. Confirmations and goods receipts are usually posted without reference to the kanban process.

3.3.6   Engineer-to-Order Production

Experience has shown that conventional production processes are not particularly successful for complex make-to-order production processes.

The production orders used for the MRP II system are scheduled and handled separately without any coordination support between processes of different production orders. For example, process 25 of production order A-100 cannot start until process 10 of production order B-50 has started. Therefore, engineer-to-order production uses network techniques for scheduling and coordinating processes and cost accounting.

MRP II uses the BOM to split up the production of the finished product into smaller units, while engineer-to-order production divides the overall production process into work packages, which are specified in a *work breakdown structure (WBS)*. There is not always a one-to-one correspondence between these structures and the units defined in the BOM.

MRP keeps technology, maintenance, and other customer-specific activities from production. Engineer-to-order production, on the other hand, requires that production-specific and non-production-specific processes be handled together.

Another difference is that standard costs are used for MRP II, while actual costs are used for engineer-to-order production.

Classic network systems are not very suitable for production management. They do not support inventory management, material requirements planning, or scheduling and tracking tasks within the factory. What engineer-to-order production needs is a system that combines the best of both procedures. You need a solution that can execute production orders, inventory management, and material requirements planning, like MRP II, and also handle task coordination, budget planning, and actual cost calculation.

You also need a system for processing complex production processes for industry, such as those for aircraft, ships, and large machines. A significant part of the lead time and added value of these product types is not taken into account in production-based processes such as design, work scheduling, and order costing.

Work breakdown structure For these reasons, engineer-to-order production uses work breakdown structures and networks. A WBS is a hierarchical model of the tasks that need to be carried out in a project and is the basis for the organization and coordination of the project. It contains the work, the time, and the costs that are associated with every task. A provisional WBS is created for the preparatory planning stage (that is, during the tender procedure). It then can be extended dynamically during the lifetime of the project.

Network *Networks* are use to model detailed processes, such as the staff, capacities, materials, production resources, tools, and services that are required for the project. Networks also can describe extensive relationships between processes. They are connected to the WBS and thus provide an extra level of detail for representing the overall structure of the work.

The starting-point is to set up a *project structure* in order to create a customer quotation. Once the project structure has been set up, detailed cost plans are developed and integrated into the budget. Based on the level of detail, plans are developed from bottom to top, while budgets are developed from top to bottom. Capacities are also checked, and the project details are combined to form a customer quotation. A sales order can be created as a special order type with project reference (project order). The project is then released for project structure plan-driven and network plan-driven processing. Down payments, invoice payments, and any other customer payments are assigned to the relevant WBS element. Costs and material withdrawals are posted directly to the network or WBS elements. The system monitors the availability of the budgeted funds. The costs are invoiced at regular intervals or at the close of the project, either to the general ledger, the cost center, or directly to the revenue calculation system.

Project structure

The finished products are listed in the sales order and are managed using the make-to-order production scenario. Production orders are created either manually or automatically by the system. These orders are then linked to the relevant WBS element. Thus, production is controlled by conventional production orders, and the actual production costs and milestones are posted to the relevant assigned WBS element.

The structure of the company is modeled with the organizational structures of the SAP ERP system. For the area of production planning and control, the organizational units of Company Code, Plant, and Storage Location are the most important. A different type of organizational element is represented by the different types of planners that represent individuals within the company and are linked to areas of responsibility.

4   Organizational Structures

4.1   Meaning of Organizational Structures

For the German-speaking countries, Nordsieck (1972, p. 7–8) characterized a company's organizational structure by the design of the structural and process organizations that mutually determine each other.

Organization modeling deals with a company's structural organization, unlike the process organization, which deals with the logical time structuring of the work processes. To manage complex social structures, as represented by companies with their many employees, it is necessary to subdivide these into manageable units. Organization modeling therefore refers to the mapping of a company's organizational structure into the structures of a standard application system. The organization model therefore describes the organizational units, their structural relationships, and the users of an information system (see Keller, 1993, p. 626). These organizational structures are shown using organization charts.

Structural and process organization

The traditional approach of organizational structuring places the main emphasis on the structural organization (see Kosiol, 1962). It considers the association of basic task-sharing, functional, and organizational elements such as the job, instance and management for an organizational structure, and the associated relationships between them. Jobs, as the smallest action unit of a company, arise either from the combination of the same tasks at the work object and differing performance tasks, or they consist of the same performances for differing objects. Instances summarize the management tasks of different jobs into a higher job (see Wöhe, 1996, p. 186).

The job classification as the design product represents the relationship between the jobs as a hierarchical structure, in that it links these together from the point of view of the authority. We can derive different structural types that express, on the one hand, the ranking ratio with the formal information flow and communication flow within the organization and, on the other hand, the development of the organizational forms as a reaction to changing market conditions. These include the line organization, the functional organization, the team organization, the object-oriented models, and the matrix organization.

Line organization   Within each *line organization,* there is a specialist disciplinary superior to be uniquely assigned. Each job is linked to all superior instances through a single decision, information, and communication line. The benefits of this are a simple organizational design, a precise delimitation of competencies, and a precise assignment of responsibility and communication relationships. In contrast, you will notice the adverse effects of overloads on the superordinate instances, because jobs of the same rank are linked to each other through the superordinate instance.

Functional organization   The *functional organization* provides for a specialization of the management. Here, the principle of the work distribution is also applied to the management tasks. Instances should have specialized knowledge from which a multiple chain of command for subordinate jobs is derived. That is, with this type of command and control, individual or multiple jobs each have several direct superior instances. Because the requirements for the management's expertise increase as greater areas of responsibility grow, it is useful to define the area of responsibility, as unclear terms of reference can lead to responsibility conflicts. The fundamental idea behind the functional organization is the correlation of the formal decision-making responsibility with the professional competence (specialist knowledge) in an instance.

Team organization   The *team organization* unites the advantages of the clear competence and responsibility definition of the line system with the advantages of the specialization of the functional organization. Staff positions are established in the team organization that are neither instances nor executing jobs, but rather management supports. Here, the tasks of decision preparation, control, and specialist consulting are performed without the decision-making authority.

Object-oriented models are also referred to as divisional organizations, branch organizations, or business area organizations. With these models, the company is structured according to an object characteristic or by a category; for example, a product. Companies design their organizational structure according to the object principle, by forming categories by product, product group, market, customer, or region. A category organization develops with similar business divisions that group the operational functions under responsible management. The business divisions are thus given a profit responsibility in the sense of a profit center; that is, they are managed like companies in the company.

Object-oriented models

In the *matrix organization*, elements of the function orientation such as design, production, and development, and elements of the object orientation such as material, markets, and customers are joined together, generating synergy effects. For the project management or product management, different projects or products thus form the elements of the object orientation. This organizational model shows that we are turning away from strictly hierarchical pyramid models through the use of multi-dimensional arrangements, with holistic project tasks becoming increasingly important.

Matrix organization

4.2 Organizational Structure Overview in SAP ERP

The structure of a company can be mapped by different organizational units for accounting, logistics, and human resources management. Organizational units help to depict a company's structural and process organization.

The complexity of the company structure can be mapped by the multiple relationships of the SAP ERP organizational units. In some cases, there are several possibilities for displaying an issue in the SAP ERP system. For instance, a company can consist of several legal entities, for each of which separate, individual financial statements must be prepared at the end of the financial year.

The internal arrangement of companies is defined, among other things, by the responsibility for particular customer or product groups, which are grouped into strategic business areas. The activities within a business area can be distributed across several companies. Finally, a location can be used by several companies and within various business areas. To map a company you first need, as a minimum, a SAP ERP system in which all accounting and logistics functions are shown.

Profitability analysis is performed in the results area in the SAP ERP system. The cost-center and cost-element accounting are performed in the controlling area. Finally, the company code controls financial accounting and legally represents the enterprise. The creation of internal financial statements for the business areas is supported by the business divisions, and the individual locations are described by plants. Figure 4.1 shows an example of how company structures can be depicted in the SAP system. The human resources functions have no effect on the arrangement of the logical SAP ERP organizational units.

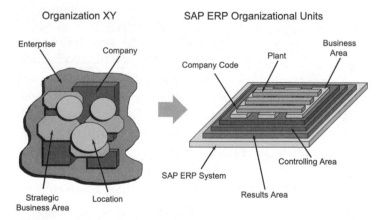

Figure 4.1 Mapping a Real Organization in Logical SAP ERP Organizational Units

The key organizational elements of the SAP ERP system will be described below. In addition to the organizational elements for the production logistics, we also will discuss the most important overall organizational units.

In the context of *production planning and control*, the company code, the plant, and the storage location are the most important organizational units. Figure 4.2 shows their dependencies.

A plant is always uniquely assigned to a company code, which can contain several plants. Each plant can contain several storage locations. A storage location is already defined with a plant reference, which means that the name of the storage location is only unique within a plant. All organizational structures are assigned to a client in SAP ERP.

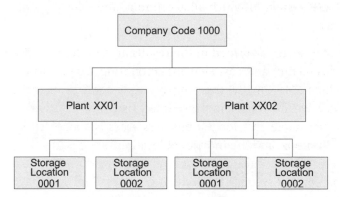

Figure 4.2 Organizational Structures for Production Planning and Control in SAP ERP

The client is a unit that is organizationally self-contained and also self-contained in terms of commercial law and data technology, within a SAP ERP system; it has separate master records and an independent set of tables. It represents the highest element of the SAP ERP organizational structure. The additional organizational elements and the master and transaction data are created and managed within a client. Often the client represents a concrete company or a group, within which there are several independent company units. A SAP ERP system can contain several clients; that is, logical units. A user always logs on to the SAP ERP system with his or her user ID in a client (see Figure 4.3).

Client

The *company code* is an organizational unit for accounting that is used to map independent units for which accounts are prepared in line with legal requirements. The legally prescribed balance sheets and income statements are prepared at the level of the company code. A company that has activities in several countries will require a company code to be set up for each country. The company code is defined with the Customizing Transaction EC01 and only contains **City**, **Country**, **Currency**, and **Language** (see Figure 4.4). Most objects are directly or indirectly linked to the company code.

Company code

Figure 4.3 Logging On to the SAP ERP System

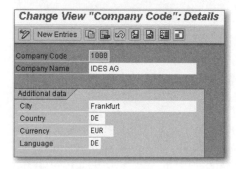

Figure 4.4 Company Code

Plant A *plant* is an organizational unit within logistics. Different production locations are mapped with the plant in SAP ERP. The company can be classified here from the point of view of production, procurement, maintenance, and planning. The plant can be, for instance, an operating site or a subsidiary within a company. It organizes the tasks for the production logistics, and it can be a physical production site or the logical grouping of several sites in which materials are produced or goods and services are provided. The following tasks, among others, are performed at this level:

▶ Inventory management

▶ Evaluation and physical inventory of stocks

▶ Demand management and production planning

▶ Production control

▶ Requirements planning

A plant can have various purposes. As a maintenance plant, it contains the maintenance objects that are spatially located in this plant. The maintenance measures to be performed are laid down within a maintenance planning plant. As a retail site, it provides goods for distribution and sale.

Plants belong to exactly one *company code*. A company code can represent several plants. From a logistical point of view, the plant is the central organizational unit and is maintained with Customizing transaction EC02 (see Figure 4.5).

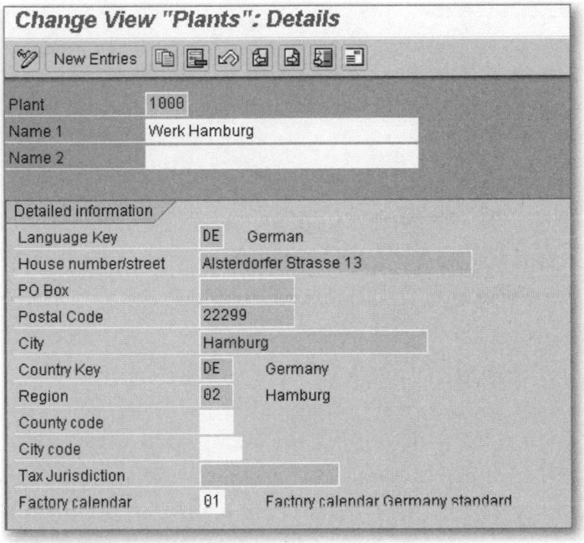

Figure 4.5 Plant

As well as the address, the organization structure **Plant** contains the **factory calendar**, the meaning of which is discussed in more detail in Chapter 10, *Production Order Creation*, in the context of scheduling. The assignment of **Plant** to company code is performed using Customizing Transaction OX18 (see Figure 4.6).

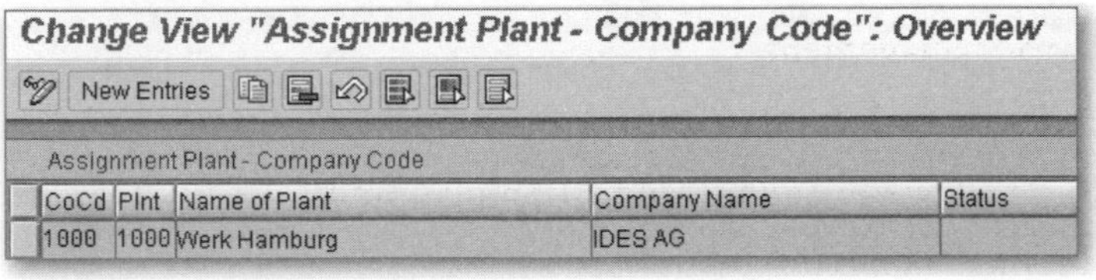

Figure 4.6 Assignment "Plant" to Company Code

Storage location Several storage locations can be defined within a plant. A *storage location* is the place where materials are physically stored. Different materials may be stored at one storage location. Storage locations are maintained plant-specifically with Customizing transaction OX09, as shown in Figure 4.7.

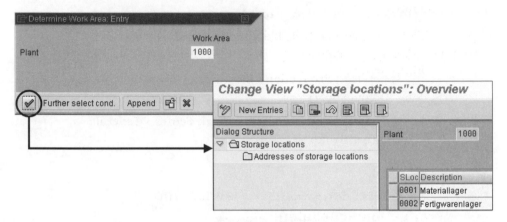

Figure 4.7 Plant-Specific Maintenance of Storage Locations

4.3 Planners in Design and Work Scheduling

The tasks of *Design* focus on the development, setup, and structure of the products. From the point of view of production planning, the creation of the *bill of material (BOM)* is the most important design task. *Work scheduling* plans the machines and processes for the production and is thus closely linked to the maintenance of the master data *work center* and *routing*. Table 4.1 lists the relevant planners in SAP ERP, which are responsible for the master data, and the areas to which they belong.

Area	SAP ERP Planner	Master Data
Design	Lab/design office	BOM
Work scheduling	Work center supervisor	Work center
	Planner group	Routing

Table 4.1 Assignment of the Areas to the SAP ERP Planners and the Master Data

The *work center supervisor* and *planner group* are plant-dependent settings; for example, the work center supervisor 001 in plant XX01 is a different person than the work center supervisor 001 in plant 1000. In contrast, the *laboratory/design office* is unique throughout the plant. The roles listed in Table 4.1 are maintained with the following Customizing paths:

▶ Design office: **Production • Basic Data • BOM • General Data • Set Up Laboratory/Design Office**

▶ Work center supervisor: **Production • Basic Data • Work Center • General Data • Define Supervisor**

▶ Planner group: **Production • Basic Data • Work Center • General Data • Set Up Planner Group**

4.4   MRP Controller, Capacity Planner, and Production Scheduler

While the planners listed in Section 4.3 are only responsible for the maintenance of master data, production planning, and control fall into the task area of the following planners: *MRP controller*, *capacity planner*, and *production scheduler*. These three planners correspond to the roles that SAP sees for production planning and control. Several, or even all, roles can be assigned to one person in a company.

These roles are significant primarily because they allow the fast selection of planning objects according to responsibility.

The *MRP controller* is responsible for production planning, that is, for the quantitative coverage of the requirements. The area of responsibility covers the creation of procurement proposals and the monitoring of material availability. Operations planning also often falls into this area of responsibility. In the short-term, the transition to the tasks of the production scheduler is smooth because postponements lead to only brief shortages due to irregularities or disruptions in production.

MRP controller

MRP controllers are maintained with the Customizing path **Production • Requirements Planning • Master Data • Define MRP Controller** and contain the name and the contact data of the corresponding person (see Figure 4.8).

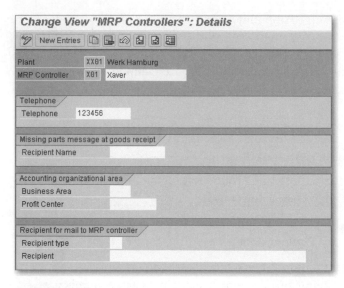

Figure 4.8 MRP Controller

Capacity planner The job of the *capacity planner* is to schedule production operations in such a way that they fulfill the following conditions.

▸ They are feasible in terms of capacity

▸ As far as possible, no delays arise with respect to customer requirements or subsequent production operations

▸ Production costs remain low (setup times can increase due to the sequence of the operations, or unfavorable work center utilizations may arise)

Capacity planners are maintained with the Customizing path **Production • Capacity Planning • Master Data • Capacity Data • Set Up Capacity Planner** (see Figure 4.9).

Figure 4.9 Capacity Planner

Production scheduler The *production scheduler* is the person who is responsible, at the outset, for the smooth running of production. Regarding detailed planning, there may be overlapping or a crossover with the capacity planner. Unlike the MRP controller, the production scheduler does not create any new procurement proposals, but rather produces the planned orders. Production schedulers are maintained with Customizing transaction OPJ9 (see Figure 4.10).

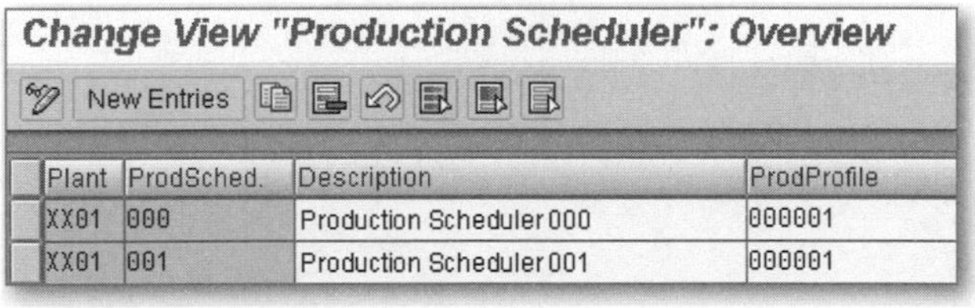

Change View "Production Scheduler": Overview

New Entries					

	Plant	ProdSched.	Description	ProdProfile
	XX01	000	Production Scheduler 000	000001
	XX01	001	Production Scheduler 001	000001

Figure 4.10 Production Scheduler

The only information the production scheduler contains is the production-scheduling profile, which contains a large number of settings. The production scheduling profile is described in Chapter 10, *Production Order Creation*.

Table 4.2 provides an overview of the planning and evaluation functions for which the MRP controller, capacity planner, and production scheduler are used as selection criteria. The significance of this table can only be fully appreciated after reading the book, and is therefore more for later reference.

Selection criteria

Function	Transaction	MRP Controller	Capacity Planner	Production Scheduler
Overall requirement, demand management	MD73	x		
Collective display, MRP list	MD06	x		
Collective display requirements/stock list	MB07	x		
Requirement for the scenario (long-term planning)	MS65	x		
Mass processing of production orders	COHV COMAC	x		x

Table 4.2 MRP Controller, Capacity Planner, and Production Scheduler as Selection Criteria

Function	Transaction	MRP Controller	Capacity Planner	Production Scheduler
Order information system	COOIS	x		x
Missing parts information system	CO24	x		x
Capacity evaluation	CM01 CM02 CM04 CM05 CM07		x	
Capacity leveling	CM21 CM22		x	
Use of production resources and tools	CF10 CF13			x

Table 4.2 MRP Controller, Capacity Planner, and Production Scheduler as Selection Criteria (cont.)

Master data contains the description of the product structure as material master and bill of materials, and it contains the description of the production structure as work center and routing. In addition, master data comprises numerous control parameters. For this reason, the careful maintenance of master data is a prerequisite for the SAP ERP system to function properly.

5 Master Data

5.1 Master Data Overview

The term "master data" includes data concerning the product structure, production processes, and available capacities. Parameters contained within the master data control the planning and execution processes to a large extent. For these reasons, master data is of essential importance. Your discipline with regard to the maintenance of master data can be crucial for the success or failure of an implementation.

The most important types of master data with regard to production planning and control in SAP ERP are the material master, the bill of materials (BOM), the routing, and the work center. BOM and routing can be combined into production versions, which can be advantageous for the selection of master-data alternatives. Their combination is required for the integration with SAP APO. Figure 5.1 provides an overview of how items of master data can be assigned to each other.

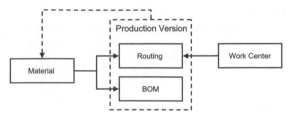

Figure 5.1 Master Data for Production Planning and Control in SAP ERP

Both the BOM and the routing are created with reference to a material. The work center does not have any direct reference to a material and can be used in several routings.

5.2 Material

Material master

The material master is a central element of basic data within production logistics. This basic data has manifold relationships to other important basic data, which are necessary in order to establish efficient and accurate production planning. The master data, *Material*, generally characterizes the used and generated goods in an industrial operation. A material also can be a trading good, for example in retail, distribution, or wholesale. The identifying characteristic of a material is that it is assigned a unique material number. In addition to the identifying date (supplier reference number), the material is also assigned additional descriptive information (see Kilger, 1986, pp. 284–296).

Sales logistics, for example, concerns the article description, the sales price, and component-based discount rates. Price calculation requires the underlying cost unit rates, and procurement logistics requires information on the replenishment lead times and order quantity in order to achieve the best-possible price and the lowest-possible storage costs. The many different integration relationships of the material that are important for production of goods are described in the following sections with reference to the corresponding relevant process areas (see Figure 5.2).

The structural relationships between different materials included in an assembly or end product are stored in the BOM. The BOM specifies whether a material is superior or inferior to another material or assembly. In addition to the structural relationships, the BOM also stores the quantities required for the production of an end product or assembly as well as information on lead times for the individual components. The geometrical relationships for a material are saved in a drawing. Moreover, additional documents can exist to describe a material, such as a patent (see Glaser et al., 1991, pp. 10–13). A drawing contains the following types of information.

▶ **Geometrical data**
Dimensions, patterns, views

▶ **Technological data**
Form tolerances, position tolerances, surface structure

▶ **Organizational details related to the drawing**
Drawing number, processor, creation date, reference to associated detail drawings

▶ **Organizational details related to the drawing content**
Identification number, classification number, description

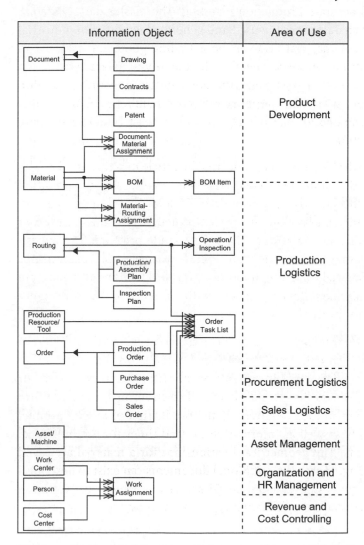

Figure 5.2 Structural Relationships of Information Objects and Their Classification

Creating the material master

Materials must be created using Transaction MM01. In addition to the material number, the material master is also assigned the **Industry sector** and **Material Type** during the creation (see Figure 5.3).

Figure 5.3 Creating a Material

Industry sector

The *industry sector* determines the screen sequence and field selection in the material master. In this context, field references and field selection groups can be used to hide specific fields or declare them as optional or mandatory fields (see Figure 5.4). Once a material has been assigned to an industry sector, this action cannot be undone.

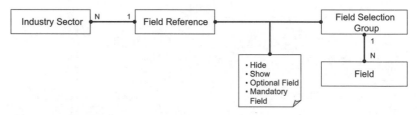

Figure 5.4 Field Selection Based on Industry Assignment

Material type

The *material type* can be defined using the following Customizing path: **Logistics – General • Material Master • Basic Settings • Material Types**. The material type is responsible for an external or internal number assignment. It determines which views are available in which sequence and whether the material can be configured, and it controls the inventory management requirement as well as the accounts in the case of goods movements. Figure 5.5 displays a portion of the maintenance screen for material type, **FERT**.

Views

The material is the central basic data in SAP ERP and is used by all modules. Materials are unique in an entire system and contain some organization-based parameters. The parameters of the material master are maintained in *views* that group different parameters according to specific subjects. The most important data for SAP Production Planning (PP) are the basic data and the plant-dependent Material Requirements Planning (MRP) data. The basic data contains information that describes the material irrespective of the organization, for example the weight and volume as well as the basic quantity unit. Figure 5.6 shows the **Basic data 1** view for the **Airconditioner 110** material with material number **KOOLIX110**.

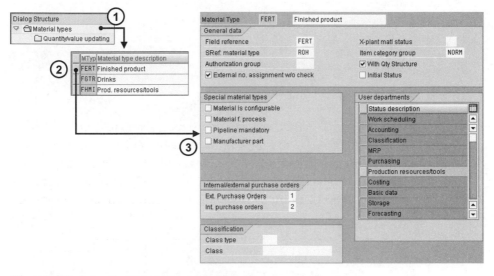

Figure 5.5 Defining the Material Type (Excerpt)

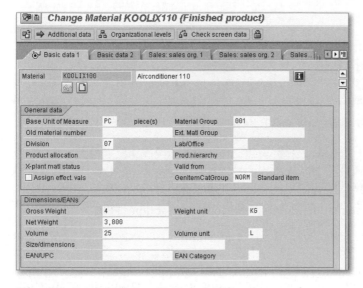

Figure 5.6 Material Master—"Basic data 1" View

The material master contains a large quantity of data and control parameters that are grouped in different views. Table 5.1 provides an overview of the different material views for material type **FERT** and indicates whether these views are organization-dependent.

Material View	Organization-Independent	Plant	Storage Location	Storage No.	Sales and Distribution
Basic data 1 & 2	x				
Classification	x				
Sales: Sales org. 1 & 2	x				x
Sales: general/plant	x	x			
Foreign trade/export data		x			x
Sales text		x			x
Purchasing	x	x			
Foreign trade/import data		x			
Purchase order text	x				
MRP 1– 4		x			
Forecasting		x			
Work scheduling					
Plant data/storage 1 & 2	x	x	x		
Warehouse management 1 & 2		x		x	
Quality management		x			
Accounting 1 & 2		x			
Costing 1 & 2		x			

Table 5.1 Material View and Organizational Unit

For maintaining the material type, the user departments shown in Figure 5.5 correspond to the views listed in Table 5.1. You can maintain both organization-independent and organization-specific parameters in a view. Views that are particularly relevant to production include the following.

▸ **MRP view**
The MRP view enables you to define how to procure a material and how to plan and control this material within the production

process. The definition of the procurement type specifies whether a material is to be externally procured or produced in-house, or if both scenarios are possible. The entry of a value in the **MRP Planner** field defines the ownership for a specific material. The MRP characteristic indicates whether a material is to be planned as demand-driven or consumption-based (stochastic MRP, reorder-point planning). Another attribute within the MRP view represents the strategy group that supports different planning requirements at end-product level. Examples of this include make-to-order production, anonymous make-to-stock production, and production by lot size for sales and warehouse orders and for consideration of planning requirements at subordinate levels (for example, planning with final assembly and planning at assembly level). In addition, the discontinuation indicator allows you to control the point in time after which a material can no longer be used.

► **Design view**
The design view enables you to enter product-related data such as the gross weight, including the weight unit, the volume and volume unit, as well as a reference to the design drawing. Moreover, using the document-management system in this view allows you to manage the design drawings and to store several design drawings for a specific material.

► **Classification view**
The classification view is used to classify specific materials with identical or similar characteristics into groups, and to categorize those groups based on specific characteristics. The SAP ERP system supports the classification process by means of a cross-module and cross-department classification system that allows you to classify materials, customers, supplier, and so on. When classifying a material, you can assign a specific material to several classes.

► **Work-scheduling view**
The work-scheduling view enables you to enter data that is relevant for production execution. Here it is important that you define the in-house production time per operation, which can be specified either as a complete, lot-size-independent time unit or as lot-size-dependent for the individual parts, setup time, transition time, and processing time. If the material must be handled in batches, as is the case in the chemical and food industries, for

example, the material can be explicitly marked. Furthermore, you can specify tolerance values for allowed over-deliveries and under-deliveries.

▶ **Forecasting view**
The forecasting view enables you to define how to carry out the consumption forecast. In this context, the consumption is usually updated for withdrawals from stock. The consumption is divided into an overall consumption and an unplanned consumption. For consumption-based materials, it is always the overall consumption that's updated; i.e., the total of planned and unplanned consumption. The unplanned consumption, on the other hand, is updated for demand-driven materials. This can occur if materials are withdrawn from stock when no reservation exists or if materials must be withdrawn from stock because of a reservation and the withdrawn quantity exceeds the quantity specified in the reservation.

The individual parameters of the different views will be described in further detail when we discuss the corresponding functions.

View selection When you create a material, the system provides all views defined for the material type. You will not want to create and maintain all these views. In order to reduce the maintenance work, you can store a user-specific selection of views and organizational structures as default values (see Figure 5.7).

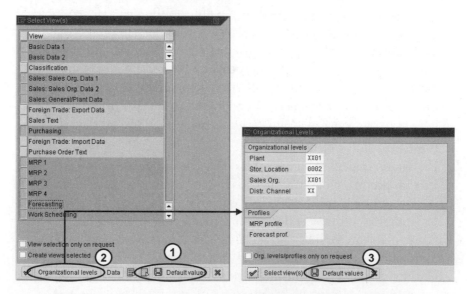

Figure 5.7 Default Values for Material Views and Organizational Structure

5.3 BOM

5.3.1 Areas of Use and Types of BOMs

Similar to the material master, the BOM can also contain information relevant to different user departments. The *BOM* contains the total of all components necessary for production of an end product or assembly, such as sub-assemblies, individual parts, and raw materials. In addition, depending on the relevant BOM type, the BOM contains the structural relationships among the individual components. The term "bill of material (BOM)" is used in industrial enterprises with unit-based production; industrial enterprises with process-based production such as the food industry and the chemical and pharmaceutical industries use the term *recipe* instead.

To carry out requirements planning (BOM explosion) you need, among other things, information on the MRP level, quantity, and the lead-time offset, whereas work scheduling requires quantity information for creation of assembly work centers and for cost determination. For design, BOM information is needed as a basis for implementing changes, while sales and distribution uses BOM information as a basis for aftermarket activities.

The management and alignment of engineering/design and production BOMs plays a major role in many industrial enterprises. In product development, the products are categorized according to functional aspects based on the design drawing, while the production BOM is based in a categorization according to the production process.

Engineering/ design BOM and production BOM

For example, from the design viewpoint the exhaust system can be regarded as a component of the combustion engine, whereas, from the point of view of the assembly, the exhaust is a part of the bodywork. For this reason it can be necessary to maintain the engineering/design and production BOM in parallel. However, in case of changes, you must then align the different BOMs across the different user departments in order to preserve consistency. If the different BOMs match to a large extent despite the different categorization criteria, it makes sense to treat them as you would variants.

In addition to the differentiation of BOMs according to their purpose, BOMs can also be differentiated according to their structure. Basically, BOMs are differentiated by their level and by the degree of

BOM categories

structuring. Depending on the product structure, a differentiation is made between single-level and multilevel BOMs. With single-level BOMs, the assembly to be sold or the end product is directly produced on the basis of the raw materials (for example, the production of screws) or purchased materials (for example, equipping motherboards with individual parts). With multilevel BOMs, the production is carried out via several production and assembly levels that must be planned. First, a raw material is added to an assembly, which in turn becomes part of the end product. With unstructured BOMs, it is merely the quantity of required components that must be specified (as a summarized BOM). For structured BOMs, the structural relationships between the individual components are specified. Based on these two basic principles the following BOM categories exist (see Scheer, 1990, pp. 79–113).

▶ **Single-level BOM**
The single-level BOM contains assemblies and individual parts that are assigned to the next subordinate level. The specified quantities always refer to the assembly that's named in the BOM header. The two-level presentation of the BOM ensures a clear overview. However, the entire context of multi-part products that contain several assemblies at different MRP levels can only be displayed if the BOM is output as a multilevel BOM.

▶ **Multilevel BOM**
The multilevel BOM presents the internal structure of a product; in other words, the logical relationships of a product structure. For the component (assembly or end product) described in the BOM header, the multilevel BOM shows all assemblies and individual parts included along with the respective quantities at all structure levels.

▶ **Summarized BOM**
A summarized BOM presents all quantities of subassemblies and individual parts without structure information for the components (assembly or end product) described in the BOM header.

▶ **Variant BOM**
Variant BOMs are used to map similar product structures in which variants differ in only a few BOM items. The purpose of this BOM category is to avoid having to create a complete data record for each variant type, thereby minimizing the storage and maintenance requirements.

The use of a specific BOM category depends in part on its intended purpose. Single-level BOMs are often used in mechanical-engineering companies, such as those that produce partly standardized product families or multilevel product series with high degrees of standardization. Multilevel BOMs are primarily required in the context of BOM explosion and are thus often used in mechanical-engineering companies that build special-purpose or large machines. Summarized BOMs are frequently used for costing purposes, simple production and assembly structures, and to generate requirements for which one only needs to determine the quantities of individual parts and raw materials. Variant BOMs are used in mechanical-engineering companies whose products have a high degree of similarity. These companies include mechanical engineering companies with vendor-specific variants. Figure 5.8 shows the relationship between the product structure and BOM categories.

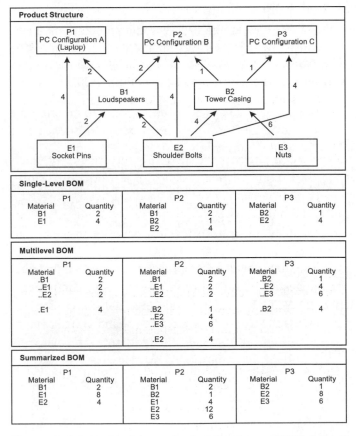

Figure 5.8 Relationship Between Product Structure and BOM Categories

Three end products—P1, P2, and P3—are displayed with their components in the product structure. The required quantity of the component is indicated by the numbers next to the arrows. While the single-level BOM contains only those components that are used directly for manufacturing the end product, the multilevel BOM contains all components, even those of the subassemblies used. The level of the component—that is, if and where it is used in an assembly—is indicated by the prefixed points. For example, for end product P1, two units of component E1 are used for assembly B1 and four units are used for end product E1 itself. The summarized BOM only lists the required quantities of all components without detailing the design structure. For this reason, the summarized BOM does not further break down the requirement of eight units of component E1 for end product P1.

5.3.2 Material BOM

In SAP ERP, the BOMs are defined in the production-planning module. The BOM consists of a header section and an item section. The header section specifies, for instance, the plant allocation, validity period, and the status (released or locked for production).

BOM maintenance   We will use the example of a *material BOM* in order to describe the BOM maintenance in SAP PP. You can create material BOMs using transaction CS01, while transaction CS02 enables you to change them (see Figure 5.9). Each material can have several BOMs, because different BOMs can exist for different purposes, while there can be several alternatives for each purpose. Thus the BOM can only be uniquely identified via the header information, purpose, and alternative.

Item overview   The *item overview* shows which components are needed in what quantities for the header product. In this case, the four components **KLKOMPR100**, **KLVNT30**, **KLGEH100**, and **KLSTE100** are required for header product **KOOLIX220** (see Figure 5.10). The individual components are entered as items of the BOM. In addition to the overview of components and their quantities, the item overview also uses the item type to provide information as to which type of component is being used (in this case a stock item) and whether the component is an assembly. This means that a separate BOM exists for the component (in this case for component **KLVNT30**; see Figure 5.11).

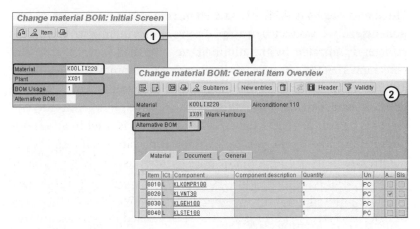

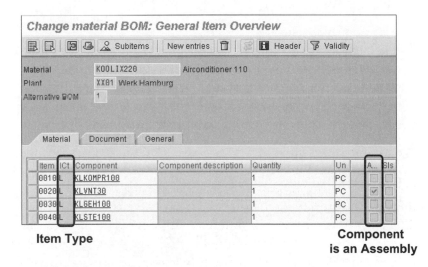

Figure 5.9 BOM Maintenance

Figure 5.10 BOM Item Overview

Figure 5.11 shows an alternative, graphical display of the BOM structure.

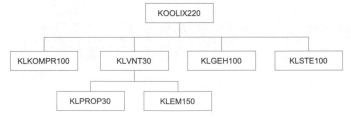

Figure 5.11 BOM Structure

The *item category* subdivides the item into different classes. Some item categories are relevant to planning and production, while others merely provide information. BOMs can map various different objects in the SAP system, such as materials, equipment, technical locations, and documents. The most important predefined item categories in SAP ERP are as follows.

▸ **L for stock item**
Stock items contain components that can be stored and included in inventory management. The parameterization also allows for a further subdivision of the items. For example, the subsets of a BOM item can differ by their installation location. The different installation locations are then mapped as sub-items. Sub-items have no operational relevance in the BOM and are not included in the production order.

▸ **N for non-stock item**
A non-stock item describes a material that is not withdrawn from the warehouse but procured directly for a production order. Consequently, a non-stock item always has an integrative relationship to purchasing. If the BOM contains a non-stock item for which a cost element has been entered, an account check is carried out. If the cost element refers to primary costs, a check is made to see whether the G/L account actually exists in the identified company code. The system finds the company code on the basis of the information provided for the plant to which the BOM is to be assigned, and on the basis of the resulting valuation area. Secondary costs are only maintained in cost accounting.

▸ **R for variable-size item**
If you specify this item category, the entered sizes and a potentially stored calculation formula can be used to automatically determine the variable-sized item quantity.

▸ **I for PM structure element**
A maintenance BOM contains items that are used to structure the design of the equipment (PM assembly). No plant data is required for those materials. For this reason, no plant inspection is carried out for materials with item category **PM structure element**. Items of this item category should only be used in maintenance BOMs (such as equipment BOMs, maintenance-relevant material BOMs, BOMs for function location, and so on).

▶ **T for text item**

The text item has a descriptive character. This item category can be assigned different texts.

▶ **M for intra material**

This item category is important in the process industry (master recipe). Materials that are temporarily used in process engineering are recorded as components with this item category.

Figure 5.12 shows the maintenance of the item categories using Customizing transaction OS13.

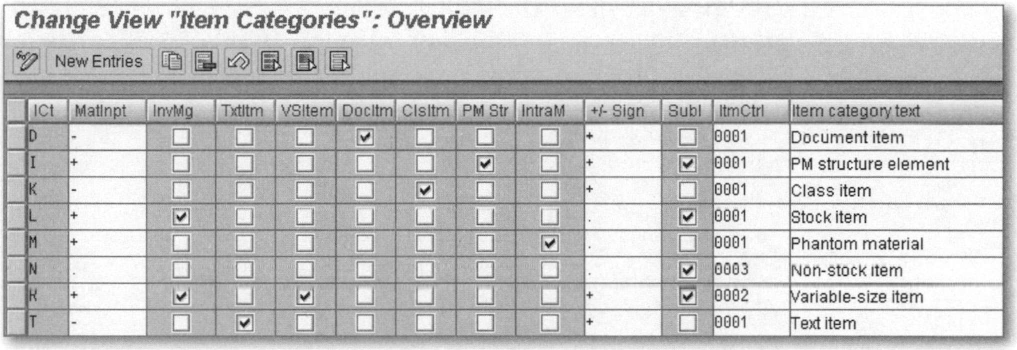

Change View "Item Categories": Overview

ICt	MatInpt	InvMg	Txtltm	VSitem	Docltm	Clsltm	PM Str	IntraM	+/- Sign	Subl	ItmCtrl	Item category text
D	-				✓				+		0001	Document item
I	+						✓		+	✓	0001	PM structure element
K	-					✓			+		0001	Class item
L	+	✓							.	✓	0001	Stock item
M	+							✓	.		0001	Phantom material
N	.								.	✓	0003	Non-stock item
R	+	✓		✓					+	✓	0002	Variable-size item
T	-		✓						+		0001	Text item

Figure 5.12 Customizing the Item Categories for the BOM

The material input parameter (**MatInpt**) indicates whether a material reference to the item exists. This is not the case with document items, for example. The inventory-management parameter (**InvMg**) allows you to control that only those materials whose quantities are managed in inventory management can be used for the item.

In addition to the item overview, the BOM contains detail views for the header and for individual components. Figure 5.13 shows the BOM header for the BOM shown in Figure 5.9. — *Header overview*

The **base quantity** is an essential piece of information contained in the header overview. The entire quantity information for the components refers to the base quantity. Correspondingly, the component requirement for an order can be calculated using the following formula, provided that no scrap is planned: — *Base quantity*

$$\text{component requirements} = \text{input quantity} * \text{order quantity} / \text{base quantity}$$

BOM status The *BOM status,* which is also assigned in the BOM header, can be used to restrict the BOM usage, if it is still being processed. You can maintain the BOM status using Customizing transaction OS23 (see Figure 5.14).

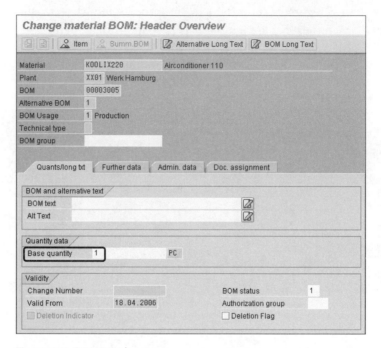

Figure 5.13 BOM Header

Change View "BOM Statuses": Overview

New Entries

BOM St	ExMs ID	MRPExplo	PlanOrd	Rel cstg	RelWkSch.	Rel ords	Coll is	SalesOrd
1		✔	✔	✔	✔	✔	✔	✔
2		☐	☐	☐	☐	☐	☐	☐
3		✔	✔	☐	✔	☐	☐	✔

Figure 5.14 BOM Status

The status defines applications for which the BOM has been released; for example, explosion in requirements planning, in the planned order, or in costing.

Item detail Additional parameters exist for each component. These parameters are contained in the *item detail* (see Figure 5.15). The parameters include parameters for scrap and scheduling, which are described in more detail in Chapters 8 and 10.

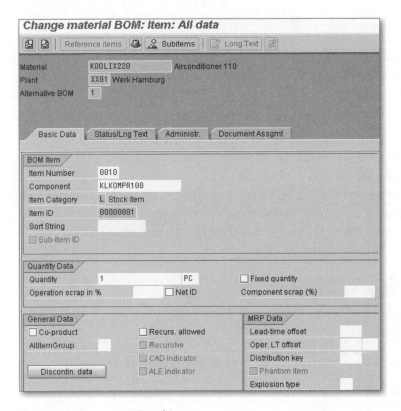

Figure 5.15 Component Detail

The *BOM usage* restricts the use of the BOM to specific areas, as explained in the previous section where we described the design requirements in comparison to production. The BOM usage must be specified for identification purposes when you create or change the BOM; it is maintained using Customizing transaction OS20 (see Figure 5.16).

BOM usage

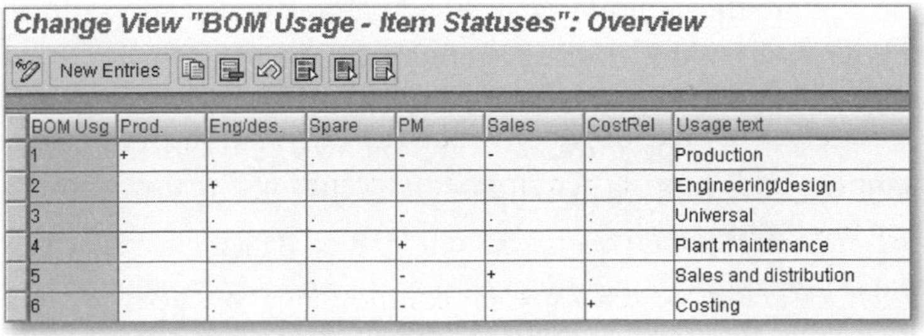

Change View "BOM Usage - Item Statuses": Overview

BOM Usg	Prod.	Eng/des.	Spare	PM	Sales	CostRel	Usage text
1	+	.	.	-	-	.	Production
2	.	+	.	-	-	.	Engineering/design
3	.	.	.	-	-	.	Universal
4	-	-	.	+	-	.	Plant maintenance
5	.	.	.	-	+	.	Sales and distribution
6	.	.	.	-	-	+	Costing

Figure 5.16 BOM Usage

For each of the areas of production, design, sales and distribution, and so on, the BOM usage defines whether the item must be relevant to one of the areas (+ indicator), can be relevant to one of the areas (. indicator), or whether it must not be relevant to one of the areas (- indicator).

Multilevel BOM explosion

Depending on the complexity of the product and product structure, a large number of BOM levels can exist for a saleable product. In these cases it can be useful to obtain an overview of all the components that are included in total; that is, across all BOM levels in the saleable product. This type of information is provided using the multilevel BOM explosion that can be called using transaction CS11. Figure 5.17 shows the multilevel BOM explosion for our example of the air-conditioning system **KOOLIX220**.

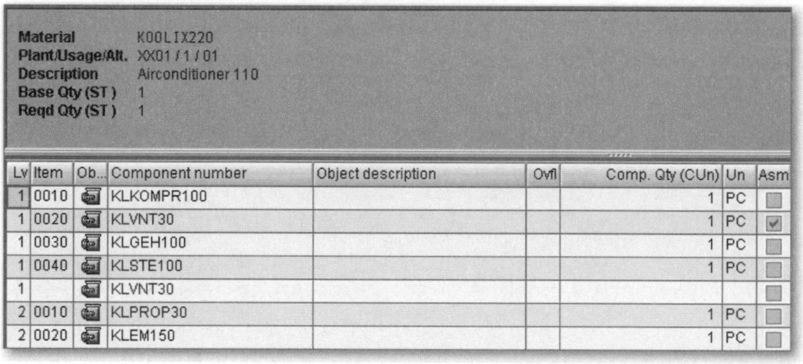

Material	KOOLIX220
Plant/Usage/Alt.	XX01 / 1 / 01
Description	Airconditioner 110
Base Qty (ST)	1
Reqd Qty (ST)	1

Lv	Item	Ob...	Component number	Object description	Ovfl	Comp. Qty (CUn)	Un	Asm
1	0010		KLKOMPR100			1	PC	☐
1	0020		KLVNT30			1	PC	☑
1	0030		KLGEH100			1	PC	☐
1	0040		KLSTE100			1	PC	☐
1			KLVNT30					☐
2	0010		KLPROP30			1	PC	☐
2	0020		KLEM150			1	PC	☐

Figure 5.17 Multilevel BOM Explosion

Here, a two-level BOM was "flattened" in that the BOM of component **KLVNT30** has been included in the overview along with its components, **KLPROP30** and **KLEM150**.

Where-used BOM

Whereas the multilevel BOM explosion analyzes which subordinate elements are required for which component specified in the BOM header, it is sometimes also necessary to know which component is required for which superordinate component. The *where-used BOM* tells you which subordinate components are needed for which superordinate components. For example, the designer needs this information when implementing changes, in order to be able to estimate the extent to which a design change of a standard element will affect other components. Similarly, in case of production problems this information enables you to identify the superordinate production processes affected by the problems so that you can take preventive action. Figure 5.18 shows the where-used BOM for a component—**KLKOMPR100**—using transaction CS15.

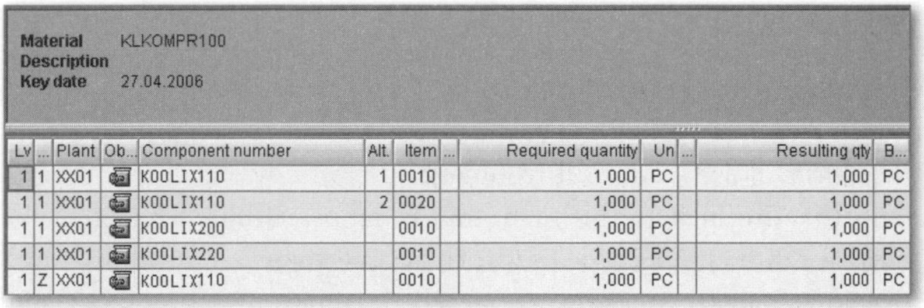

Material	KLKOMPR100
Description	
Key date	27.04.2006

Lv	...	Plant	Ob...	Component number	Alt.	Item	...	Required quantity	Un	...	Resulting qty	B...
1	1	XX01		KOOLIX110	1	0010		1,000	PC		1,000	PC
1	1	XX01		KOOLIX110	2	0020		1,000	PC		1,000	PC
1	1	XX01		KOOLIX200		0010		1,000	PC		1,000	PC
1	1	XX01		KOOLIX220		0010		1,000	PC		1,000	PC
1	Z	XX01		KOOLIX110		0010		1,000	PC		1,000	PC

Figure 5.18 Where-Used BOM

All BOMs are listed in which **KLKOMPR100** is used. As you can see in the sample BOMs for **KOOLIX110**, BOMs are defined on the basis of header material, BOM usage, and alternatives.

5.4   Work Center

5.4.1   Role of the Work Center

Work centers play a major role for two reasons. First, work centers represent the central capacity quantity within production planning. Second, personnel planning determines which employees with which qualifications should work at which types of work centers. Correspondingly, the definition of the work center can affect the way in which cost elements and activity types are handled in accounting, and it can affect payroll processes in HR management.

In the context of materials resource planning (MRP), work center resources are often regarded as PRTs such as machines, tools, devices, and NC programs. Whereas these points are based on a more or less technical view of resource planning, work centers are characterized by a more organizational point of view. For example, depending on the organizational structure within a company, a work center can correspond to a machine, a group of machines, a person, or a group of persons.

For the technical point of view, the assignment of work centers to operations are of particular importance in the context of work scheduling as well as the costing, lead- time scheduling, and capacity requirements planning that are based on those assignments. For the organizational viewpoint, the following factors are important for the remuneration of an employee (see Kilger, 1986, pp. 229–284; Marr/Stitzel, 1979, pp. 391–423).

- ▶ **Production Organization**
  Different types of production organization include shop floor production, flow manufacturing—with and without time dependence—for the manufacturing and assembly centers, and MRP-relevant scheduling of employees based on their qualifications

- ▶ **Definition of the working time**
  This includes fixed and flexible working time provision, full-time and part-time work, and shifts

- ▶ **Wage types**
  Time wage, piecework wage, and premium wage as well as summarizing and analytical job evaluation

A work center is a spatial area within the work system of a company. At the work center, an operation of an order (see Section 5.5), several operations of an order, or the entire order (work order) are executed. In the SAP ERP system, a work center can be assigned to a routing, a maintenance plan, an inspection plan, or a network. Using the data that's maintained in the work center, you can define in the operations which machines and persons are to be used, which costs will be incurred, which capacities are available, and how scheduling is structured.

In the SAP system, work centers are often used along with tasks and jobs from HR management in order to create comprehensive job descriptions. The job describes the job classification, while the tasks describe the activities included in the job, and the work center describes the location at which the work is executed. If you create a job description in HR management, you must first create jobs, then tasks, and then work centers.

If you plan an integration of the areas of production (PP) and HR (HR-PD), you must activate the integration switch in Customizing. In addition, you must set the common capacity categories using the **Capacity Category Person** flag.

5.4.2 Basic Data for the Work Center

You can create work centers using transaction CR01 and change them using transaction CR02. To create a work center, you must specify a reference to a plant and a work center category. Figure 5.19 shows the initial screen that is displayed for changing the work center **KLMNTG05** in plant **XX01**.

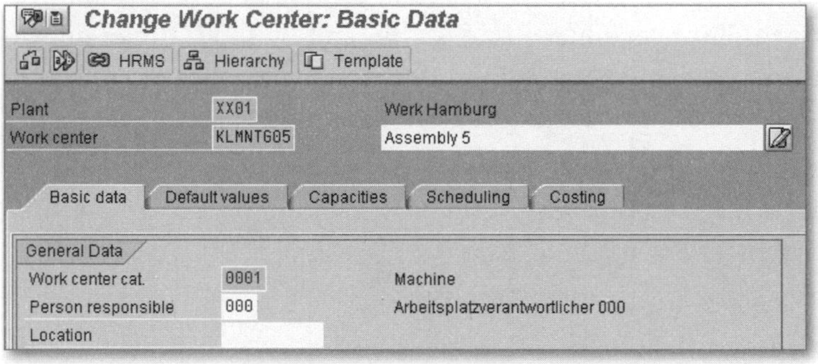

Figure 5.19 Work Center Initial Screen

The work center contains the following views and essential parameters.

▶ **Basic data**
The basic data view contains information about the person responsible for the work center, the usage of the work centers in plans, and the standard value key that is essential for scheduling and capacity requirements planning.

▶ **Default values**
Here you can maintain default values that are copied into the routing when the work center is used.

▶ **Capacities**
This view contains information on the capacities pertaining to the work center as well as formulas for calculating the capacity requirement.

▶ **Scheduling**
The scheduling view contains formulas that enable you to perform scheduling tasks.

▶ **Costing**
This view provides information on the cost center for the work center and activity types.

Work center category
In addition to the field selection, the *work center category* controls the usability in routings and must be maintained using Customizing transaction OP40. In the example shown in Figure 5.20, the work center category 0001 can be used for routings for production, maintenance, and quality assurance, whereas it cannot be used for recipes and rate-based plans.

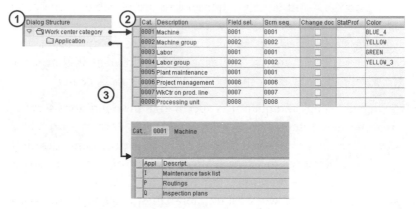

Figure 5.20 Work Center Category

Task list usage
The *task list usage* goes even further into the details of the work center categories. In the example shown in Figure 5.21, the task list usage **001** only allows for routings (category N) and reference operation sets (category S). You can maintain the task list usage via Customizing transaction OP45.

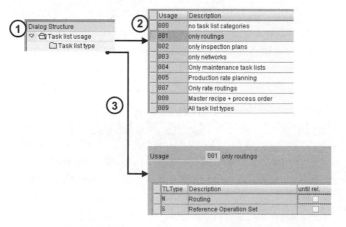

Figure 5.21 Task List Usage

5.4.3 Capacity

A capacity represents the potential to fulfill a specific task. In the SAP system, capacities define the service offering that can be provided by persons and machines within a given period. A work center can be assigned several capacities that differ by their capacity categories. For example, machine capacities, personnel capacities, spare capacities for rush orders, and energy requirements are possible work center capacities of different capacity categories. Capacity-requirements planning determines the capacity requirement of operations that pertain to specific orders. The capacity requirement is then compared with the available capacity defined in the work center.

The default values and quantities specified in the operations serve as a basis for determining the *capacity requirement*. Formulas contained in the work centers are then used in capacity-requirements planning in order to calculate the capacity requirement on the basis of the default values and quantities. Moreover, in capacity-requirements planning you can use work center hierarchies to aggregate the available capacity and the capacity requirement from subordinate work centers to work centers at superordinate hierarchy levels. The capacity allows you to store the operating time and the daily available capacity for a work center. The definition of the available capacity can refer to one or several work centers.

Capacity requirement

The starting point for defining the *available capacity* is the working time at a specific work center. The working time is defined by the work start and work finish. Moreover, the working time also plays a crucial role for date determination in the context of scheduling, because an operation can be processed at a work center only within the working time. However, the working time cannot be completely used for production. Factors such as scheduled breaks and technical and organizational incidents reduce the working time. In order to determine the productive working time, the breaks must be subtracted from the pure working time. The result is the theoretically usable working time. By subtracting the technical and organizational incidents from this, you can determine the working time that can be used for production. The system outputs the working time that can be used for production as operating time in the capacity view. The technical and organizational times that result from incidents are stored as rates of capacity utilization in the work center or capacity

Available capacity

view. The rate of capacity utilization enables you to define the percentage of the operating time shift during which you can use the capacity for production purposes.

"Capacity" object

The **Capacity** object contains the capacity required for production. Capacities are typically directly maintained from the work center. Exceptions in this context are the pooled capacities, which will be described separately in this book. Figure 5.22 shows how you can navigate to the **Capacity** object by double-clicking on the capacity category in the capacity view of the work center.

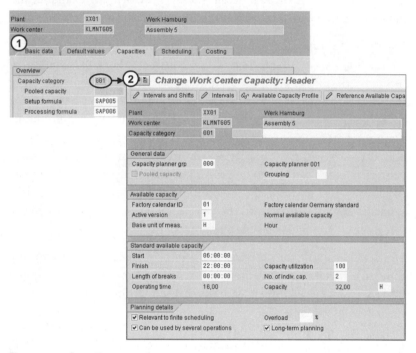

Figure 5.22 Capacity

The general data section of the **Capacity** contains the capacity planner, the factory calendar, the version of the available capacity, and other planning details that will be described in the following sections.

Standard available capacity

The **Standard available capacity** specifies the working times and the capacity of the **Capacity** object. In addition to the **Operating time** that results from **Start**, **Finish**, and the **Length of breaks**, the **rate of capacity utilization** and the number of individual capacities (**No. of**

indiv. cap.) determine the actual available capacity according to the following formula.

$$Capacity = Operating\ time * No.\ of\ indiv.\ Cap. *$$
$$Capacity\ utilization\ /\ 100$$

The *rate of capacity utilization* is usually below 100% in order to account for downtimes and maintenance work. The latter only applies if plant maintenance is not recorded automatically by the system.

Rate of capacity utilization

A capacity can contain several *individual capacities*. For example, you can summarize a group of individual work centers of the same category into one capacity in order to reduce the data maintenance work. But to be able to still carry out planning tasks at individual capacity level, you must explicitly create the individual capacities from the capacity via the following menu path: **Goto • Individual Capacity** (see Figure 5.23).

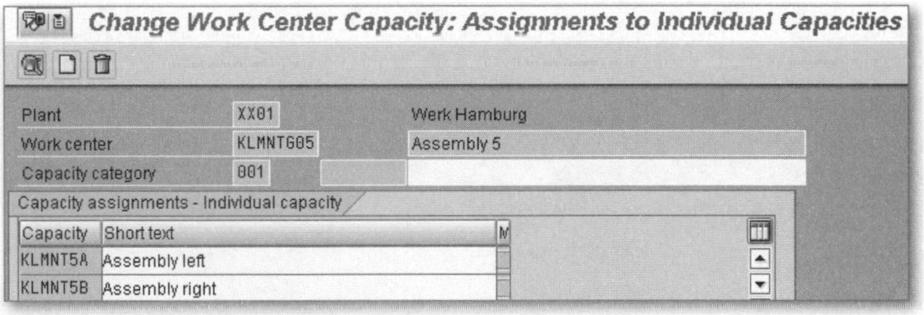

Individual capacities

Figure 5.23 Individual Capacities

A work center can contain one or several capacities, provided the capacities belong to different capacity categories. You can maintain *capacity categories* via the following Customizing path: **Production • Basic Data • Work Center • Capacity Planning • Define Capacity Category** (see Figure 5.24).

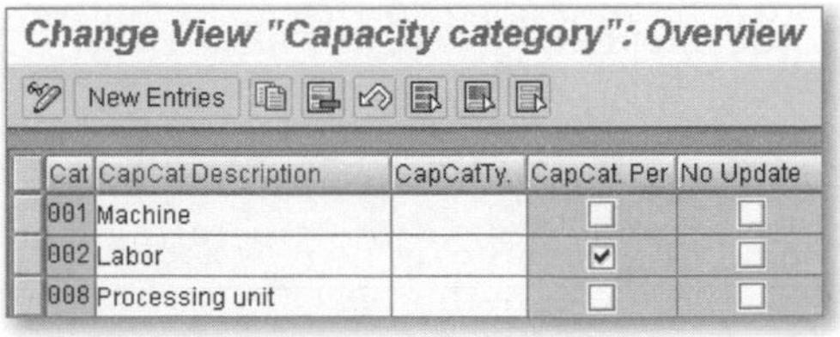

Number of capacities of the work center

Figure 5.24 Capacity Category

When the work center is created, the capacities are added to the work center by entering the capacity category in the **Capacities** view. If the work center exists already, you can add new capacities by clicking on the relevant button shown in Figure 5.25.

Shift sequences

The standard available capacity defines the working times in a comparatively rough way, given that the length of breaks is not scheduled. The breaks merely reduce the operating time. Moreover, the working times are the same for each day of the week. You can use shift sequences to carry out a more detailed modeling; for instance, if you want to specify that the working time is shorter on Fridays.

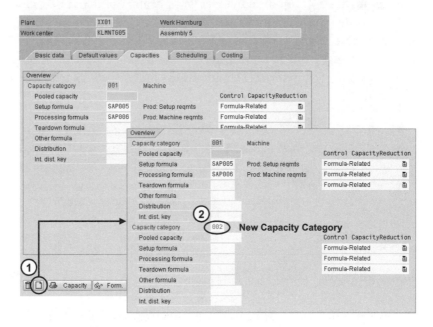

Figure 5.25 Adding a Capacity

A *shift sequence* consists of one or several shifts, each of which can be assigned a break plan. All these three objects—break plan, shift, and shift sequence—are maintained using Customizing transaction OP4A. Figure 5.26 shows the maintenance of a shift sequence, including the shifts and the break plan.

Shift sequence, shift, and break plan are assigned to a grouping. In Figure 5.26, that's grouping **51**. This grouping, in turn, is assigned to the capacity (see Figure 5.27).

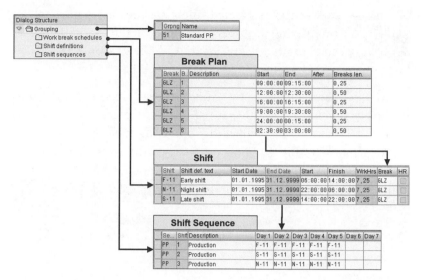

Figure 5.26 Shift Sequences

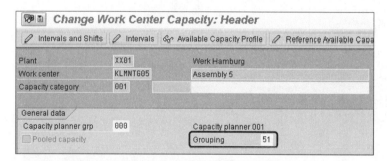

Figure 5.27 Assigning a Grouping to the Capacity

It sometimes happens that a capacity is used by several work centers. **Pooled capacity** For example, in a shop-floor production scenario, the assembly work centers could be mapped as work centers, while the workers are mapped as pooled capacities that can work at various different assembly work centers. *Pooled capacities* are directly created as capacities using transaction CR11 and are assigned the **Pooled capacity** parameter (see Figure 5.28).

The assignment to the work center occurs in the **Capacities** view, as shown in Figure 5.29.

If you navigate from the work center into the capacity, the pooled capacity is displayed. You cannot modify the pooled capacity from the work center.

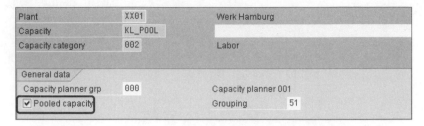

Figure 5.28 Creating a Pooled Capacity

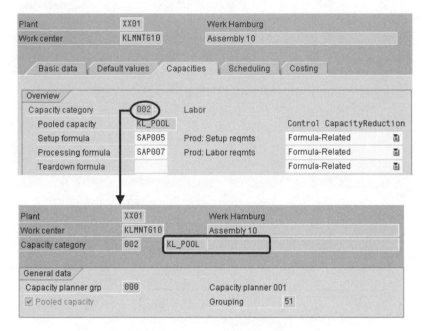

Figure 5.29 Assigning the Pooled Capacity to the Work Center

5.4.4 Formulas for Capacity Load and Scheduling

The work center determines how you can define the lengths and capacity requirements for the operations processed at this work center. Although the determination of capacity requirements and operation times is based on separate formulas, both formulas use the same standard values.

Parameters   The standard values are first defined as *parameters* using Customizing transactions OPCX or OP7B (see Figure 5.30). The parameters themselves do not contain any additional information.

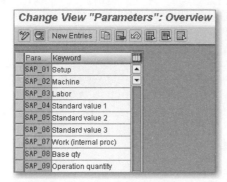

Figure 5.30 Parameters

The *standard value key* determines which of the parameters are to be assigned standard values in the routing. You can create the standard value key using Customizing transaction OPCM. The key can contain one or several parameters. Figure 5.31 displays the standard value key **SAP1**.

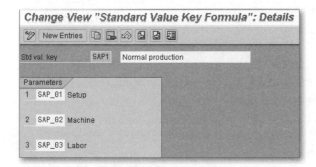

Figure 5.31 Standard Value Key

The standard value key is assigned to the work center in the **Basic data** view (see Figure 5.32).

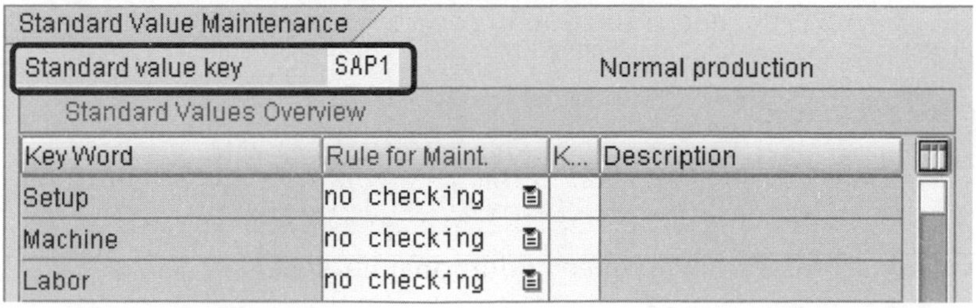

Standard Value Maintenance				
Standard value key	SAP1		Normal production	
Standard Values Overview				
Key Word	Rule for Maint.	K...	Description	
Setup	no checking			
Machine	no checking			
Labor	no checking			

Figure 5.32 Assigning the Standard Value Key to the Work Center

When an operation is created in the routing and the operation uses this work center, you can maintain standard values for the three parameters, **Setup time**, **Machine time**, and **Labor time**.

Formula The formulas used to calculate the capacity requirements and operation durations use the previously defined parameters. You can use the parameters of the standard values, and other parameters can be filled with orders values without any explicit definition, such as:

▶ SAP_08: Base quantity

▶ SAP_09: Operation quantity

▶ SAP_11: Number of operation splits

You can create the formulas using Customizing transaction OP21. In addition to the formula itself—that is the linking of the parameters— the formula stores information on which of the three following applications the formula can be used for.

▶ Capacity requirements

▶ Scheduling

▶ Costing

Figure 5.33 shows the standard formula for calculating the processing duration, **SAP002**, and the standard formula for calculating capacity requirements, **SAP006**.

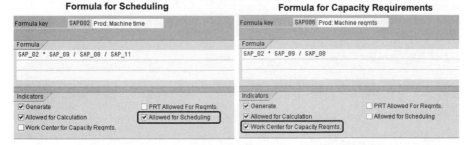

Figure 5.33 Formulas for Calculating the Processing Duration and the Capacity Requirements

As you can easily see, the formulas for the processing duration and capacity requirements are not identical. The capacity requirement can be calculated as:

*Capacity requirement = Standard value * Order quantity / Base quantity*

The processing duration can be reduced if the operation is processed simultaneously at several work centers as follows:

Duration = Standard value * Order quantity / Base quantity /
  Number of splits

The formulas are assigned to the **Scheduling**, **Capacities**, and **Costing** views. Figure 5.34 shows the assignment of the formulas **SAP001** for setup and **SAP002** for processing to the **Scheduling** view.

When applying the scheduling formulas you should note that the working times are defined in the capacity and that the work center can contain more than one capacity. For this reason, you must define in the **Scheduling** view which capacity category uses the working times. This capacity category represents the scheduling basis and is determined using the **Capacity category** parameter (see Figure 5.34).

Scheduling basis

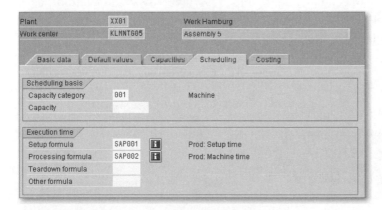

Figure 5.34 Scheduling Formulas in the Work Center

5.4.5 Costing

Costing enables you to determine the costs of the internal activities to be performed in manufacturing the products. Because of the maintenance involved with cost centers and activity types, costing establishes a link from the operation via the work center to cost accounting. If the work center is used in an operation, you can enter standard values for the activity types stored in the work center. In product costing, the evaluation of internal activities is based on the allocation records that have been planned for these activity types. Activity types define the manner in which the standard values are to be allocated in cost accounting.

Cost center
A *cost center* is a part of the company that is defined according to an area of responsibility or according to spatial or accounting-specific aspects. It is assigned to a controlling area. A cost center can be assigned work centers from different plants. The plant, in turn, is uniquely assigned to a company code. A work center is firmly assigned to a cost center within a specific period. A cost center can be assigned several work centers. However, a work center can only be assigned to one cost center at a given point in time.

Activity types
In a cost center, those activity types are evaluated that are defined in a controlling area and which can be referred to in a work center. Activity types are used to define the different types of activities that can be generated within a cost center. The activity types are defined in the controlling area. The activity types are evaluated per cost center and period by means of an allocation record that consists of a fixed (work-independent) and a variable (work-dependent) part. They enable you to define the price at which internal activities are to be settled (costing). The work center uses only those activity types that are permitted for the assigned cost center.

Assignment of a work center to a cost center and specification of activity types occurs in the **Costing** view (see Figure 5.35).

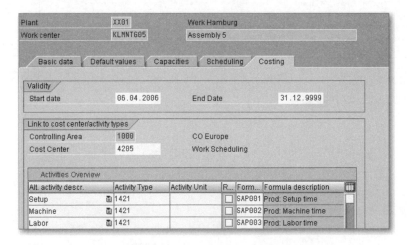

Figure 5.35 Costing Information in the Work Center

5.4.6 Work Center Hierarchy

Work centers can be arranged in a hierarchy. The *work center hierarchy* is structured by subordinating a work center to another work center. Note that a work center can be used in several hierarchies at the same time. The hierarchy enables you to determine the available capacity on the basis of aggregated data. A difference is made between statistical work centers and production work centers. Statistical work centers are used to aggregate data. Production work centers are merely used in the operations of plans and plant orders. They contain data that is required for costing, scheduling, and capacity requirements planning in the operation. Moreover, the production work centers can be used as a source of information for the production process.

You can create work center hierarchies using transaction CR21 and change them using transaction CR22. During the creation phase, the hierarchy is assigned the work centers one after the other (see Figure 5.36). When you create the hierarchy, you must first select the first **work center** (indicated in the figure by the numeral 1). In this context, it is useful to first enter the statistical work center that's used to aggregate the available capacity (2). During this maintenance process, it is important that you set the **Assigned** checkmark in the subsequent window (3). After that, you can assign additional work centers (4).

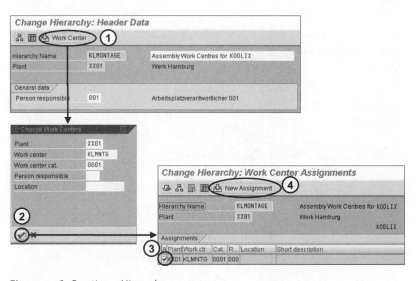

Figure 5.36 Creating a Hierarchy

You can add more work centers in the change mode; while the hierarchy structure can be changed in the graphical view (see Figure 5.37).

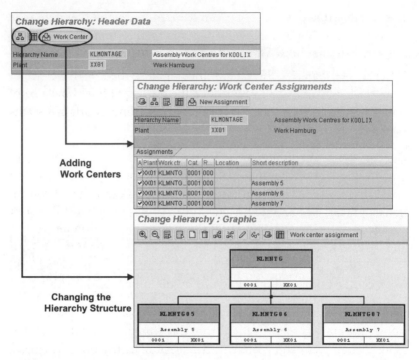

Figure 5.37 Changing the Hierarchy Structure

The assignment of a work center to a hierarchy can also be displayed in the work center itself (see Figure 5.38).

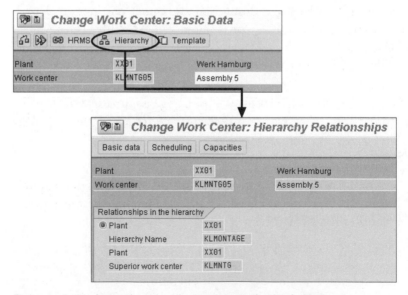

Figure 5.38 Displaying the Hierarchy Structure in the Work Center

5.5 Routing

5.5.1 Purpose and Structure of the Routing

Whereas the material, BOM, and drawing describe the properties of a material, assembly, or end product, the routing defines how a component or input material is to be converted from its original status into the final status.

During work scheduling, you describe what is to be produced, in what fashion, and what materials are needed for its production. The goal is to ensure the appropriate production of a product and continuously preserve financial efficiency.

The increasing degree of automation in industrial enterprises has led to a situation where, in addition to conventional work scheduling, computer aided production instructions are generated as programs (NC programming). Furthermore, product inspection has turned into a process of planning and anticipatory quality inspection. The inspection requirements that resulted from this situation are often created as inspection plans and written into inspection instructions. The basic procedures employed in conventional work scheduling, programming, and inspection planning have several things in common. The basic steps are therefore described on the basis of a routing creation.

The starting point of work scheduling is to include the product information provided by the product development and design departments into instructions for production and assembly. The series of operations and the sequence to follow in order to produce a part or assemble different parts or subassemblies are defined in the routing. In addition, the individual items—that is, the operations—are assigned production processes, operating resources, and capacity requirements. The creation of a routing consists of the following tasks (see Eversheim, 1989, pp. 30–56):

Work scheduling tasks

▶ **Determining the initial part**
Determination of the initial part consists of defining the variable size-item type and dimensions in consideration of the requirements of the work piece.

▶ **Determining the sequence of the series of operations**
Determination of the sequence of the series of operations includes the definition of the sequence of operations in order to convert a work piece from its initial status into its final status.

▶ **Machine selection**
The machine selection consists of assigning or selecting the required machines to carry out an operation.

▶ **Assigning production resources/tools**
The PRT assignment consists of selecting the tools and devices that are no fixed part of the machines in order to carry out the operations.

▶ **Determining the standard time and standard values**
The main task of the standard time determination is to identify target times for carrying out the individual processing operations.

Types of routing creation Several ways of creating the routing have emerged over time. The work involved in the different types of creating a routing is essentially affected by the degree of standardization of the work piece to be processed.

▶ **Regenerative planning**
Regenerative planning requires you to carry out all steps listed above. Regenerative planning is necessary whenever you must create a routing for non-standardized work pieces. New devices often must be developed and designed during regenerative planning.

▶ **Adaptive planning**
Adaptive planning involves the addition or deletion of entire operations or the replacement of individual work instructions and operating resources in order to implement changes. This procedure should be carried out along with a similarity search on the basis of a classification system. It presupposes a range of products based on partly standardized work pieces.

▶ **Variant planning**
Variant planning involves an adaptation of the routing based on the variation of individual parameters. It does not allow for adding or deleting individual operations. The prerequisite for applying the variant-planning principle is the creation of component families; that is, a grouping of components that contain identical or similar geometrical properties or identical or similar production processes. Each component family is based on a standardized basic routing, and the variants to be produced are very similar to each other.

▶ **Repetitive planning**
In repetitive planning, the existing planning results are completely reused. The order-independent routings are complemented with MRP-based order data such as delivery date, order number, and quantity. Repetitive planning involves the least work, but it presupposes a standardized range of products.

Apart from differentiating the routings according to the work involved in their creation, you can also differentiate them by their intended use. The term *reference operation set* describes a routing that is firmly assigned to a material to be produced and that contains standard information. Alternative routings indicate that a material can be produced on the basis of different routings. Variant routings contain all operations to be carried out. During creation of the routing, the variant required is derived from the overall range of products.

Core routings contain only rough information, while detailing occurs during the actual production. Core routings are used frequently in cellular or group manufacturing where the employee creates the actual routing based on his or her knowledge. This principle usually also involves the creation of component families for the individual cells so that the employee can plan a manageable range of components.

The *routing management* is of particular importance, as it efficiently supports archiving as well as the work scheduler in the search for existing or similar routings. Classifications are used to store descriptive information on work-piece groups or similar production processes and classification numbers. A text-search function enables you to quickly access data. Similarly, the routing history, validity date, expiration date, and the modification and deletion of routings are basic requirements for an efficient routing management.

Routing management

In the SAP ERP system, a routing describes the sequence of individual operations that are required to produce the end product. The routing depends on a specific plant; that is, it is clearly defined within a plant. Individual operations of a routing can be assigned to other plants at any time if the other plants are part of the same controlling area. The routing is defined as order-independent and serves as a basis for costing, lead time, and capacity scheduling, for capacity requirements planning and capacity leveling, and as a set of instruc-

Routing structure

tions for the actual production execution. The essential elements of a routing are the material and the operations.

The following options are available to assign a material to a routing.

▶ You can summarize routings to task list groups. Task list groups contain routings that are based on similar production cycles and/or used for production of similar materials. Within a task list group, the assigned routings are uniquely identified by specifying a group counter.

▶ Routings that are used to produce a material according to different production methods can be stored in different task list groups.

▶ A routing can be used to produce different materials (inverse parts such as left and right cabinet doors). In the SAP ERP system, you can even assign the different materials to different plants.

An operation characterizes the work step to be carried out, the standard value (in terms of time) for the execution, and the quantity to be produced. The minimum information that must be contained in the execution time for an operation must consist of the setup time, processing time, and teardown time. For scheduling purposes, this information can be supplemented by the following three additional pieces of time indication (see Figure 5.39).

▶ **Queue time**
This is the period of time in which the material is located at the production center until the execution of the operation begins

▶ **Move time**
This is the period of time that's needed to move the material from one production center to the subsequent production center

▶ **Wait time**
This period of time begins after the production has been finished. During this interval, the material is temporarily stored in the production center until it is moved.

It is possible that the queue and setup times overlap each other, as can be the case with the wait and teardown times, because those steps can be carried out simultaneously.

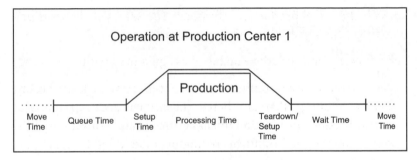

Figure 5.39 Time Periods Involved in a Production Order

You can create routings with and without material reference and without specifying a task list group, as similar routings are summarized into groups. You don't have to specify any material in the first step of the routing creation as this can also be done at a later stage. If you create a routing for an existing material, all plans that are already available for this material are listed during the creation. If you don't specify any of the existing task list groups during the creation, SAP ERP will assign a task list group internally. The SAP ERP system supports the following routing types. | **Routing types**

▶ **Routing**
The routing describes one or more sequences of operations for the production of a material. You can create several routings for one material in order to use it in different lot-size ranges, or for different usages such as production processing, post-processing, or the processing of prototypes. To reduce the effort of entering data in a routing, you can reference or copy reference operation sets as many times as required and in any sequence. Because materials, routings, and plants can be linked with each other in any way, routings can be used very flexibly. For example, you can map in a single routing the production of inverse parts such as the left and right car doors.

▶ **Reference operation set**
In contrast to a routing, the reference operation set is not assigned to a material. A reference operation set involves a sequence of operations that is repeated frequently within a production cycle and that can be referred to if required. You can use reference operation sets as a reference or template in routings or work orders. This considerably reduces the effort of entering data for routings, as existing sets of data can be referenced. Moreover, a change to

the reference operation set causes all referencing routings to be changed automatically.

▸ **Rate routing**
Rate routings are designed for maintenance of production rate-based task lists and can be used in repetitive manufacturing, among other scenarios. Whereas in normal routings the base quantity generally remains constant (for example, pieces) and the time-related data such as the processing time is maintained using standard values, rate routing works exactly the opposite. The production quantities are maintained on the basis of individual items and the reference time is constant. Thus, a rate routing describes the quantity of an item that must be produced within a given period of time. A rate routing contains a series of operations. A production rate is defined for each operation, based on the production quantity, production time, and the associated units. The production rate is determined as the quotient of the production quantity and production time. This enables you, for example, to determine the production quantity in terms of tons per shift. All other aspects of the functionality and maintenance of routings and rate routings are identical. Work centers that are assigned to the operations contained in rate routings should contain standard value keys in which the standard values for production time, setup time, and teardown time are predefined.

▸ **Reference rate routing**
Reference rate routings are used as a reference or template in rate routings. A reference rate routing contains a sequence of operations. As is the case with the rate routing, the production rate for an operation is defined on the basis of the production quantity and reference time. The functionality and maintenance of reference rate routings are similar to those of reference operation sets.

Apart from the drawing and the BOM, routings are an essential basis for production and serve as a production instruction for executing the production processes. In addition to describing the production process, the routing serves as the central basis for scheduling the individual operations. The time data specified in the routing enables you to carry out order-independent forward or backward scheduling. If the times specified in the routing exceed the latest possible permitted completion date, you can use the following three methods in order to reduce the production order time.

▶ Reduce the queue, wait, and move times to the minimum required length.

▶ Have operations overlap by having subsets transferred to subsequent operations before the previous operation has been completed.

▶ Split up an operation by having the quantity to be produced in an operation distributed to different capacities (devices or machines) so that the operation can be carried out simultaneously on one or several machines.

The creation of programming instructions for Numeric Control (NC) machines in the context of computer aided programming represents a further advancement. Depending on the degree of integration, you can refer to geometrical and technological information created by a computer (CAD/NC integration, see Diedenhoven, 1985, pp. 58–65).

Another useful development is the partial automation of conventionally created routings, wherein a variant-based routing is created by the creation of variants for a product family and the variation of parameters from a reference operation is set. Moreover, you can automate parts of adaptive planning by implementing appropriate classification systems and using core routings and reference operation sets (see Hüllenkremer, 1990, pp. 48–57).

SAP ERP supports computer aided work scheduling in that it allows you to configure your routings and by providing an automatic determination of standard values. This determination of standard values for setup, machine operation, move, inspection, and queue times is based on stored tables and formulas. In addition to automating the creation of routings, it is useful to enter specific information on subsequent operations. In the SAP ERP system, you can do that by assigning a control key to an operation.

5.5.2 Routing

Routing is the most frequently used routing type in discrete manufacturing. You can create a routing using Transaction CA01, and change it using transaction CA02. You can access the routing either via the **Material** and **Plant** items or via the **Planning Group** (see Figure 5.40).

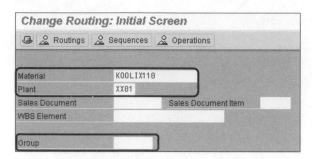

Figure 5.40 Accessing the Routing

Alternative routings A planning group can contain several routings. Similar to the BOM, these routings are uniquely identified by their intended use and group counters. In our example, three different routings exist for material **KOOLIX110** within the planning group. The three routings are displayed for selection when you access the routing (see Figure 5.41).

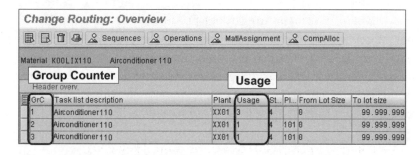

Figure 5.41 Alternative Routings

Once you have selected one of the alternatives, you can access the routing header that contains an assignment to the work scheduler, the status of the routing (creation phase, released, and so on), and the valid lot-size range (see Figure 5.42).

Lot-size range The **From Lot Size** and **To lot size** parameters indicate that the planned order is only selected for those orders whose order quantity corresponds to this interval.

Material assignment A planned order can be assigned to several materials. This makes sense if similar materials are produced in identical production steps. You can display and change the assignment by clicking on the **MatlAssignment** button. The example in Figure 5.43 shows that one routing applies to the two materials **KOOLIX110** and **KOOLIX300**.

Change Routing: Header Details

◀ ▶ ✐ ♟ Routings ♟ MatlAssignment ♟ Sequences ♟ Operations ♟ CompAlloc

Material K00LIX110   K00LIX110

Task list
Group	50001323
Group Counter	2 Airconditioner110
Plant	XX01 ☐ Long text exists

Production line
Line hierarchy

General data
☐ Deletion flag
Usage	1	Production
Status	4	Released (general)
Planner group	101	Planergruppe 101
Planning work center		
CAPP order		
From Lot Size		To lot size 99.999.999 PC
Old task list no.		

Figure 5.42 Routing Header

The essential information regarding production is contained in the operations. The individual operations—including the work centers at which production takes place, the control key, and the standard values—are entered in the operation overview. The operation overview in Figure 5.44 shows a production structure that consists of three operations: **Pre-Assembly (0010)**, **Main Assembly (0020)**, and **Finishing (0030)** including their assignments to work centers **KLMNTG05**, **KLMNTG06**, and **KLMNTG07** as well as control key **PP01**.

Operations in the routing

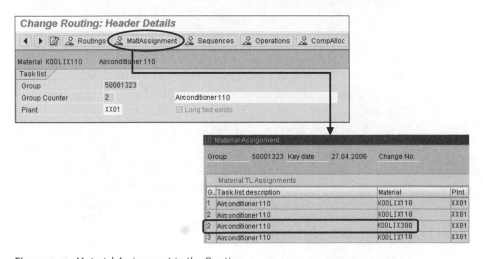

Figure 5.43 Material Assignment in the Routing

131

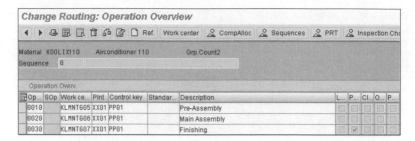

Figure 5.44 Operation Overview in the Routing

Control key — The *control key* contains various parameters that determine whether the operation is relevant to scheduling or capacity planning, whether confirmations are possible, and much other information. The following chapters describe the parameters of the control key whenever these parameters are used. You can maintain the control key using Customizing transaction OPJ8 (see Figure 5.45).

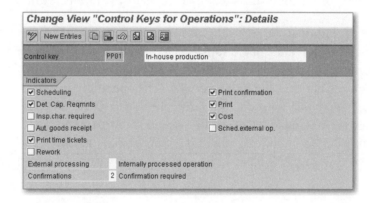

Figure 5.45 Control Key

The control key contains various flags that are optional or mandatory, depending on the control key, and that can be maintained in Customizing. For example, the control key enables you to define how to handle an operation or sub-operation. Similarly, you can use the control key to define whether you want to calculate the costs or carry out capacity requirements planning for the operation or sub-operation. Depending on the control key, different plausibility checks are carried out. For example, splittings and overlappings are only allowed if the operation is scheduled. The **External processing** flag makes sure the purchase requisitions are generated during production order creation.

As an essential piece of information, the operation details contain the standard values related to the base quantity of the operation. In Figure 5.46, operation **0010** contains standard values for the **Setup time** (30 minutes) and **Machine time** (60 minutes) in relation to 10 units. The standard value key of the work center defines which standard values can be maintained (see Section 5.4). In the example shown in Figure 5.46, these are the **Setup time**, **Machine time**, and **Labor time**. In addition, the operation details contain various other parameters which will also be described in later chapters. Figure 5.46 shows a section of the operation details.

Operation details and standard values

By default, all components are assigned to the first operation, which implies that the requirement for the components occurs at the beginning of the first operation. However, it often happens that certain components are not required until the end of the order is reached, which can lead to unwanted material buffers, particularly with regard to long production times that involve many operations. However, the **CompAlloc** button (component assignment) enables you to explicitly assign the components to specific operations. Figure 5.47 illustrates in numerical sequence the procedure for assigning components in the operation overview screen of the routing.

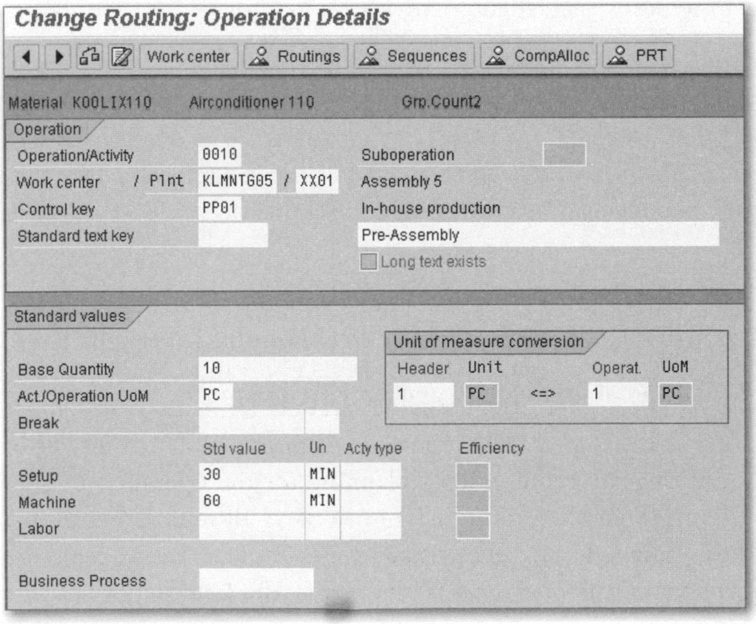

Component assignment

Figure 5.46 Operation Details (Excerpt)

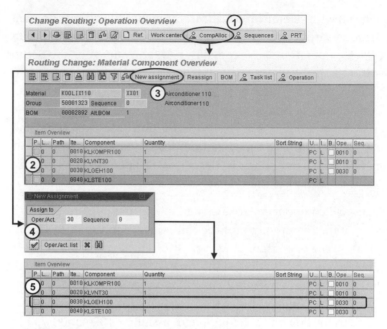

Figure 5.47 Assigning Components to Operations

The assignment is based on the BOM of the header material. If several alternative BOMs are available, the assignment is based on a specific, previously selected alternative.

Sequences The routing is maintained as a linear chain of operations. *Parallel sequences* enable you to split up the production process if specific production steps of an order can be carried out simultaneously. *Alternative sequences* represent an alternative in the production process if a product can be produced in different ways.

You can call the sequence overview by clicking on the **Sequences** button in the routing. The sequence overview displays all parallel and alternative sequences contained in the routing (see Figure 5.48).

The sequences are numbered and contain a sequence category. The standard sequence contains sequence category 0. Parallel sequences contain sequence category 1, while alternative sequences contain sequence category 2.

The example shown in Figure 5.48 contains the standard sequence (which is always created when you create an operation), and an alternative sequence (sequence 1 with reference to standard sequence 0). It also contains parallel sequences both for the standard sequence

(sequence 2 with reference to standard sequence 0) and for the alternative sequence (sequence 3 with reference to alternative sequence 1).

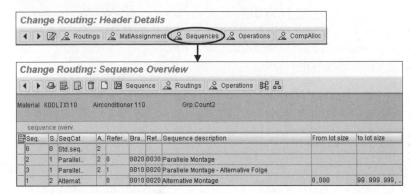

Figure 5.48 Sequence Overview

The branch operation—related to the referenced sequence—and the return operation are important pieces of information for sequences. While it is not necessary to specify a branch operation, the entry of a return operation is mandatory.

As shown by the numbered steps in Figure 5.49, you can create new sequences in the sequence overview. When doing so, you must decide in a first step whether you want to create an **Alternative Sequence** or a **Parallel Sequence**. The important information to enter here is the definition of the **Branch operation** as well as the **Return operation** and the **Reference sequence**.

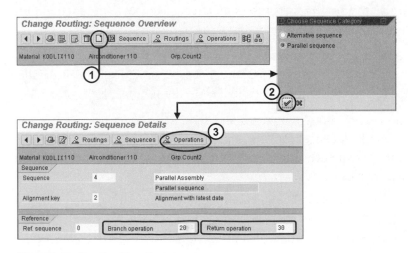

Figure 5.49 Creating New Sequences

If you click on the **Operations** button, you can go to the operation overview, where you can maintain the operations of a sequence.

Production resources/tools

Production resources/tools (PRTs) are movable operating resources that can be assigned to internal and external operations in the routing. Examples of PRTs include tools, devices, NC programs, drawings, and test equipment.

You can assign a PRT to an operation in the **PRT Overview**, as shown in Figure 5.50. Here, you must specify on which date which quantity of the PRT is required and for what period of time.

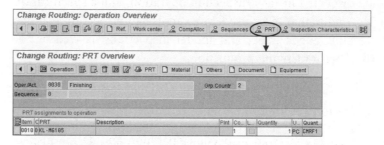

Figure 5.50 Assigning PRTs to an Operation

PRTs can be of the following types: **Material**, **Document**, **Equipment**, or **Others**, the last named being PRTs with a separate master record.

PRTs with master record

You can create PRTs with master record using transaction CF01. They contain a separate status and task list usage (see Figure 5.51).

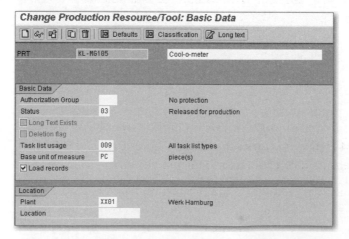

Figure 5.51 PRT with Master Record

However, you should remember that no procurement can occur based on a PRT-based master record.

PRTs for which a material master record has been created can be produced in-house or procured externally. It is important to know that a PRT with material master can be assigned to an operation if the **PRT** view has been maintained in the material master and the status flag of the material allows the assignment.

PRTs with material master

The *inspection plan* is closely related to the routing. An inspection plan contains the individual inspection operations, the characteristics to be inspected in each inspection operation, and a specification of the test equipment to be used. You can use an inspection plan for goods receipt, goods issue, and model inspections as well as for inspections accompanying production.

Inspection plan

In SAP ERP, you don't need to create inspection plans, because the inspection characteristics are directly stored in the routing. You can either assign the inspection characteristics directly to an operation or declare an operation as an inspection operation and define inspection item in the routing. Among other things, an inspection characteristic contains a characteristic description, the inspection method, and the sampling procedure. Quality-relevant characteristics include the specification of physical and geometrical properties. The inspection method defines the procedure based on which the inspection is to be carried out. The sampling procedure defines the sample size for an inspection. That is to say, it defines whether to use a full sample, a percentage of a sample, a fixed sample, or a sample from the sampling scheme.

A *production version* is created for a material and combines a routing with a BOM. You can use production versions to select master data. The following chapters explain how you can do that. Note that production versions are mandatory for the integration with SAP APO.

Production version

You can define the production version in the material master either in the **MRP4** view or in **work scheduling**. Figures 5.52 and 5.53 illustrate the steps needed to create production versions.

In the second step, you create the production version, including its validity dates. The content of the production version—that is, the assignment of the routing and BOM—is defined in the production version details (see Figure 5.53).

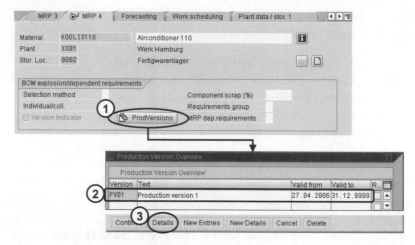

Figure 5.52 Creating Production Versions, Step 1

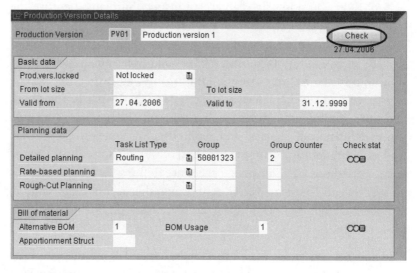

Figure 5.53 Creating Production Versions, Step 2

Prior to saving the production version, it is advisable to make sure that both the routing and BOM actually exist and have been assigned to the material. You can do that by clicking on the **Check** button.

Sales planning, also referred to as demand planning, covers future requirements without considering stocks and available capacities. The sales history often serves as a basis for sales planning. Operations planning uses the results of the sales-planning process to plan the production quantities, and takes initial stocks and capacities into account on a general level.

6   Sales and Operations Planning

6.1   Process Overview

The main purpose of sales and operations planning (SOP) is to define the product types and quantities to be sold for a medium- to long-term planning period. This includes the requirement figures for aggregated end products (for example, product groups), for end products and spare parts that can be sold separately as assemblies (for example, electric motors), and for individual parts (such as a casing or a propeller for a ventilating shaft).

The goal of sales and operations planning is to obtain the corresponding planning data for production. This goal comes into play, for instance, in the consumer goods industry, the food industry, or at a company that specializes in repetitive manufacturing. Moreover, the planned sales data determined by means of market analyses or based on historical data (such as actual sales orders) are to be harmonized with the actual production capabilities at a high level. That is, they are to be harmonized without BOM explosion and work scheduling at plant or operating resource group levels.

Sales planning defines the range of products and the sales quantity for the coming planning period on the basis of the production capabilities and the product demand in the sales market (see Meffert, 1986, pp. 216–240). "The goal of sales planning is to define the sales program and to forecast the sales quantities and prices" (Wöhe, 1996, p. 601). The sales plan forms the basis from which the other business-related functional plans are derived, because the quantity you want to produce depends on the sales options you have. Therefore, the production plan is aligned with the sales plan.

Sales and operations planning only considers quantities. For this reason, the sales plan in this context also refers only to quantities. The operations plan also takes into account the resource capacities, but only at an aggregated level as they are stored in the rough-cut planning profile. In contrast to this, the sales and profit planning from CO-PA contains a value-based sales plan.

Sales and operations planning thus links the market-oriented sales and profit planning and the production-oriented demand management and production planning.

Tasks and integration into enterprise planning Based on the production plan, we define the procurement plan for provisioning the production factors (see Wöhe, 1996, pp. 595–607). Sales planning provides information that must be differentiated in terms of time, space, and content in order to determine which products are to be sold at what quantities.

In SAP ERP, sales planning is part of enterprise planning, which consists of sales planning, revenue planning, and sales and profit planning. The total scope of planning within sales and profit planning comprises the following tasks (see SAP—Profitability and Sales Accounting and Sales and Distribution Controlling, 1996, pp. 4.7–4.15).

► Sales planning for a profitability segment (planning object); that is, planning at product group level or for individual products.

► Determination of planned gross/net revenues by evaluating the sales volume on the basis of the values stored in the sales and distribution system (revenues, discounts, bonuses, and so on). This would mean, for example, that a company tries to achieve revenue of $2 million for a planned period and wants to reduce the production costs as much as possible.

► Sales and profit planning on the basis of costs planned in controlling (for example, cost of goods manufactured and cost-center overhead). For example, enterprise planning provides for a budget of $500,000.

► Gradual planning of all fixed costs

The interface with the profitability analysis (CO-PA) enables you to use the sales and profit plan as a basis for the sales plan. Working in reverse, it is also possible to transfer the result of sales and operations planning to sales and profit planning, cost- center accounting, or to activity-based costing. This enables an integration of quantity planning and value planning.

The result of sales and operations planning is the operations plan that is transferred as planned independent requirement to demand management. The operations plan is created on the basis of the sales plan, which is also a result of this process. Figure 6.1 illustrates the integration of sales and operations planning into the neighboring processes.

Data flow

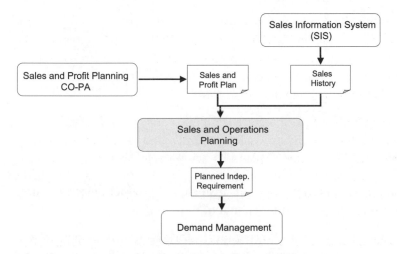

Figure 6.1 Process Overview of Sales and Operations Planning

Sales and operations planning first carries out the individual steps for creating a sales plan. Then, a resource-leveling step is performed in order to define the operations plan. The sales plan is created either interactively on the basis of the planner's experience or is supported by a forecast based on the historical sales data. Event planning represents another optional step, which considers the influence of promotions and other events (such as the Super Bowl,) on the sales volume. Events are particularly important in the consumer goods industry.

The sales plan considers solely the requirements side and does not take the available production capacity into account. A rough-cut resource leveling step at aggregate level makes sure that no requirement quantities are transferred to production that significantly exceed the feasible quantities. Figure 6.2 illustrates the individual process steps.

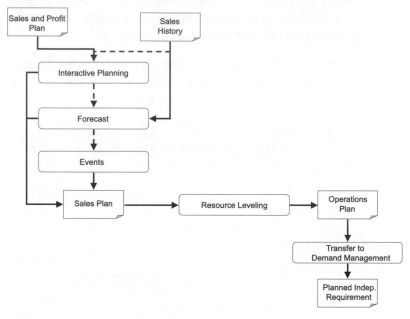

Figure 6.2 Process Steps Involved in Sales and Operations Planning

Finally, the operations plan is transferred to production as a requirement-relevant planned independent requirement.

Sales and operations planning in ERP

Planning can occur at different levels, for example at the level of the product or product group. Depending on the specific requirements, the planning tables can be configured individually and different types of data retention can be used.

SAP provides standardized planning tables that enable you to carry out planning at defined levels in the product group hierarchy. In this case, SOP is referred to as standard sales and operations planning (standard SOP). In contrast, planning tables and planning levels can be configured per your requirements in the context of flexible planning. The plant planning level is not mandatory, and the operations plan can be distributed to different plants according to a distribution key.

In flexible planning, the screen layout for entering the plan figures can be freely defined. This way, you can define the planning level and the value fields of a planning session. The layout of the data-entry screen for the planning data is defined in a planning type with regard to both the position of input fields and the associated meaning. Based on its position within the data-entry screen, each input field is firmly assigned a row and a column. The content of each input field is determined by specific information that is stored in the associated rows and columns of the planning layout.

Sales and operations planning in SAP ERP uses objects whose names do not necessarily indicate their meaning. These objects include the following:

SAP terms and objects for sales and operations planning

► **Information structure**
Data structure that stores the planning. Planning data is stored in key figures for combinations of characteristic values.

► **Planning method**
The storage, aggregation, and disaggregation of data with regard to the planning level occurs either as consistent planning or as level-by-level planning.

► **Planning hierarchy**
The planning hierarchy contains the characteristic values combinations for the characteristics of the information structure.

► **Planning table**
This is where the actual planning is carried out.

► **Planning type**
The planning type defines the format of the planning table.

Figure 6.3 provides an overview of the objects and their interdependencies.

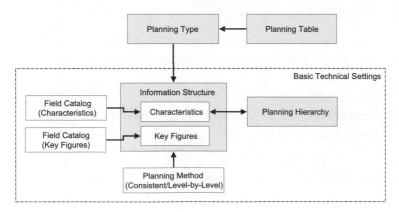

Figure 6.3 Objects of Sales and Operations Planning

143

Another important term is that of the *product group* that contains materials or other product groups. The product group is primarily important in standard SOP.

Each information structure can be assigned only one planning hierarchy. The following section dealing with the technical basics of sales and operations planning describes the information structure, planning methods, planning hierarchy, and product group objects in greater detail. The planning type and planning table objects are described in Section 6.3.

SAP provides three standard planning types. If these three types are used, the process is called standard SOP. If not, you must create your own information structures and planning types. This is what is referred to as flexible planning. Because the functions described in the following sections often require a case distinction, it is important to understand the relationships between planning methods. Standard SOP and flexible planning are opposing concepts, while the level-by-level and consistent planning methods are opposites at another level. Figure 6.4 compares the different objects used in standard SOP and flexible planning.

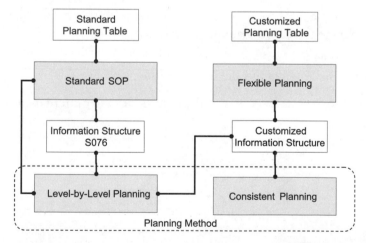

Figure 6.4 Standard SOP, Flexible Planning, Level-by-Level Planning, and Consistent Planning

Note that standard SOP uses the level-by-level planning method, whereas flexible planning can use both level-by-level and consistent planning. Table 6.1 provides an overview of the most important properties of standard SOP and flexible planning.

Standard SOP	Flexible planning
Pre-set configuration	Individual configuration
Planning based on product groups	Planning based on planning hierarchies
Level-by-level planning	Consistent planning or level-by-level planning
Standard planning table	Individual planning table

Table 6.1 Properties of Standard SOP and Flexible Planning

The wider range of options in flexible planning is offset by higher configuration efforts. Standard SOP allows for the use of preconfigured settings, but its capabilities are much more limited.

6.2 Basic Technical Principles in Sales Planning

6.2.1 Information Structures

Planning is based on data structures that store *key figures* (for instance, the delivery quantity) for *characteristics* (for example, product and customer). These data structures are referred to as information structures. They can be created and changed using the following Customizing path: **General Logistics • LIS • Logistics Data Warehouse • Data Basis • Information Structures • Maintain Custom Information Structures**. Alternatively you can use Transaction MC21 to create information structures, and Transaction MC22 to change them. Information structures contain characteristics and key figures. The characteristics correspond to the planning levels. The key figures contain the actual information, whereas the characteristics are used as keys for accessing the information. Standard SOP is based in information structure S076 (see Figure 6.5).

In this case, the following planning levels are available: **Prod. group/material** (product group or material), **Plant**, and **Production version**. The order of the characteristics in the information structure defines the hierarchy levels: The product groups or materials are planned at the top level. For each material, you can make a detailed plan of the plant and an even more detailed plan of the production version within the plant.

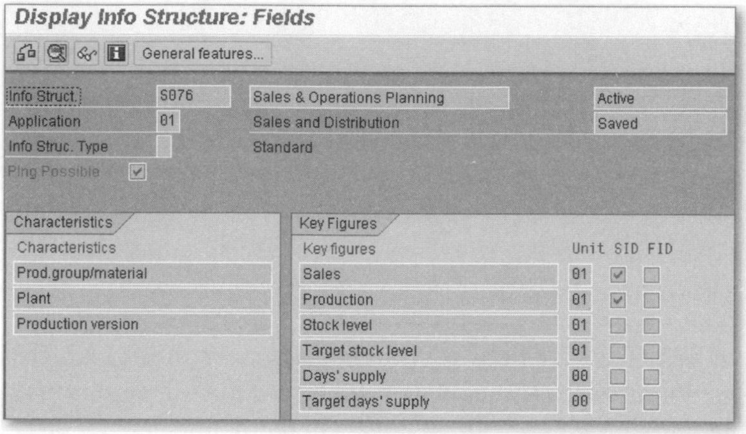

Figure 6.5 Information Structure S076

The information structure contains the following key figures: **Sales**, **Production**, **Stock level**, **Target stock level**, **Days' supply**, and **Target days' supply**. The planning result is stored for each characteristic values combination among these six key figures. Values for other key figures, such as special order, for example, cannot be stored in this information structure.

The decisive aspects of the information structure are that it can be used for planning and that it be active. You can maintain additional planning parameters using Transaction MC7F (see Figure 6.6). The most important items are the **Planning method**, the **Statistics currency**, and the **Base Unit of Measure**. If the base unit of measure of the information structure is not identical to the base unit of measure of a planned characteristic, you must maintain the base unit of measure of the information structure as an alternative unit of measure for the material. Another property of the information structure is the planning periodicity with which the data is stored.

Maintenance of these planning parameters is the prerequisite for creating a planning hierarchy. The planning parameters for the key figures enable you to define for each key figure whether, for example, a forecast is possible or whether the figure should be aggregated by creation of a total or in a different way (see Figure 6.7).

Usually, it is advisable to create a total for the aggregation. The options to calculate an average or have no aggregation at all are only advisable if the total creation doesn't make sense.

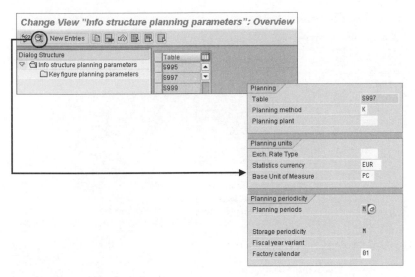

Figure 6.6 Planning Parameters for the Information Structure

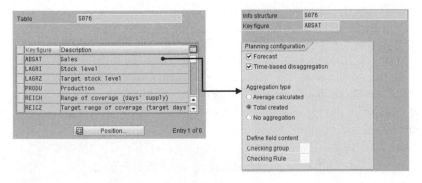

Figure 6.7 Planning Parameters for Key Figures

To carry out flexible planning, you must first create custom information structures. You can create them using transaction MC21, while transaction MC22 enables you to change them. For this purpose, the information structure must be marked as planning-relevant, and first you must select the characteristics and key figures to be used for planning. Figure 6.8 shows how to proceed when selecting the characteristics from the field catalogs. A field catalog contains a group of characteristics or key figures that are grouped by different topics. The sequence of the characteristics is important, as it must correspond to the planning hierarchy. In our example, the sales organization is at the highest planning level, while the material is at the lowest level.

Creating information structures

147

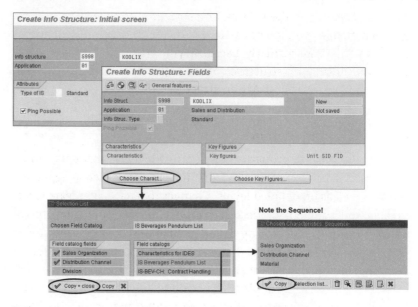

Figure 6.8 Selecting Characteristics for Information Structures

The selection of key figures is carried out in a similar way. In our example, the key figures were selected from field catalog **SOP Key Figures**. Once you have saved the information structure, you must generate it so that it gets activated. Figure 6.9 displays the process of generating the information structure and shows the activation log.

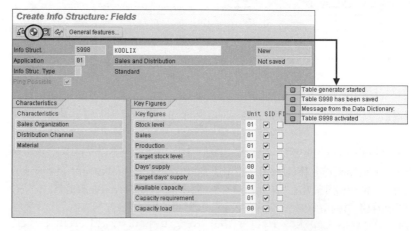

Figure 6.9 Generating/Activating Information Structures

Finally, you must maintain the planning parameters via transaction MC7F, as described earlier in this section.

The data is stored in the information structure. However, copy management enables you to copy data from one information structure to another. This is particularly useful if you want to copy data from standard information structures of the Logistics Information System (LIS) into your own information structures.

Copy management

6.2.2 Planning Methods

The most important properties of planning levels is that data can be aggregated in different ways and that it can be modified at aggregate levels as well as on detailed levels. Changes to data at aggregate levels involve the problem of disaggregation and raise the question of which level to use for storing data. The planning method determines the way in which the data is disaggregated and stored. Two different planning methods are available: consistent planning and level-by-level planning. A third planning method—delta planning—is no longer available. For more information on this matter, see SAP Note 725135 in the OSS system.

You can assign the planning method to the information structure using Customizing transaction MC7F (**Set Planning Parameters for Information Structures and Key Figures**, see Figure 6.10).

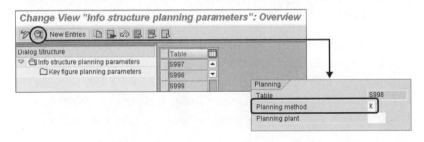

Figure 6.10 Planning Method for Information Structures

You can enter the planning method in the **Planning method** field, with **I** being level-by-level planning and **K** being consistent planning. The planning method for the information structure used in standard SOP (S076) is level-by-level planning.

In consistent planning, the data is directly disaggregated to the most detailed level, where it is also stored. The display at higher levels is obtained by aggregating the detailed data. This way, the data is consistent across all planning levels. This means that if planning is car-

Consistent planning

ried out at different levels, at product and product group levels for example, the planning results are transparent for all levels. Figure 6.11 illustrates an example in which planning occurs alternately at a higher and a lower level.

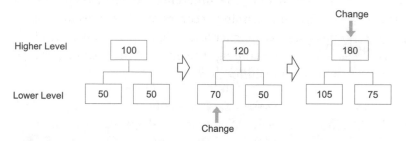

Figure 6.11 Data in Consistent Planning

In this example, the proportional factor for the disaggregation was 50 % at the beginning. Then it was adapted at a detailed level to the new planning values of 58 % (70/120) and 42 % (50/120). A change at a higher level includes planning that is detailed in such a way that the relationships between the individual members of the lower level remain unchanged. Correspondingly, a change to the detailed level that is implemented at aggregate level results in a proportionate change to detailed planning; the ratio of 58 % vs. 42 % is preserved.

Level-by-level planning

In contrast to consistent planning, the planning values in level-by-level planning are stored at the level at which they are entered. The aggregation or disaggregation of data from one level to the next can only occur as an explicit planning step. This enables you to generate at different levels plans that are not compatible with each other. Figure 6.12 shows the same example as was used for consistent planning, to the first planning at a lower level.

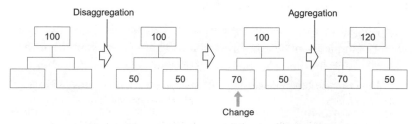

Figure 6.12 Data in Level-by-Level Planning: Planning at a Lower Level

As long as the disaggregation is not explicitly triggered, no data exists at the detailed level. A planning change at detailed level can be included in an aggregation step at a higher level. The detailed planning result at the higher level is not displayed until the aggregation step has been carried out. The difference between level-by-level planning and consistent planning becomes more obvious in a subsequent planning change at a higher level. Figure 6.13 shows the effect of that for level-by-level planning. The effect of the planning change is similar in consistent planning.

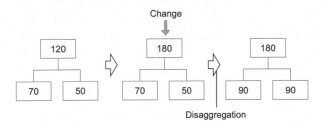

Figure 6.13 Data in Level-by-Level Planning: Planning at a Higher Level

At first, a planning change at a higher level does not affect the detailed plan. However, during a disaggregation step the detailed plan is completely overwritten so that all the information previously entered at the detailed level gets lost.

The main difference between consistent planning and level-by-level planning is that in consistent planning the data is automatically aggregated and disaggregated. The disaggregation occurs along the planning levels defined in the planning hierarchy or product group, in correspondence with the proportional factors (see Section 6.2.5). In level-by-level planning, both the aggregation and disaggregation must be explicitly triggered. Table 6.2 compares the most essential properties of both planning methods.

Comparison between consistent and level-by-level planning

Consistent planning	Level-by-level planning
Planning hierarchy	Product group
Storage at the lowest level, planning data at all levels	Storage at each level, planning data only at maintained level
Automatic aggregation and disaggregation	Aggregation and disaggregation as a planning step

Table 6.2 Properties of Consistent Planning and Level-by-Level Planning

Only consistent planning allows you to fix key figure values in the planning table in order to avoid overwriting specific values during aggregation or disaggregation. Moreover, you can only use standard analyses in consistent planning. In both cases, you can configure the opening stocks automatically in the background.

6.2.3 Product Group

The product groups used in SAP ERP have different meanings. In the context of production planning and control, the product groups represent combinations of materials for sales and operations planning, aggregated using **level-by-level planning**. For this purpose, you can use products that are similar with regard to their sales behavior, and production requirements. Examples would be iPod 30GB, iPod 60GB, iPod Mini, and so on. Product groups can be single-level or multilevel. In multilevel product groups, the individual product groups are nested, that is, one product group contains another product group. Product groups are used in conjunction with level-by-level planning. You can maintain product groups using transactions MC84 (creation) and MC85 (change).

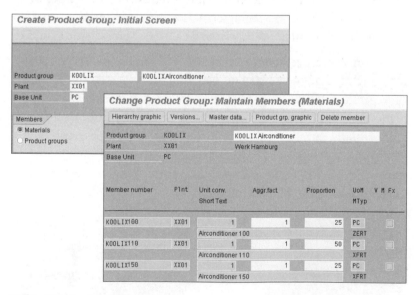

Figure 6.14 Product Group

Similar to the planning hierarchy, the product group (see Figure 6.14) also contains proportional factors for the disaggregation of its members. In addition to the interactive entry, you can also calculate proportional factors on the basis of historical data via the following menu path: **Edit • Calculate Proportional Factors**. Moreover, you can equally distribute the proportional factors via **Edit • Distribute Proportional Factors**.

Transaction MC91 enables you to graphically display product groups. Figure 6.15 shows an example of such a graphic.

Graphical display

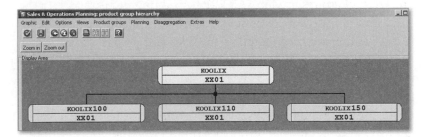

Figure 6.15 Product Group Graphic

6.2.4 Planning Hierarchy

The consistent planning method requires the definition of a planning hierarchy. Although the characteristics of the information structure fine-tune the planning levels, you must assign characteristic values to them in order to be able to carry out planning at those levels. Based on the custom information structure S997 that contains the characteristics **Sales Organization**, **Distribution Channel**, and **Material**, the planning hierarchy could be structured as shown in Figure 6.16.

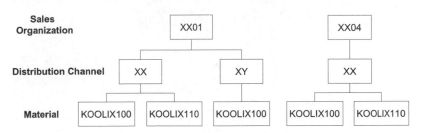

Figure 6.16 Logical Planning Hierarchy

This planning hierarchy allows planning, for instance, at the **Sales Organization** level for the actual sales organizations XX01 and XX02. To map this planning hierarchy, the characteristic values combinations listed in Table 6.3 are necessary.

Sales organization	Distribution channel	Material
XX01	XX	KOOLIX100
XX01	XX	KOOLX110
XX01	XY	KOOLIX110
XX04	XX	KOOLIX100
XX04	XX	KOOLIX110

Table 6.3 Characteristic Values Combinations for Mapping the Logical Planning Hierarchy

In SAP ERP, the planning hierarchy can be created using transaction MC61. The planning hierarchy is always related to an information structure. To be able to create a planning hierarchy, the planning parameters of the information structure must be maintained. Figure 6.17 shows the maintenance of the planning hierarchy for the first two values from Table 6.3 or the left-hand branch of Figure 6.16.

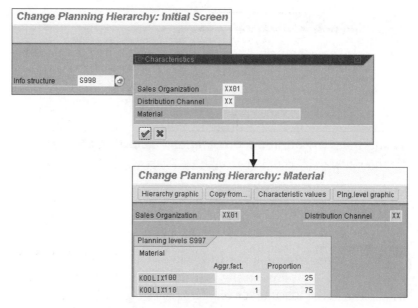

Figure 6.17 Maintaining the Planning Hierarchy

The sequence defined during creation of a planning hierarchy is also used in the planning table when changing from one characteristic values combination to the next. A planning object number is assigned in chronologically ascending order in the background.

The aggregation factor (**Aggr.fact.**) only exists for historical reasons and is no longer used. The proportional factor, in contrast, is actually used (**Proportion**). This factor has different effects, depending on the planning method and—in the case of consistent planning—on the calculation method. Section 6.2.5 provides more details on this.

You also can use transaction MC61 for adding more characteristic value combinations. However, note that you must select the **Revise** command from the menu to do that (Figure 6.18, step 1). In the second step, you must specify the information structure and the action (**Add member**, step 2). In the window that opens next you must enter the characteristic values combination to be added and trigger the enhancement (step 3). The successful creation of the characteristic values combination is stored in a log file (step 4).

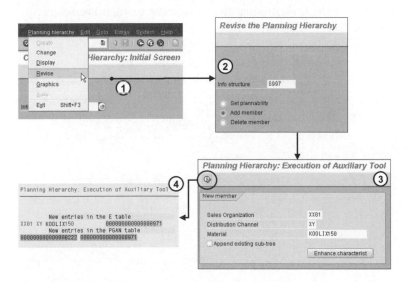

Figure 6.18 Adding Characteristic Values Combinations to a Planning Hierarchy

During creation of the characteristic values combinations, the system checks if the objects are actually available in the system, for example whether material **KOOLIX100** exists for sales organization **XX01** and distribution channel **XY**.

Transaction MC62 enables you to edit the proportional factors as shown in Figure 6.19. You can predefine a specific characteristic values combination, and you can leave some values open. If you leave some values open, the system displays all combinations that have not been restricted.

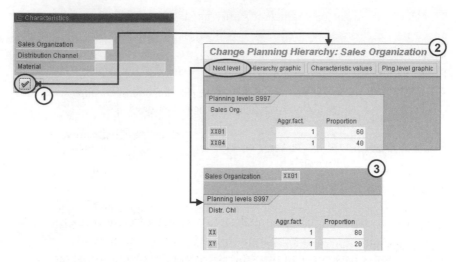

Figure 6.19 Maintaining Proportional Factors and Navigation in the Planning Hierarchy

First, you must define the proportions at the highest planning level and then click on the **Next level** button to navigate to the next lower level. The position of the cursor determines the branch that is navigated to. This way you can navigate through the entire planning hierarchy. As with the product group, you can also display the planning hierarchy as a graphic.

If the information structure already contains data—historical data, for example—you can use Transaction MC9A to generate the master data for flexible planning.

6.2.5   Proportional Factors and Disaggregation

The propagation of planning data from a higher level to a lower one is carried out by means of disaggregation. The proportional factors determine how the values are to be distributed from the aggregate level to the detailed level. Section 6.2.2 that dealt with the planning methods already described the concept of disaggregation for consistent and level-by-level planning.

Only in level-by-level planning are the proportional factors maintained in the planning hierarchy used directly. In consistent planning, they can be used as a basis for disaggregation. Table 6.4 provides an overview of how the proportional factors maintained in the product group or planning hierarchy are used in disaggregation.

Planning mode	Calculation method	Usage of proportional factors	Number of levels
Level-by-level planning	–	direct	one
Consistent planning	Calculation based on the planning hierarchy	Multiplication of proportional factors of multiple levels	multiple
Consistent planning	Calculation based on actual data	–	multiple

Table 6.4 Usage of Proportional Factors

You can calculate the proportional factors either directly from the planning hierarchy or in a separate step. Two different methods are available for consistent planning: the calculation of proportional factors based on actual data (Transaction MC8U), and calculation based on the planning hierarchy (Transaction MC9B).

The calculation on the basis of actual data totals the data for the given period at the detailed level, and the proportion of the characteristic values combination is calculated for each key figure. Figure 6.20 shows an example of how Transaction MC8U can be used to calculate the proportional factors for information structure S997 on the basis of the historical values of key figure **Sales**.

Proportional factors based on actual data

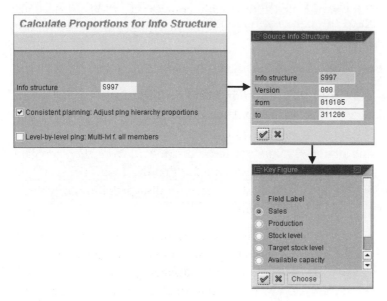

Figure 6.20 Calculating the Proportional Factors Based on Historical Data

The historical data are summarized for the period from May 1, 2005 through December 31, 2006 and used as a basis for the calculation of the proportional factors.

Proportional factors based on the planning hierarchy

In the alternative case, the proportional factors are evaluated across the entire planning hierarchy by multiplying the proportional factors of the individual levels with each other and across all levels. Figure 6.21 shows the result of this calculation for our example.

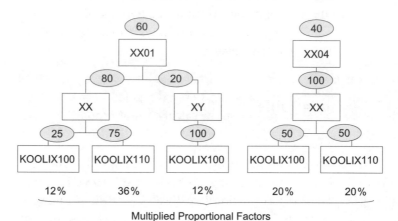

Figure 6.21 Calculating the Proportional Factors Based on Maintained Proportional Factors

For example, the proportion of 12 % for **KOOLIX100** in sales organization **XX01** through distribution channel **XX** can be calculated as follows:

Proportion XX01/XX/KOOLIX100 = 0.6 * 0.8 * 0.25 = 12 %

Figure 6.22 displays Transaction MC9B for the calculation of proportional factors for information structure **S997**.

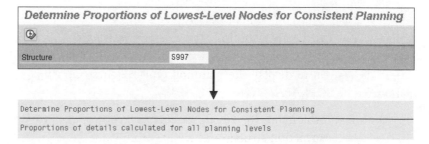

Figure 6.22 Calculation of Proportions for Planning Hierarchies by Multilevel Multiplication

Because you can only disaggregate one level at a time in level-by-level planning, the factor is used in the planning hierarchy in this case.

6.2.6 Versioning

Within the information structure, the planning data is retained in versions. This enables you to carry out simulations. Versions can be assigned any number, with the exception of two specific versions that have defined meanings: Version 000 always contains actual data, and version A01 is the active version.

6.3 Planning Table

6.3.1 Planning Type

The planning type defines the format of the planning and thus represents the link between the planning table (where the actual planning is carried out) and the information structure (where the planning is stored). You can create several planning types for one information structure. Because the data is stored in the information structure, the different planning types depend on each other, as they use the same set of data. If you use level-by-level planning, you must create a separate planning type for each planning level.

The following three planning types are available for standard SOP:

- ▸ SOPKAPA for planning product groups

- ▸ SOPKAPAM for planning materials

- ▸ SOPDIS for two-level planning of planning hierarchies

Because standard SOP uses level-by-level planning, separate planning types are required for the different levels of product group and material. You can create planning types using Transaction MC8A. Transaction MC8B enables you to change them, while Transaction MC8C allows you to display the planning types. Figure 6.23 shows planning type SOPKAPA.

The planning type contains the key figures (**Sales**, **Production**, and so on) from the information structure as well as from some key figures such as **Sales/Day** that are required for specific calculations and are not stored. You can display the attributes for each key figure via the following menu path: **Edit • Line Attributes** (see Figure 6.24).

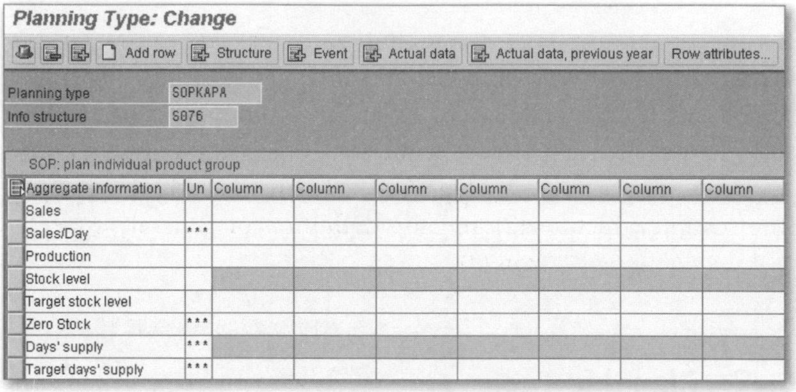

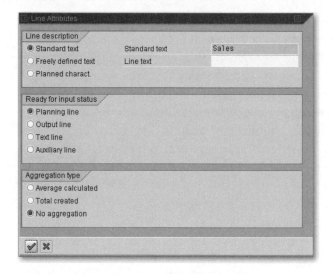

Figure 6.23 Standard Planning Type SOPKAPA for Product Groups

Figure 6.24 Line Attributes in the Planning Type

The **Ready for input status** controls whether the line values can be planned (**Planning line**) or only displayed (**Output line**). Auxiliary lines can, for instance, be used for intermediate calculations and only appear in the planning type, not in the planning table.

The planning type contains several macros for the execution of arithmetic operations within the context of planning. You can edit macros via the following menu paths: **Macro • Create** and **Macro • Edit**. You can display the planning type as it is also displayed in the planning table via the menu path, **Goto** • **Format** • **Layout**. Accordingly, the auxiliary lines are hidden in this case.

If you want to use flexible planning, you must first create separate planning types. You can create planning types using Transaction MC8A, while MC8B allows you to change them. The names of these separate planning types must begin with Y or Z. Figure 6.25 displays the creation of a planning type (1), including its assignment to the information structure (2) and the definition of general properties and the planning horizon (3).

Creating planning types

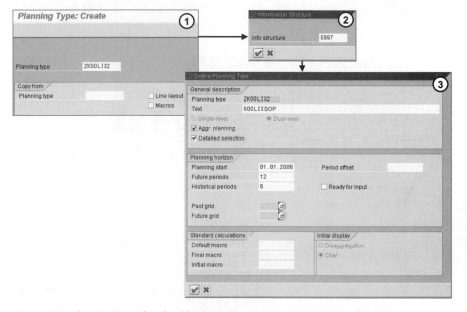

Figure 6.25 Planning Type for Flexible Planning

If you use the level-by-level planning mode, you can define whether you want the planning type to support only single-level planning— that is, only the header level—or whether you want it to support both the header and member levels (two-level planning). For consistent planning, the two-level planning is firmly defined.

The creation of the planning type also involves the definition of the planning horizon: the number of periods that reach into the future and into the past. Usually, the historical key figures are not included, but if you want to extend the planning to the past, you must set the corresponding flag. The planning start defines the date on which you want the planning to begin when the planning table is called. If you don't enter any value in this field, the planning begins on the current date. The planning grid is not defined in the planning type, but in the information structure.

In addition, you can specify macros to be executed after each entry (**Default macro**), at the planning start (**Initial macro**), or at the end of the planning (**Final macro**). The following section describes macros in further detail.

First, start with an empty planning book consisting of empty rows. These must be filled with key figures, provided they are available in the information structure, or with auxiliary key figures (see Figure 6.26).

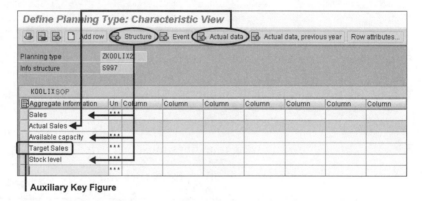

Figure 6.26 Row Selection for the Planning Type

You can add key figures from the information structure by clicking on the **Structure** button, while you can create other key figures by clicking on **Add row**.

6.3.2 Macros

Macros enable you to automate the linking of key figures in the planning table by using calculation rules. For example, standard SOP provides macros for the calculation of the projected stock level and for the creation of an operations plan on the basis of the sales plan. You also can use macros in aggregation and disaggregation during level-by-level planning. You can create your own macros as well. You also can define macros in the planning type via the menu item, **Macro** (Transaction MC8A for creating; MC8B for changing).

An example of a macro is the **DEFAULT** macro that is used to calculate the projected stock level and the number of days of supply (see Figure 6.27).

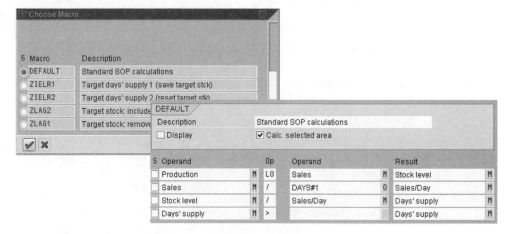

Macro for stock level and days' supply

Figure 6.27 Default Macros for Calculating the Stock Level

This macro calculates the days' supply as follows:

Days' supply = max {Stock level / (Sales/Day); 0}

For this purpose, the following four steps must be carried out:

1. Stock level = Stock balance resulting from sales and production

2. Sales/Day = Sales/Number of workdays

3. Days' supply = Stock level/(Sales/Day)

4. Days' supply = max {Days' supply; 0}

The stock level is determined on the basis of planned production and sales using the special operator L0, which includes the opening stock. Table 6.5 lists other special operators for macros.

Special operators

Operator	Description
<	Minimum {element; value}
>	Max {element; value}
AM	Aggregation of members
DM	Disaggregation of members

Table 6.5 Special Operators for Macros (Selection)

Operator	Description
LO	Stock balance (stock of previous period + receipts – issues)
PR	Production
RW	Days' supply

Table 6.5 Special Operators for Macros (Selection) (cont.)

Creating macros

You can create macros in the planning type via menu path, **Macro •
Create**. Existing rows can be linked with each other via standard or
special operators. In addition, function module EXIT_SAPMMCP6_
002 enables you to integrate your own logic. To be able to call the
macro from the planning table, you must set the **Display** parameter
(see Figure 6.28).

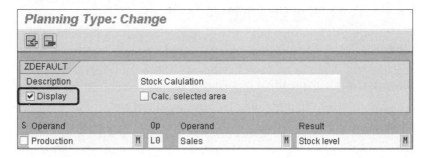

Figure 6.28 Definition of a Macro for Calculating the Stock Level

You can either call macros explicitly from the planning table via
menu path, **Edit • Macro**, or define them as default, final, or initial
macros in the planning type. Figure 6.29 displays the assignment in
the planning type information (menu path: **Goto • Planning Type
Info**).

The **Default macro** is carried out after each data entry, while the **Ini-
tial macro** is executed when the planning table is called, and the
Final macro is run when the planning table is closed. Complex
Default macros can have a negative effect on the runtime behavior.

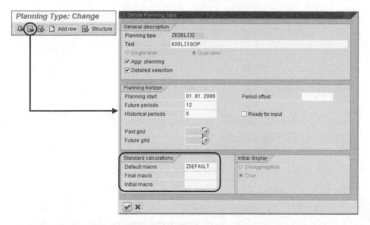

Figure 6.29 Defining Macros as Default, Initial, and Final Macros

6.3.3 Planning in the Planning Table

The planning table allows the planning for the objects defined in the product group or planning hierarchy. Standard SOP already contains preconfigured planning tables, whereas for flexible planning, you must first create the planning tables. The transactions for calling standard SOP and the flexible planning are different.

You can start standard SOP either at material level (Transaction MC87 for creating; Transaction MC88 for changing) or at product group level (Transaction MC81 for creating; Transaction MC82 for changing). Each plan is stored for a version. If you want to edit the active version or an already existing version, you must choose the change mode. Figure 6.30 displays the planning in the planning table for the entry at product group level in the active version.

Planning in standard SOP

Change Rough-Cut Plan

Product group	KOOLIX	KOOLIX Airconditioner	
Plant	XX01		
Version	A00 Active version		Active

SOP: plan individual product group

Planning table	Un	M 07.2006	M 08.2006	M 09.2006	M 10.2006	M 11.2006	M 12.2006	M 01.2007
Sales	PC	400	500	400	328	200	200	100
Production	PC	500	300	300	300	200	50	50
Stock level	PC	600	400	300	272	272	122	72
Target stock level	PC	300	300	300	200	200	200	200
Days' supply	***	31	18	15	17	28	11	15
Target days' supply	***							

Figure 6.30 Planning in the Standard Planning Table

Opening
stock level

The stock level is calculated as the difference between the opening stock level and production on the one hand and sales on the other. The opening stock level is not an aggregate of the members of the product group, but must be entered interactively in the planning table via the following menu path: **Goto • Opening Stock Level** (see Figure 6.31).

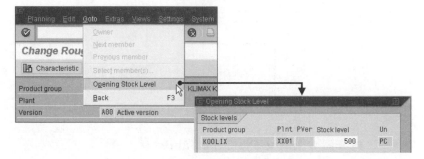

Figure 6.31 Defining the Opening Stock Level in the Standard Planning Table

The interactive entry of the opening stock level is also necessary if planning occurs at material level. Alternatively, you can schedule the determination of the opening stock level (per information structure) as a background job via Transaction MC8M.

The target stock level and target days' supply are set in the planning table and can be used for creating a production plan.

Row totals

The display of row totals can be used to support interactive planning, for example in order to compare all sales and production figures across the entire planning period. You can call the display of row totals from the menu, as shown in Figure 6.32.

Creating the
sales plan

Standard SOP provides automated functions for creating the sales plan, or for creating a suggested sales plan. You can call these functions via **Edit • Create Sales Plan** from the menu. The functions contain the following options:

▶ Copy plan from sales information system (SIS)

▶ Copy plan from CO-PA

▶ Forecast (see Section 6.4)

You can revise all results interactively.

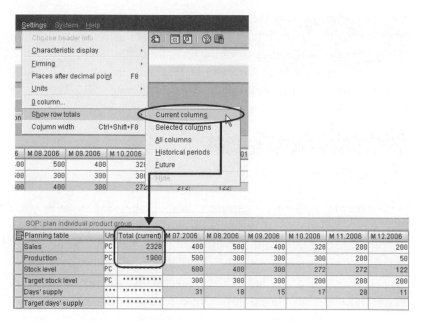

Figure 6.32 Displaying Row Totals

Similar to the creation of the sales plan, the standard SOP also provides automated functions for creating the operations plan. These functions are as follows.

Creating the
operations plan

▸ **Synchronous to sales**
This means that the sales figures are used as operations plans.

▸ **Target stock level**
The operations plan is configured in such a way that the target stock level is reached in each period.

▸ **Target days' supply**
The operations plan is configured in such a way that the target stock level is reached in each period.

▸ **Stock level = zero**
The operations plan is configured in such a way that the entire stock level is consumed.

You can call these functions via the following menu path: **Edit • Create product plan** (see Figure 6.33).

The difference between the **Synchronous to sales** and **Stock level = zero** functions is that the opening stock is reduced to zero in the latter case.

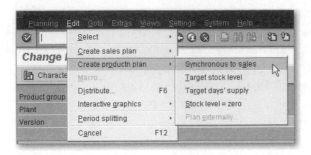

Figure 6.33 Functions for Creating the Production Plan

Disaggregation and aggregation In the case of level-by-level planning, both disaggregation and aggregation are carried out using macros. For standard SOP, you can use the two planning tables for this purpose, which can call using transactions MC76 (create) and MC77 (change). When you open the planning table in the change mode, the system displays the proportional factors from the product group. These proportional factors can be overwritten during aggregation and disaggregation (see Figure 6.34). The modified proportional factors are stored in the product group.

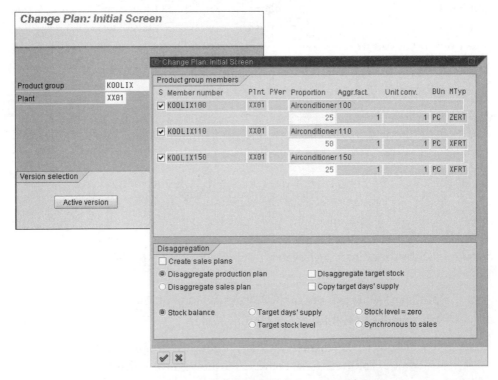

Figure 6.34 Initial Screen of the Standard Planning Tables

At this stage, the user must already define whether the production or sales should be disaggregated. Both disaggregation and aggregation are carried out using macros. Figure 6.35 shows the disaggregation of the operations plan for product group **KOOLIX** (see circled section) to the product members. The only product member shown here is **KOOLIX100**.

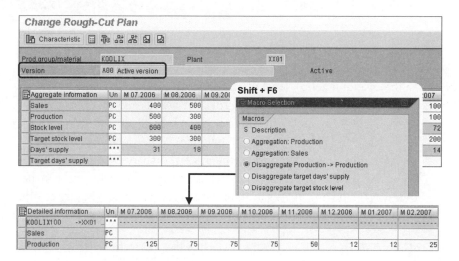

Figure 6.35 Disaggregation in Standard SOP

You can call macros either via menu path **Edit • Macro** or using the key combination **Shift + F6**.

You can start flexible planning by calling Transaction MC93 (create) and Transaction MC94 (change). In contrast to standard SOP, flexible planning only provides the custom key figures and macros.

Planning in flexible planning

If you use flexible planning with the consistent planning method, you must select the planning level at the beginning. If all characteristics are assigned a value, planning takes place at the most detailed level. If some characteristics are not assigned a value, planning occurs at a correspondingly aggregated level (see Figure 6.36).

Flexible planning with consistent planning method

If you entered flexible planning at the aggregate level, you can change the planning levels within the planning table. Figure 6.37 illustrates the change of levels in the planning table.

Another useful tool is the display of a key figure for subordinate characteristic values combinations. Figure 6.38 shows how to do that in the planning table.

You can display the key figure by clicking on the looking-glass icon. Be sure to place the cursor on the key figure to be displayed.

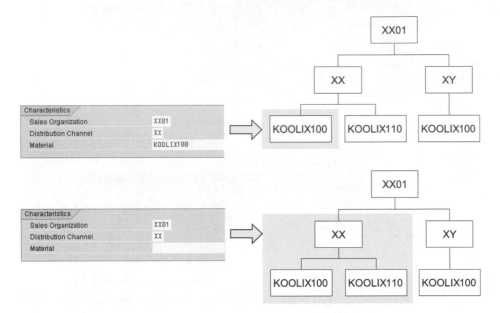

Figure 6.36 Entry Level for Flexible Planning (with Consistent Planning Method)

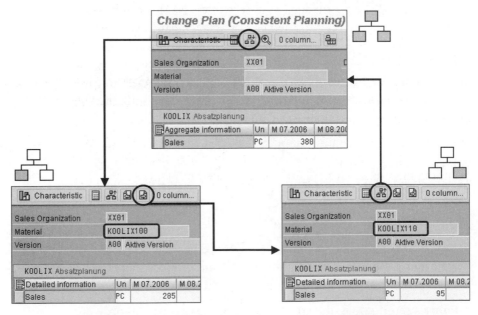

Figure 6.37 Change of Levels in Flexible Planning (with Consistent Planning Method)

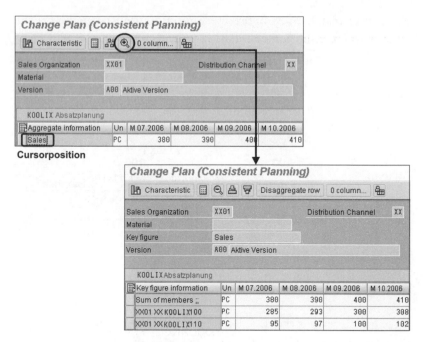

Figure 6.38 Details of a Key Figure for Several Characteristic Values Combinations

If planning occurs at different levels, it is often useful to protect specific values from being changed at different levels. This can be done by fixing the values either at a detailed or an aggregate level. The following scenario provides an example of fixing values at a detailed level. You know that the requirement for **KOOLIX100** will be 50 units in the distribution channel of sales organization **XX01**, regardless of what is being planned for the entire sales organization. In this case, you don't want a change—for example, an increase of the planned quantity at sales organization level—to affect **KOOLIX100**. This change is supposed to affect only the other members of the planning hierarchy. This situation is illustrated in Figure 6.39.

Fixing values

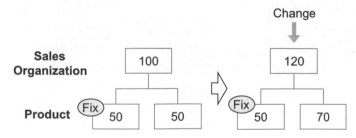

Figure 6.39 Fixing at Detailed Level: Schema

This process can happen in reverse. Suppose, for instance, that at the level of the distribution channel you want to assign a certain planning value to the sales figures, even though a change is carried out at a subordinate level. In this case the change to one of the members must be balanced by automatic changes to other members. Figure 6.40 illustrates this scenario.

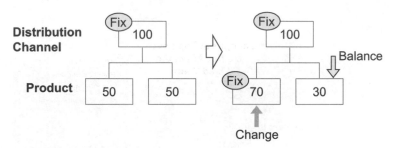

Figure 6.40 Fixing at a Higher Level: Schema

If the higher level is fixed, a change at a lower level entails a fixing of the changed element.

You can carry out the fixing process in the planning table by clicking on the corresponding button or by selecting **Settings • Firming • Switch On** from the menu Note that you must adhere to the following sequence of steps:

1. Activate fixing

2. Change value

3. Deactivate fixing

The value to be fixed must differ from the previous value. Once a value has been fixed, it is displayed in red. Figure 6.41 illustrates this procedure. The figure shows the sales figures for two products and the next higher level. The value to be fixed for **KOOLIX100** is changed to 50 units, which increases the planning quantity at the higher level to 110 units (**Sum of members**). Due to the fixing, an increase by 10 units at a higher level does not affect **KOOLIX100**. Instead, the entire difference quantity is assigned to **KOOLIX110**.

You can deactivate the fixing via the following menu path: **Settings • Firming • Unfirm Period**. Values can only be fixed if you use the consistent planning method.

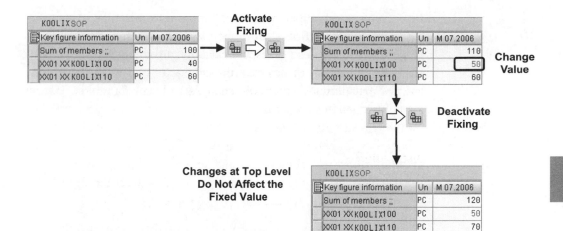

Figure 6.41 Fixing in the Planning Table

6.4 Forecast

A forecast is the prediction of the future development of a time series. The forecast calculates the sales quantities for a specific period of time. These calculations can consist of estimates from the sales and distribution areas or from the market planning as part of strategic enterprise planning. Moreover, historical figures can be extrapolated using mathematical-statistical forecasting procedures in order to calculate the requirements. For this reason, the forecast calculation can also be used in profitability analysis or in materials management (see Section 8.3.4).

In the context of material requirements planning, historical data such as the consumption figures of a specific material is used in order to estimate the future requirements for this material. To do that, you can use forecast models that enable you to derive forecast values from the historical data.

Forecast model

The future requirements are forecast on the basis of past consumption values. The consumption values indicate what quantity of a material was consumed within a specific period in the past. These values have been updated automatically during material withdrawals. If you create a new material, the consumption values must either be entered manually or transferred from a different source into the system by means of a batch input.

Before you can create a forecast for a material, you must define forecast parameters. The forecast model is of central importance in this respect. If you consider the historical consumption values for a material, you will realize that there are some patterns at work. For example, the consumption can have been relatively constant over time or it can have followed a certain trend. Depending on the development of the consumption, the material is assigned a specific forecast model, based on which the forecast values are then calculated. There are numerous forecast models available. To name but a few, there are the constant model, the moving average model, the trend model, the seasonal model, and the seasonal trend model.

The choice of forecast model depends primarily on the consumption development of the material to be planned. For example, it makes sense to use the moving average model if the consumption development is constant. The second-order exponential smoothing and the regression analysis, on the other hand, provide reliable forecast values if the consumption development follows a trend. In addition to selecting an appropriate forecast model based on the time-series development, you also must define the right smoothing factor to be used in the mathematical-statistical calculation in order to carry out useful forecasts. Smoothing factors include the following.

▶ **Alpha factor**
The alpha factor is used to smooth the basic value.

▶ **Beta factor**
The beta factor is used to smooth the trend value.

▶ **Gamma factor**
The gamma factor is used to smooth the seasonal index.

The overview in Table 6.6 shows which forecast models should be used with which smoothing factors on the basis of the time-series development.

Time series development	Forecast model	Forecast strategy	Parameter
Constant progression	Constant model	10	—
Constant progression	Constant model of first-order exponential smoothing	11	Alpha factor

Table 6.6 Forecast Models and Forecast Strategies

Time series development	Forecast model	Forecast strategy	Parameter
Constant progression	Moving average model	13	Number of historical values
Constant progression	Weighted moving average model	14	Weighting group
Trend-like pattern	Linear regression	20	—
Trend-like pattern	Trend model of second-order exponential smoothing	22	Alpha and beta factors
Season-like pattern	Seasonal model (Winters procedure)	31	Alpha and gamma factors, periods per season
Seasonal trend pattern	Seasonal model of first-order exponential smoothing	40	Alpha, beta, and gamma factors, periods per season

Table 6.6 Forecast Models and Forecast Strategies (cont.)

The forecast strategies are firmly predefined and are assigned to the forecast profile.

For the forecast—as for the entire sales planning process—the planning level is of major importance. The *planning level* defines the product basis on which the planning is to be carried out. Thus, companies with a very wide range of products must face the challenge of having to plan the sales quantities for numerous different products. In this context it makes sense to carry out the forecast at product group level for a specific product family instead of forecasting individual products. This is often the case in large-scale production and repetitive manufacturing, whereas in small-scale production it can be more useful to forecast the requirements at assembly level or at individual materials level, for instance for frequently used materials.

Planning level

In the SAP system, the forecast calculation can be based on various different sources of information, such as deliveries, sales, consumption, and incoming payments. The forecast can be carried out entirely at the level of an individual material, or it can be performed at plant level so that it includes all materials produced in a particular plant. For this purpose, the planner can create flexible planning hierarchies on the basis of product families, product groups, sales and distribution areas, or other market or organizational units. Moreover, the planner can store the model selection, including the associated parameters, in forecast profiles in order to ensure a uniform usage throughout the company.

An interactive forecast is carried out for the planning level that is currently processed in the planning table. In standard SOP, you can forecast the sales quantities for product groups and materials. The forecast for a material is based on that material's historical consumption data, and it aggregates these values at product group level. Flexible planning, on the other hand, allows you to forecast any key figure you like, provided the key figures have been created in Customizing. Standard SOP is solely carried out as level-by-level planning, whereas flexible planning can be performed as level-by-level planning or consistent planning.

Forecasting   You can call the forecast using the following path from the menu: **Edit • Create Sales Plan**. This applies to both standard SOP and flexible planning. Whereas in standard SOP the forecast always fills the **Sales** key figure, in flexible planning the forecast refers to the key figure on which the cursor is currently placed. Figure 6.42 shows the settings screens for the forecast horizon and forecast procedures as they are displayed when you call the forecast. Once you have selected the period intervals and forecast models (step 1), you can adjust the forecast models and smoothing factors in the window that displays next (step 2).

The important parameters here are the number of historical periods used, the number of periods to be forecast, and the model. These parameters are pre-assigned values by the forecast profile, but can be changed interactively. In the example shown in Figure 6.42, the system selects a trend model with a basic value of **320** and trend value **10**. This selection is made on the basis of historical sales data. The result is shown in a pop-up window and is not written to the key figure until it is explicitly transferred. Figure 6.43 illustrates the transfer of the interactively performed forecast into sales planning. The forecast is calculated as of the fifth month and transferred into the **Sales** key figure. These values can be changed interactively.

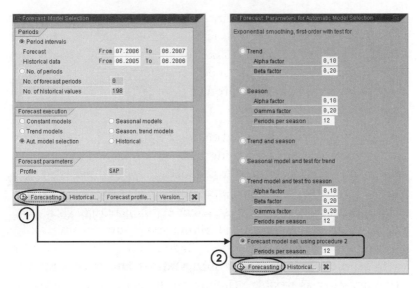

Figure 6.42 Calling the Forecast from the Planning Table

As shown in Figure 6.42, the parameters needed for forecasting are **Forecast profile** predefined via the forecast profile. You can create the forecast profile using Customizing Transaction MC96. It can be assigned to the forecast when you call the forecast, as shown in Figure 6.44.

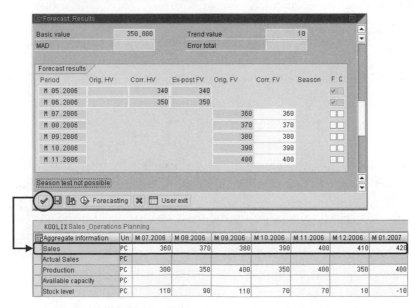

Figure 6.43 Transferring the Forecast

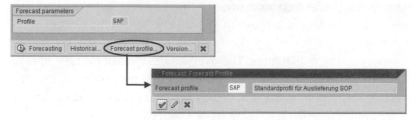

Figure 6.44 Assigning the Forecast Profile

At this stage, you can also change the most important items of the forecast profile, such as the forecast strategy, forecast parameters, historical periods, and forecast periods. Figure 6.45 illustrates these options.

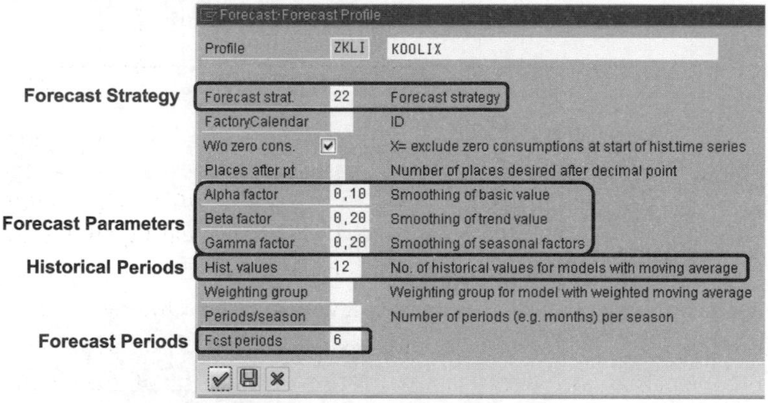

Figure 6.45 Customizing the Forecast Profile

6.5 Event

Sometimes the sales volume can be affected by events that are already known. This applies particularly to the consumer goods industry, where promotions can be used to generate short-term sales increases. Other events, such as the Super Bowl, can also affect sales. These events are limited in time and scope and it often happens that a slight decrease in the sales figures occurs at the end of an event. Figure 6.46 shows a typical sales development that is affected by events.

SAP ERP provides two ways of modeling an event: *cumulative modeling* and *percentage modeling*. In the case of cumulative events, the sales quantity affected by the event is maintained as a difference quantity in absolute figures. The overall sales quantity is represented as the total of "normal" sales plus the event. In the case of percentage events, the sales quantity affected by the event refers to the quantity planned in the **Sales** key figure.

Event modeling

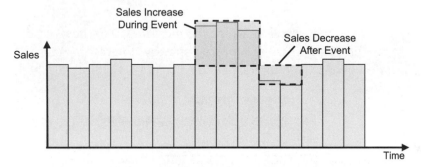

Figure 6.46 Effects of an Event on Sales

You can create events using Transaction MC64, and change them using Transaction MC65 (see Figure 6.47). When creating an event, you must define the **Event type** and the length of the event period (**Length 1: event per.**) at the header level (step 1). Once you have defined the values (step 2), you must assign the event to one or several information structures (step 3). The periodicity of the event period must exist in the information structure.

To be able to use the event in sales and operations planning, you must assign it to the planning type, as shown in Figure 6.48.

You can do that in the planning type maintenance (Transaction MC8B) by clicking on the **Event** tab (step 1). The window that opens next displays the key figures of the information structure that are not yet used. One of them must be used to save the event values, in our case that's the **Target stock level** key figure (step 2). As a result of this assignment, the planning type now contains additional key figures for planning the events (step 3).

Thus, in addition to the sales key figure, flexible planning with results also includes the event key figure that cannot be changed in the planning table, as well as the total of sales and event as the corrected sales figure (see Figure 6.49).

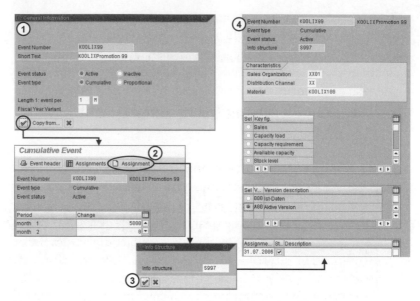

Figure 6.47 Creating an Event and Assigning It to an Information Structure

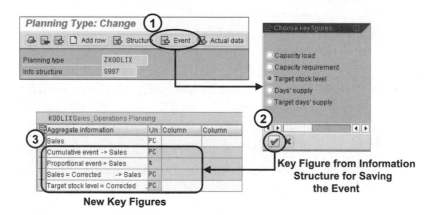

Figure 6.48 Assigning Events to the Planning Type

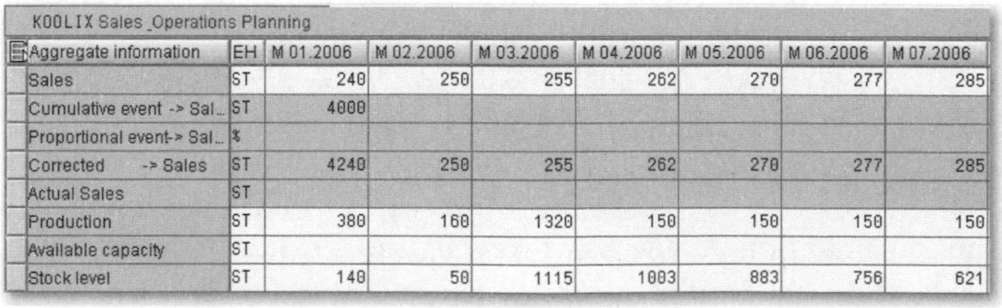

KOOLIX Sales _Operations Planning								
Aggregate information	EH	M 01.2006	M 02.2006	M 03.2006	M 04.2006	M 05.2006	M 06.2006	M 07.2006
Sales	ST	240	250	255	262	270	277	285
Cumulative event -> Sal..	ST	4000						
Proportional event-> Sal..	%							
Corrected -> Sales	ST	4240	250	255	262	270	277	285
Actual Sales	ST							
Production	ST	380	160	1320	150	150	150	150
Available capacity	ST							
Stock level	ST	140	50	1115	1003	883	756	621

Figure 6.49 Sales Planning with Events

As you can see in this figure, the total sales quantity displayed as a corrected sales quantity (**Corrected • Sales**) represents the total amount of sales planning (**Sales**) and event (**Cumulated event • Sales**).

6.6   Resource Leveling Using a Rough-Cut Planning Profile

Based on a rough-cut planning profile, resource leveling calculates the resource load for the operations plan and thus enables you to quickly estimate feasibility in terms of capacity. You can define a capacity load for a specific base quantity at different levels, such as the material and plant levels, the product group and plant levels, or at the information structure level. The resource-leveling process scales the resource load maintained in the rough-cut planning profile with the production plan and thus calculates the resource load for the production plan. Figure 6.50 illustrates this relationship.

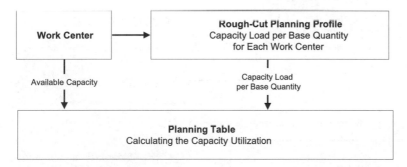

Figure 6.50 Resource Leveling Using a Rough-Cut Planning Profile: Schema

The available capacity is imported from the work center and used as a basis for calculating the percentage of resource utilization.

You can create rough-cut planning profiles using Transaction MC35, while Transaction MC36 enables you to change them. Similar to the routing, you must maintain the status, usage, and lot-size range for the rough-cut planning profile. In addition, you must define the base quantity, which is the number of units of a product to which the capacity load to be further maintained refers. Apart from this, you must define the period pattern in which you want to maintain the capacity load. Figure 6.51 illustrates the creation of a rough-cut planning profile.

Rough-cut planning profile

To be able to calculate the percentage of resource utilization in the resource-leveling process, you must first create the resources to be checked in the rough-cut planning profile, following the steps shown in Figure 6.52. In this example, we only use work centers as resources, but note that other restricting entities such as production resources/tools or materials could also be used.

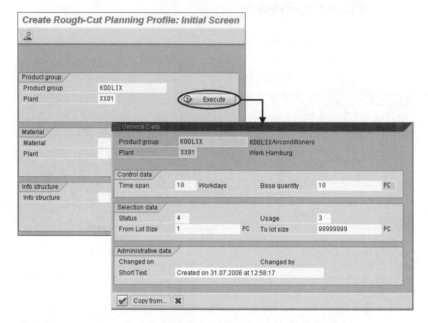

Figure 6.51 Creating a Rough-Cut Planning Profile

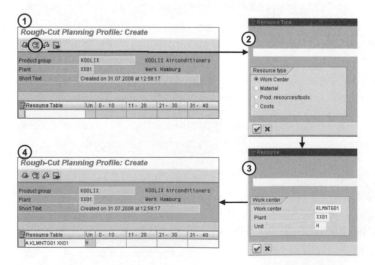

Figure 6.52 Assigning Resources in the Rough-Cut Planning Profile

The capacity consumption to be expected per period is indicated separately for each resource. In this example, it is 10 workdays each (see Figure 6.53). The consumption refers to the base quantity (10 units in this example) and is aggregated for each resource.

Rough-Cut Planning Profile: Create

Product group	KOOLIX			KOOLIX Airconditioners
Plant	XX01			Werk Hamburg
Short Text	Created on 31.07.2006 at 12:58:17			

Resource Table	Un	0 - 10	11 - 20	21 - 30	31 - 40
A KLMNTG01 XX01	H	1	1,5		
A KLMNTG02 XX01	H	2	1	2	

Figure 6.53 Capacity Consumption in the Rough-Cut Planning Profile

The planning table allows you to display the available capacity and the capacity requirement via the following menu path: **Views · Capacity Requirements Planning · Rough-Cut Planning · Show** (see Figure 6.54).

Change Rough-Cut Plan

Prod.group/material	KOOLIX		Plant		XX01		
Version	A00 Active version				Active		

Planning table	Un	M 07.2006	M 08.2006	M 09.2006	M 10.2006	M 11.2006	M 12.2006	M 01.2007	M 02.2007
Sales	PC	600	750	850	1200	1400	1900	1800	1200
Production	PC	50	600	900	1200	1400	2300	1800	1000
Stock level	PC	200	50	100	100	100	600	600	400
Target stock level	PC	300	300	300	300	300	300	300	300
Days' supply	***	7	1	2	1	1	6	7	6
Target days' supply	***								

Resource load	Un	M 07.2006	M 08.2006	M 09.2006	M 10.2006	M 11.2006	M 12.2006	M 01.2007	M 02.2007
KLMNTG01 XX01 002	***	--------	--------	--------	--------	--------	--------	--------	--------
Available capacity	H	32	736	672	672	672	608	704	640
Capacity reqmts	H	13	150	225	300	350	575	450	250
Capacity load	%	39	20	33	44	52	94	63	39
KLMNTG02 XX01 002	***	--------	--------	--------	--------	--------	--------	--------	--------
Available capacity	H	48	1104	1008	1008	1008	912	1056	960
Capacity reqmts	H	25	300	450	600	700	1150	900	500
Capacity load	%	52	27	44	59	69	126	85	52

Figure 6.54 Capacity Utilization in the Standard Planning Table

If a capacity is overloaded, a corresponding message is displayed in the footer. In our example, this will be the case for December 2006 (see Figure 6.55).

Figure 6.55 Overload Notification in the Footer

The capacity utilization is immediately calculated when the plan changes, and this facilitates the interactive adjustment of the operations plan to the capacities. However, the resource-leveling process does not provide any standard function for adapting the production plan to the available capacity.

When the rough-cut planning profile is changed, the changed capacity requirement is only accounted for if the planning data changes.

6.7   Transfer to Demand Management

The transfer of planning data to demand management can be triggered interactively or automatically. Moreover, it can run in parallel or in the background as a mass processing job. The most commonly used method is the background transfer. An interactive transfer usually occurs only if changes to sales and operations planning must take immediate effect on the requirements.

Transferring the standard SOP
The transfer of planning data to demand management from standard SOP can be done via Transaction MC74 for planning at material level, and via Transaction MC75 for planning at product group level. Figure 6.56 shows the transfer of planning data to demand management for planning at product group level.

Transfer Planning Data to Demand Management

Transfer now | Other PG or material

Product group	KOOLIX	KOOLIX Airconditioners
Plant	XX01	Werk Hamburg
Version	A00	Active version

Transfer strategy and period
○ Sales plan for material or PG members
○ Sales plan for mat. or PG members as proportion of PG
○ Production plan for material or PG members
◉ Prod.plan for mat. or PG members as proportion of PG

From   31.07.2006   To   31.12.2006
☑ Invisible transfer

Independent requirement specifications
Requirements type   VSF
Version   00
☑ Active

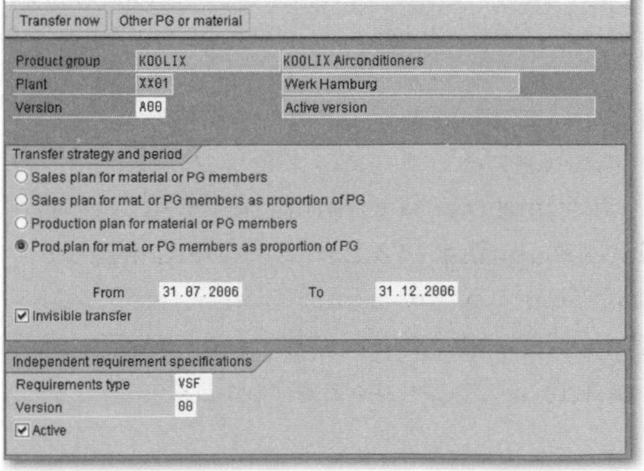

Figure 6.56 Transfer of Standard SOP to Demand Management

At this point, you can choose whether you want to transfer the sales plan or production plan as a planned independent requirement. The planned independent requirement is always created at material level. If you select the transfer using the option **as proportion of PG**, the proportion of materials is determined based on the proportional factors of the product group. Otherwise, if the **direct** option is selected, planned values must already exist at material level. As a result, the system displays planned independent requirements in the stock/requirements list. Chapter 7, *Demand Management*, describes planned independent requirements in more detail.

The transfer of planning data from flexible planning to demand management using Transaction MC90 occurs at the **Material** and **Plant** levels (see Figure 6.57). In this case, you must select the key figure you want to transfer.

Transferring the flexible planning

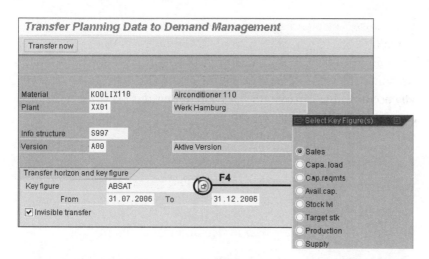

Figure 6.57 Transferring the Flexible Planning to Demand Management

If the plant reference is not contained as a characteristic in the planning structure, you can distribute specific materials to specific plants. You can carry out a plant distribution via Customizing path **Production • Sales and Operations Planning • Functions • Define Proportional Distribution Across Plants** or by using Transaction MC7A. Figure 6.58 shows an example in which 80 % of the requirements for material **KOOLIX100** are distributed to plant **XX01** and 20 % to plant **XX02**.

Plant distribution

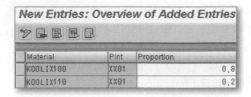

Figure 6.58 Plant Distribution

The plant distribution is maintained at material level. Note that in this context no check is carried out as to whether the material has actually been created for the respective plant. If no plant reference exists in the planning and no plant distribution is maintained, the planning data is distributed equally to all plants in which the material is maintained.

6.8 Mass Processing

In sales and operations planning, it is often necessary to carry out planning steps for a large number of products. Some planning steps require the knowledge and experience of the planner and must therefore be carried out interactively. Many planning steps, however, can be automated, such as these:

▶ Forecasting

▶ Determining the opening stock level

▶ Running a macro

▶ Transferring planning data to demand management

To carry out these planning steps, it makes sense to employ mass processing.

The basic principle of mass processing is that you must define activities that describe the steps to be carried out and their assignment to mass-processing jobs. The exception occurs when determining the opening stock level, which has already been described in Section 6.3.3. Figure 6.59 illustrates this relationship as well as the creation of activities using Transaction MC8T.

Activities are assigned a name (**Key f. plng.activity**) and can contain several planning steps. The sequence of the activities is defined via **Sequence in activity**. However, some activity categories must be carried out without any further planning steps, such as **UEBERGABE**. In addition, there is a unique reference to the planning type.

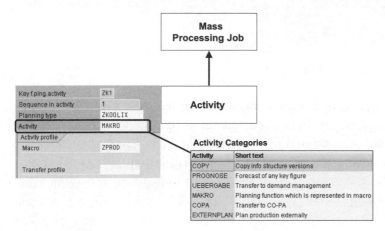

Figure 6.59 Activity

Activities can have different categories, such as **MAKRO** or **PROG-NOSE**. Depending on the activity category, additional information may be required that can be assigned to the activity in its profile. Table 6.7 lists the required information for each activity category.

Activity category	Information
COPY	Copy profile
PROGNOSE	Forecast profile and key figure ("Field name")
UEBERGABE	Transfer profile
MAKRO	Macro
COPA	Assignment of plan/actual indicator
EXTERNPLAN	SCPI planning profile

Table 6.7 Activity Categories and Profiles

Section 6.4 already described the forecast profile to be used for the forecast. Likewise, the macros were described in Section 6.3.2. The following pages of this chapter describe additional profiles.

To transfer planning data to demand management, you must create an activity of the **UEBERGABE** category and assign a transfer profile to it. Transfer profiles can be created using Transaction MC8S (see Figure 6.60).

Transfer profile

187

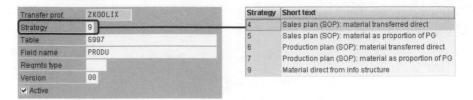

Figure 6.60 Transfer Profile

You can use the strategies 4 through 7 shown in Figure 6.60 to transfer planning data from standard SOP, depending on whether you want to transfer the sales or the operations plan and whether the respective plan was created directly at material level or at product group level. If you want to transfer planning data from flexible planning to demand management, you should choose strategy 9, and you must define the information structure (**Table**) and the key figure. The following chapter describes the requirements type and version.

Copy profile

If you want to copy key figures between information structures using activity category **COPY**, you must create a copy profile via Transaction MC8Z. When doing this, you must specify the source and target information structures as well as source and target key figures.

Creating mass processing jobs

You can create a mass-processing job using Transaction MC8D (MC8E to change it; M8F to delete it). This involves several steps.

1. Assign a name to the mass-processing job

2. Assign the information structure and version

3. Assign the planning type

4. Assign a name to the variant

5. Select selection screens

6. Define characteristic values, activity, and aggregation level

7. Save the variant

Figure 6.61 shows the first 5 steps in the system.

The remaining two steps are illustrated in Figure 6.62. An important step in defining the mass processing job is the restriction of the area of application carried out through the definition of the characteristic values. As is the case when you start flexible planning, you do not need to assign values to all characteristic values combinations.

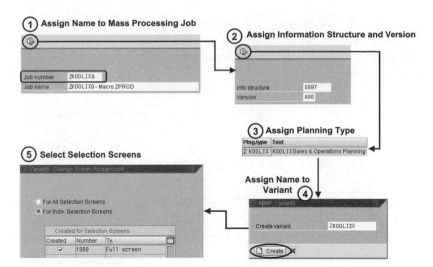

Figure 6.61 Creating a Mass Processing Job, Steps 1 through 5

⑥ **Define Characteristic Values, Activity, and Aggregation Level**

Maintain Variant: Report RMCA9976, Variant Z KOOLIX9

Attributes

⑦ **Save Variant**

Variant Attributes

Copy Screen Assignment

Variant Name	ZKOOLIX9
Meaning	Macro ZPROD

Characteristics

Sales Organization	XX01	to
Distribution Channel		to
Material		to

Control Parameters for Batch Planning

Job numbe	ZKOOLIX9
Planning activity	ZK1

Aggregation Level

○ Sales Organization
○ Distribution Channel
◉ Material

Planning Run Information

Info structu	S997
Version	A00
Planning type	ZKOOLIX

Figure 6.62 Creating a Mass Processing Job, Steps 6 and 7

By selecting the aggregation level, you can define whether you want to carry out the activity at a higher or a more detailed level.

This differentiates mass processing from interactive planning in the planning table, because in the latter case you must carry out the planning at a higher level if you enter it at a higher level. Figure 6.63

illustrates the influence of the aggregation level for a simple macro that adds 10 to each existing value. The example is based on the assumption that all materials of a distribution channel are selected and that the consistent planning method is used.

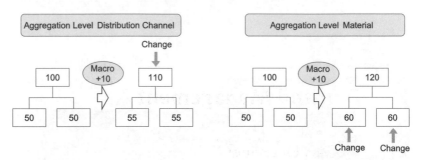

Figure 6.63 Aggregation Level

You can schedule the mass processing job using Transaction MC8G. Here, you must specify the variant name and use the standard batch scheduling function. Correspondingly, you can monitor the mass processing jobs using Transaction SM37. Moreover, you can use Transaction MC8I to obtain an overview of a specific job.

Demand management combines sales planning with customer requirements according to the planning strategy and thus determines the independent requirements for production.

7 Demand Management

7.1 Process Overview

The goal of *demand management* is to establish what quantities are to be produced at what times. This is done by creating planned independent requirements that already trigger planning. Unlike operations planning, the planned independent requirement is given a precise date and can be consumed with specific customer requirements. Figure 7.1 shows the process flow for demand management.

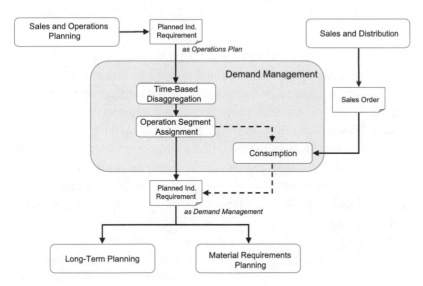

Figure 7.1 Process Steps for Demand Management

In *Sales and Operations Planning*, the operations plan is usually created with a monthly or weekly granularity. During transfer to demand management, the planned independent requirement is first given a date, or several dates, if it is disaggregated based on time.

Production type   One criterion often cited in the technical literature for differentiating the different requirements of production planning and control systems is the production type (see Glaser et al., 1991; Schäfer, 1969). This criterion is already taken into account within demand management. The characteristic feature for describing the production type is the frequency of the same activity output in production, that is, the level of certainty that the same activity type will recur (see Kilger, 1986, p. 29–33). Often, the production type is differentiated into mass, large-series, medium-series, small-series, and make-to-order production (see Keller, 1993, pp. 246–247; Schäfer, 1969, pp. 59–79).

Make-to-order
production   If the company is a make-to-order manufacturer—that is, a company that plans, develops, constructs, and produces certain products based on specific existing customer requirements—it is difficult to plan the independent requirement for the subsequent periods. In this case, when the order is placed, the products to be created are not yet specified in all details, and the delivery date may shift due to changes within the planning and production phase. Such make-to-order manufacturers typically include companies building special-purpose machines.

In order to ensure that reasonably reliable planning can be performed for such types of companies, a make-to-order manufacturer should first be able to perform a *rough-cut planning* with regard to the sales and production program, taking capacity, material and financial restrictions into account, and then simulate the production run. The initial data required will be information on the current capacity load, the likely number of assembly and production steps required to create the product, the production and assembly duration of those steps for simulating the likely capacity requirement, and the anticipated order end date. This information is stored in a rough-cut planning file and is updated with completion messages for orders and part orders. Particularly during make-to-order production, it is important to perform the planned independent requirements planning with great care, because errors in the early phase will lead to irregular capacity utilization. Errors or mistakes made during the planned independent requirements planning will also inevitably result in a poor requirements planning. This can lead to the issuing of externally processed orders when there are overloads, or to the payment of contractual penalties if there are delayed deliveries.

The planned independent requirements planning looks a little different for a repetitive manufacturer. A repetitive manufacturer's planned independent requirement may arise due to existing sales orders and be based on forecast figures for the additional quantity to be sold. The rough-cut planning is based here on partially assured values; the company can obtain forecast figures through marketing promotions. Nevertheless, we must pay attention to the forecast quality here, because problems can arise due to poor forecast values: If too many products are produced, certain unsellable products can remain in the warehouse. If too few products are produced, however, employees can close these gaps.

Repetitive manufacturing

Accompanying the production type, the planning of planned independent requirements is significantly affected by the type of order placement used and by the product spectrum, that is, the product structure and the product standardization. The type of order placement specifies in what form production and assembly are triggered during order processing. The product structure describes the assembly of a product from subordinate components. The product standardization specifies to what extent an end product has reached a certain level of standardization. This standardization level may involve geometric, structural, or procedural aspects. In conjunction with the type of order placement, these may impact the activities of construction, costing, production, and sales logistics (see Keller, 1993, pp. 239–306).

Type of order placement

With the order-triggering type *Sales orders as individual orders*, the problem can arise that fluctuations will be greater in one period than in another. If there are more orders than planned, there may be capacity overloads in the individual planning periods. If the incoming orders remain below the planned values, either the capacity utilizations must be reduced or components must be produced for stock. With the order-triggering type *Sales orders based on outline agreements*, the product, delivery date, and quantity may be firmly agreed upon. The outline agreement with the customer corresponds to a kind of basic load that can be easily scheduled based on the available data. If the product is defined but not the quantity and delivery date, then end products or incoming assemblies must be produced for stock prior to the expected or provision date, in order to meet the delivery dates. If only the product group is known—for example, orthopedic seats—but not the precise product, the quantity, and the delivery date, different orders may be called in various variants at irregular time intervals. Strong order fluctuations may be processed through the prefabrication of non-variable parts; i.e., parts or assemblies that appear in different variants. The order triggering can also be performed through internal development orders of the development and construction department for products that cannot be sold yet on the market. Depending on the urgency, these orders can be freely planned and may be brought forward or postponed during periods of lower capacity utilization, without affecting scheduled sales orders. If a development order is related to a sales order, for instance for the manufacturing of special-purpose tools, it must be handled and planned like a sales order.

Planning strategy

To create the demand program in the form of planned independent requirements, you must specify the planning strategy with which a particular product is planned. The planning strategies represent the procedures that make sense from a business point of view for planning and manufacturing or procuring a product. As a matter of principle, you can differentiate here whether production should be triggered directly by a specific sales order (order production) or only sales order-anonymously (warehouse production). It is also possible to allow both sales orders and warehouse orders to flow into the demand program. If the production time is relatively long in proportion to the usual market delivery time, the products or certain assemblies should already be prefabricated before sales orders arrive. The sales quantities are preplanned for this (using the sales planning, for example).

The planning strategy determines whether the planned independent requirement is used purely for planning purposes, or whether it may trigger production, and whether the planned independent requirement can be consumed with actual customer requirements. If you are already manufacturing for a planned independent requirement, the planned independent requirement is created in the make-to-stock segment; otherwise this will occur in the planning segment. The planning strategy is assigned in the **Strategy Group** field to the material in the **MRP 3** view (see Figure 7.2).

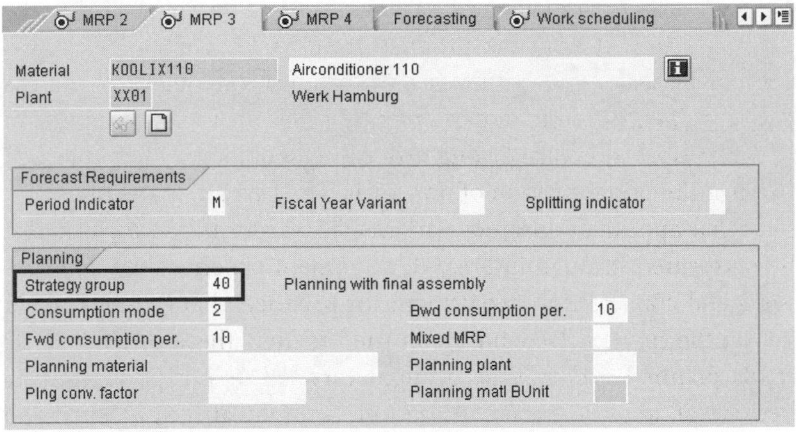

Figure 7.2 Planning Strategy in the Material Master

7.2 Time-Based Disaggregation

When demand management is transferred from the rough-cut sales and operations planning, a time-based disaggregation is required. The reason is that planning is carried out in periods of weeks or months in sales and operations planning, whereas the planned independent requirement has a current date. Without any further configuration, the requirement of the period is scheduled for the first working day of the period. A finer distribution is also possible. However, for this you need to define **distribution strategies** and period splits (**PSplt**). Figure 7.3 shows how you determine the **distribution type** in the distribution strategy (**Distr**) and assign the **function**. The distribution strategy is assigned to the period split for weekly (**Distr W.**) and monthly (**Distr M.**) distribution. The period split, in turn, is assigned to **Plant** and planning group (**PGp**).

The function determines the distribution function, in that we define for any number of times (modeled as a percentage of the overall duration) what proportion of the overall requirement is transferred. The distribution strategy uses the function and also defines the distribution type: whether the values are distributed continuously or discretely. For a function for which 100 % of the requirement is to be transferred after 100 % of the duration, a continuous distribution thus corresponds to an equal distribution while a discrete distribution corresponds to a concentration at the end.

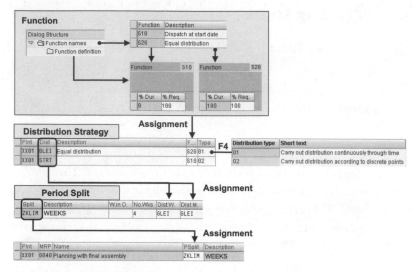

Figure 7.3 Distribution Strategy and Function for Time-Based Disaggregation

The period split defines into what periods, and into how many periods, the operations planning should be divided. The number of weeks in the first column is divided into days as per the distribution strategy, and the number of weeks in the second column is divided into weeks. The rest remains as a monthly requirement, unless the sales and operations planning already has been performed in weekly periods. In this case, the second column of the period split is ignored. Finally, the period split is assigned plant-specifically to a Materials Requirements Planning (MRP) group. The values listed in Figure 7.2 are maintained in Customizing as sub-items for the following Customizing path: **Production • Production Planning • Demand Management • Planned Independent Requirement • Automatic Distribution** (see Figure 7.4).

Figure 7.4 Sub-Items for the Customizing Path for Automatic Distribution

Furthermore, in the interactive processing of the planned independent requirements you also can initiate a time-based distribution of the planned independent requirements into smaller periods. This process is discussed in Section 7.4.

7.3   Planning Strategy

7.3.1   Selected Planning Strategies

Planning strategies can be set for each customer in Customizing. SAP already offers many different preconfigured planning strategies in the standard system. The most common strategies will be described briefly below.

With *make-to-stock production*, the entire planning is solely performed based on the planned independent requirement. The underlying assumption is that the products must be in stock for customers to buy them. This also means that sales orders do not affect requirements. Make-to-stock production is often used in the consumer goods industry.

Make-to-stock production

Make-to-order production is the exact opposite of make-to-stock production: Production is only initiated by the specific sales order, and the sales order is only catered for well after the order receipt. Planning is performed individually for each sales order (or more precisely: for each sales order item). Separate individual customer sections are created to keep the requirements apart for different sales orders for the same product. This implies that there is no sales and operations planning and no planned independent requirements are created. Make-to-order production is used especially often for more complex products that are frequently configurable. Examples include special-purpose machines or automobiles.

Make-to-order production

You can control whether the make-to-order production extends to semi-finished products using the indicator **Individual/coll.** flag in the material master (see Figure 7.5).

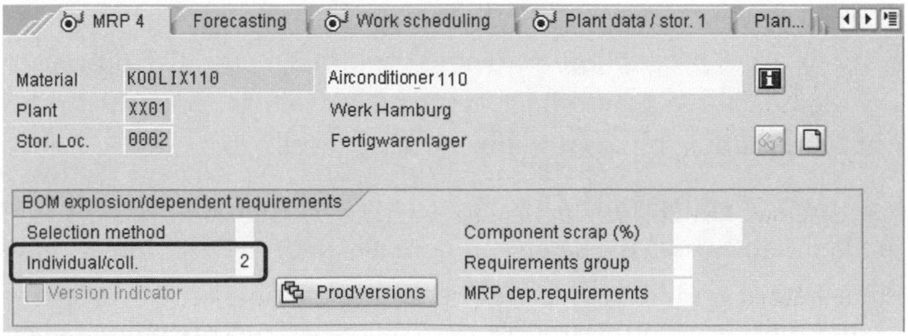

Figure 7.5 Individual/Coll. Flag

If the Individual/coll. flag is set to **1** (individual requirement), the component is also manufactured in an individual customer segment. Otherwise, the components are planned anonymously in the make-to-stock segment. However, this flag can be overridden in the BOM.

Planning with final assembly

Planning with final assembly is the same as make-to-stock production in many respects, but has one important difference. Unlike the make-to-stock production, sales orders are requirements-relevant during planning with final assembly. In this case the planned independent requirements are settled with the sales orders, to avoid duplicate manufacturing. The maximum from the sales orders and the planned independent requirements is thus always planning-relevant. The advantage of this planning strategy is that where the planning is estimated too low, production and procurement will nevertheless be triggered in order to cover the actual customer requirement.

Planning without final assembly

The particular feature of *planning without final assembly* is that the final production stage will only be produced if there is an actual customer requirement. Otherwise, the planning without final assembly behaves the same way as planning with final assembly. On the upstream stages (that is, semi-finished products and raw materials), production, and procurement are already triggered on the planned independent requirement. This strategy is especially suitable for reducing the risk of capital tie-up in cases where the last production level contains a proportionately high added value. It also helps deal with diverging material flow on the last stage to avoid delivery problems, if the requirement was forecast for the wrong product. Planning without final assembly can be used in conjunction both with make-to-order production and with make-to-stock production.

Planned orders for semi-finished products that are also produced as make-to-order production (Individual/coll. flag 1) are also only actually manufactured when the specific sales order is received. In this way, you can flexibly choose the stocking level.

Planning with planning material

If a group of end products has many logistical similarities—that is, it predominantly uses the same components and requires similar manufacturing processes—using a planning material represents a simplification of the planning. In this case, the sales and operations planning and creation of the planned independent requirement are performed for the planning material. With this planning strategy, sales orders for the final product are settled against the planned independent requirement of the planning material. In the subsequent material requirements planning, planned orders are then reduced for the planning material and planned orders are created for the end product. As is the case for planning without final assembly, the advantage of the planning strategy is that the components for the end product could already be produced or procured. This planning strategy also can be used in conjunction with make-to-order production or make-to-stock production.

The planning material is exclusively used for planning and is never actually manufactured. The planning strategy must be entered both in the planning material and in the end product; however, the parameters for the settlement are only used from the planning material. In the material master of the end product, you must also enter the planning material (**planning material**), the planning plant (**planning plant**), and the conversion factor between the planning material and the end product (**Plng conv. factor**). This is shown in Figure 7.6

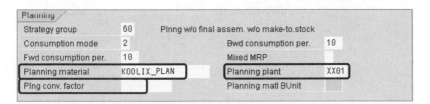

Planning				
Strategy group	60	Plnng w/o final assem. w/o make-to.stock		
Consumption mode	2	Bwd consumption per.	10	
Fwd consumption per.	10	Mixed MRP		
Planning material	KOOLIX_PLAN	Planning plant	XX01	
Plng conv. factor		Planning matl BUnit		

Figure 7.6 Planning Material in the Material Master of the End Product

Even if make-to-order production is used for the end product, the components must be produced anonymously to stock (Individual/coll. flag 2).

Planning at assembly level is similar to planning without final assembly from a business point of view. During planning at assembly level, the planned independent requirement is not created for the end product, but exclusively for the assembly (that is, the semi-finished product). When a sales order is received, a planned order is created for the end product whose secondary requirements consume the planned independent requirements for the assembly. This strategy is particularly appropriate in cases where it is easier to perform a reliable planning for assemblies than for end products. This applies even more if the planned assemblies account for a considerable part of the

Planning at assembly level

overall replenishment lead time. The planning strategy must be assigned to the assembly and the key figure for mixed MRP must be set.

Planning Strategy (Key)	Planning Strategy
10	Make-to-stock production
20	Make-to-order production
40	Planning with final assembly
50	Planning without final assembly (make-to-order)
52	Planning without final assembly (make-to-stock)
60	Planning with planning material (make-to-order)
63	Planning with planning material (make-to-stock)
70	Sub-assembly planning

Table 7.1 Planning Strategies in SAP ERP (Selection)

Table 7.1 lists the described planning strategies and their keys in the SAP ERP system. The principles of the most frequent planning strategies are described in detail in other works, where examples are provided (see Dickersbach, 2005b). This book concentrates on describing the way planning strategies work.

7.3.2 Consumption

The principle of consumption is that sales orders reduce the planned independent requirement. Whether consumption will take place depends on the planning strategy, and this issue is described in detail in Section 7.3.4. As a matter of principle, the planning strategies *Planning with final assembly*, *Planning without final assembly*, and *Planning with planning material* require a consumption. The sub-assembly planning is a special case where the planned independent requirement is consumed against a secondary requirement or a reservation.

Usually, planned independent requirements are entered with weekly or monthly granularity, and in many cases there is no time-based disaggregation. If a sales order is entered and there is no planned independent requirement for the corresponding date, one then must determine whether a planned independent requirement is consumed, and if so, which one. This is defined using the **consumption mode** and the consumption intervals (backward and forward) in the material master. Figure 7.7 shows the maintenance in the **MRP 3** view and the possible values for the **consumption mode**, as they are displayed with the F4 function key.

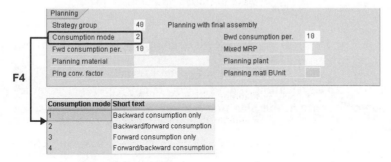

Figure 7.7 Consumption Mode

The consumption intervals are specified in terms of days, and the mode is self-explanatory. In choosing the consumption intervals, you must make sure that they are not too restrictive, in order to prevent overproduction by the planned independent requirement and customer requirement (see Dittrich et al., 2003, pp. 88–98).

7.3.3 Planning Segments

Material requirements planning is performed in different segments, depending on the strategy and requirements class.

During an anonymous make-to-stock production, scheduling is performed in the make-to-stock segment, where all requirements and receipt elements are added. While usually the exact lot size is used in the individual customer segment, all lot size types are used in the make-to-stock segment.

Make-to-stock segment

The planning segment represents a special case. For the planning strategies *Planning without final assembly* and *Planning with planning material,* it is essential that the planned orders that are created for the end products are not converted into production orders. This is done by creating these planned orders in a planning segment. Planned orders in the planning segment have the status **Planning** and cannot be converted into production orders. Figure 7.8 shows the status for planned orders.

Planning segment

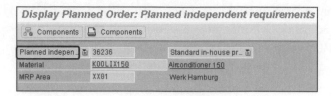

Figure 7.8 Status of Planning in the Planned Order

Another sspecial attribute of these planned orders is that they cannot be changed interactively.

For the capacity evaluation, it does not make any difference whether planned orders are in the planning segment or in the make-to-stock segment.

Make-to-order segment

If you use make-to-order production, a separate planning segment is created for each sales order item so that the assignment of requirements and resources is preserved. This case is not of interest for demand management, because by definition planned independent requirements can never be saved in a make-to-order segment.

7.3.4 Planning Strategy and Requirements Class

The requirements class for planned independent requirements is the central control element to determine whether and how consumption occurs and into what segment—be it make-to-stock segment or planning segment—the planned independent requirement is copied. The requirements class is assigned to a requirements type, which in turn is assigned to the planning strategy. The planning strategy contains both the requirements class for the planned independent requirement and the requirements class for the customer requirement. The planning strategy is in turn assigned to the planning strategy group, which is then finally assigned to the material in the **MRP 3** view. Figure 7.9 illustrates this relationship.

Requirements class

The requirements class for planned independent requirements is maintained with Customizing Transaction OMPO. This requirements class contains the following parameters.

▶ **Planning Indicator (PI)**
This indicator controls whether the material requirements planning is performed as net requirements planning, as gross requirements planning, or by a make-to-order segment.

▶ **Consumption Indicator (ConI)**
This indicator controls the extent to which the planning is consumed by sales orders.

▶ **Configuration Indicator (C)**
This determines whether a configuration using variant configuration is allowed.

▶ **Indicator for Requirements Reduction (RRd)**
This controls when the planned independent requirement is reduced.

▶ **Requirement Type (RT)**
The requirement type defines whether the requirements class is relevant for planned independent requirements or for customer requirements.

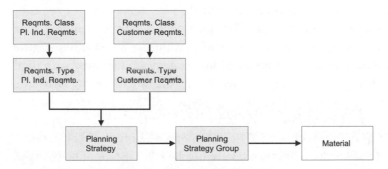

Figure 7.9 Relationship Between Requirements Class, Requirements Type, and Strategy

Figure 7.10 shows the Customizing for the requirements classes. The consumption indicator is decisive for the transfer of the planned independent requirement into the make-to-stock segment or into the planning segment.

The requirements class for customer requirements is maintained with Customizing Transaction OVZG. The only common parameter it contains is the consumption indicator, which is described there as an assignment indicator. Otherwise, the requirements class for customer requirements contains other, sales-relevant parameters, which is why we will not explore this any further in the context of this book.

The requirements type for planned independent requirements is maintained with Customizing Transaction OMP1 and only contains the requirements class.

Requirements type

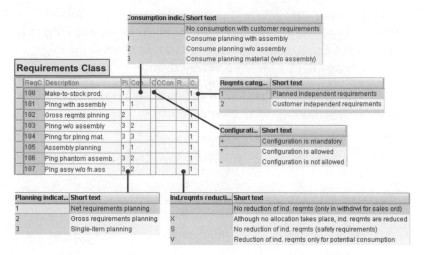

Consumption indic.	Short text
	No consumption with customer requirements
1	Consume planning with assembly
2	Consume planning w/o assembly
3	Consume planning material (w/o assembly)

Requirements Class

ReqC	Description	Pl	Con...	C	CCon	R...	C.
100	Make-to-stock prod.	1			•		1
101	Plnng with assembly	1	1				1
102	Gross reqmts plnning	2					
103	Plnng w/o assembly	3	2				1
104	Plnng for plnng mat.	3	3				1
105	Assembly planning	1	1				1
106	Plng phantom assemb.	3	2				1
107	Plng assy w/o fn.ass	3	2				1

Reqmts categ...	Short text
1	Planned independent requirements
2	Customer independent requirements

Configurati...	Short text
+	Configuration is mandatory
*	Configuration is allowed
-	Configuration is not allowed

Planning indicat...	Short text
1	Net requirements planning
2	Gross requirements planning
3	Single-item planning

Ind.reqmts reducti...	Short text
	No reduction of ind. reqmts (only in withdrwl for sales ord)
X	Although no allocation takes place, ind. reqmts are reduced
S	No reduction of ind. reqmts (safety requirements)
V	Reduction of ind. reqmts only for potential consumption

Figure 7.10 Requirements Class for Planned Independent Requirements

Planning strategy The planning strategy finally brings together the requirements data and classes from the planning and customer requirements. Figure 7.11 shows, as an example, planning strategy **40–Planning with final assembly**. You will see that what are consumed are the planning requirements of the requirements type VSF and the requirements class 101 with customer requirements of the requirements type KSV and requirements class 050. Furthermore, a number of key parameters of the requirements classes are displayed that cannot be changed at this point.

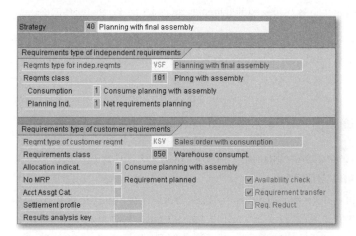

Figure 7.11 Strategy 40 for Planning with Final Assembly

The Customizing path for maintaining the strategy is as follows: **Production • Production Planning • Demand Management • Planned Independent Requirement • Planning Strategy • Define Strategy** or **• Define Strategy Group for the Strategy Group**.

Table 7.2 provides an overview of the most common strategies and their requirements classes and requirements types.

Strategy	Requirements Type Planning	Requirements Class Planning	Requirements Type Customer Requirement	Requirements Class Customer Requirement	Assignment (Consumption Indicator)
10	LSF	100	KSL	030	–
20	–	–	KE	040	–
40	VSF	101	KSV	050	1 – Planning With Final Assembly
50	VSE	103	KEV	045	2 – Planning Without Final Assembly
52	VSE	103	KSVS	049	2 – Planning Without Final Assembly
60	VSEV	104	KEVV	060	3 – Planning Material
63	VSEV	104	KSVV	070	3 – Planning Material
70	VSFB	105	–	–	1 – Planning with Final Assembly

Table 7.2 Requirements Types and Requirements Classes for Planning Strategies (Selection)

The strategy group is assigned to the material master in the **MRP 3** view, as was shown in Figure 7.2.

7.4 Editing Planned Independent Requirements

7.4.1 Interactive Planning with Planned Independent Requirements

Planned independent requirements are created during the transfer of the sales and operations planning to demand management. However, it is possible to create or to change planned independent requirements directly—that is, without sales and operations planning—using Transactions MD61 or MD62 (see Figure 7.12).

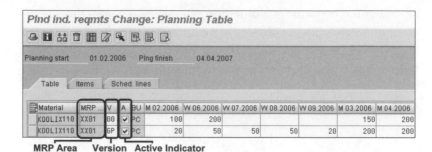

Figure 7.12 Interactive Changes to the Planned Independent Requirement

This example shows planned independent requirements for the **Material KOOLIX110** in **MRP area XX01** for two versions: **00** and **GP**. Here, version **GP** contains the planned independent requirement from sales and operations planning and version **00** contains the interactively added planned independent requirements. The **Active Indic.** determines whether the relevant version affects requirements for the material requirements planning. Further information within this transaction is provided by the **Items** and **Schedule Lines** views. The **Items** view represents the overall quantity of the planned independent requirements for each material and version and also gives requirements type and strategy (see Figure 7.13). The **Schedule Lines** view also displays the value of the planned quantities, in addition to the quantity.

	Table	Items	Sched. lines															
Material	Short Text			MRP ...	V	A	Req Plan	Plan Qty	BU	RTyp	Cl	St...	M...	MRP...	M...	S	H	T..
KOOLIX110	Airconditioner 110			XX01	00	✔		1.150	PC	VSF	1	40	PD	0040	X01	✔	✔	
KOOLIX110	Airconditioner 110			XX01	GP	✔		1.790	PC	VSF	1	40	PD	0040	X01	✔	✔	

	Table	Items	Sched. lines	
Material	KOOLIX110		Airconditioner 110	
Plant	XX01	Reqmts type	VSF	Version/active	00 / ✔	Reqmts Plan	
Plan Qty	1.150	PC		MRP Area	XX01

P..	ReqmtDate	Planned qty	Spl.	S	Value / EUR	PVer	BOMExpNo	StandardVal.	T	Hi
M	02.2006	100			23.000,00					✔
W	06.2006	200			46.000,00					
M	03.2006	150			34.500,00					

Figure 7.13 Interactive Changes to the Planned Independent Requirement

Transaction MD73 allows you to get an overview of the planned independent requirements and their consumption status. You can display both the assignment of the sales orders to the planned independent requirements (**Output List 1**) and, in reverse, the assignment of the planned independent requirements to the sales orders (**Output List 2**). Figure 7.14 shows the assignment of the sales orders to the planned independent requirements for material **KOOLIX110**.

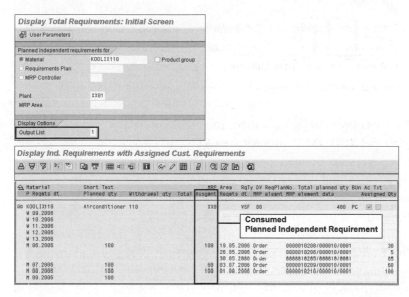

Figure 7.14 Assigning the Sales Orders to Planned Independent Requirements

The **Assignment** column shows the proportion of the planned independent requirement that has been consumed by sales orders. The maximum that can be consumed is the planned quantity, even if the requirements quantity of the sales orders exceeds the planned quantity. This information can be taken from Output List 2. Figure 7.15 shows this list for the same planning situation.

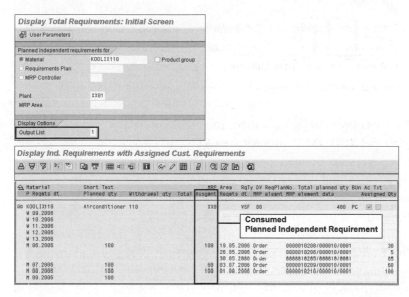

Figure 7.15 Assigning the Planned Independent Requirements to Sales Orders

The sales orders whose requirement exceeds the consumed quantity are assigned a yellow traffic light. In Figure 7.15 these are the orders **10205** and **10210**.

7.4.2 Reducing the Planned Independent Requirements

The planned independent requirements are reduced during the goods issue. Unlike consumption, the planned independent requirements are actually reduced and not just consumed. During anonymous make-to-stock production, the oldest planned independent requirement is reduced first. However, the reduction can also affect planned independent requirements in the future. If strategies are used with consumption, the reduction is performed according to the definition of the consumption mode and the consumption intervals. For this to work, the transaction data must be set accordingly (see Figure 7.16).

Figure 7.16 Requirements Reduction in the Movement Type

Customizing for the transaction data is performed with Customizing Transaction OMJJ. During assembly planning, the planned independent requirement is reduced when goods are withdrawn for the production order.

7.4.3 Reorganizing Planned Independent Requirements

Planned independent requirements can still be consumed by customer requirements if they are already completed. You need to delete this in order to avoid having planned independent requirements that result from an over-optimistic planning reduced by goods issues. This deletion is described as a reorganization and is performed using Transaction MD74 (see Figure 7.17).

The planned independent requirements should be reorganized at regular intervals.

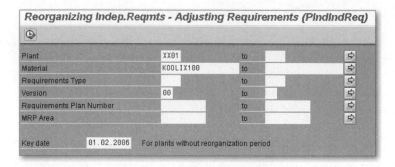

Figure 7.17 Reorganizing Planned Independent Requirements

Material requirements planning is the central function of production planning. It calculates procurement proposals for all low-level codes, based on the demand program and taking into account lead times, lot sizes, and scrap quantities.

8   Material Requirements Planning

8.1   Process Overview

The material requirements planning (MRP) phase determines the requirements in terms of the assemblies, individual parts, and raw materials for fulfilling the agreed demand program. It also defines the required quantity and the requirements date. Calculations for planned requirements have to take into account the materials, components and assemblies in stock. Planned stock also has to be taken into account; that is, materials, individual components, and assemblies that are not available now but will be available when required. To calculate this information, the requirements planner has to have access to data on stock movement, production status, and planned orders. If the calculated requirements cannot be matched up with an economical lot size, the optimal lot size of the production orders is calculated for the components that will be produced in-house. The *production orders* are then transferred to the order-planning phase of production logistics (time management, capacity management, and order release). The procurement proposal for the components to be procured externally, in other words the *purchase requisitions*, is communicated to the purchasing department or to *procurement logistics* (see Grochla, 1978, pp. 33–141; Schneeweiß, 1993, pp. 157–185). Figure 8.1 illustrates the input and output elements involved in material requirements planning.

The influencing factors for the execution of the requirements determination are the product structure, the type of order (make-to-stock production or make-to-order production), as well as the value of the parts to be planned (A, B, or C parts).

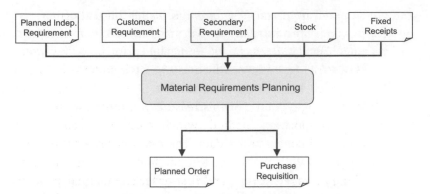

Figure 8.1 Input and Output Elements in Material Requirements Planning

The value of those parts often determines which of the two most common methods of MRP—*consumption-based planning* or *material requirements planning*—should be used. Consumption-based planning derives the new requirement from historical consumption data. The simplest example of this is reorder point planning. Reorder-point planning triggers a procurement proposal as soon as the stock level falls below a defined quantity. In addition, there are more elaborate methods that determine the requirement on the basis of forecasting procedures. These forecasting procedures are based on part consumption data from past periods. In contrast, material requirements planning, which is typically used for A and B parts, is based on planned independent requirements or concrete customer requirements. The basis for the requirement determination at lower low-level codes is the bill of material (BOM). To put it simply, one can say that consumption-based planning is oriented towards the past as it is based on historical consumption patterns, whereas material requirements planning is future-oriented because it is based on actually existing requirement quantities that refer to a date in the future.

Consumption-based planning

The goal of *consumption-based planning* or *forecast-based requirement determination* is to determine the necessary material requirement on the basis of mathematical-statistical calculations. Different statistical methods are used in this context in order to derive future requirements from historical consumption data. Many business books recommend the use of consumption-based planning for low-value goods as well as for goods with high requirement fluctuations and for goods that are not directly affected by production changes. Here, a differentiation is made between secondary products such as nails and glue, operating materials such as lubricating oil and office supplies, and primary products such as bar material, plates, springs, and gaskets (see Grochla, 1978, pp. 58–69). The quantity of low-value goods in industrial operations, which can be high under certain circumstances, must be planned as accurately as possible despite the low value of a single good. For this reason, you must use the most appropriate extrapolation method, which must be based on the recorded material consumption data. The *constant material requirement* is supported with the forecasting methods of mean value creation, moving average creation, and first-order exponential smoothing. For the *trend-based material consumption*, the linear trend model (least squares method), first-order exponential smoothing with trend correction, and second-order exponential smoothing are used. Seasonally fluctuating material requirements use first-order and second-order exponential smoothing (see Arnolds et al., 1996, pp. 95–116; Hoitsch, 1985, pp. 372–383).

Material requirements planning or *deterministic requirement determination* is characterized by an analytic procedure in which a *dependent demand* is derived step by step from an existing *independent requirement*. Using gross-net calculation within material requirements planning, a *BOM explosion* is carried out from the finished product to the individual component. Based on the independent requirement data provided by the sales and distribution or controlling departments, you can obtain the dependent demand of components. Based on the dependent demand, material requirements planning determines the *gross requirement* of components by adding up the requirements of spare parts and scrap quantities. After that, the *net requirement* is calculated by deducting the available stock, plant, and order quantities (see Arnolds et al., 1996, pp. 81–93; Hackstein, 1989, pp. 132–154; Grochla, 1978, pp. 37–58; Hoitsch, 1993, pp. 360–372; Scheer, 1990, pp. 79–130).

Material requirements planning consists of the following steps.

1. *Check the planning file* in order to avoid planning materials that are not needed

2. Determine the material shortage quantity (or surplus quantity) by carrying out a *net requirements calculation*

3. Calculate *procurement quantity* in order to include lot sizes for planned orders or purchase requisitions

Material requirements planning

Steps involved in material requirements planning

4. *Scheduling*

5. Select the source of supply by *determining the procurement proposal*

6. Determine the requirement of subordinate parts on the basis of the BOM explosion by carrying out a *dependent demand determination*

Figure 8.2 illustrates these steps.

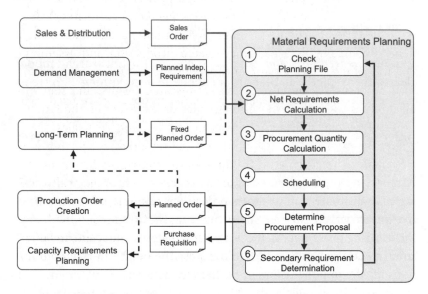

Figure 8.2 Process Steps Within Material Requirements Planning

Material requirements planning must meet certain requirements. It must be possible to determine the *optimal purchase order quantity* for goods that must be procured externally, and to determine the *optimal production lot size* for goods that are produced in-house. In addition, it must also be possible to explode the BOM automatically, and the MRP controller must be allowed to interfere at each level. An important aspect is the consideration of the lead time within the BOM explosion. This ensures that the subordinate material is available prior to the make-to-order production date of the superordinate component. The component-based lead time can be stored in the material master, the BOM, or the routing. For this reason, this basic data must be accessed during the requirements breakdown. The material master contains the component-specific lead time if the lead time is not included in superordinate components. If the lead time depends not only on the material itself but also on which superordinate component the material is included in, the lead time is stored in the BOM master. If several series of operations must be carried out to produce a material, the overall lead time is determined by summing up the lead times of individual operations. The overall lead time is then stored in the routing and assigned to the base planning object.

The type of order placement or order triggering indicates how the production and assembly processes are triggered. It correlates closely with the type of product creation. For example, a customer-related development entails a customer-related production and assembly. On the other hand, customer-independent product development may be occurring because of market-research results, and that the assembly is triggered by a concrete sales order. After all, the type of order placement indicates the way in which a concrete sales order affects the internal processes and material requirements planning in a company. In particular, it is important to know how far the development and design processes can be separated chronologically and logically from the concrete sales orders. For example, in the automotive industry the customer thinks that a car is configured individually for him or her, whereas the manufacturer sees this "customizing" strictly as an assembly phase made possible by the internal definitions of product development and production.

Order placement

The possible types of order placement range from anonymous make-to-stock production, whereby the individual sales order is fulfilled entirely from stock, to the customer-specific make-to-order production in which the individual sales order decisively affects the processes from development to work scheduling to production and assembly. The different options are mapped in the company by different planning strategies.

In the case of make-to-stock production, production is based on a planned independent requirement that is defined by the company. A mixture of the different types can provide for planning according to both planned independent requirements and concrete customer requirements. In this context, the customer requirements consume the planned independent requirements. The relationship between the sales order and period-based dependent demand that is relevant to production cannot be clearly assigned, especially if lot-sizes are created in order to summarize several sales orders of a planning period. In requirements planning (requirements breakdown), lot formation and the transfer of dependent demands to other periods cause the information relationships between requirements and the order to be lost. This makes it impossible to identify the origins of individual material requirements. However, this information is important if the company carries out customer-specific production and has to be able to inform the customer of each change in the status of the order. For this reason, planning is carried out in a separate segment for each sales order in those cases. Section 7.2 describes the effects of the different order-placement types on the requirement with regard to the sales order and forecasting in greater detail.

Stocks — To be able to carry out *exact material requirements planning*, you also must record the stock quantities. In addition to a company's *physical stocks*, you must also consider the *on-order and production stocks* that are not yet available at the time of scheduling, but must be on the date on which they are physically required. Similarly, your calculation must include stocks that physically exist in the warehouse and are reserved for other orders as well as reserved purchase and production orders. The consideration of goods-receipt and goods-issue inspection stocks plays an important role when determining the warehouse stock. These inspection stocks contain all those stocks for which the usage cannot be guaranteed with complete certainty, perhaps because quality information is lacking (as described in Section 8.4 on net requirements calculation). In addition to the *quantity-based stock determination*, it must also be possible to carry out a *value-based inventory management*. This information is for instance required for accounting tasks related to commercial and tax laws.

8.2   Influencing Factors in Material Requirements Planning

8.2.1   Lot Size

The MRP lot size defines the number and quantity of the planned orders created for the requirements during the planning run. The predominant lot-sizing procedures are static lot sizes such as the exact and fixed lot sizes, periodic lot-sizing procedures, and optimizing lot-sizing procedures. Apart from the lot-sizing procedure, the MRP lot size contains additional information on the characteristics of the lot-sizing procedure as well as on the scheduling of the procurement proposals. Table 8.1 provides an overview of the standard MRP lot sizes.

MRP lot size	Lot-sizing procedure	Lot-size indicator
DY – Dynamic lot size creation	Optimization lot size	D – Dynamic planning
EX – Exact lot size calculation	Static lot size	E – Exact lot size
FK – Fixed lot size for customer make-to-order production	Static lot size	F – Fixed lot size
FS – Fixed/splitting	Static lot size	S – Fixed with splitting
FX – Fixed order quantity	Static lot size	F – Fixed lot size
GR – Groff lot-sizing procedure	Optimization lot size	G – Procedure according to Groff
HB – Replenish to maximum stock level	Static lot size	H – Replenishment to maximum stock level
MB – Monthly lot size	Lot size according to flexible period length	M – Monthly lot size
PK – Lot size according to flexible period length and planning calendar	Lot size according to flexible period length	K – Period based on planning calendar
SP – Part period balancing	Optimization lot size	S – Part period balancing
TB – Daily lot size	Lot size according to flexible period length	T – Daily lot size
WB – Weekly lot size	Lot size according to flexible period length	W – Weekly lot size
WI – Least unit cost procedure	Optimization lot size	W – Least unit cost procedure

Table 8.1 MRP Lot Sizes and Lot-Sizing Procedures (Selection)

Figure 8.3 illustrates the effects of exact, fixed, and period-based lot sizes on the basis of a requirement situation. Depending on the MRP lot size and the value (fixed lot size of 40 units and fixed lot size of 35 units), different numbers of planned orders are determined.

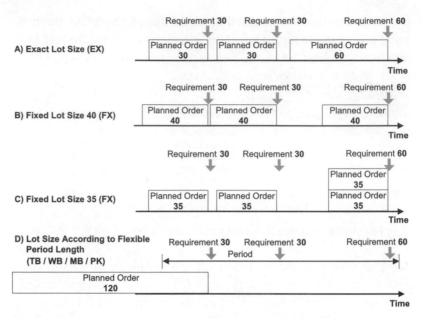

Figure 8.3 Lot Sizes

In situation C, the fixed lot size results in the planning of more receipts (namely 140 units) than are needed to fulfill the requirement of 130 units. Because material requirements planning does not consider any capacity restrictions, the two planned orders of 35 units each in situation C are planned in parallel. This would have to be corrected, for example, in a detailed planning step (see Chapter 11, *Capacity Requirements Planning*).

Lot size with splitting It is possible to split fixed or period-based lot sizes into rounding values. The orders can be shifted by a certain *takt time*, meaning a control parameter for scheduling based on *takts*; i.e., physical areas of a production line. This avoids the simultaneous scheduling of numerous orders and thus ensures that the actually required lead time is observed. Figure 8.4 illustrates situation C from Figure 8.3 by using the fixed lot size with splitting (FS) and a takt time.

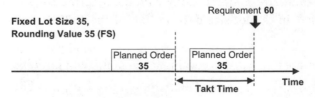

Figure 8.4 Lot Size with Splitting

If you use splitting in combination with a fixed lot size, the rounding value must be a multiple integer of the fixed lot size. The takt time indicates the offset between order dates in terms of workdays. Figure 8.5 displays the entries required for this.

Lot size data			
Lot size	FS	Fixing and splitting	
Minimum Lot Size		Maximum Lot Size	
Fixed lot size	35	Maximum stock level	
Ordering costs		Storage costs ind.	
Assembly scrap (%)		Takt time	1
Rounding Profile		Rounding value	35
Unit of Measure Grp			

Figure 8.5 Entries Required for Using Lot Sizes with Splitting

The production or purchase of materials entails fixed lot-size costs such as setup costs for machines or purchase-order costs and variable costs, which is referred to as capital tie-up due to stockholding. To minimize the variable costs, you should procure quantities as small as possible, whereas to minimize the fixed costs, you should procure quantities as large as possible. Optimizing lot-sizing procedures consider variable and fixed costs, and based on these costs they determine optimal lot sizes according to different procedures. To determine the variable costs, you must use the storage costs percentage that is specified in the storage costs indicator. Both the MRP lot size and the storage costs indicator are maintained using Customizing Transaction OMI4 (see Figure 8.6).

Optimizing lot-sizing procedures

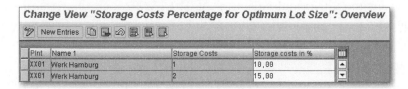

Change View "Storage Costs Percentage for Optimum Lot Size": Overview

Plnt	Name 1	Storage Costs	Storage costs in %	
XX01	Werk Hamburg	1	10,00	
XX01	Werk Hamburg	2	15,00	

Figure 8.6 Storage Costs Indicator

The storage costs indicator is stored along with the ordering costs in the material master in the **lot size data** section of the **MRP 1** view (see Figure 8.7).

The variable costs are calculated according to the following formula:

*Variable costs = Requirement * Price * Storage costs[%] * Storage duration / 365*

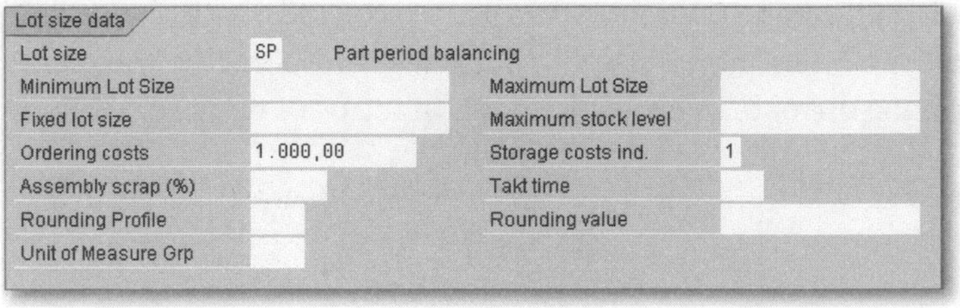

Figure 8.7 Assigning the Storage Costs Indicator to the Material Master (Section Taken from MRP 1 View)

The price is maintained in the **Accounting 1** view of the material master (see Figure 8.8).

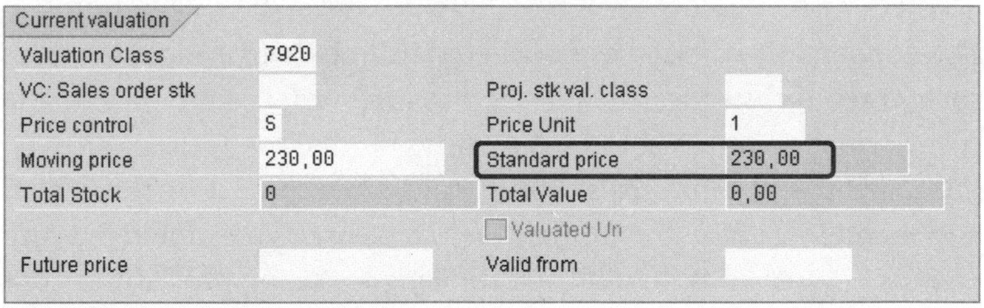

Figure 8.8 Price in the Material Master

The lot-sizing procedures of part-period balancing, least-unit cost procedure, and dynamic lot size creation use the fixed and variable costs to determine the lot size in different ways. Let us take a look at an example in order to illustrate the effect of lot sizes. The example contains monthly requirements as of 01/01/2007, and the optimizing lot-sizing procedures are now used to determine the lot size for the first procurement by 01/01/2007.

Table 8.2 contains the key figures used by the various lot-sizing procedures. The example uses a material with a price of US$ 230, 10 % storage costs, and ordering costs of US$ 500.

The selected lot size must cover the cumulated requirement of one or several periods. If the lot size fulfills the requirement of an additional period, the additional variable costs are calculated as capital tie-up or stockholding costs. These accrue for each additional period from the availability date—here 01/01/07—to the requirement date. The overall variable costs thus correspond to the total of additional variable costs, whereas the overall costs represent the total of variable and ordering costs. The unit costs are calculated from the overall costs in relation to the lot size; the lot size corresponds to the cumulated requirement.

Date	01/01/07	02/01/07	03/01/07	04/01/07	05/01/07	06/01/07	07/01/07	08/01/07	09/01/07	10/01/07
Requirement	100	100	30	20	50	50	20	10	30	100
Cumulated requirement	100	200	230	250	300	350	370	380	410	510
Additional variable costs	0	190	114	114	380	475	228	133	456	1710
Variable costs	0	190	304	418	798	1273	1501	1634	2090	3800
Ordering costs	500	500	500	500	500	500	500	500	500	500
Overall costs	500	690	804	918	1298	1773	2001	2134	2590	4300
Unit costs	5	3.45	3.49	3.67	4.32	5.06	5.11	5.61	6.31	8.43
Lot size (SP)				250						
Lot size (WI)		200								
Lot size (DY)									410	

Table 8.2 Key Figures for Determining Optimal Lot Sizes

Part period balancing (MRP lot size SP) determines the lot size in which the amount of variable costs is just under that of the fixed costs. In the example above, the lot size for the first lot was 250 units because in this case the variable costs of US$ 418 are below the fixed costs of US$ 500. The variable costs of the next lot size of 300 units (US$ 798) would exceed the amount of fixed costs.

Part period balancing

The *least unit cost procedure* (MRP lot site WI) is based on the minimum amount of unit costs. This minimum amount of US$ 3.45 is reached at a lot size of 200 units.

Least unit cost procedure

The *dynamic lot size creation* (MRP lot size DY) combines different requirements until the additional variable costs exceed the fixed costs. This procedure determines a lot size of 410 units because the fixed costs of US$ 500 are not exceeded until the next step increases the lot size to 510 units with additional variable costs of US$ 1,710.

Dynamic lot size creation

<table>
<tr><td>Groff lot-sizing procedure</td><td>Another optimizing lot-sizing procedure is the *Groff lot-sizing procedure* (MRP lot size GR). In this procedure, the increase in additional variable costs corresponds to the gradient of the decreasing ordering costs.</td></tr>
<tr><td>Customizing the MRP lot sizes</td><td>Transaction OMI4 enables you to define your own MRP lot sizes, though not lot-sizing procedures. Figure 8.9 displays the definition of MRP lot size EX for an exact lot-size calculation.</td></tr>
<tr><td>Short-term and long-term lot sizes</td><td>You can also create two different lot-sizing procedures for the short-term and long-term horizons. This is often useful in order to reduce the number of requirement coverage elements, especially if fixed lot sizes are used that are smaller than the average requirement quantity. Typically, a period-based lot size is used for the long-term horizon.</td></tr>
<tr><td>Last lot exact</td><td>If you use fixed lot sizes, you may find that the quantity that's produced or externally procured exceeds the existing requirement, see also situation C in Figure 8.3. If fixed lot sizes are used for financial or practical reasons (without any technical need, that is), you can avoid surplus procurements by setting the **Last lot exact** flag. This is particularly applicable for higher value goods.</td></tr>
</table>

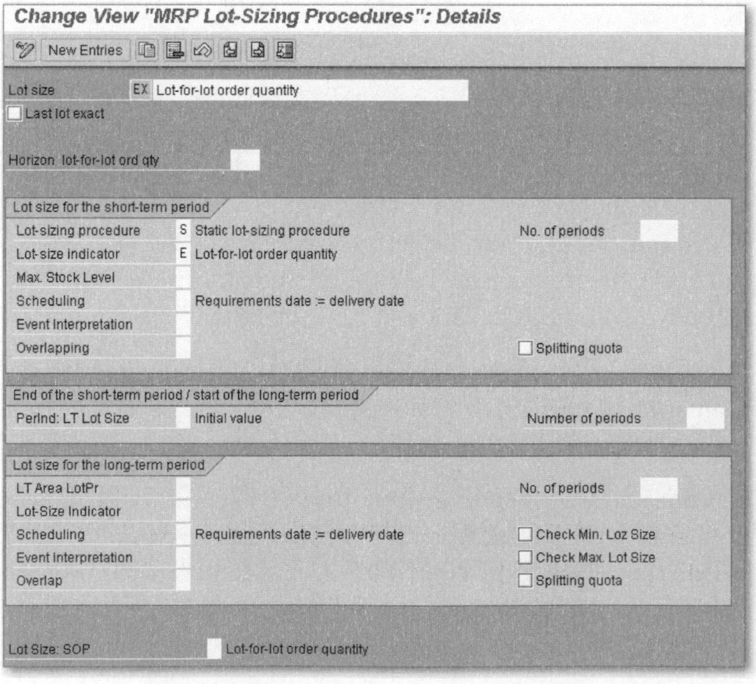

Figure 8.9 Customizing the MRP Lot Sizes

The MRP lot size and other parameters needed for the lot-sizing procedure are maintained in the **MRP 1** view of the material master (see Figure 8.10).

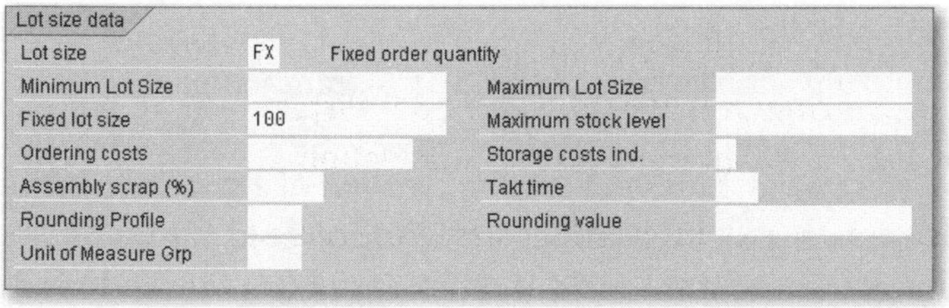

Lot size data			
Lot size	FX	Fixed order quantity	
Minimum Lot Size		Maximum Lot Size	
Fixed lot size	100	Maximum stock level	
Ordering costs		Storage costs ind.	
Assembly scrap (%)		Takt time	
Rounding Profile		Rounding value	
Unit of Measure Grp			

Figure 8.10 Parameters for the Lot-Sizing Procedure in the Material Master

Some of the MRP lot sizes require additional entries. Table 8.3 provides an overview of the required fields for the more complex MRP lot sizes. These must be maintained in the lot size data section (see Figure 8.10).

MRP lot size	Fields
DY – Dynamic lot size creation	Ordering costs, storage costs indicator
FS – Fixed/splitting	Fixed lot size, rounding value, takt time
FX – Fixed order quantity	Fixed lot size
GR – Groff lot-sizing procedure	Ordering costs, storage costs indicator
HB – Replenish to maximum stock level	Maximum stock level
SP – Part period balancing	Ordering costs, storage costs indicator
WI – Least unit cost procedure	Ordering costs, storage costs indicator

Table 8.3 MRP Lot Size and Required Parameters

Moreover, you can maintain a minimum and maximum lot size. The minimum and maximum lot sizes are used for exact and period-based lot-size calculations.

In some cases it is useful to round the quantities. In the simplest scenario, this can be done using a rounding value. In this case, the order quantity of the requirement coverage element always represents a multiple of the rounding value. In more complex scenarios where the rounding value depends on the requirement quantity, you can use a rounding profile. The rounding profile enables you, for example, to model different pack sizes.

The SAP ERP system provides static and dynamic rounding profiles. The static rounding profiles round up the value once a threshold value has been reached. If the rounding value has been exceeded, the values are continuously rounded to the rounding value until the next threshold value has been reached. You can create rounding profiles using Customizing Transaction OWD1. This transaction differentiates between static and dynamic rounding profiles, among other things (1). Figure 8.11 shows the sample creation of a static rounding profile. The rounding logic is defined by the **Threshold value** and the corresponding **Rounding value** (2). From the creation of the rounding profile, you can simulate (4) the rounding logic within the specified limits (3).

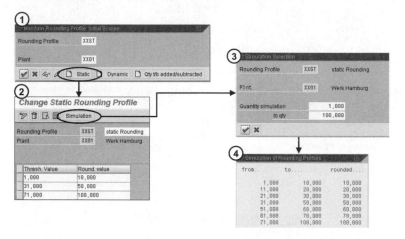

Figure 8.11 Rounding Profile

This example uses pack sizes of 10, 50, and 100 units. Although a rounding value of 10 already ensures that no products remain unpacked, it is planned that from a quantity of 31 units the value should be rounded up to the next higher pack size of 50 units. In the area between 50 and 70 units, a medium pack size of 50 units and one or two small packs of 10 units each are used. From 71 units onwards we round up to a large pack size of 100 units, instead of 80 units.

Dynamic rounding profiles allow for a rounding on the basis of master data parameters such as the distribution lot size as well as the use of Business Add-Ins (BAdIs).

Both the rounding value and the rounding profile are maintained in the lot-size data section of the **MRP 1** view in the material master.

8.2.2 Scrap

The dependent demand is calculated on the basis of the BOM; that is, in accordance with the relationship between the input quantity of components and the order quantity, in relation to the base quantity of the BOM. This relationship is stored in the BOM.

Dependent demand = (Order quantity * Base quantity) / Input quantity

Factors that also increase the dependent demand are the different scrap types that account for the scrap in production. The scrap types contained in SAP ERP are assembly scrap, component scrap, and operation scrap.

Assembly scrap represents the scrap created during the production of an assembly or finished product at the level of the finished product. An example of using assembly scrap is the automated production of switching elements, in which it is decided in the final step of quality inspection whether the product can be used or if it is scrap. Accordingly, the demand for all components increases by the amount of assembly scrap:

Assembly scrap

Dependent demand = (Order quantity * Base quantity) * Input quantity
* (1 + Assembly scrap)

The assembly scrap is maintained for the finished product in the **MRP 1** view of the material master (see Figure 8.12). It refers to all components contained in the BOM used.

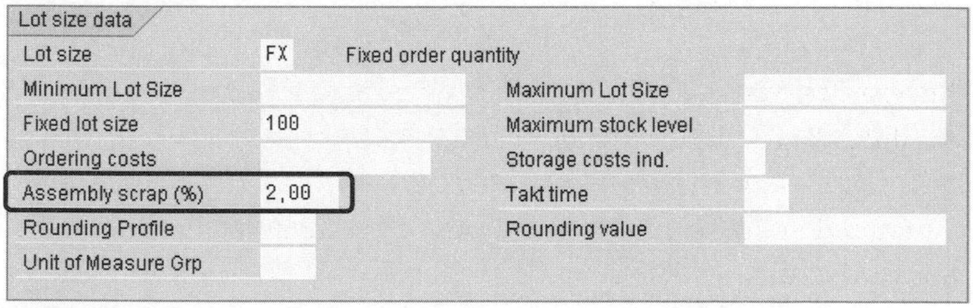

Lot size data			
Lot size	FX	Fixed order quantity	
Minimum Lot Size		Maximum Lot Size	
Fixed lot size	100	Maximum stock level	
Ordering costs		Storage costs ind.	
Assembly scrap (%)	2,00	Takt time	
Rounding Profile		Rounding value	
Unit of Measure Grp			

Figure 8.12 Maintaining the Assembly Scrap in the Material Master

A fixed lot size refers to the yield, not to the input quantity. Correspondingly, the input quantity in SAP ERP varies depending on the assembly scrap, unlike SAP Advanced Planner and Optimizer (SAP APO).

Component scrap   Component scrap refers to cases in which individual components in production are subject to a higher amount of scrap. In this case, the components are inspected prior to the assembly. The formula used or calculating the component scrap is similar to that used for calculating the assembly scrap:

$$Dependent\ demand = (Order\ quantity * Base\ quantity) * Input\ quantity$$
$$* (1 + Component\ scrap)$$

In contrast to assembly scrap, component scrap only refers to a single component. You can maintain the component scrap either in the material master of the component, provided it is a material-specific property, or in the BOM, if the scrap is specific to the production. Material-specific component scrap is maintained in the **MRP 4** view of the component material (see Figure 8.13).

Figure 8.13 Maintaining the Component Scrap in the Material Master

The BOM-specific scrap is maintained in the item details section of the component in the BOM. You can create material BOMs using Transaction CS01, while Transaction CS02 enables you to change them (see Figure 8.14).

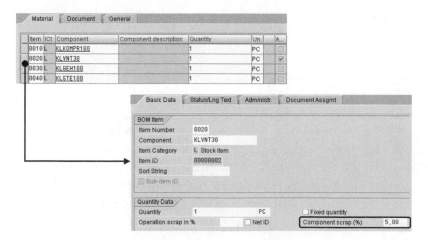

Figure 8.14 Maintaining the Component Scrap in the BOM

The net identifier (**Net ID**) flag enables you to ignore the assembly scrap for the component. You can set this flag as well in the BOM item details section. If the operation scrap is maintained in the BOM item details section, you must set the net identifier flag.

Operation scrap represents the type of scrap that results from a critical or susceptible production step. Correspondingly, only those components are affected by scrap that is already used in this production step. Components that are used in a later production step are not affected by scrap. The quantity reduction for downstream operations is considered in the scheduling and costing processes.

Operation scrap must be maintained in the operation of the routing (see Figure 8.15). You can create the routing using Transaction CA01, while CA02 enables you to change it.

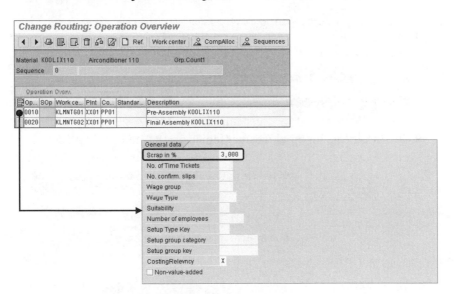

Figure 8.15 Maintaining Operation Scrap in the Routing

Figure 8.16 provides an overview of how the combination of assembly and component scrap affects the calculation of the dependent demand of the different components. The figure is taken from another book (see Dickersbach 2005b) and has been adapted to the example of the air-conditioning system.

The assembly scrap for **KOOLIX110** and the component scrap for the control unit are maintained in the material master in this example. The scrap data for the fan, the casing, and the mains system (lines, pipes, and hoses) of the air-conditioning unit is maintained in the BOM. It is evident that the component scrap adds to the assembly scrap and that the net identifier overrides the assembly scrap.

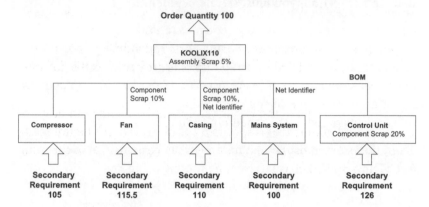

Figure 8.16 Effects of Different Scrap Types on the Dependent Demand (Dickersbach 2005b)

8.2.3 Safety Stock

The SAP ERP system supports two types of safety stock: absolute safety stock and safety days' supply. In both cases, you must enter the data in the material master (see Figure 8.17).

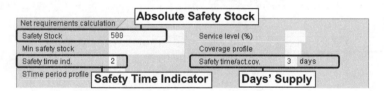

Figure 8.17 Safety Stock and Safety Days' Supply

Both entries are contained in the **MRP 2** view. The planning of a safety days' supply is referred to as safety time. In order to consider the safety time, you must set the safety time indicator to 1 (for independent requirements) or 2 (for all requirements).

Absolute safety stock   In MRP, the safety stock is regarded as an additional requirement that must be covered. The safety stock is explicitly listed in the stock/requirements list (see Section 8.7) and it reduces the available quantity for the net requirements calculation (but not for the availability check). Figure 8.18 displays this interpretation of the safety stock.

A.	Date	MRP ...	MRP element data	Reschedul...	E..	Rec./reqd.qty	Available qty
☑	02.08.2006	Stock			96		410
	02.08.2006	SafeSt	Safety stock			500-	90-

Figure 8.18 Safety Stock as a Requirement Element in the Stock/Requirements List

Although no additional requirement exists and a stock of 400 units is available, a planned order for 100 units is created in order to cover the safety stock.

The safety time causes the goods receipts to be planned in advance by the period of time that is specified as safety time (see Figure 8.19). Thus, the planned days' supply of the stock corresponds to the number of days specified as safety time.

Days' supply/
safety time

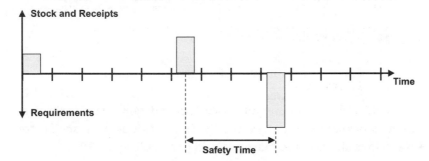

Figure 8.19 Effect of the Safety Time

Figure 8.20 displays the effect of the safety time in the stock/requirements list. As you can see, the planned order is created on a date that shifted back by the safety time. The factory calendar is automatically included in the calculation.

A.	Date	MRP ...	MRP element data	Reschedul...	E..	Rec./reqd qty	Avail. quantity
☑	02.08.2006	Stock					100
☑	29.08.2006	PlOrd.	0000037329/Stck		01	200	300
☑	01.09.2006	IndReq	VSF			300-	0

Figure 8.20 Effect of the Safety Time in the Stock/Requirements List

8.2.4 Master Data Selection

To create planned orders, you need the BOM and—optionally—the routing. Because there can be several alternatives for both master data objects, you can control the selection of the alternatives.

The BOM can be selected via the *order quantity*, the *explosion date*, or according to the *production version*. The selection method field (**Selection method**) in the material master controls which of those variants is used for selecting the alternatives (see Figure 8.21).

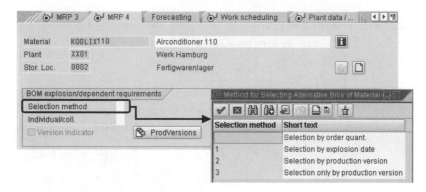

Figure 8.21 Controlling the Selection of Alternatives for BOMs

If you select the BOM on the basis of the order quantity, the system checks whether the lot size falls within the lot-size range defined in the BOM. For the selection by the explosion date, you must maintain the validity period of each individual material in a table (see Figure 8.22). You can maintain the table using Transaction OPPP.

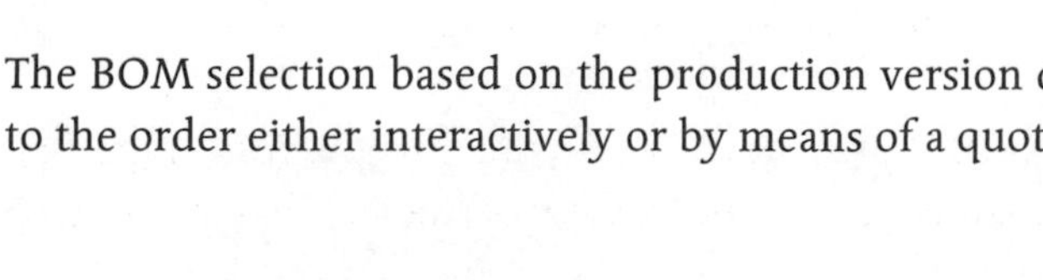

Figure 8.22 BOM Selection by Validity

The BOM selection based on the production version can be assigned to the order either interactively or by means of a quota arrangement.

8.3 MRP Procedures

8.3.1 Overview

As noted at the beginning of this chapter, the two essential MRP procedures are *material requirements planning* and *consumption-based planning*. Within MRP, a basic differentiation is made between a full

BOM explosion and master production scheduling for critical parts. Consumption-based planning is carried out as reorder-point planning, forecast-based planning, or as time-phased materials planning (see Figure 8.23).

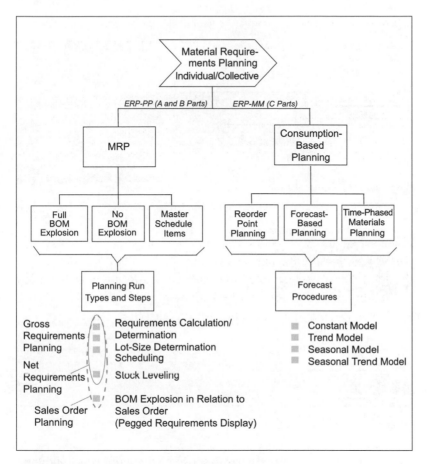

Figure 8.23 Overview of Material Requirements Planning

In SAP ERP, the MRP procedure is contained in the MRP type flag that can be maintained in the **MRP 1** view of the material master (see Figure 8.24).

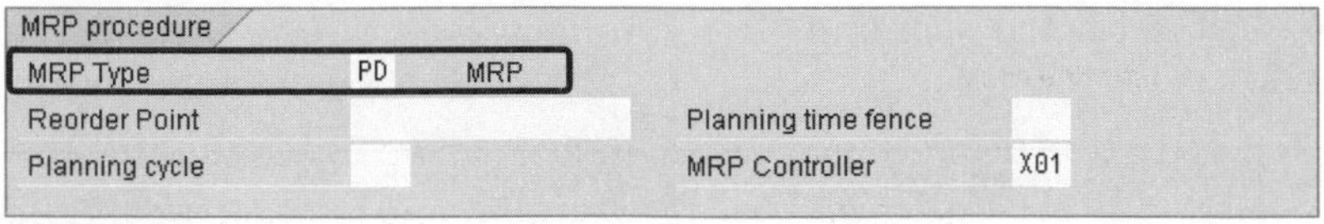

MRP procedure			
MRP Type	PD	MRP	
Reorder Point		Planning time fence	
Planning cycle		MRP Controller	X01

Figure 8.24 MRP Type in the Material Master (Excerpt from the MRP 1 View)

You can define the MRP type in Customizing via the following path: **Production** • Material **Requirements Planning** • **Master Data** • **Check MRP Types** (see Figure 8.25).

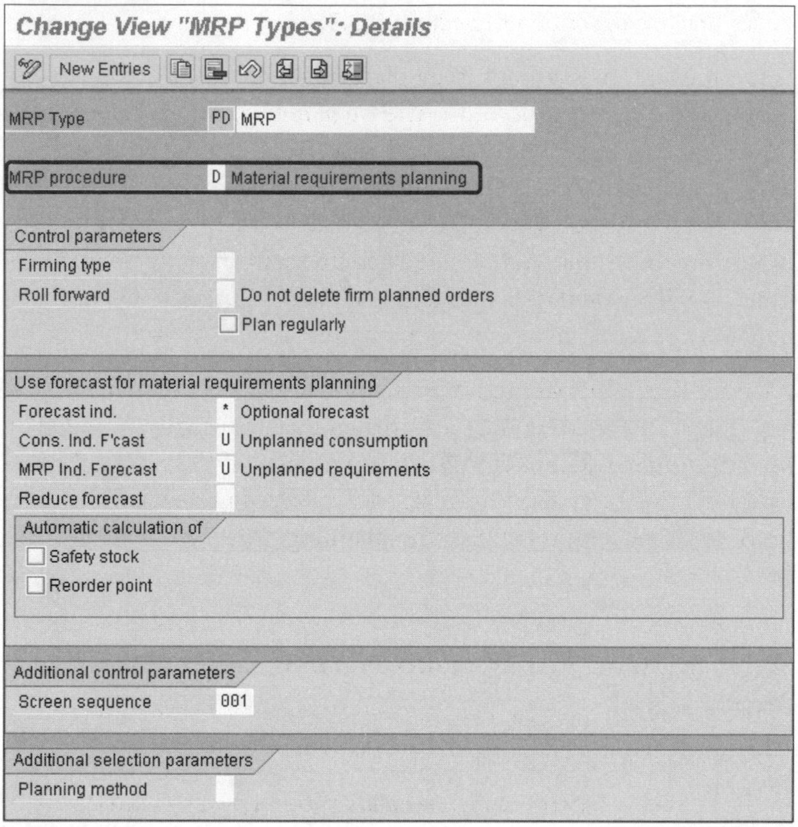

Change View "MRP Types": Details

MRP Type	PD MRP
MRP procedure	D Material requirements planning

Control parameters
Firming type
Roll forward ☐ Do not delete firm planned orders
☐ Plan regularly

Use forecast for material requirements planning
Forecast ind. * Optional forecast
Cons. Ind. F'cast U Unplanned consumption
MRP Ind. Forecast U Unplanned requirements
Reduce forecast
Automatic calculation of
☐ Safety stock
☐ Reorder point

Additional control parameters
Screen sequence 001

Additional selection parameters
Planning method

Figure 8.25 Customizing the MRP Types

As MRP procedures in the narrow sense of the word, the following alternatives are available:

- Reorder point planning (B)
- Material requirements planning(D)
- No planning (N)
- Forecast-based planning (S)
- Master production scheduling (M)
- Time-phased materials planning (R)
- No planning, with BOM explosion (X)

The *material requirements planning* (D) and *master production scheduling* (M) procedures are described in greater detail in Section 8.3.2, while *reorder point planning* (B), *forecast-based planning* (S), and *time-phased materials planning* (R) are consumption-based MRP procedures that are described in Section 8.3.3.

If specific materials are not to be planned automatically, you can use the *No planning* (N) procedure. The *No planning, with BOM explosion* (X) procedure represents a special case. This procedure is used in conjunction with SAP APO. Planning itself is carried out in SAP APO, while the BOM explosion for planned orders occurs in SAP ERP. The reason for this is that in APO not all components need to be planned. Thus, the dependent demands are generated in SAP ERP by means of a BOM explosion, instead of copying them from SAP APO.

As a result of material requirements planning, procurement proposals—that is, planned orders—are created that are usually available on the requirement date. Exceptions to this occur if the replenishment lead time does not allow for this, if a safety time has been configured, or if the requirement in the planning time fence changes (see Section 8.5).

8.3.2 Material Requirements Planning

In the process of *material requirements planning* you can differentiate if and how the materials should be planned.

In the context of *material requirements planning with full BOM explosion*, the SAP ERP system carries out a requirements calculation for all requirement quantities to be planned. After that, it determines the lot sizes or defines the input quantities for assemblies that are produced in-house. Moreover, it determines the material staging dates for the required assemblies in a scheduling process. For each new procurement proposal of an assembly, the BOM is exploded in the planning run. For existing procurement proposals, the BOM is only exploded if the quantity or date of the procurement proposal has changed or if the BOM structure has been modified. If you still want to carry out a BOM explosion in the planning run, you can make the appropriate setting in the *Planning mode* in the initial screen. The quantities and dates for all assemblies that are necessary for the production can be set in the way described below. The depen-

Material requirements planning with full BOM explosion

dent demand quantity is determined by the quantity factor of the BOM item. The dependent demand date is determined on the basis of the in-house production time of the superordinate component. This means that the planned start date of the planned order for the superordinate assembly determines the dependent demand date of the BOM item.

Material requirements planning without BOM explosion

Material requirements planning without BOM explosion includes sales orders and material reservations directly in the planning process. For this reason, we assign it to the plan-based procedures because it refers to actually existing requirements. In this context a check is made to find out whether the stock level can cover the requirement. If necessary, a procurement proposal is generated.

Master production scheduling

In industrial operations it is often necessary to process a large quantity of date because of the many different components to be included in the production process. The data quantity involved requires a lot of computing power. To ease this problem, you can carry out planning runs only for critical parts: the so-called master schedule items. Master schedule items are raw materials, assemblies (semi-finished products), or finished products of a BOM that have a great influence on the supply chain (A parts) or occupy critical production resources. The purpose of master production scheduling is to optimally use cost-intensive resources and to avoid production bottlenecks by efficiently planning the master schedule items. Master-schedule items have a high added value and therefore tie up a substantial amount of capital. To reduce this capital tie-up caused by stockholding and to increase planning stability, the planning of specific products and main assemblies should be harmonized as much as possible. The production plan of those products has a powerful influence on the overall production process. Careful planning of those specific parts leads to a reduction of stocks and at the same time increases the on-time delivery performance as well as the service level. By restricting the planning process to master schedule items, the MRP controller can carry out fast planning and thus create alternative production plans in several planning runs in order to compare those plans. In addition, the MRP controller can interactively change the automatically created results with regard to quantity, date, and time, and then calculate the results again to reflect those results.

8.3.3   Consumption-Based Planning

Consumption-based planning is based on historical consumption data and uses forecasts and statistical methods to predict the future requirement. The methods used in consumption-based planning do not refer to the production plan; that is, the net requirements planning is not triggered by a independent or dependent demand. The requirement determination is triggered when a fixed reorder point is not met or when is triggered by forecast requirements calculated on the basis of historical consumption values. Consumption-based planning requires a well-functioning inventory management that is always up to date.

The MRP procedures of consumption-based planning are primarily used in areas without in-house production or for planning B and C parts, as well as operating supplies in manufacturing companies. The type of procurement proposal that is automatically generated during planning depends on the procurement type of the material. In-house production always requires the creation of a planned order. In the case of external procurement, the MRP controller can choose between creating a planned order and a purchase requisition. If the MRP controller wants to use a planned order, the order must be converted into a purchase requisition at a later stage, and this, in turn, must be forwarded to purchasing. The benefit of this procedure is that the MRP controller carries out an additional check of the procurement proposals. The purchasing department cannot order the material until the MRP controller has checked and converted the procurement proposal. If the MRP controller does not want to use a planned order, the procurement proposal is directly made available to the purchasing department, which takes on the responsibility for the availability of the material and for the stock level.

Let's now look at the MRP procedures used in consumption-based planning: *reorder point planning*, *forecast-based planning*, and *time-phased materials planning*.

Reorder point planning compares the available stock at plant level with the reorder point. The reorder point is made up of the safety stock and the average material requirement to be expected during the replenishment lead time. Accordingly, when defining the reorder point, you must take into account the safety stock, the historical consumption, or the future requirement as well as the replenishment

Reorder point planning

lead time. The safety stock needs to cover the excess material consumption during the replenishment lead time as well as the additional requirements if delivery is delayed. Accordingly, you must consider the historical consumption as well as the future requirement and the timeliness of service provision of the supplier or the production department when defining the safety stock. Figure 8.26 shows the principle of reorder point planning.

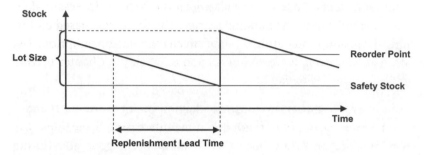

Figure 8.26 Principle of Reorder Point Planning

The reorder point and safety stock are thus central control parameters to be used in reorder point planning and can be manually defined by the MRP controller or calculated automatically by the system. For this reason, reorder point planning distinguishes between the two procedures of *manual* and *automatic reorder point planning*. Manual reorder point planning requires the users to define the reorder point and safety stock by themselves and store these parameters in the corresponding material master record. In automatic reorder point planning, the reorder point and safety stock are determined by the integrated forecast program. Using historical material consumption values, the program determines the future requirements. Depending on the service level to be defined by the MRP controller and on the replenishment lead time of the material, the reorder level and the safety stock are then calculated and transferred to the respective material master record. Because the forecast program is run at regular intervals, the reorder point and safety stock are adapted to the current consumption and delivery situation and thus help to reduce the stock level.

If you use manual reorder point planning (**MRP type VB**), you must maintain the reorder point in the material master (see Figure 8.27).

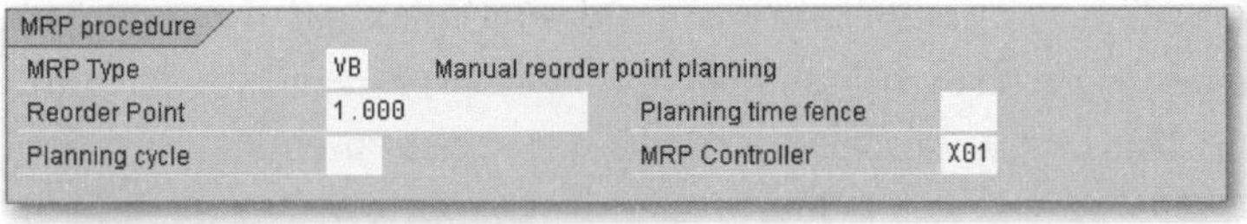

Figure 8.27 Parameters for Manual Reorder Point Planning in the Material Master

In automatic reorder point planning (**MRP type VM**), the reorder point and safety stock are calculated on the basis of forecast values and then written to the material master. The forecast is based on historical consumption data and adapts to changes in consumption. The topic of *forecasting* is treated in Section 8.3.4 and in Chapter 6, *Sales and Operations Planning*.

If the available stock is below the reorder point, the system generates a procurement proposal. However, if the purchasing department has already planned a purchase order or production order, the system does not generate any procurement proposal. The system calculates the quantity specified in the procurement proposal according to the selected lot-sizing procedure. You can define a separate lot-sizing procedure for each individual material. Moreover, the procurement proposal is scheduled; that is, the system calculates the date on which the supplier or the production department must deliver the corresponding quantity.

The inventory management program is responsible for the continuous monitoring of the stock level in reorder point planning. With each material withdrawal, a check is carried out to determine whether the withdrawal causes the stock level to fall below the reorder point. In this case, an entry is created in the planning file for the next planning run. When material is returned, the system also checks if the available stock exceeds the reorder point again. If this is the case, another planning file entry is created so that the planning run can delete redundant procurement proposals. If planned goods receipts become redundant due to returns or similar circumstances these goods receipts are proposed for cancellation by the planning program. In this case, the MRP controller needs to check together with purchasing or production if the purchase order or the production order can be cancelled.

In reorder point planning, net requirements calculation is only triggered if the stock level falls below the reorder point. Requirements elements such as customer requirements, planned independent requirements, or reservations are merely displayed in reorder point planning and remain unconsidered in net requirements calculation. The available stock can be determined by the following calculation:

> *Plant stock*
> + *open order quantity (purchase orders, production orders, firm planned orders, fixed purchase requisitions)*
> --
> = *Available stock*

If the available stock falls below the reorder point, the material shortage quantity represents the difference between the reorder point and available stock. The system uses the date of the planning run as the requirement date. The safety stock does not play any role when calculating the material shortage quantity. When the stock level falls below the reorder point, the MRP controller receives an exception message.

Reorder point planning with external requirements represents a special case. This MRP procedure uses sales orders and manual reservations to calculate the available stock. The corresponding MRP types are **V1** for manual and **V2** for automatic reorder point planning. Choosing the MRP type allows you to define whether you want to consider the external requirements only within the replenishment lead time or in the entire planning time fence (see Figure 8.28).

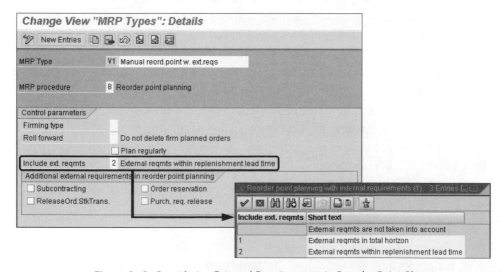

Figure 8.28 Considering External Requirements in Reorder Point Planning

Like reorder point planning, forecast-based planning (**MRP type VV**) is based on material consumption data, and the integrated forecast program determines forecast values for future requirements. But in contrast to reorder point planning, these values form the basis for the planning run in forecast-based planning. Forecasting is carried out at regular intervals in order to forecast future requirements based on historical data. The advantage is that the automatically determined requirement is adjusted to the current consumption behavior. If material has already been withdrawn in the current period, the forecast requirement is reduced by these material withdrawals in order to avoid the inclusion of this part of the forecasted requirement in the new planning process.

Forecast-based planning

The period pattern for the forecast (day, week, month, or posting period) and the number of prediction periods can be defined separately for each material. However, the period pattern of the forecast may not be detailed enough for MRP. For this reason, you can use the splitting indicator to define for each material how the forecast requirement values must be distributed to a more detailed period pattern for MRP purposes. For each plant, the splitting indicator must be maintained using the following Customizing path: **Production • Requirements Planning • Forecast • Define splitting of forecast requirements for MRP**. The splitting indicator contains the number of periods to be considered as well as the number of days and/or weeks for which the splitting is to be carried out (see Figure 8.29).

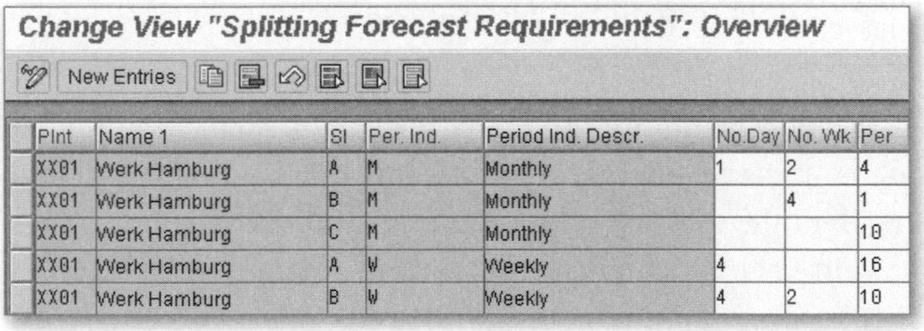

Period pattern

Change View "Splitting Forecast Requirements": Overview

New Entries

Plnt	Name 1	SI	Per. Ind.	Period Ind. Descr.	No.Day	No. Wk	Per
XX01	Werk Hamburg	A	M	Monthly	1	2	4
XX01	Werk Hamburg	B	M	Monthly		4	1
XX01	Werk Hamburg	C	M	Monthly			10
XX01	Werk Hamburg	A	W	Weekly	4		16
XX01	Werk Hamburg	B	W	Weekly	4	2	10

Figure 8.29 Distributing the Forecast Values to Different Periods

The splitting indicator is assigned to the material in the **MRP 3** view (see Figure 8.30).

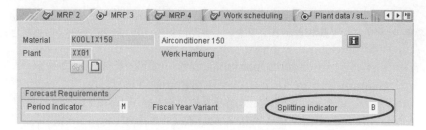

Figure 8.30 Splitting Indicator in the Material Master

The requirement quantities forecast by the system are copied during the planning phase, and a net requirements calculation is carried out. During the net requirements calculation, a check is performed for each period in order to see whether the forecast requirement is covered by the available stocks or by the goods receipts that have been firmly scheduled by purchasing or production. In the case of a shortage for a forecast requirement, the system generates a procurement proposal. The system calculates the quantity specified in the procurement proposal according to the selected lot-sizing procedure. Depending on the lot-sizing procedure used, several requirement quantities are combined into a lot size. For each procurement proposal, the system calculates the date on which the proposal must be converted into a purchase order or production order so that the purchase order can be sent to the supplier on time and the production order can be forwarded to production. Only if the supplier receives the purchase order on time and if production receives the production order on time can the ordered quantity be delivered on the scheduled date.

In forecast-based planning, the forecast of the overall requirement serves as the basis for the net requirements calculation. The system only considers the forecast requirement quantities as goods issues. Other requirements elements such as customer requirements, planned independent requirements, or reservations are merely displayed in forecast-based planning and remain unconsidered in net requirements calculation. Each forecast requirement is checked as to whether it is covered by plant stock and/or goods receipts (purchase orders, production orders, and fixed procurement proposals). The available stock can be determined for each requirement using the following calculation:

    Plant stock

  − *Safety stock*

  + *Open order quantities (purchase orders, production orders,*
     fixed procurement proposals),

  − *Requirement quantity (forecast requirements)*

  = *Available stock*

A shortage occurs when the available stock becomes negative; that is, when the requirement quantities are bigger than the receipts. The material shortage quantity is stored by the system. The system uses the date of the forecast requirement as the requirement date. This is based on the assumption that the forecast requirement exists at the beginning of the period. Thus, the requirement date is the first work day of the respective period.

If a vendor always delivers a material on a certain day of the week, it makes sense to carry out a planning run that follows the same cycle and is displaced by the delivery time. This can be done using the MRP procedure of time-phased materials planning. To be able to plan a material based on time phases, you must enter the MRP type for time-phased planning and the planning cycle in the material master (see Figure 8.31).

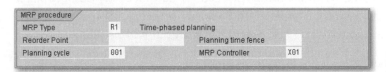

Figure 8.31 Parameters for Time-Phased Materials Planning in the Material Master

A planning calendar is used as a planning cycle. You can define planning calendars using the following Customizing path: **Production • Requirements Planning • Master Data • Maintain Planning Calendar** (see Figure 8.32).

As is the case in forecast-based planning, forecast requirements are determined for materials planned on the basis of time phases. These forecast requirements are then used in the net requirements calculation.

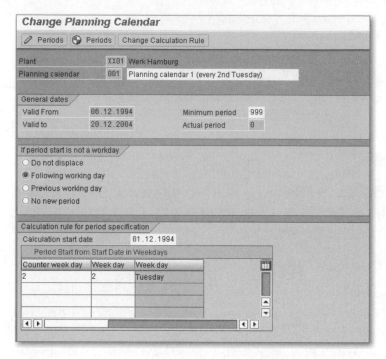

Figure 8.32 Planning Calendar for Time-Phased Materials Planning

Materials planned in this time-phased way are assigned a planning date in the planning file. This date is automatically reset when a material master is created and then after every planning run. The date matches the day on which the material will be planned for the next time. It can be calculated on the basis of the planning cycle specified in the material master. This procedure ensures that a material can be planned only on specific days that are defined by the user. For example, if all materials of a supplier are assigned to the same planning cycle, all those materials are always planned on the same days. The MRP controller can edit the purchase requisitions that are generated in the purchasing module of SAP ERP in the case of a material shortage separately for each supplier. Moreover, it is possible to specify a planning date in the planning run. This is useful as it enables you to bring the planning run forward to an earlier date. If the planning run is set for Monday, for example, you can perform this run on Saturday.

8.3.4 Consumption Forecast

Some of the consumption-based MRP procedures require a consumption forecast before material requirements planning can be carried out. These procedures include forecast-based planning and time-phased materials planning. For automatic reorder point planning, we recommend creating a forecast, as it will be required for calculating the reorder point.

Forecasting has already been described in detail in Section 6.4. Based on a requirements history, we forecast the future requirement that eventually affects the planned independent requirement of saleable products. In contrast, the consumption forecast for components is based on material withdrawals, as opposed to a calculation based on a BOM explosion.

You can maintain the forecast parameters in the **Forecast** view of the material master, as shown in Figure 8.33. The parameters include the granularity of the forecast; that is, whether it is carried out on the basis of monthly, weekly, or daily values. The granularity can be defined using the **Period Indicator**. Other entries specify the number of historical periods based on which the forecast is carried out, as well as the number of forecast periods. You can either specify the forecast model directly or have it determined automatically. Possible forecast models include the following:

Forecast parameters

▶ Constant model (D)

▶ Trend model (T)

▶ Seasonal model (S)

▶ Seasonal trend model (X)

▶ Moving average (G)

However, if entries exist for the tests regarding the model selection (**Model selection** field), an automatic model selection is carried out in any case (see Figure 8.33).

The **Execute forecast** button enables you to carry out a forecast in the material master, while the other two buttons allow you to edit the historical values and the forecast values.

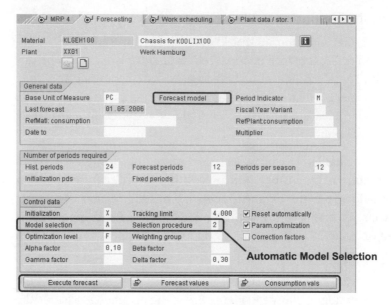

Figure 8.33 Forecast Parameters in the Material Master

Executing the forecast You can run the forecast as an individual forecast for a material or as an overall forecast for several materials. Figure 8.34 displays the initial screen for an individual forecast called via Transaction MP30.

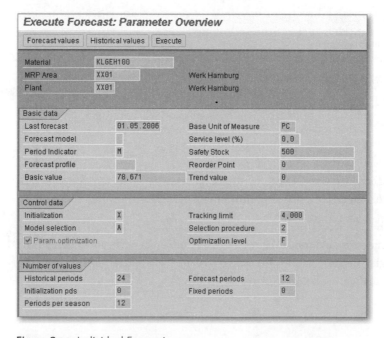

Figure 8.34 Individual Forecast

The result of the forecast is displayed in a separate window (see Figure 8.35). In this case, the automatic model selection has determined a constant model. The forecast contains the value **91** for the coming three months, **90** for the subsequent three months, and so on.

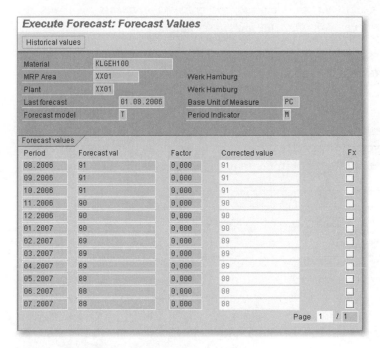

Figure 8.35 Individual Forecast: Forecast Result

The determined forecast value is displayed in the grey **Forecast val** column and represents the proposed value for the **Corrected value** column. You can change the corrected value interactively.

The forecast can be changed using Transaction MP31, while Transaction MP32 enables you to display it. Although the different consumption-based MRP procedures take into account the forecast values, the values are not displayed in the stock/requirements list.

For the overall forecast via Transaction MP38 you can restrict the planning scope by plants, materials, and ABC indicators. The ABC indicator can be maintained in the **MRP 1** view of the material master.

8.4 Executing Material Requirements Planning

8.4.1 Net Requirements Calculation Logic

With regard to material requirements planning, SAP ERP distinguishes between the methods of *gross requirements planning*, *net requirements planning*, and *sales order planning*.

Gross requirements planning

In gross requirements planning, a BOM explosion including lot-size calculation and scheduling is carried out *without* considering warehouse and plant stocks. The planning run merely includes the expected receipts (planned orders and purchase requisitions). For materials for which you want to carry out gross requirements planning, you must specify the gross requirements planning indicator in the **Mixed MRP** field in the material master (see Figure 8.36).

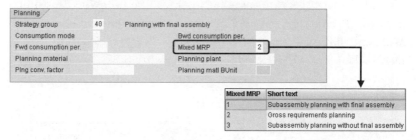

Figure 8.36 Parameters for Gross Requirements Planning in the Material Master

Stocks

Net requirements planning and sales order planning include available stocks in the planning process. SAP ERP recognizes different types of stocks. For all storage locations of a plant that have not been excluded from the planning process and are not planned separately, the following stocks are summarized into the plant stock:

▶ Unrestricted valuated stock

▶ Stock in quality inspection

In case of a consignment—that is, stock which is located in the warehouse of the manufacturing company but is owned by the supplier until it is withdrawn from the warehouse—the plant stock consists of the same types of stocks (unrestricted-use stock, stock in quality inspection).

Transaction MMBE enables you to display a stock overview of the different stock types (see Figure 8.37).

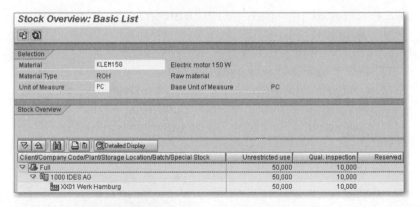

Figure 8.37 Stock Overview

You can define whether or not you want to include the stock in transfer and blocked stock in the plant stock via the following Customizing path: **Production** • Material **Requirements Planning** • **Planning** • **MRP Calculation** • **Stocks** • **Define Availability of Stock in Transfer/Blocked Stock/Restricted Stock** (see Figure 8.38).

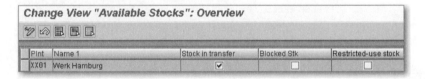

Figure 8.38 Defining the Plant Stock

In this case the blocked stock is not available for MRP, as you can see in the stock/requirements list shown in Figure 8.39.

In net requirements planning, a BOM explosion is carried out involving lot-size calculation and scheduling that *includes* warehouse and plant stocks.

Net requirements planning

Net requirements planning means that the system checks for each requirement date if the requirement is covered by the plant stock or by one or several goods receipts. If that's not the case, the system calculates the material shortage quantity. The lot-size calculation determines the quantity of the goods to be received. In net requirements calculation, the available stock can be determined according to this formula:

> *Plant stock*
> - *Safety stock*
> + *Open order quantity (purchase orders, production orders, fixed procurement proposals),*
> - *Requirement quantity (planned independent requirements, customer requirements, material reservations, forecast requirements for unplanned additional requirements)*
>
> --
>
> = *Available stock*

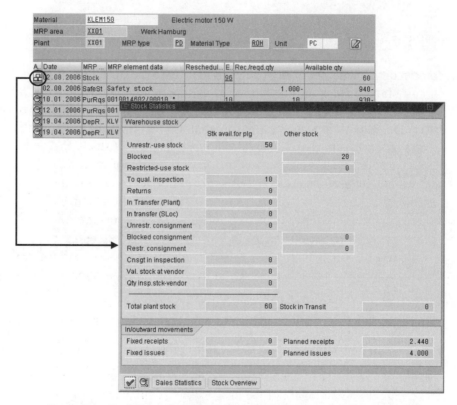

Figure 8.39 Stock Types in the Stock/Requirements List

Let's take a look at an example in the stock/requirements list in order to describe net requirements planning (see Figure 8.40).

In this example, the available stock quantity is 400 units of the finished product, **KOOLIX110**. The defined safety stock is 500 units, which means there is already a shortage of 100 units. The production order of 50 units reduces the shortage quantity to 50 units. However, we have a planned independent requirement of 200 units, which increases the shortage quantity to 250 units. Thus, the available quantity is 250 units, as displayed in the bottom row of the **Available qty** column.

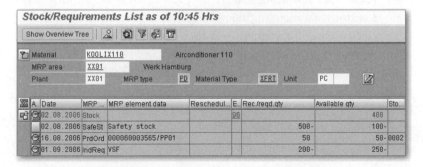

A.	Date	MRP ...	MRP element data	Reschedul...	E.	Rec./reqd.qty	Available qty	Sto...
	02.08.2006	Stock			96		400	
	02.08.2006	SafeSt	Safety stock			500-	100-	
	16.08.2006	PrdOrd	000060003565/PP01			50	50-0002	
	01.09.2006	IndReq	VSF			200-	250-	

Figure 8.40 Example of Net Requirements Planning in the Stock/Requirements List

To plan a specific sales order, you must use the sales order planning run. Sales order planning enables you to track a sales order across several production levels, to maintain separate sales order stocks that pertain to specific sales orders, and to collect the costs of individual sales orders. In sales order planning, a procurement proposal is created for each sales order without prior lot-size calculation. Current production orders or purchase orders for those sales orders are considered as well as finished and delivered part quantities handled as special stock. Furthermore, you can use a specific evaluation based on the sales order in order to obtain an overview of the production status of the entire BOM structure.

Sales order planning

When designing the *BOM structure*, you must distinguish between the *production* and *MRP structures* in the product structure description. The production structure tells you what quantity of a material or assembly must be available at which point in time during the production process (assignment of the material or assembly to a production level). Consideration of the low-level code supports the provisioning of a material or assembly at the right time for the entire production. The procedure of *low-level coding* takes into account that a material may appear in several products and at more than one production levels of a product. The low-level code is the lowest level that a material appears in any product structure. The low-level coding procedure summarizes the entire requirement of a material at the lowest level at which the material is used.

Low-level codes

The materials are planned according to the sequence of their low-level code. The highest low-level code, that is, the saleable product, is low-level code 0. The components that are directly used for the salable product are low-level code 1 and so on. In SAP, the low-level code is stored in a *planning file*. The planning file enables the MRP controller to view the structure of the low-level codes at any time. Thus, it is possible to view planning file entries for all materials of a plant, to display the planning file entry for a specific material by entering the material number, to restrict the selection to certain low-level codes, or to view only the master schedule items by setting the *master production scheduling* (**MPS**) flag Figure 8.41 displays the low-level codes in the planning file.

R	Cde	Material	MRP Area	MPS ind.	NChge plng	NChgePHor.	ResetProps	ExplodeBOM	Plng date
B	000	K00LIX100	XX01	☐	X	X	X	X	
B	000	K00LIX110	XX01	☐	X	X	X	X	
B	000	K00LIX200	XX01	☐	X	X	X	X	
B	000	K00LIX220	XX01	☐	X	X	X	X	
B	001	KLGEH100	XX01	☐	X	X			
B	001	KLKOMPR100	XX01	☐	X	X			
B	001	KLSTE100	XX01	☐	X	X			
B	001	KLVNT30	XX01	☐	X	X			
B	002	KLEM150	XX01	☐	X	X			
B	002	KLPROP30	XX01	☐	X	X			

Low-Level Code 000 { (rows 000)
Low-Level Code 001 { (rows 001)
Low-Level Code 002 { (rows 002)

Figure 8.41 Display of Low-Level Codes in the Planning File

During the planning run you can define whether you want to plan all materials or only selected ones and what type of planning you want to use. If you use total planning, you must plan all planning-relevant materials for a plant, whereas in single-item planning the planning run is carried out only for the selected material. Single-level single-item planning only plans the BOM level of the selected material. Multilevel single-item planning plans the BOM level of the selected material, including all subordinate BOM levels. The planning file contains all materials that are relevant to a planning run. This means that as soon as you create a material master with planning data and a valid MRP type, the material is automatically included in the planning file.

8.4.2 Parameters for Material Requirements Planning

In addition to the master data parameters, there are other parameters that affect material requirements planning and that must be set directly during the execution of MRP. The parameters are the following.

- ▶ **Processing key or planning run type**
  The processing key defines whether a regenerative planning, a net change planning, or a net change planning in the planning horizon must be carried out.

- ▶ **Creation of purchase requisitions**
  You can create either planned orders or purchase requisitions for externally procured materials. Another option is the creation of purchase requisitions in the opening period, and of planned orders outside the opening period.

- ▶ **Delivery schedules**
  If you use delivery plans for procurement purposes, you can choose whether you want to create delivery schedules or whether you want to create them only in the planning horizon.

- ▶ **Create MRP list**
  This parameter defines if an MRP list is always created or never created, or if it is created only in the case of exception messages. The MRP list is described in greater detail in Section 8.7.

- ▶ **Planning mode**
  The planning mode controls whether the planned orders are adjusted or created from scratch, or if a new explosion of the master data must be carried out.

- ▶ **Scheduling**
  The scheduling parameter defines whether the basic dates are determined for a planned order based on the in-house production time defined in the material master, or whether a lead time scheduling is performed on the basis of the routing. The determination of basic dates is the more commonly used type of scheduling in material requirements planning and is described in greater detail in Section 8.5. Lead time scheduling is described in Chapter 10, *Production Order Creation*.

Figure 8.42 displays the screen for executing material requirements planning.

Figure 8.42 Control Parameters for Material Requirements Planning

Processing key or
planning run type

In the SAP ERP system, the planning run type is defined via the **processing key.** When starting a planning run, the following three principles can be distinguished.

▶ **Regenerative planning** (NEUPL)
Regenerative planning plans all MRP-relevant materials. In this context, quantities that have been firmly scheduled in an earlier planning run are released and completely planned anew on the basis of the current planning situation.

▶ **Net change planning** (NETCH)
Net change planning or the net change principle plans anew only those quantities that are affected by data changes due to the new situation. To be able to carry out net change planning, the materials are assigned a total change indicator in the planning file for each MRP-relevant change. The indicator is thus an entry for NETCH. Usually, the total change indicator is automatically set by the system when an MRP-relevant change to the current situation of a material occurs. Such changes can be as follows:

  ▷ Changes in stock, provided they affect the stock/requirements list of the material.

  ▷ Additional purchase requisitions, purchase orders, planned orders, sales requirements, forecast requirements, dependent demands, or reservations.

  ▷ Changes to MRP-relevant fields of those goods receipts and issues or of the material master

  ▷ Deletions of goods receipts and issues

▶ **Net change planning in the planning horizon** (NETPL)
Net change planning in the planning horizon plans only those materials that have been affected by an MRP-relevant change

within the period of time that has been defined as the planning horizon. If a planning horizon has been defined, an additional indicator—the net change planning indicator, which is an entry for NETPL—is assigned to the material for each MRP-relevant change within the planning horizon. If the planning of a material is cancelled, the entry for this material remains contained in the planning file so that the material will be included in the next net change planning run. Customizing enables you to define whether you want to delete these entries despite the cancellation of the planning run. This might occur, for example, if a specific material is not available in the planning plant.

MRP-relevant changes generate an entry in the planning file. You can display the planning file using Transaction MD21. In addition to the planning entries, the file also contains information on the low-level code (000 being the highest low-level code) as well as an indication as to whether the material is a master schedule item (see Figure 8.43).

Planning file entry

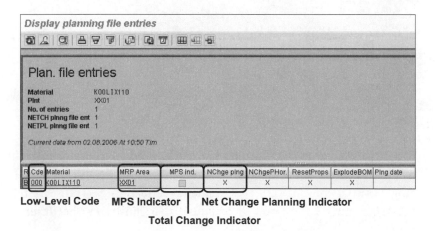

Figure 8.43 Planning File

Regenerative planning (processing key NEUPL) plans all materials. However, if you carry out net change planning (NETCH) or net change planning in the planning horizon (NETPL), the system first checks whether the planning file contains a corresponding entry. For reasons of runtime, only those materials are planned in cases that have a corresponding planning file entry. Entries are generated by MRP-relevant changes; that is, changes to requirements or receipts. A dependent demand created in the planning run also generates a planning file entry. The planning run resets the respective indicators except for the interactive planning carried out using Transaction MD43.

The indicator for a new BOM explosion also causes the BOM explosion for existing planned orders. This indicator is set by changing the BOM.

8.4.3 Planning Scope

You can call material requirements planning via Transaction MD01. The scope of material requirements planning typically refers to a specific plant, but it also can refer to several plants if you define a corresponding planning scope. You can define the planning scope using the following Customizing path: **Production** • **Material Requirements Planning** • **Planning** • **Define Scope of Planning for Total Planning** (see Figure 8.44).

Figure 8.44 Planning Scope for Material Requirements Planning

You can also restrict the planning scope to a product group or material. In the latter case, a distinction is made between multilevel planning (Transaction MD02) and single-level planning (Transaction MD03). Figure 8.45 shows an example that illustrates the differences.

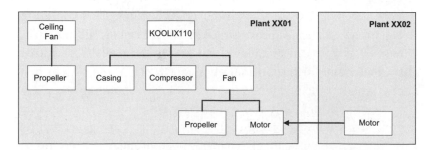

Figure 8.45 Sample Definition of the Planning Scope

Material requirements planning for the planning scope of plants **XX01** and **XX02** includes all materials of the example. If planning is carried out only for plant **XX01**, a stock transport requisition is sent to plant **XX02**. However, a requirement coverage element is not yet created in plant **XX02**.

A multilevel single-item planning run for **KOOLIX110** includes all components for the header product, whereas a single-level single-item planning considers only the header product, **KOOLIX110**.

8.5 Scheduling

8.5.1 Forward and Backward Scheduling

If the lot sizes needed to cover the requirement are available, you must define the dates for the materials to be produced and externally procured in the final step. In this context, you can make a distinction between the scheduling type—whether you want to use forward or backward scheduling—and the procurement type, whether production takes place in-house or externally. Similarly, the following interdependencies exist with the different MRP procedures.

▶ For materials that are planned in *forecast-based planning* and in *material requirements planning*, the future requirement dates are known. The materials must be available on those dates. The determination of basic dates for in-house production and of the release date for purchasing therefore occurs as *backward scheduling* in these procedures. Only if the basic or release date determined during scheduling is in the past does the system automatically switch to forward scheduling from the planning date onwards.

▶ In *reorder point planning*, the dates are defined by means of *forward scheduling*. Once the reorder point is fallen short of during the planning run, the procurement activities must be initiated. Based on the date of the material shortage, the availability date of the materials is determined.

In in-house production, the planning run distinguishes between the order start and order finish dates. The order finish date defines the latest finish date of the production, while the order start date specifies the earliest possible start of the production. In this context, both the goods receipt processing time defined in the material master and the in-house production time in terms of work days are taken into account. The in-house production time can be stored as lot-size-dependent or lot-size-independent in-house production time. In the case of external procurement, the order finish date corresponds to the delivery date, while the order start date corresponds to the release date. Here, the processing time in purchasing is taken into account as well as the goods receipt processing time in terms of work days and the planned delivery time of the material in terms of calendar days.

In the case of in-house production, the system always creates *planned orders*. These planned orders are used to plan the production quantities. Once the planning has been completed, the planned orders are converted into production orders. In the case of external procurement, the system creates either a *planned order* or a *purchase requisition*. Purchase requisitions for external procurement plan the external procurement quantity. Once the planning has been completed, the planned order is converted into a purchase requisition or the purchase requisition is converted into a purchase order. In the initial screen of the planning run, you can use the creation indicator for purchase requisitions in order to define whether the system should directly create purchase requisitions or whether it should first create planned orders. If a delivery plan exists for a material and if the source list contains an MRP-relevant entry, you can directly generate *delivery schedules* in material requirements planning. You can do this by specifying the creation indicator for delivery schedules in the initial screen of the planning run.

8.5.2 Scheduling In-House Production (Basic Date Determination)

You can schedule in-house production, in other words the planned orders, in two different ways.

▶ **Basic date determination**
Scheduling occurs based on the in-house production time that's stored in the material master

▶ **Lead time scheduling**
Scheduling occurs on the basis of the evaluation of the routing

The scheduling parameter that is to be set when you start material requirements planning enables you to decide which of the two alternatives you want to use (see Section 8.4.2). The basic date determination based on in-house production time is the more commonly used method in material requirements planning and is described in the following section.

Basic date determination is a type of scheduling that determines the basic dates within which production is to take place. For this reason, the in-house production time defined by the basic dates should be bigger than or equal to the in-house production time that is defined by the routing explosion. In this context, no operation dates are defined and no capacity requirements are generated. The determination of the in-house production time can be carried out as quantity-dependent or independent. In both cases, the entries in the material master are reverted to, and both cases they also take factory calendars into account.

Basic date determination

The easiest way to specify the in-house production time is to maintain the **In-house production time** parameter in terms of days in the material master. Figure 8.46 displays the maintenance of this parameter in the **MRP 2** view.

Quantity-independent in-house production time

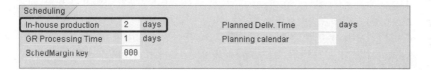

Figure 8.46 Quantity-Independent In-House Production Time in Material Master (Excerpt from MRP 2 View)

This in-house production time does not depend on the order quantity; that is, small quantities require the same amount of time as large quantities. This assumption is valid for planning if the order quantity is limited via the lot-sizing procedure, if experience has shown that order quantities usually don't differ very much, or if the daily granularity can cover the fluctuations of the order quantity.

If the influence of the order quantity on the in-house production time can no longer be neglected, you can also calculate the in-house production time as quantity-dependent. For this purpose, you must carry out detailed modeling of the in-house production times and maintain the **Setup time**, **Interoperation**, and **Processing time** fields

Quantity-dependent in-house production time

as well as the **Base quantity** in the **Work Scheduling** view of the material master (see Figure 8.47).

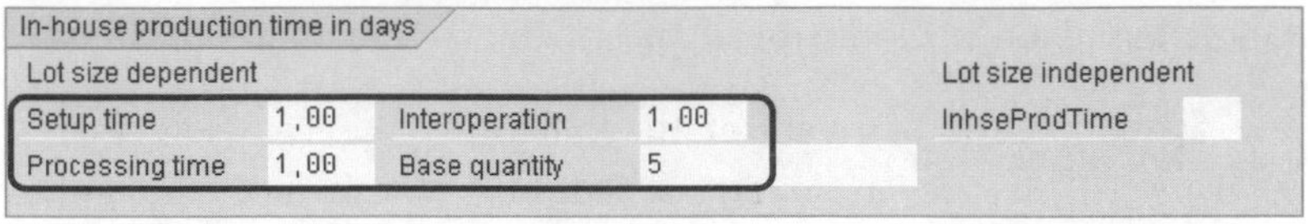

In-house production time in days				
Lot size dependent				Lot size independent
Setup time	1,00	Interoperation	1,00	InhseProdTime
Processing time	1,00	Base quantity	5	

Figure 8.47 Quantity-Dependent In-House Production Time in Material Master (Excerpt from "Work Scheduling" View)

The interoperation time represents a summary of move times, wait times, and safety times. Only the processing time is quantity-dependent, as it depends on the base quantity. The setup and interoperation times are quantity-independent and are added to the processing time. The following formula describes the quantity-dependent in-house production time:

$$In\text{-}house\ production\ time = Setup + (Order\ quantity\ /\ Base\ quantity)\ * $$
$$Processing\ time + Interoperation\ time$$

You can maintain parameters either for the quantity-independent or for the quantity-dependent in-house production time.

Lead time scheduling Scheduling on the basis of the routing occurs according to the order quantity, the standard values of the routing, and the scheduling formulas of the work center. This type of scheduling is described in great detail in Chapter 10, *Production Order Creation*.

Order dates In the case of backward scheduling, you can derive the dates for the planned order from the requirement date. To do this, you must deduct the three periods—opening period, in-house production time, and goods receipt processing time—from the requirement date (see Figure 8.48).

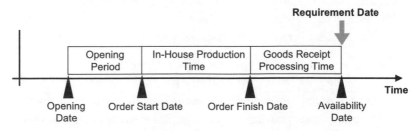

Figure 8.48 (Backward) Scheduling and the Dates of the Planned Order

In the case of forward scheduling, the order start date is shifted to today's date and the opening period is omitted. Forward scheduling only occurs in material requirements planning if the requirement date is too close to the current date.

The opening period is part of the scheduling margin key that is described in Section 10.5. The scheduling margin key and goods receipt processing time are maintained below the in-house production time in the **MRP 1** view, as shown in Figure 8.46.

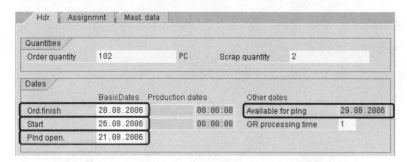

Hdr	Assignmnt	Mast. data

Quantities

Order quantity	102	PC	Scrap quantity	2

Dates

	BasicDates	Production dates		Other dates	
Ord.finish	28.08.2006		00:00:00	Available for plng	29.08.2006
Start	26.08.2006		00:00:00	GR processing time	1
Plnd open.	21.08.2006				

Figure 8.49 Opening, Order Start, Order Finish, and Availability Dates In the Planned Order

Figure 8.49 displays the opening, order start, order finish, and availability dates from Figure 8.48 in the planned order.

8.5.3 Scheduling External Procurement

When planned orders for externally procured materials or purchase requisitions are created, they are not immediately assigned to a supplier. For this reason, the **planned delivery time** parameter in the material master is used for scheduling (see Figure 8.50).

Scheduling

In-house production		days	Planned Deliv. Time	7	days
GR Processing Time		days	Planning calendar		
SchedMargin key	000				

Figure 8.50 Planned Delivery Time in the Material Master

The planned delivery time refers to workdays that appear in the factory calendar, provided that no planning calendar is explicitly specified. As an alternative to determining the planned delivery time from the material master, you can determine the planned delivery time from the purchasing info record. If you want to do that, this scheduling type must be allowed in the plant parameters (see Figure 8.52). Moreover, the source list must contain a corresponding entry.

The scheduling process for external procurement is carried out similarly to that of in-house production except that is uses four periods (for backward scheduling). These periods are:

► Opening period

► Purchasing department processing time

► Planned delivery time

► Goods-receipt processing time

These periods are deducted from the requirement date.

Figure 8.51 External Procurement Time in the Material Master

The planned delivery time corresponds to the in-house production time in in-house production, and the opening period and goods receipt processing time are similarly maintained and used. The purchasing department processing time is maintained in the plant parameters (see Figure 8.52). The plant parameters are described in Section 8.8.

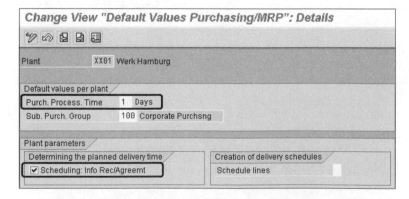

Figure 8.52 Purchasing Department Processing Time in the Plant Parameters

8.5.4 Planning Time Fence

For reasons of system stability, you generally should avoid automatically creating planned orders until the very last day in order not to confuse the production plan. The planning time fence allows for the definition of a range within which material requirements planning does not create or delete any procurement proposals. You can maintain the planning time fence in the **MRP 1** view (see Figure 8.53).

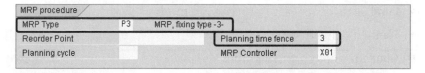

Figure 8.53 Firming Parameters in the Material Master

If and how the planning time fence is taken into account depends on the firming type. You can define the firming type in the MRP type. Four firming types are available, and these differ with regard to the automatic firming of elements within the planning time fence and with regard to the creation of new elements. Table 8.4 lists the properties of the respective firming types.

	New procurement proposals at the end of the planning time fence	No procurement proposals in the case of material shortages in the planning time fence
Automatic firming of procurement proposals in the planning time fence	Firming type 1	Firming type 2
No firming of procurement proposals in the planning time fence	Firming type 3	Firming type 4

Table 8.4 Firming Types

If the procurement proposals are not firmed in the planning time fence, they are deleted in the case of a surplus. Figure 8.54 illustrates the different behaviors of the firming types on the basis of a sample shortage. In this example, a requirement of 10 units within the planning time fence confronts a planned order of five units. The figure shows the situation after the planning run.

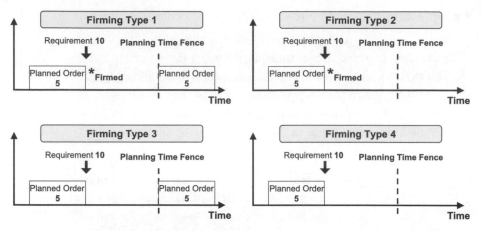

Figure 8.54 Influence of the Firming Types on Material Requirements Planning

In none of the four cases illustrated here does material requirements planning create procurement proposals within the planning time fence.

8.6 Procurement Proposals

8.6.1 Planned Order and Purchase Requisition

Materials are either produced in-house, procured externally, or both. The **procurement type** in the **MRP 2** view of the material master defines which of the alternatives applies to the material in the plant (see Figure 8.55).

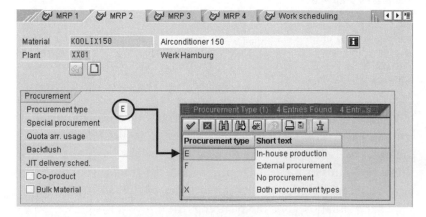

Figure 8.55 Procurement Type in the Material Master

If both in-house production and external procurement are allowed, material requirements planning assumes in-house production by default.

The element required for in-house production is the planned order, which later is converted into a production order. If external procurement is allowed, the planned order can also be converted into a purchase requisition, and this, in turn, is converted into a purchase order or purchase order item.

Planned orders contain an order quantity, a start date, and a finish date. The start and finish dates are the result of the scheduling process and are based on the factory calendar. The MRP-relevant date can occur after the finish date if a goods-receipt processing time has been maintained. In addition, the planned order contains the dependent demands from the BOM explosion as well as organizational data. You can change the planned order either by using Transaction MD12 or as a detail within the stock/requirements list (see Figure 8.56).

Planned order

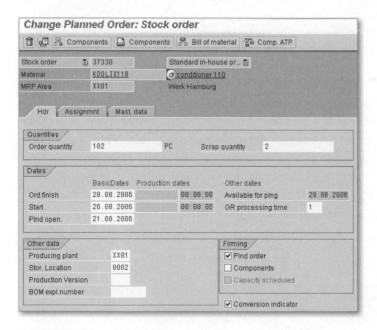

Figure 8.56 Planned Order

The planned order is assigned a number—in this case 37330—and it contains the reference to the header material (**KOOLIX110**) as well as the order profile (**stock order**). The header data contains, among other things, the order quantity, the dates, and the conversion indicator. The **Assignment** view contains information on the settlement, while the **Master data** view displays the BOM that is used. If you click on the **Components** button or press the **F5** key, you can display and change the components of the planned order (see Figure 8.57).

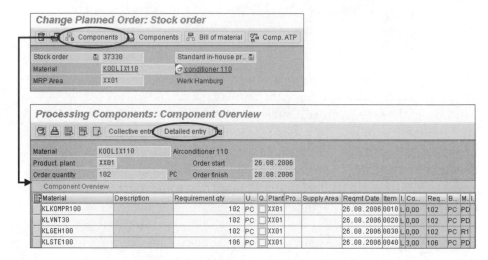

Figure 8.57 Components of the Planned Order

Order profile

Planned orders have an order profile. In the examples illustrated here, that's the **stock order** profile. You can define the order profile in Customizing via the following path: **Production** • Material **Requirements Planning** • **Procurement Proposals** • **Planned Orders** • **Define Order Profile**. The order profile is used for both planned orders (object type 1) and purchase requisitions (object type 2) and it contains information on the permitted procurement types and special procurement types (see Figure 8.58).

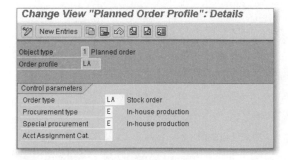

Figure 8.58 Planned Order Profile

For externally procured materials you either can create a planned order and convert it into a purchase requisition at a later stage, or you can directly create a purchase requisition. You can change purchase requisitions using Transaction ME52N (see Figure 8.59).

Purchase requisition

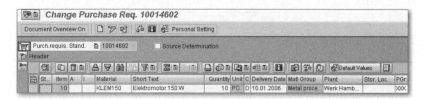

Figure 8.59 Purchase Requisition

8.6.2 Interactive Planning

Interactive planning can be carried out by specifically creating planned orders using Transaction MD11 or by using interactive material requirements planning for material and plant via Transaction MD43. In the latter case, the system displays the current requirement and stock situation. The **Planning** button enables you to trigger material requirements planning (see Figure 8.60).

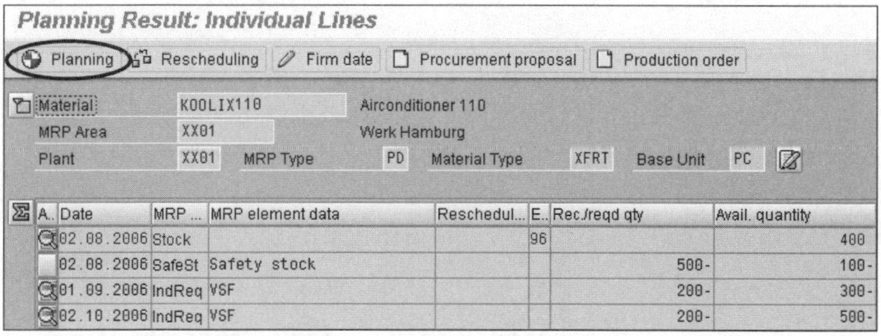

Figure 8.60 Interactive Material Requirements Planning

As a result, planned orders are created (see Figure 8.61). The system displays the planning result, which is still just a simulation at this point. The planned orders are not created until the results are saved. Moreover, this transaction enables you to create and reschedule specific procurement proposals.

You also can change planned orders or purchase requisitions in the stock/requirements list. In this case, the procurement proposals are firmed, which is then indicated by the asterisk (see Figure 8.62).

A.	Date	MRP ...	MRP element data	Reschedul...	E.	Rec./reqd qty	Avail. quantity	Sto...
	02.08.2006	Stock			96		400	
	02.08.2006	SafeSt	Safety stock			500-	100-	
	01.09.2006	PlOrd.	0000037337/Stck		01	100	0	0002
	01.09.2006	PlOrd.	0000037338/Stck		01	100	100	0002
	01.09.2006	PlOrd.	0000037339/Stck		01	100	200	0002
	01.09.2006	IndReq	VSF			200-	0	
	02.10.2006	PlOrd.	0000037340/Stck		01	100	100	0002
	02.10.2006	PlOrd.	0000037341/Stck		01	100	200	0002
	02.10.2006	IndReq	VSF			200-	0	

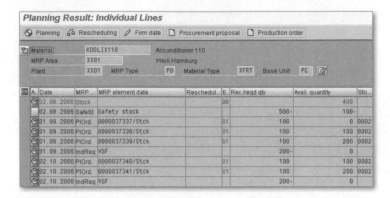

Figure 8.61 Result of Material Requirements Planning

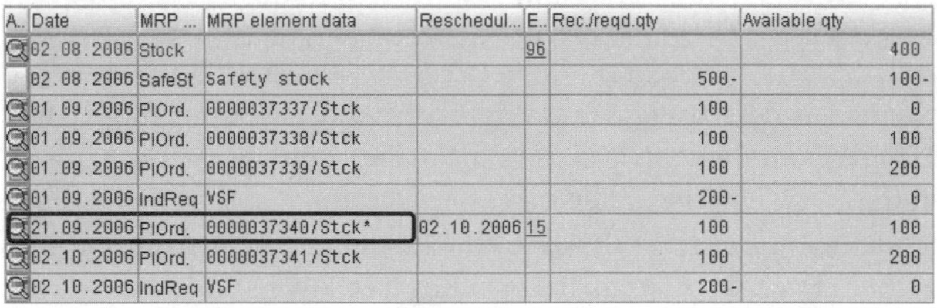

A..	Date	MRP ...	MRP element data	Reschedul...	E..	Rec./reqd.qty	Available qty
	02.08.2006	Stock			96		400
	02.08.2006	SafeSt	Safety stock			500-	100-
	01.09.2006	PlOrd.	0000037337/Stck			100	0
	01.09.2006	PlOrd.	0000037338/Stck			100	100
	01.09.2006	PlOrd.	0000037339/Stck			100	200
	01.09.2006	IndReq	VSF			200-	0
	21.09.2006	PlOrd.	0000037340/Stck*	02.10.2006	15	100	100
	02.10.2006	PlOrd.	0000037341/Stck			100	200
	02.10.2006	IndReq	VSF			200-	0

Figure 8.62 Firmed Planned Orders in the Stock/Requirements List

The firming indicator is set in the planning order details (see Figure 8.63).

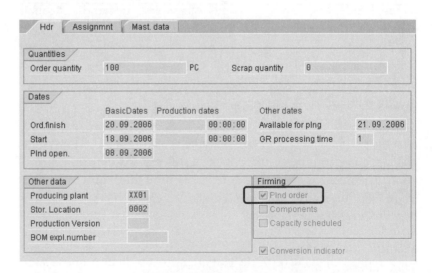

Figure 8.63 Firming Indicator in the Planned Order

8.7 Analysis

8.7.1 Stock/Requirements List and MRP List

The SAP ERP system provides two similar lists with which to present the planning situation: the stock/requirements list (Transaction MD04) and the MRP list (Transaction MD05). While the MRP list shows the planning situation at the time of the last material requirements planning run, the stock/requirements list shows the current planning situation. The current situation can deviate from the situation of the last planning run because changes might have occurred in the meantime due to goods receipts and issues, confirmations, or sales orders. You can compare the two lists via the menu path **Goto • MRP List Comparison** or **Goto • Stock/Requirements List Comparison** respectively. Figure 8.64 illustrates some of the options provided by the stock/requirements list:

▶ Display of exception messages

▶ Jump into the detail view

▶ Jump into the order report

▶ Display goods receipt date or availability date

▶ Show the replenishment lead time

The stock/requirements list describes all MRP-relevant elements for a material within a plant. These include the stock, customer and planned independent requirements, dependent demands, planned orders, and production orders. In addition, it shows parameters that are relevant to material requirements planning such as the safety stock or the planning time fence. For all elements, details can be displayed and changed, if that's permitted. However, you cannot create procurement proposals interactively.

Usually, the system displays the availability date of a goods receipt. But you can also display the goods receipt date instead, for example in order to plan actions in case of delays.

Each element of the stock/requirements list contains a (positive) receipt quantity or a (negative) requirement quantity. The purpose of material requirements planning is to make sure that the available quantity does not become negative. This is indicated in the right-hand column of the stock/requirements list.

Available quantity

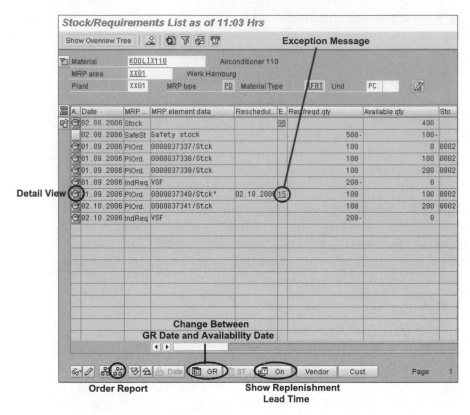

Figure 8.64 Stock/Requirements List

Period totals   The use of many elements can increase the degree of complexity of the planning situation. In this case it is useful to present them as period totals. The button marked in Figure 8.65 enables you to toggle between the presentation of period totals and the individual presentation.

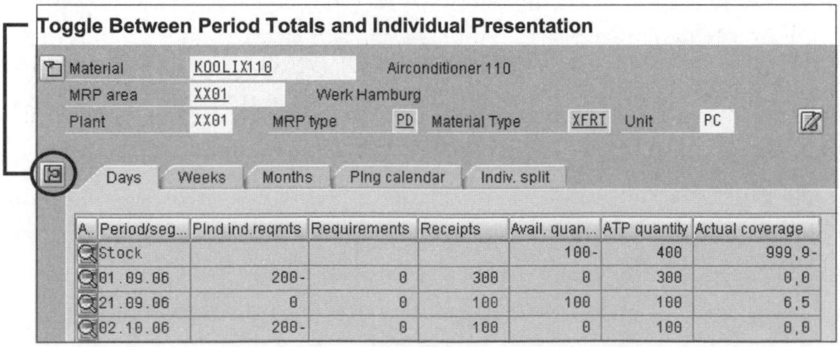

Figure 8.65 Period Totals

Replenishment lead time

You can display the replenishment lead time to help you interpret the planning situation. Like the planning time fence, the replenishment lead time is then displayed as an information row (see Figure 8.66).

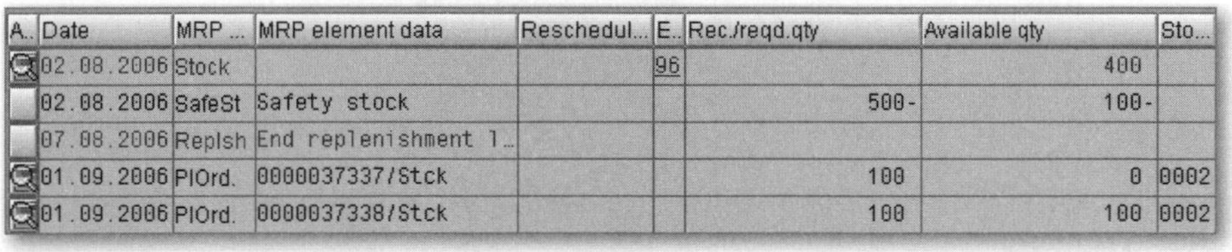

A..	Date	MRP ...	MRP element data	Reschedul...	E..	Rec./reqd.qty	Available qty	Sto...
	02.08.2006	Stock			96		400	
	02.08.2006	SafeSt	Safety stock			500-	100-	
	07.08.2006	Replsh	End replenishment 1..					
	01.09.2006	PlOrd.	0000037337/Stck			100	0	0002
	01.09.2006	PlOrd.	0000037338/Stck			100	100	0002

Figure 8.66 Replenishment Lead Time in the Stock/Requirements List

Order report

Because the stock/requirements list shows only one material, you can use the order report in order to display the relationship with the requirement and receipt elements in other low-level codes (see Figure 8.67).

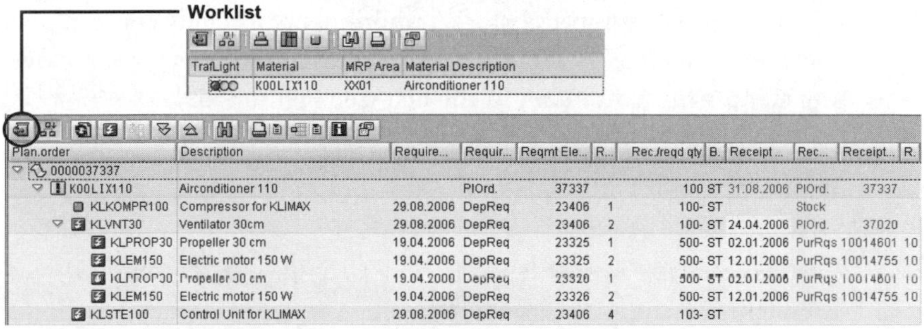

TrafLight	Material	MRP Area	Material Description
	K00LIX110	XX01	Airconditioner 110

Plan.order	Description	Require...	Requir...	Reqmt Ele...	R...	Rec./reqd qty	B.	Receipt ...	Rec...	Receipt...	R.
0000037337											
K00LIX110	Airconditioner 110		PlOrd.	37337		100	ST	31.08.2006	PlOrd.	37337	
KLKOMPR100	Compressor for KLIMAX	29.08.2006	DepReq	23406	1	100-	ST		Stock		
KLVNT30	Ventilator 30cm	29.08.2006	DepReq	23406	2	100-	ST	24.04.2006	PlOrd.	37020	
KLPROP30	Propeller 30 cm	19.04.2006	DepReq	23325	1	500-	ST	02.01.2006	PurRqs	10014601	10
KLEM150	Electric motor 150 W	19.04.2006	DepReq	23325	2	500-	ST	12.01.2006	PurRqs	10014755	10
KLPROP30	Propeller 30 cm	19.04.2006	DepReq	23326	1	500-	ST	02.01.2006	PurRqs	10014601	10
KLEM150	Electric motor 150 W	19.04.2006	DepReq	23326	2	500-	ST	12.01.2006	PurRqs	10014755	10
KLSTE100	Control Unit for KLIMAX	29.08.2006	DepReq	23406	4	103-	ST				

Figure 8.67 Order Report

Problematic materials are assigned a corresponding icon and—depending on the severity of the problem—are transferred into the pool of orders/operations. Here, the MRP controller can navigate into the stock/requirements list of the materials in question in order to find the cause of the problem. It is also possible to set threshold values and traffic lights (see Figure 8.68).

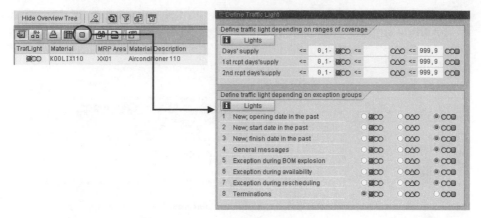

Figure 8.68 Threshold Values

8.7.2 Exception Messages

Exception messages are generated in material requirements planning when problems occur during the planning run. The exception messages are displayed in the stock/requirements list, but you can also view the elements for which exception messages exist via the following menu path: **Edit • Find in the List** (see Figure 8.69).

Figure 8.69 Display of Exception Messages in the Stock/Requirements List

Table 8.5 provides an overview of some of the exception messages.

Exception message	Text of exception message
96	Stock fallen below safety stock level
98	Abnormal end of requirements planning
70	Max. release quantity – quota exceeded
63	Production start before order start date
64	Production finish date after order finish date
50	No BOM available

Table 8.5 Exception Messages (Selection)

Exception message	Text of exception message
52	No BOM selected
55	Phantom assembly has not been exploded
56	No requirement coverage
05	Opening date is in the past
06	Start date is in the past
07	Finish date is in the past
10	Bring operation forward
30	Schedule operation on time
25	Excess stock quantity
42	Procurement proposal changed
44	Procurement proposal newly exploded

Table 8.5 Exception Messages (Selection) (cont.)

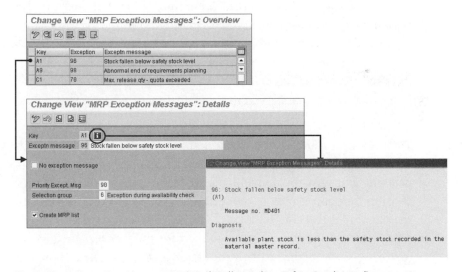

Figure 8.70 Exception Message 96 (Stock Fallen Below Safety Stock Level)

You can define the exception messages in Customizing using the following path: **Production** • Material **Requirements Planning** • **Evaluation** • **Exception Messages** • **Define and Group Exception Messages**. They contain detailed information on each exception type. Figure 8.70 displays the information for exception message **96: Stock fallen below safety stock level**.

8.8 Plant Parameters and MRP Group

The plant parameters contain a view of numerous Customizing settings that are relevant to material requirements planning. You can call the plant parameters using Customizing Transaction OPPQ (see Figure 8.71).

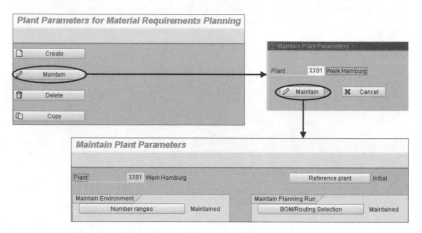

Figure 8.71 Plant Parameters

The plant parameters screen shows whether certain Customizing settings have been maintained or if they are still in their initial status. Using this screen enables you to navigate directly to the relevant Customizing area.

MRP group The MRP group allows you to maintain the settings and default values of numerous parameters, not only for material requirements planning but also for demand management and production order creation purposes. Some of the settings in the MRP group also relate the standard settings to the MRP group level. The MRP group is specific to each plant and must be defined for each material using the following Customizing path: **Production • Material Requirements Planning • MRP Groups • Define MRP Group for each Material Type**. Once it has been defined, it must be assigned to the relevant material type. Alternatively, you can also assign the MRP group directly to the (plant-specific) material master (see Figure 8.72).

You can maintain the MRP group using Customizing Transaction OPPR (see Figure 8.73).

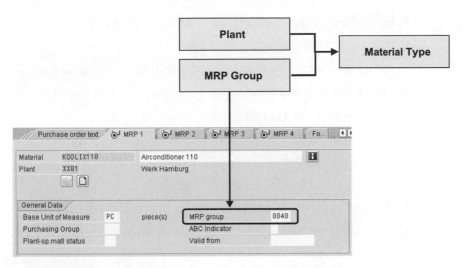

Figure 8.72 Assigning the MRP Group

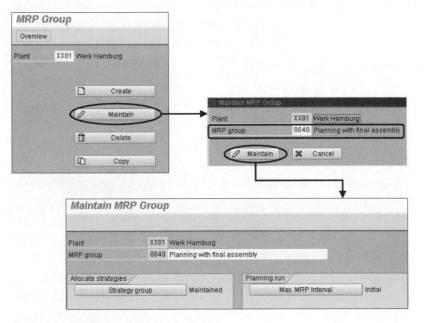

Figure 8.73 MRP Group

The MRP group contains entries for the following items:

▶ Strategy group

▶ Settlement type and horizon

▶ Rescheduling horizon, planning horizon, and planning time fence

- ▶ Production storage location selection
- ▶ Order types for converting the planned order
- ▶ Period split for distributing the independent requirement
- ▶ Maximum MRP intervals
- ▶ Availability of safety stock for MRP
- ▶ BOM explosion
- ▶ Direct procurement of non-stock items
- ▶ Creation indicators for purchase requisitions
- ▶ Order start date in the past
- ▶ Scheduling of external procurement according to information record
- ▶ Checking rule for dependent demand

Some of these values also can be maintained at a more detailed level, for instance in the material master. In this case, the values of the material master override the values maintained here.

Long-term planning is basically a simulation of planning. It can examine how a change in planned independent requirements would affect capacity utilization, stocks, and external procurement. Long-term planning is also suitable for short-term simulations.

9 Long-Term Planning

9.1 Process Overview

The purpose of long-term planning is to simulate planning. This simulation is not limited to a long-term or medium-term period, but also can be done for the short term. Long- and medium-term projects usually have objectives that are different from those of short-term periods.

▶ **Long-term simulation**
The goal of long-term simulation is to obtain information on long-term to medium-term requirements and capacities. In this context, average stocks and exact lot sizes are usually sufficient.

▶ **Short-term simulation**
The goal of short-term simulation is to check the effects of short-term planning changes before they effect material requirements planning. Here, the actual planning situation must be mapped as accurately as possible.

Simulation typically occurs on the basis of an inactive version of the program plan through use of tools that are similar to those used in material requirements planning. All simulation-relevant transaction data such as planned independent requirements, planned orders, sales orders, and firm receipts are maintained in a *planning scenario*. In addition to this data, the planning scenario contains the parameters needed for the simulation and is thus the central object for long-term planning.

The following functions are available to evaluate the simulation carried out in long-term planning:

- Comparison with operative planning
- Analysis of capacity utilization
- Analysis of external procurement data
- Requirements and inventory analysis
- Cost-center planning

Planned independent requirements, which are usually inactive, serve as a basis for long-term planning. Long-term planning also can be based on sales orders, stocks, and firm receipts. Figure 9.1 provides an overview of the long-term planning process.

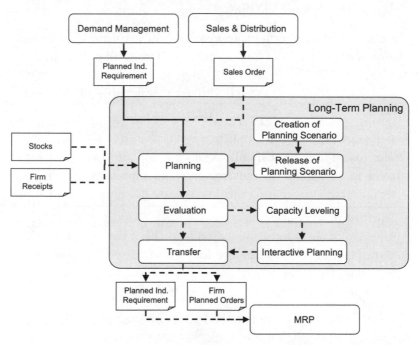

Figure 9.1 Overview of Long-Term Planning Process

Particularly in the case of short-term simulation, it is useful to achieve more or less identical basic conditions using operative planning. For this reason, the default settings for a short-term simulation provide for the consideration of all transaction data: planned independent requirements, customer requirements, current stocks, and firm receipts. For a long-term simulation, on the other hand, accounting for an average stock and the planned independent requirement can be sufficient to obtain a more transparent planning result than achieved in a short-term simulation.

It is possible to carry out interactive planning in the planning scenario that results in firmed planned orders. These firm planned orders can be transferred to material requirements planning; strictly speaking, they are adopted by material requirements planning. This is relevant to short-term simulation.

9.2 Planning Scenario

The simulations for long-term planning are carried out in a planning scenario. The planning scenario contains the complete set of transaction data of the simulation; that is, it contains the requirement elements and, optionally, stocks and firm receipts. The simulation itself is carried out similarly to material requirements planning, the only difference being that all requirement coverage elements are created only within the planning scenario and thus are invisible to operative planning. In addition to the transaction data from operative planning that are used for long-term planning, the planning scenario defines which parameters are to be taken into account for the simulation. These parameters are described in the following sections.

A planning scenario is identified by a three-digit number and can be created using Transaction MS31. To change the planning scenario, you must use Transaction MS32 (see Figure 9.2).

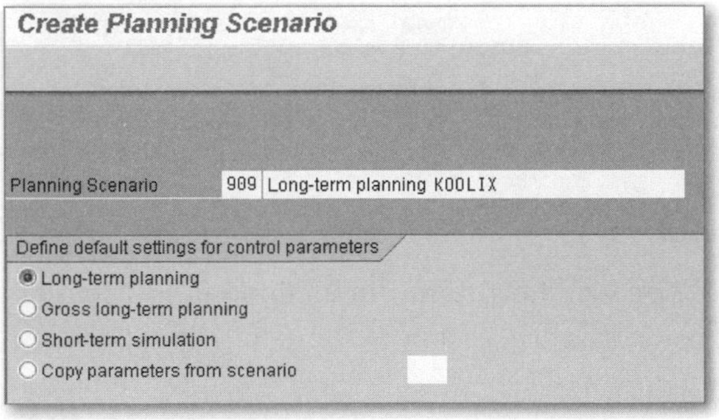

Create Planning Scenario

| Planning Scenario | 909 | Long-term planning KOOLIX |

Define default settings for control parameters

- ⦿ Long-term planning
- ◯ Gross long-term planning
- ◯ Short-term simulation
- ◯ Copy parameters from scenario

Figure 9.2 Creating a Scenario

There are three standard scenario types:

- ▶ Long-term planning
- ▶ Gross long-term planning
- ▶ Short-term simulation

The difference between these scenario types can be found in the default values of the parameters. These default values can be complemented or changed in all three cases. Another option is to copy the parameter values of a different scenario.

In addition to the parameterization, the planning scenario allows for assigning the planned independent requirement version (or versions), the plant (or plants), and the release. Figure 9.3 provides an overview of the definition of the planning scenario.

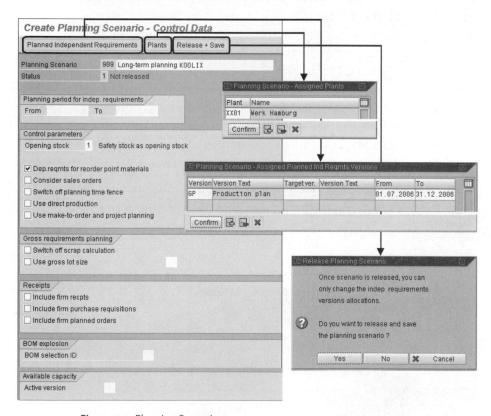

Figure 9.3 Planning Scenario

Note that once the scenario has been released, the parameters can no longer be changed.

The planning period refers to the planned independent requirement. For the evaluation of the planning scenario, you should take into account the fact that, because of the lead times involved, planned orders, and purchase requisitions occur before the planning period begins.

Table 9.1 lists the parameters of the planning scenario as well as the default values for the different standard scenario types. Depending on the type of scenario, some of the parameters are already set by default in the SAP system.

Parameter group	Parameter	Long-term planning	Gross long-term planning	Short-term simulation
Control parameter	Opening stock	Safety stock	No stock	Plant stock
	Dependent requirements for reorder point materials	x	x	x
	Consider sales orders			x
	Switch off planning time fence			
	Use direct production			x
	Use make-to-order and project planning			x
Gross requirements planning	Switch off scrap calculation		x	
	Use gross lot size		x	
Receipts	Include firm receipts			x
	Include firm purchase requisitions			x
	Include firm planned orders			x

Table 9.1 Parameters of the Planning Scenario and Their Default Values

These parameters can be changed interactively for the planning scenarios. Some of them are self-explanatory, and we will describe others in the following sections.

Opening stock

The **Opening stock** control parameter is used to define whether stocks are used for the long-term planning and, if so, which ones. The following alternatives are available for long-term planning:

▶ Zero stock

▶ Safety stock

▶ Plant stock

▶ Average plant stock

Whereas no stock is used for gross requirements planning, the actual plant stock is needed for a short-term simulation. For long-term simulations, you can use the safety stock or the average plant stock, as both can be more reliable than the current plant stock. To be able to use the average plant stock, you must first determine it. This can be done using Transaction MS29 (see Figure 9.4).

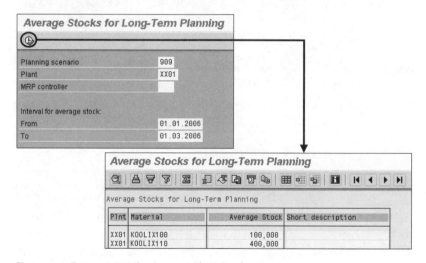

Figure 9.4 Determining the Average Plant Stock

The calculation of the average plant stock for the planning scenario specified in the transaction is based on the period in question. This period is also defined in the transaction.

Sales orders

Another control parameter defines whether sales orders are to be considered. This is primarily important for the short-term simulation. In a long-term simulation, you can usually assume that the customer requirements are sufficiently represented by the planned independent requirements. Customer requirements are consumed by the planned independent requirement version selected for the planning scenario, using the same logic as in the active version.

The consideration of make-to-order and project planning is also relevant mostly to short-term simulations, unless the portion of make-to-order and project planning affects the medium-term capacity utilization considerably.

Gross requirements planning is mainly used for cost analysis and budgeting purposes and is carried out without considering stocks, lot sizes, and scrap. In addition to using zero stock, the parameters relevant to gross requirements planning are: **Switch off scrap calculation** and **Use gross lot size**. These parameters are assigned default values when you create a gross long-term planning scenario.

Gross requirements planning

In order to obtain a picture of the current planning situation that is as accurate as possible—which is preferable for the short-term simulation—you can include firm receipts in the simulation. Figure 9.5 displays the corresponding parameters in the planning scenario.

Receipts

Figure 9.5 Parameters for Including Firm Receipts (Excerpt from the Planning Scenario)

Firm receipts include production orders, purchase orders, shipping notifications, and manual reservations, as well as scheduling agreement delivery schedules and scheduling-agreement releases. These cannot be changed in long-term planning; neither can firm purchase requisitions be changed. Firm planned orders represent an exception in this context as they can be changed within long-term planning.

When firm planned orders are included, it is actually only the planned order headers that are transferred. As a result, changes to the planned order structure get lost.

Long-term planning does not require any separate master data. However, it is possible to use different master data for long-term planning. Within the planning scenario, you can control whether a different bill of materials (BOM) or other available capacities are to be used.

Master data selection

BOM: selection ID The selection ID enables you to use separate BOMs for long-term planning purposes. To do this, you must create a separate BOM usage and assign it to a selection ID by using the order of priority for BOM usages (Transaction OS31; see Figure 9.6).

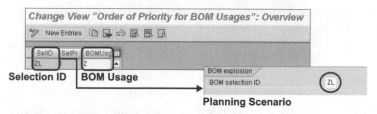

Figure 9.6 BOM Selection

You must employ the BOM usage when creating the BOM for long-term planning.

Capacity version You can maintain different capacity versions in the work center. The default versions are: normal available capacity (01), minimum available capacity (02), and maximum available capacity (03). In the planning scenario, you can select the version you want to use for the simulation (see Figure 9.7).

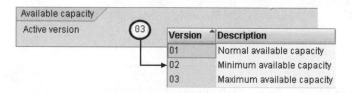

Figure 9.7 Versions of Available Capacity

The work center is described in detail in Section 5.4, while Section 11.2 contains detailed information on the available capacity.

9.3   Executing Long-Term Planning

9.3.1   Release and Planning File Entries

The first step in executing the long-term planning consists of releasing the planning scenario. When the scenario is released, planning file entries for the planning scenario are written at the same time. These planning file entries are stored in a separate planning file and can be displayed using Transaction MS21 (see Figure 9.8).

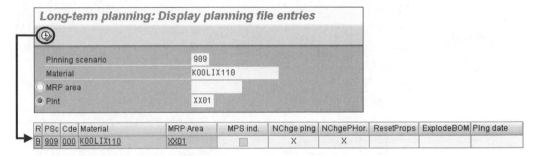

Figure 9.8 Planning File Entries for Planning Scenarios

Once a planning scenario has been released, you can no longer change its parameters. However, you can undo the release within the planning scenario.

9.3.2 Material Requirements Planning in the Planning Scenario

Long-term planning employs means similar to those used in material requirements planning. Separate transactions are available in which you must specify the planning scenario. These transactions are as follows:

- MS01—Online planning run
- MSBT—Background planning run
- MS02—Single-item planning, single-level
- MS03—Single-item planning, multilevel

Long-term planning results in simulative planned orders that exist only in the planning scenario. In other words, they are invisible to operative planning and to the stock/requirements list. In addition, you can interactively change the planned independent requirement using Transaction MS65, while Transaction MS04 enables you to perform interactive changes to the planning situation. You can create simulative planned orders using Transaction MS11 (see Figure 9.9).

Both interactively changed simulative planned orders and newly created simulative planned orders are firm. You can recognize newly created simulative planned orders by the different number range.

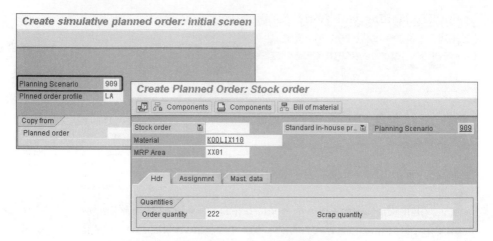

Figure 9.9 Creating Simulative Planned Orders

9.3.3 Evaluating the Planning Scenario

To evaluate the long-term planning, you can use tools that are similar to those used in material requirements planning and capacity requirements planning. As already mentioned in the previous section, you must use specific transactions to do this that allow you to enter a reference to the planning scenario. These are the following transactions:

- MS04—Requirements/Stock List
- MS05—MRP list
- MS44—Material Planning Situation
- MS47—Product Group Planning Situation
- CM38—Capacity Requirements Work Centers
- MFS0—Graphical Planning Table

Chapter 11, *Capacity Requirements Planning*, describes the transactions for capacity evaluation that correspond to CM38 and MFS0. In general, long-term planning can make use of the same options.

The ability to compare long-term planning to operative planning or another planning scenario is a unique feature. You can call this comparison as material specific and plant specific for a planning scenario by using Transaction MS44. In this context, you can choose whether you want to run a comparison with the current operative planning situation (corresponding to the requirements/stock list), with the last operative planning run (corresponding to the MRP list), or with another planning scenario. Figure 9.10 displays a comparison between long-term planning and operative planning.

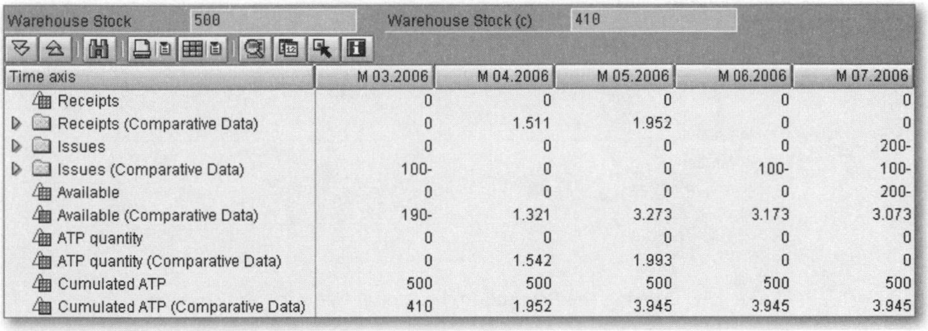

Warehouse Stock	500	Warehouse Stock (c)	410		
Time axis	M 03.2006	M 04.2006	M 05.2006	M 06.2006	M 07.2006
Receipts	0	0	0	0	0
▷ 🗀 Receipts (Comparative Data)	0	1.511	1.952	0	0
▷ 🗀 Issues	0	0	0	0	200-
▷ 🗀 Issues (Comparative Data)	100-	0	0	100-	100-
Available	0	0	0	0	200-
Available (Comparative Data)	190-	1.321	3.273	3.173	3.073
ATP quantity	0	0	0	0	0
ATP quantity (Comparative Data)	0	1.542	1.993	0	0
Cumulated ATP	500	500	500	500	500
Cumulated ATP (Comparative Data)	410	1.952	3.945	3.945	3.945

Figure 9.10 Comparison Between Long-Term Planning and Operative Planning

You can define the presentation of the comparison by means of a layout; in this case we chose the standard layout, SAPSOP. This layout displays the issues, receipts, and the available quantity for long-term planning and operative planning (indicated by **Comparative Data** in this case).

Furthermore, you can use Transactions MCB& and MCB) to evaluate inventory controlling (from info structure S094). You also can obtain analyses for materials (Transaction MCEC), suppliers (MCEA), and the material group (MCEB) for the planning scenario from the purchasing information system (info structure S012). For this purpose, you must first build up the data using Transaction MS70.

9.3.4 Transferring the Planning Scenario

It is possible to transfer planned independent requirements and firm planned orders from long-term planning into operative planning.

The transfer of planned independent requirements occurs in one of two ways. Either you activate the new planned independent requirement version and deactivate the previous one using Transaction MD62 (see Section 7.4), or you copy the new planned independent requirement version using Transaction MS64 (see Figure 9.11). The advantage of copying the new version is that this method allows you to select the period for which you want to transfer the planned independent requirement.

Transferring planned independent requirements

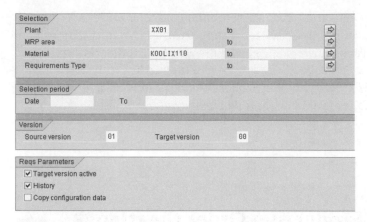

Figure 9.11 Copying the Planned Independent Requirement Version

In the selected period, the planned independent requirement of the target version is overwritten by the planned independent requirement of the source version.

Copying firm planned orders

Firm planned orders can be copied from the planning scenario into operative planning. This means that they are also firm in operative planning. The copy process itself is performed from material requirements planning using Transaction MD43 (see Figure 9.12).

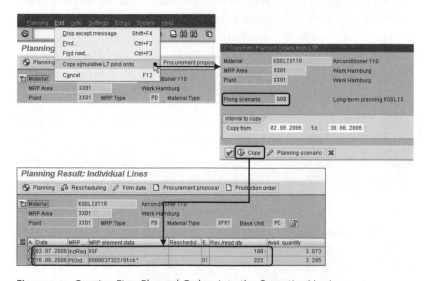

Figure 9.12 Copying Firm Planned Orders Into the Operative Version

The time fence for copying firm planned orders must be explicitly defined via the copy interval.

The central factor in controlling and recording the production process is the production order. This chapter describes how the production order is created—whether by converting a planned order or by means of interactive creation—and the functions that are executed in this process, such as masterdata selection, scheduling, and availability checking.

10 Production Order Creation

10.1 Process Overview

The previous chapters have dealt with the planning, from the sales and operations planning through the demand management and material requirements planning to the optional simulation in long-term planning. In the context of planning, the following three chapters cover the execution of production and how this is mapped in SAP ERP. The central object for production in SAP PP with its control, monitoring, and recording is the production order. Figure 10.1 shows the sequence of production-order functions.

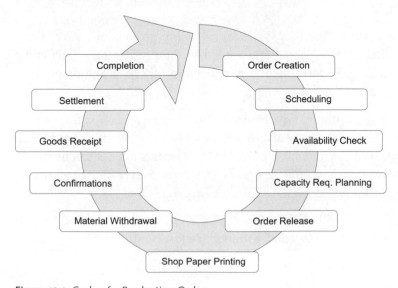

Figure 10.1 Cycle of a Production Order

When the order is created, the production order is created; the operations and material requirements then are determined based on the master data (*BOM* and *routing*). Closely associated with the creation of the order is the scheduling, which determines detailed activity dates that are required for, among other things, the capacity requirements and the material reservations. An availability check can be performed when the order is created, both for material components and capacity. These steps will be explained in the following sections.

Capacity requirements planning

To create a feasible production plan, you need to bring the operations of the production order into a sequence that is capacity-adjusted. This task is done using the planning and is described in Chapter 11, *Capacity Requirements Planning*. Often, capacity-requirements planning is performed based on production orders, to adjust the production dates to the available capacity. However, this step is optional. In special cases, the capacity requirements planning can also be performed earlier or later. These situations also are described in Chapter 11.

Production execution

The *production execution* is started when the order is released. This causes the status of the production order to change and functions as the technical system requirement for the subsequent steps. These include the shop paper printing, material withdrawal for the components, confirmation to the goods receipt, and invoicing through to completion. Another availability check can be performed during the release.

This chapter describes the creation of the production order. Here, the master data is read and copied to the production order, and a scheduling is performed. An availability check is optionally performed as a further step.

The most common type of production-order creation is the conversion of a planned order. An interactive creation of a production order without reference to a planned order is also possible, however. Figure 10.2 shows the process overview for the creation of a production order.

Chapter 12 will explain the steps for controlling, monitoring, and recording the production with the production order.

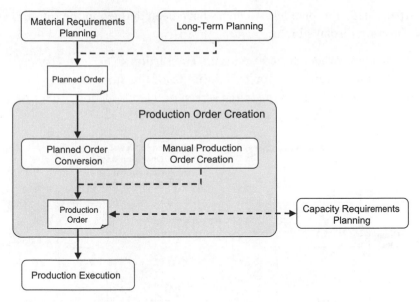

Figure 10.2 Process Overview Production Order Creation

10.2 Production Order

10.2.1 Structure of the Production Order

The task of the production order is both to control production and to record production in terms of quantity and costs. Controlling production includes, among other things, providing the information as to what product should be manufactured in what quantity and with what resources at what time. To this end, the production order needs to contain master data and control parameters. In line with the master data *Routing* and *BOM*, the production order primarily comprises the following.

▶ *Header data*, which contains organizational information such as the order number and costs, quantities and dates for the order as a whole

▶ *Operation data*, which contains detailed operations dates, default values, and the confirmed quantities and dates

▶ *Component data* on the operations, such as the requirements quantity and reservation number

If alternative or parallel sequences have been defined in the routing, these are displayed in the *sequence overview*.

Production orders are created with Transaction CO01 and changed with Transaction CO02 or by editing from the stock/requirements list. Figure 10.3 shows the initial screen of the production order processing.

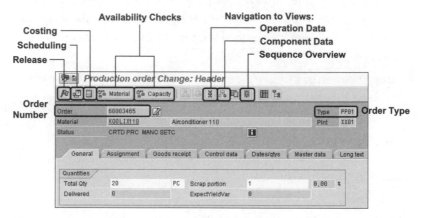

Figure 10.3 Production Order Initial Screen

We'll now describe the views for **header data**, **operation data**, and **component data** with the most important information.

Header data ⟶ On the initial screen, the *header data* contains the organizational data such as the order number, header material, plant, and order type. In addition, in the **General** view, it provides the information on the order's total and scrap quantity, and the quantity that has already been confirmed. Furthermore, you will find the basic dates here—copied from the planned order—and the dates calculated during the creation of the order via finite scheduling. The dates are based on the routing, from the beginning of the first transaction to the end of the last transaction. The scheduling parameters and buffer times used for this are also shown (see Figure 10.4).

Some additional views of the production order are as follows, with a number of selected fields.

▸ **Assignment**
Here the responsible MRP controller and production scheduler, as well as the cost center, are entered.

▶ **Goods receipt**
This contains control parameters for goods movements, deviation tolerances, the goods-receipt processing time and the production location.

▶ **Control**
This contains the parameters for the calculation, the production-scheduling profile and control parameters for scheduling. These are: creating capacity requirements, scheduling allowing for breaks, and automatic rescheduling in the event of scheduling-relevant changes.

▶ **Dates/Quantities**
This view contains the overview of planned and actual times and quantities.

▶ **Master data**
This view lists the production version, routing and BOM that were used.

▶ **Long text**
Here you can maintain a long text.

▶ **Administration**
This view keeps the date and user of the last change, and also of the creation.

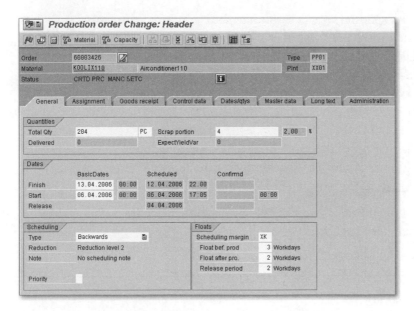

Figure 10.4 Production Order Initial Screen (Header Data)

We also can access the view **SAP Event Management**, which is only relevant when used in conjunction with the *Event Management* program to monitor production progress.

The structure of the production process is mapped in the so-called **operation overview**. This screen lists the operations that have been copied from the routing and that are scheduled for the order (see Figure 10.5). For each operation, there is an operation number, and possibly a sub-operation number. The work center is specified, and so is the control key, which determines how the operation should be handled; e.g., whether it must be confirmed, whether it can be scheduled, or whether it can be printed. Other listed data includes the status of the operation (whether it is already created or released), the operation's start and end date, the short description and the assignment flag for material components, production resources/tools (PRTs), and trigger points. From the operation overview screen, depending on the application and requirements, you can branch to the individual detail screens. Figure 10.3 shows the initial screen for the operation data and the detail operation screens, which you reach by double-clicking on the specific operation.

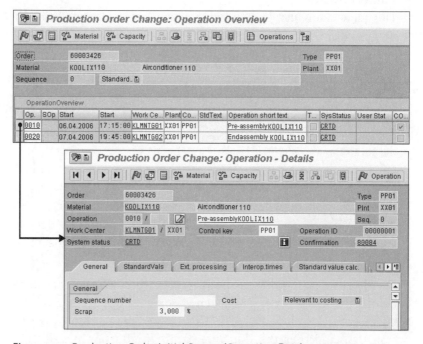

Figure 10.5 Production Order Initial Screen (Operation Data)

The most important steps for the operation data are listed as follows.

▶ **General**
This contains general information on the operation, such as the percentage scrap, number of shop floor papers to be printed, wage group, and setup type key. It also contains the calculation relevance indicator, which specifies whether the operation is included in the calculation.

▶ **Default values**
This view contains the default values from the routing, related to the operation quantity; i.e., planned values for performing the operation and the corresponding units. Costs, cycle times, and capacity requirements are calculated using the default values.

▶ **External processing**
This view contains information on externally processed operations such as subcontracting, which involves operations processed at a supplier. The purchasing info record, for example, is stored here. It is only relevant for operations that are externally processed according to the control key.

▶ **Transition times**
This view contains scheduling data that affects the operation segments outside the execution time. This includes the reduction strategy and level and the pertinent transition times: wait time, queue time, and move time. This screen is only relevant for operations that can be scheduled according to the control key.

▶ **Default value determination**
Aside from manually assigning default values, you can determine default values through the system. On this screen, you can maintain data that specifies how the default values are determined (e.g., via CAP or by estimating), in what year the default values were determined, what document was used to determine the default values, and through what default value code the default values were calculated (e. g. a table containing planned times).

▶ **Splitting**
On the detail operation screen **splitting** you can maintain data that controls whether, how and when an operation may or must be split during the scheduling. This data affects the operation's execution time and thus the lead time in the production order. This

screen is only relevant for operations that can be scheduled according to the control key.

▶ **Overlapping**
On the detail operation screen **overlapping,** you can maintain data on operations that are to be overlapped during the scheduling. The question here is thus whether the operation should be overlapped, and by what overlapping time. This data affects the lead time in the production order. This screen is only relevant for operations that can be scheduled according to the control key.

▶ **Dates**
This view contains the results of the finite scheduling for the operation. It is only relevant for operations that can be scheduled according to the control key. The scheduling determines dates for the operation segments setup time, processing time, tear-down time, and wait time. For each of these operation segments, the duration and the earliest and/or latest start date, with time, are determined. In determining the earliest dates and times, the system assumes that only the minimal queue and wait time are used. In determining the latest dates and times, the system assumes that the normal queue and wait times are used.

▶ **Quantities/activities**
Here the confirmed quantities and activities for the operation are displayed.

▶ **Dates confirmed**
This view contains the actual dates for the processing

▶ **Capacity requirement assignment**
On this screen, you can split the total requirement of the operation into sub-requirements.

Component data If there are components in the routing, they always must be assigned to an operation in the production order. The components that have not already been assigned to a particular operation in the routing are automatically assigned to the first operation by the system when the production order is created. However, you have the option at any time of assigning components from one operation to another. Components that are to be procured for specific orders can be assigned a flag in the bill of materials (BOM). When the order is created, purchase requisitions are generated automatically for these materials. The components are ordered order-specifically through the purchase functions of the materials management and provided for the production order. For operations that are performed by another company (external processing), purchase requirements are also generated for the purchase. Close integration with the purchase functions also guarantees a smooth operation processing here (see *SAP Production Planning*, 1996, p. 9.1–9.5).

The component data lists the components of the BOM, or the components of the planned order in the case of planned order conversion, with their respective requirements quantities (see Figure 10.6). The component requirements already contain the planned scrap.

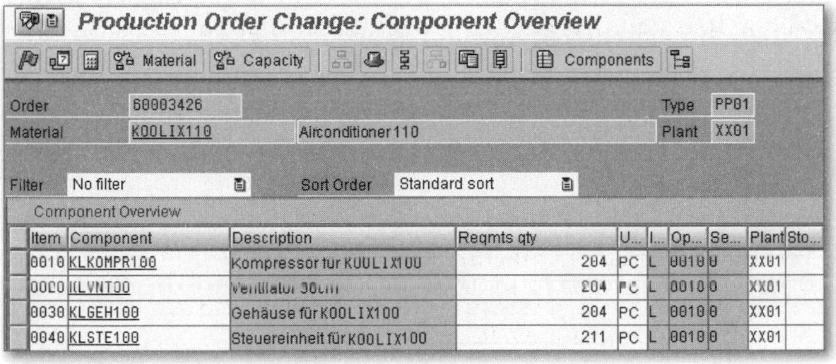

Figure 10.6 Production Order Initial Screen (Component Data)

Similar to the operation data, detailed views are also available for the components. Unlike the operation data, however, these are only relevant under particular conditions. These conditions include **purchase data** for non-stock items or **variable-size item data** for variable-size items. The **general data** specifies, among other things, the assignment to the operation and the reservation number for the component requirement.

10.2.2 Order Type

The order type is an important control quantity for the production order. It is maintained with the Customizing Transaction OPJH and controls the following functions directly or through these additional profiles:

▶ Internal and external number assignment

▶ Classification

▶ Commitments management

▶ Status management for the different production statuses

▶ Settlement

▶ Scheduling

The order type also controls additional functions—such as the availability check—which are performed status-dependently in the production order.

During the interactive creation of a production order, the order type is explicitly specified. When a planned order is converted, it is determined using the production scheduler, which is assigned to the material through the production scheduling profile. Figure 10.7 shows the relationship between the order type, production scheduling profile, production scheduler, scheduling profile, and check control. Apart from the order type and the settlement profile, all objects are plant-dependent.

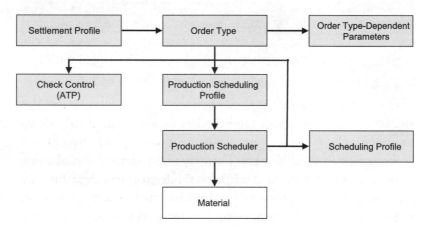

Figure 10.7 Order Type and Dependent Profiles

The settlement profile is defined in Customizing for the controlling and determines which of the costs that arise for the production order can be settled and in what way.

Order type-dependent parameters

The order type-dependent parameters are maintained with Customizing Transaction OPL8 for the combination of order type and plant. They contain control parameters for:

▶ **Planning**
Master data selection, batch determination, purchase requisition, quality check

▶ **Realization**
Status change documents, production information system, documentation of goods movements

▶ **Cost accounting**
Calculation variants, planned cost determination, distribution rules

▶ **Display profiles**

Section 10.2.3 discusses the parameters of the master data selection in detail.

The check control defines whether and how you can perform a check of the material availability, the capacity availability, and the availability of PRTs. There are two separate check controls: one for the check during creation and one for the check during the release of the production order. In other words, you can set a different check behavior for the creation and for the release; for example, no check for creation, but only for the release. The check control is created with Customizing Transaction OPJK and described in detail in Section 12.3.

Check control

The production scheduling profile defines what functions of the production order are executed automatically during creation and release and what order types are used for make-to-stock production, make-to-order production, project planning, and production without material reference. Furthermore, the production scheduling profile contains additional control parameters for the availability check of material and capacity, for the confirmation and for the transport. These are described in Chapter 12, *Production Execution*. Figure 10.8 shows a segment from the production- scheduling profile. The production-scheduling profile is maintained with Customizing Transaction OPKP.

Production scheduling profile

The scheduling profile determines, depending on the order type and production scheduler, control parameters for the scheduling. This could include what type of scheduling is used (backward or forward) and how reductions are made. The scheduling profile is maintained with Customizing Transaction OPU3 and is described in detail in Section 10.5.

Scheduling profile

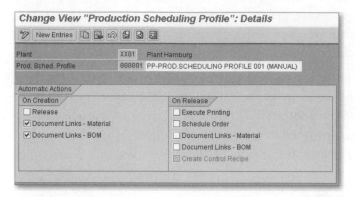

Figure 10.8 Production Scheduling Profile (Section)

The production scheduler and the assignment to the material are described in Section 4.3.

10.2.3 Master Data Selection

The master-data selection for the production order is maintained in the order type-dependent parameters with Customizing Transaction OPL8 (see Section 10.2.1). Figure 10.9 shows these parameters.

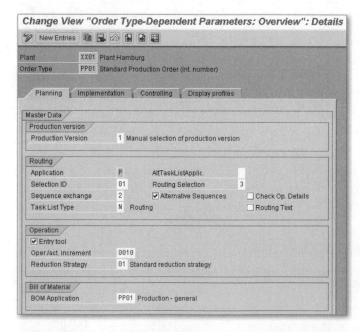

Figure 10.9 Master Data Selection Parameters in the Order Type-Dependent Parameters

We will now outline the rules for the selection of the routing, BOM, and production version. The entry aid for operations is only relevant for the interactive creation without a routing.

The parameter for the **routing selection** in the order type-dependent parameters controls whether a routing must be used; that is, as an absolute requirement or as a suggestion. It also controls whether the selection is performed manually or automatically and whether standard routings are allowed (see Figure 10.10).

Routing selection

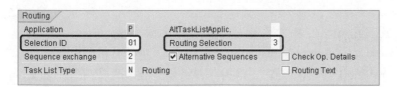

Routing			
Application	P	AltTaskListApplic.	
Selection ID	01	Routing Selection	3
Sequence exchange	2	✔ Alternative Sequences	☐ Check Op. Details
Task List Type	N	Routing	☐ Routing Text

Figure 10.10 Routing Selection Parameters in the Order Type-Dependent Parameters

The selection ID specifies a selection sequence according to the planned type, usage, and status of the plan. The selection ID is defined through the Customizing Transaction OPJF (see Figure 10.11).

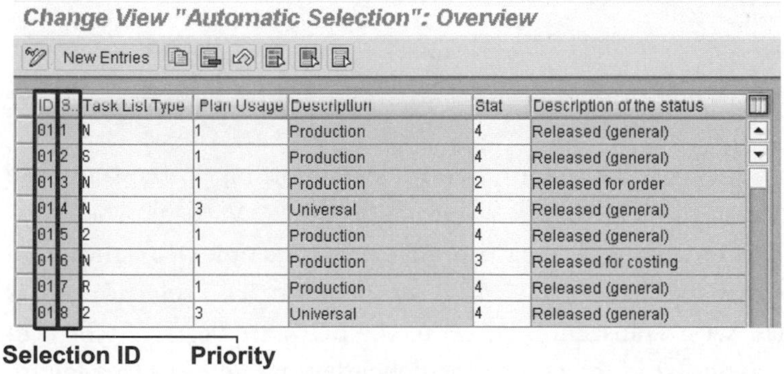

Change View "Automatic Selection": Overview

New Entries

ID	S.	Task List Type	Plan Usage	Description	Stat	Description of the status	
01	1	N	1	Production	4	Released (general)	
01	2	S	1	Production	4	Released (general)	
01	3	N	1	Production	2	Released for order	
01	4	N	3	Universal	4	Released (general)	
01	5	2	1	Production	4	Released (general)	
01	6	N	1	Production	3	Released for costing	
01	7	R	1	Production	4	Released (general)	
01	8	2	3	Universal	4	Released (general)	

Selection ID   Priority

Figure 10.11 Selection ID

In order for a routing to be selected, it must be permitted for the lot size of the order, and it must be valid at the order's start date.

If it has been defined in the material master that a selection according to production versions should be run, the routing selection set by selection ID is overridden. This is defined with the alternative selection parameter (**AlternSelection**) in the view **MRP 4**, as shown in Fig-

Selecting the production version

ure 10.13 for the BOM selection. If there are several production versions, the selection is performed either manually or automatically, depending on the entry in the order type-dependent parameters (see Figure 10.12).

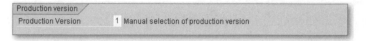

Figure 10.12 Production Version Selection Parameters in the Order Type-Dependent Parameters

BOM selection The selection of the BOM is also determined using the alternative selection parameter (**AlternSelection**) in the material master (see Figure 10.13). Here you can select by quantity, date, or production version.

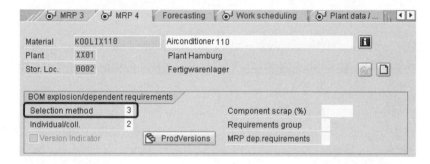

Figure 10.13 Selection ID

When you select by quantity, you select according to the sequence specified in the selection ID according to the BOM usage. The selection ID is created with the Customizing Transaction OPJI, shown in Figure 9.6 in Chapter 9, *Long-Term Planning*. The selection ID is assigned with Transaction OPJM to the BOM application, which in turn is assigned to the order type-dependent parameters (see Figure 10.14).

The selection by dates is performed according to the alternative BOM selection specified with Transaction OS32.

Here, a BOM alternative is assigned in each case for different validity dates. Thus, in the example shown in Figure 10.15, the BOM alternative 1 is valid as from 1.1.2005, but BOM alternative 2 as valid from 1.8.2006.

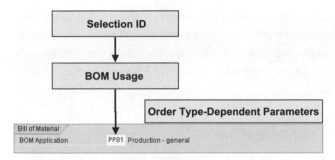

Figure 10.14 BOM Selection by Quantity

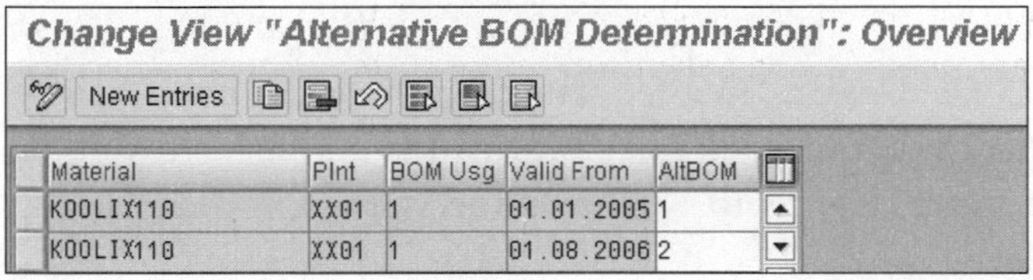

Change View "Alternative BOM Determination": Overview

Material	Plnt	BOM Usg	Valid From	AltBOM	
KOOLIX110	XX01	1	01.01.2005	1	
KOOLIX110	XX01	1	01.08.2006	2	

Figure 10.15 BOM Selection by Date

The production version is selected as described earlier in this chapter.

Once the production order is created, subsequent changes to the BOM or routing are not copied to the production order. However, if this is not desired, it is possible to read the master data from the production order via the menu path **Functions • Read PP Master Data** (see Figure 10.16).

Reading master data

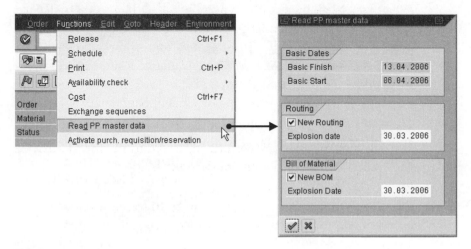

Figure 10.16 Reading the Master Data

When you read the BOM, the components of the production order are deleted; the operations are deleted when you read the routing. Interactive changes are thus lost. If the editing of the production order has already progressed too far, it is no longer possible to read the master data.

10.2.4 Status and Trigger Point

The production order has status indicators at header level and at operation level that show what functions the production order has already run. Here a distinction is made between the system status and the user status. The system statuses are set by the program according to fixed rules. The user status, on the other hand, can be freely defined, to obtain additional information on the history of the production order. Figure 10.17 shows the status at header and at operation level.

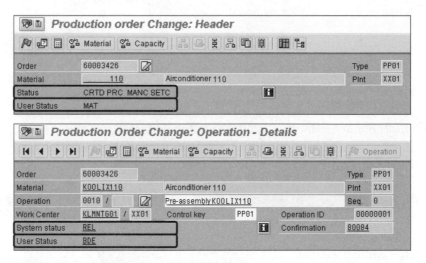

Figure 10.17 Status at Header and Operation Level

The status of the production order becomes inactive if it no longer applies because of a subsequent function. Through the filter button in the status detail, you can control whether only the active statuses or both active and inactive statuses are displayed (see Figure 10.18).

Trigger point Often we want predefined functions to be triggered when a particular event occurs in the production order. This can be achieved with so-called *trigger points*. Trigger points define functions—such as the release of directly following operations or the triggering of a work-flow—that are started automatically for an operation when an event occurs. An example of such an event would be a status change from "created" to "released." Trigger points are directly assigned to the operations in the routing or production order.

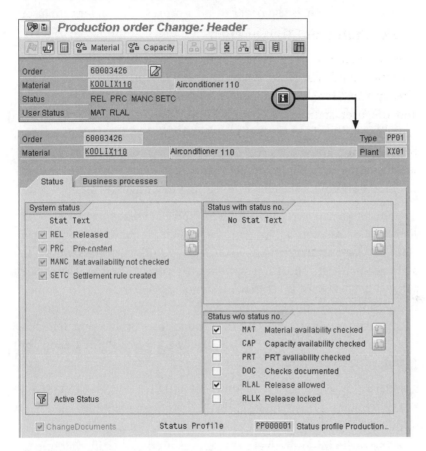

Figure 10.18 Status Detail

With trigger points, the following functions can be executed.

► **Release of directly following operations**
The occurrence of the event (e.g., operation was released) triggers the automatic release of the subsequent operations.

► **Release up to release point**
The occurrence of the event triggers the release of all subsequent operations, up to and including the next operation, which is given the **Release Stop** indicator.

▶ **Release of previous operations**
The occurrence of the event triggers the release of all previous operations.

▶ **Create order with template**
The occurrence of an event (e.g., material is faulty) means that a new order, such as the order to post-process the material, can be created. The order is created using a standard routing without reference to a material.

▶ **Include standard routing**
Because of an event, a standard routing can be incorporated into an existing order. In this case, operations must be specified between which the standard routing should be inserted.

▶ **Trigger workflow**
The occurrence of an event (e.g., material is not available) can trigger a workflow task, such as e-mailing to a buyer.

To reduce the creative work involved, you can create *standard trigger points*. They serve as a copy template when you are creating trigger points. Various different standard trigger points can be assembled in a trigger-point group. If a trigger point group is used as a template when a trigger point is created, all standard trigger points are copied to the operation automatically. Trigger point groups are created in Customizing under the menu path **Production • Production Scheduling • Master Data • Trigger Point • Define Trigger Point Group for Standard Trigger Points**.

Standard trigger points are maintained with Transactions CO31 and CO32. They are either copied directly or as a template into the operation of the routing or are copied directly to the production order. The **Trigger Point Functions** parameter is used to specify that one of the above-described functions is to be controlled by the trigger point. In the event that a trigger point with the function **Release up to release point** is used for an operation, an additional trigger point with the **Release Stop** parameter is required. The additional trigger point must be assigned to the corresponding operation, after which no more releases are to be performed.

The functions to be executed in the trigger point must be selected and parameterized. The parameters include the following.

▶ **System status (SystStat)**

Here you determine which system status triggers the function. Only a subset of the system status can be selected, such as Release (REL), Confirmation (CONF), Partial Confirmation (PCONF), or Operation is Scheduled (SCHD). This is the system status of the operation.

▶ **Change (Chng)**

This specifies whether the function is executed when setting, resetting, or both.

▶ **Triggering (Trggr)**

This defines whether the function is triggered by a status change and/or manually.

Figure 10.19 shows a standard trigger point that automatically releases the subsequent operation for the system status FREE.

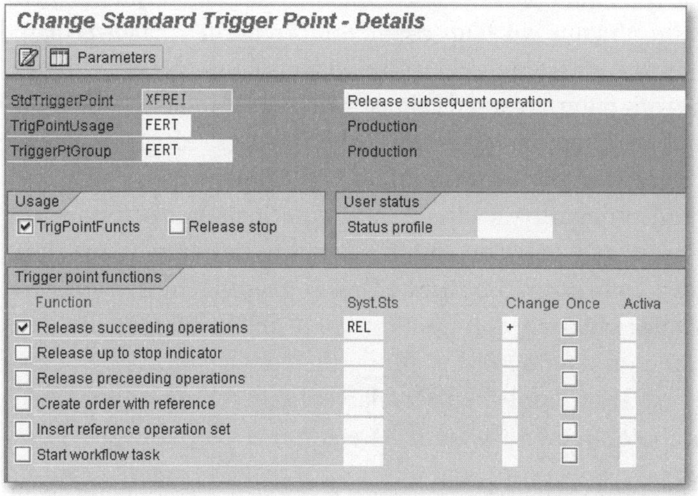

Figure 10.19 Standard Trigger Point

Assignment to the routing is performed using the menu path **Goto • Trigger Point Overview** from the operation detail. Figure 10.20 shows the trigger point overview.

Trigger points can be copied using the **StdTriggPnt** button. Alternatively, trigger points can also be defined directly in the routing.

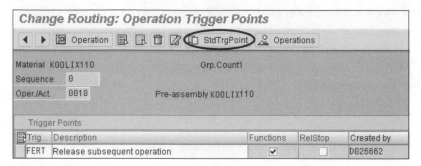

Figure 10.20 Trigger Point Overview in the Routing

10.3 Conversion from the Planned Order

The planned orders created in the upstream planning are generally the starting point for creation of the production order. Planned orders that were generated in the context of the requirements planning for requirements coverage contain information as to what material must be manufactured, when, and in what quantity, to cover the existing requirements. These planned orders (elements of the planning) are now converted into production orders (elements of the control). Here, the data contained in the planned order (material number, order quantity, start and end date, material components, etc.) is copied and enhanced with additional order-relevant data, such as operation data. The material components required for production that are contained as items in the planned order are directly copied to the production order during the conversion. The BOM is not exploded again, and the secondary requirements generated in the material requirements planning are automatically converted into reservations. The operation and PRT data are taken from the routing of the material to be manufactured. If the requirements quantity copied from the planned order or the basic finish date are changed during the conversion, a planning file entry is generated that triggers a rescheduling of the material and its components during the next material requirements planning.

A prerequisite for a planned order conversion is that you must have the basic data of BOMs and routings, as well as the functionality of the material requirements planning. The planned order conversion can be performed as an individual or collective conversion.

If you want to convert a particular planned order into a production order, the easiest way to do this is interactively as an individual conversion, for example from the requirements/stock list (Transaction MD04). Figure 10.21 shows this conversion from the detail screen of the planned order.

Individual conversion

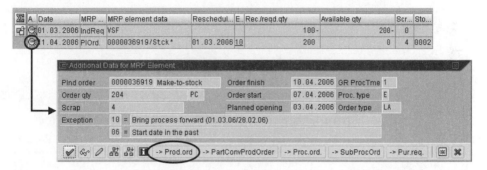

Figure 10.21 Individual Conversion from the Stock/Requirements List

An alternative to this method is the individual conversion of a planned order with Transaction CO40. As a result of the conversion, a production order is created in each case for the planned order, which must still be saved in the dialog.

When you convert a planned order into a production order, the following main steps are performed.

- Material components are copied from the planned order.
- Reservations are created for the material components.
- Routing is determined and operations are transferred.
- Finite scheduling of operations is completed.
- Planned costs are calculated (optional).

The calculation of the costs during the settlement of the production order is described in Chapter 12, *Production Execution.*

It is also possible to partially convert planned orders. During a partial conversion, the planned order quantity is divided into different sub-quantities. A separate production order is generated for each subset. The planned order is then reduced by the corresponding quantity.

Partial conversion

In the productive environment, the planned order conversion is generally performed as a collective conversion with Transaction CO41.

Collective conversion

The time of the conversion is guided by the opening date, which occurs around the opening period prior to the order start date of the planned order and allows for the lead times that are required from an organizational point of view. Further selection criteria include plant, MRP controller, production scheduler, and material (see Figure 10.22).

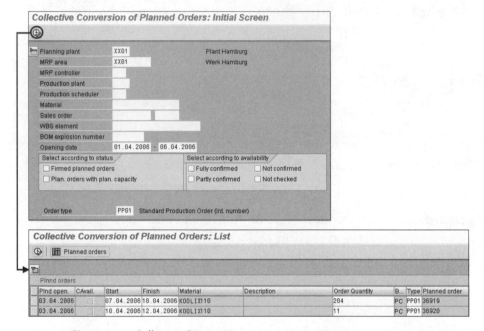

Figure 10.22 Collective Conversion

The scheduling of the opening date based on the opening period is illustrated in Figure 8.44. The opening period forms part of the scheduling margin key (see Section 10.5.4).

10.4 Interactive Production Order Creation

Another method of production order creation is to interactively create a production order. There are two alternatives: creation with reference to a material, and creation without material reference.

With material reference

The production order relates specifically to a material that is to be manufactured with a plant specified. An important control field for the *Production order* document is the order type on the initial screen (see Section 10.2.2). The operation overview screen lists all operations copied from the routing and scheduled for the order. Interactive production-order creation with reference to a material is performed with Transaction CO01.

You also can create a production order without a reference to a material; for example, you may wish to create a capacity placeholder for post-processing or for maintenance works without using the maintenance orders. The interactive production order creation without a material reference is performed with Transaction CO07 (see Figure 10.23).

Without material
reference

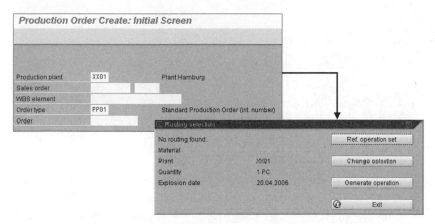

Figure 10.23 Production Order Creation Without a Material Reference

The production order requires the mandatory entry of a short text at header level, as a replacement for the material number. Then, you must decide whether the processing should take place with a standard routing. If no standard planning has been provided, a standard sequence is generated automatically by the system with an operation. In addition to the production order, the desired allocation receiver is determined with the necessary data for the settlement rule.

10.5 Scheduling

10.5.1 Dates of the Production Order

Unlike the planned order, which is used for the material requirements planning in the first instance, you need to set dates for the individual operations with the production order for controlling production. As well as the pure processing duration of the operation, here you must also add transition times (wait time, queue time, move time) and safety times (float before production, safety time). Figure 10.24 offers an overview of the dates of the production order. In this example, three operations are involved.

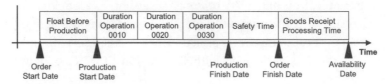

Figure 10.24 Dates of the Production Order

These dates are shown in the initial screen of the production order, as shown in Figure 10.25.

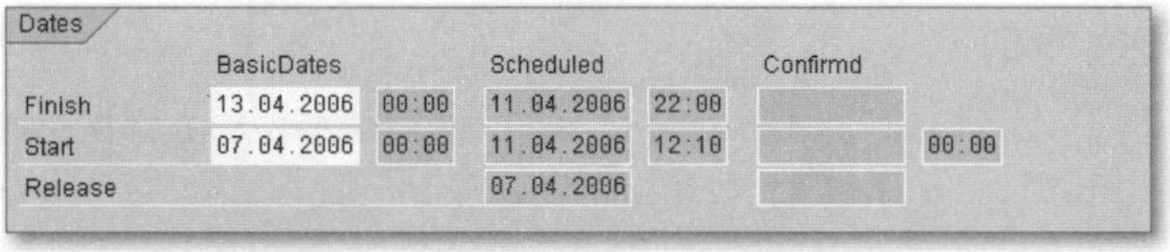

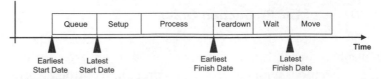

Figure 10.25 Dates of the Production Order at Header Level

In this example, the order start date is 7.4.2006, and the order finish date is 13.4.2006. No time is specified in either case. The scheduled finish date—11.4.2006 at 22:00—has been arrived at through backward scheduling, by deducting the safety time based on the order-finish date. The latest time on 11.4, according to the working time, is 22:00. It is from this time that the routing is resolved and the operation durations are calculated and scheduled according to the working times. The order start date is determined by deducting the float before production from the scheduled start date. The float before production and safety time are discussed in greater detail in Section 10.5.5.

Operation dates The duration of the operation is made up of waiting, setup, edit, teardown, storage, and transport (see Figure 10.26).

Figure 10.26 Dates of the Operation

In the production order, the operation dates are displayed in the operation detail in the view **Dates** (see Figure 10.27). However, only the start dates and the duration of the operation segments are listed here.

| Splitting | Overlap | Dates | User fields | Suboperation Dates | Qty/activit... |

Dates for Operation Segments

	Earliest Dates		Latest Dates		Duratn	Unit
Queue					70,0	MIN
Setup	11.04.2006		11.04.2006		30,0	MIN
	12:10:00		13:20:00			
Processing	11.04.2006		11.04.2006		120,0	MIN
	12:40:00		13:50:00			
Teardown	11.04.2006	11.04.2006	11.04.2006	11.04.2006	0,0	MIN
	14:40:00	14:40:00	15:50:00	15:50:00		
Wait	11.04.2006	11.04.2006	11.04.2006	11.04.2006	10,0	MIN
	14:40:00	14:50:00	15:50:00	16:00:00		
Move					60,0	MIN

Figure 10.27 Dates of the Operation in the Detail Operation Screen

The difference between the earliest dates and the latest dates is derived from the queue time. While the normal queue time is assumed for the backward scheduling between the wait time and the move time, it still acts as a buffer at the start of the operation because of the splitting into earliest and latest dates. The process-determined wait time is also given start and end dates for the teardown, because these can work in parallel. Figure 10.28 illustrates the dates of the operation segments from Figure 10.27.

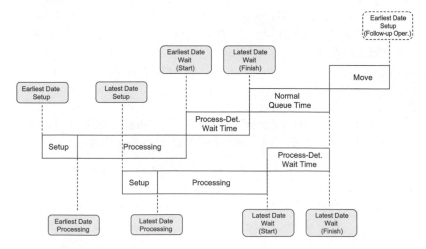

Figure 10.28 Earliest and Latest Dates of the Operation Components

The starting point for the backward scheduling is the earliest date for setting up the follow-up operation or—if it is the last operation—the scheduled finish date.

10.5.2 Finite Scheduling

In finite scheduling and lead-time minimizing, we first define the start dates and end dates of the process steps pertaining to a production order without regard to capacity restrictions. The purpose is to test the feasibility of the finish date of the production order that was specified in the materials-management process.

Forward scheduling and backward scheduling are the procedures used for this purpose. Backward scheduling determines the start date of the production order based on the latest finish date; that is, the order-finish date of the planned order. During the forward scheduling, the finish date of the production order is determined based on the earliest start date; that is, the order start date of the planned order. However, you should note that the planned date is only realistic within forward scheduling if all planned materials are available at the start date.

Finite scheduling is carried out individually for each order; any interdependencies that may exist between various orders are not taken into account. If the date cannot be kept to, you can minimize the lead time by overlapping, splitting, and reducing the transition times (see Section 10.5.5). Through the splitting, you can divide a production lot into several sub-lots, which then are manufactured at the same time on alternative machines. During overlapping, processed parts of the total lot are directly passed on to the next machine. Reducing the transition times means that any lead time portions that do not belong to the processing time can be reduced. The execution of the finite scheduling and reduction tasks depends partly on the production organization. Because of the high wait times, lead-time reduction measures are especially relevant in workshop production.

When the production order is created, lead-time scheduling is performed that calculates detailed dates for each scheduling-relevant operation and takes into account transition times between the operations and safety times. Here, the factory calendar and the working times of the relevant resources are taken into account. During scheduling, we proceed based on the existing basic dates. The basic dates (basic start date for forward scheduling and basic finish date for backward scheduling) are either copied from the planned order or entered on the header area of the production order for manual creation. The results of the finite scheduling are the production dates, both at header and at operation level.

The operation durations are calculated based on the default values of the routing and the scheduling formulas of the work center (see Section 5.4). Transition and safety times are explained in subsequent sections.

Operation durations

The factory calendar determines what days are worked. The factory calendar is defined with the Customizing Transaction SCAL. It includes the definition of the working days and the assignment of the public holiday calendar defined with the same transaction. The factory calendar for the capacity is decisive for scheduling. If no factory calendar is maintained in the capacity, we refer to the factory calendar of the plant.

Factory calendar

The working times of the resources are explained in Section 5.4. A work break causes the operation to lengthen.

Working times

The capacity's rate of capacity utilization reflects reduced downtime. The scheduling takes the rate of capacity utilization into account by extending the operation duration accordingly. Figure 10.29 shows the maintenance of the rate of capacity utilization in the capacity of the work center.

Rate of capacity utilization

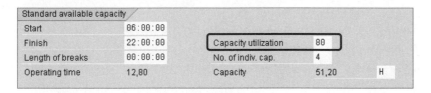

Standard available capacity				
Start	06:00:00			
Finish	22:00:00	Capacity utilization	80	
Length of breaks	00:00:00	No. of indiv. cap.	4	
Operating time	12,80	Capacity	51,20	H

Figure 10.29 Rate of Capacity Utilization of the Capacity

The rate of capacity utilization only affects the determination of the operation dates, not the determination of the operation durations. This is illustrated in Figure 10.30 by the operation dates of the production order.

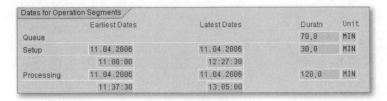

Figure 10.30 Effect on Scheduling

For example, for the earliest dates, you can identify that **setup** begins at 11:00 and lasts for 30 minutes, but that processing can only begin after 37:30 minutes due to the reduced rate of capacity utilization.

Scheduling type   You control how scheduling should be performed through the following scheduling types.

▸ During *backward scheduling* you proceed from the basic finish date and determine the other dates in a backwards calculation.

▸ During *forward scheduling* you proceed from the basic start date and determine the other dates in a forwards calculation.

▸ The *today scheduling* corresponds to the forward scheduling. Here, today's date is used as the basic start date.

▸ With the scheduling type *only capacity requirements*, only the capacity requirements are calculated. The individual operations are not scheduled, and the basic dates are copied as operation dates.

The scheduling types are defined with Customizing Transaction OPJN.

During the backward scheduling, the production finish date, production start date, and basic start date are determined based on the basic finish date. During forward scheduling, the production start date, production finish date, and basic finish date are determined based on the basic start date.

Scheduling profile   The scheduling type is assigned to the production order type with the Customizing Transaction OPU3 in the scheduling profile. Figure 10.31 shows a section from the scheduling profile. In this case, the parameters are valid for all production schedulers; however, production scheduler-specific maintenance would also be possible.

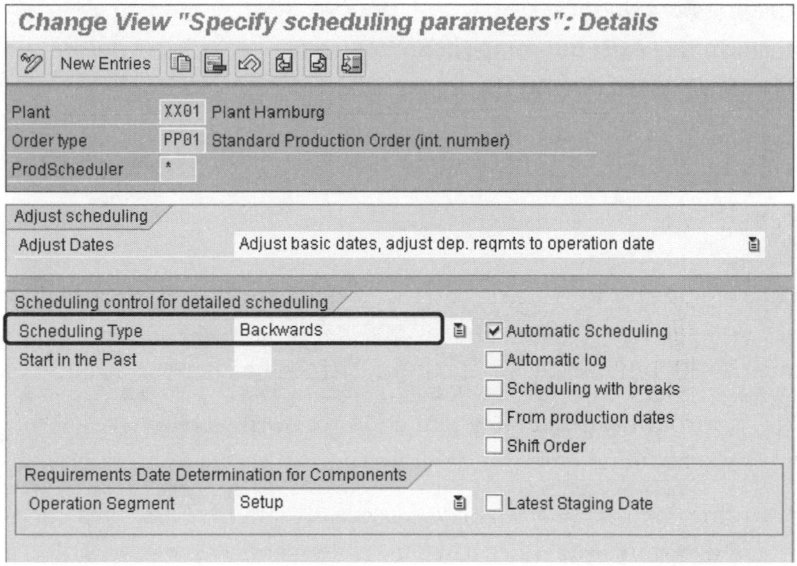

Figure 10.31 Scheduling Profile (Section)

The parameter **Start in the Past** specifies how many days in the past the basic start date may be before the scheduling type is overridden and the today scheduling (forward scheduling from today) is used.

The parameter **Adjust dates** describes whether basic finish dates are newly determined. During backward scheduling, this would apply to the basic start dates. Alternatively, this parameter could show that the basic dates as well as the dates of the secondary requirements are transferred. Figure 10.32 illustrates the possibilities. In this example it is assumed that the components are assigned to the first operation.

Date adjustment

If the secondary requirements are to be assigned to the operations, you can use the **Operation segment** parameter of the scheduling profile to determine whether this should take place during setup, processing, or teardown.

Scheduling the secondary requirements

The component requirement can be a lead time or an interval before or after the start date of the operation. This creates a buffer as the lead time or allows for handling that is not modeled further. An interval exists if a component is only required in the advanced stage of a (long) operation. A lead time is maintained as a negative interval. The interval is maintained in days either in the BOM or directly in the production order in the general data of the component. Figure

10.33 shows the effect of a lead time on the component requirement. In this case, the component requirement is one day before the beginning of the operation.

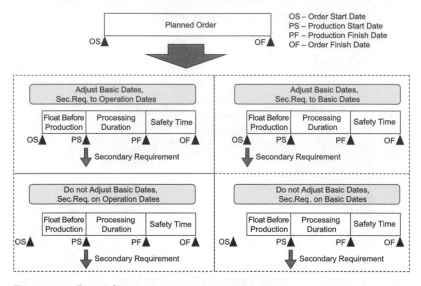

Figure 10.32 Date Adjustment

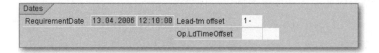

Figure 10.33 Lead time and Interval

The scheduling is always performed when the production order is created. When there are scheduling-relevant changes, you can use the parameter **Automatic Scheduling** of the scheduling profile (see Figure 10.31) to control whether a new scheduling should be performed when saving, or whether the old dates should be retained. In the latter case, the system status NTER is set.

The prerequisite for an operation being scheduled in the first place is that there must be a corresponding control key. Control keys are assigned to the operations in the routing (see Section 5.5). What is decisive in scheduling is that the **Schedule** parameter must be set. The control key is defined with Customizing Transaction OP67 (see Figure 10.34).

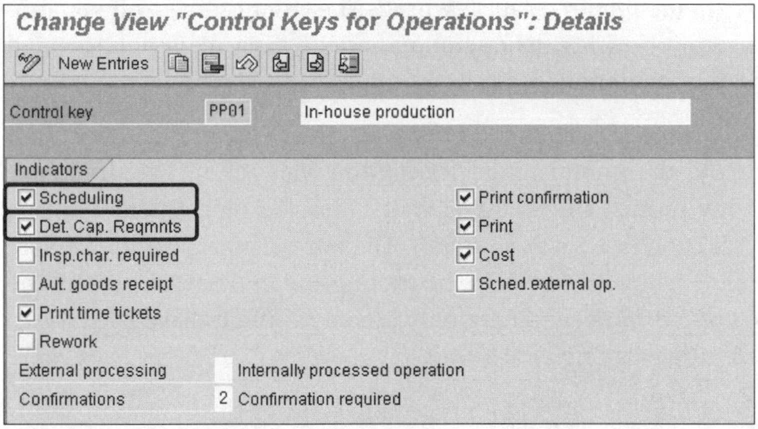

Figure 10.34 Scheduling Profile (Extract)

Unlike the determination of basic dates, which is usually used for the material requirements planning, the finite scheduling also determines capacity requirements. The prerequisite in effect here is that the **Determine CapReq.** parameter must be set in the operation's control key. The capacity requirements are calculated based on the capacity formulas of the work center (see Section 5.4) and form the basis for capacity requirements planning.

Capacity requirements

10.5.3 Transition Times

The transition times queue time, wait time, and move time relate to the operation and are maintained in the routing. Figure 10.35 shows the maintenance of the transition times in the operation detail of the routing (Transaction CA01/CA02).

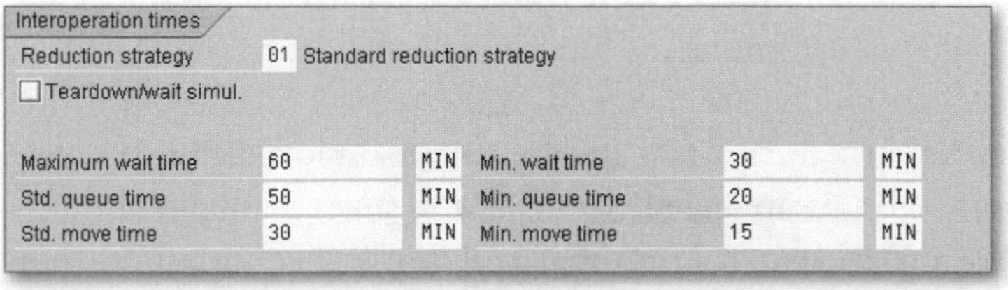

Figure 10.35 Maintenance of the Transition Data in the Routing

The queue time occurs before the production start date of the operation. It forms a buffer for a delayed material provision—in cases such as a delay of a production order for a semi-finished product—and for

Queue time

a delay in the required capacity itself. The latter can occur if you cannot begin processing the operation because capacity is still occupied with other operations.

The wait time is maintained with two values: the normal (**Nor. wait time**) and the minimal wait time (**Min. wait time**). The difference from the normal and minimal wait times can be shortened during the reduction (see Section 10.5.5). The normal and the minimal wait times are maintained both in the routing and in the work center. The values of the work center are only used if no values have been maintained in the routing.

Wait time
The wait time lies after the processing steps of the operation and is used after those processing steps that require a certain wait time until the work pieces are transportable. An example for this is the cancellation or cooling of work pieces.

Two values are also maintained for the wait time, namely the maximal (**Max. wait time**) and the process-determined wait time (**Proc-Det. wait time**). The process-determined wait time is required for technical reasons and is used for scheduling. It is possible to arrange the wait time in parallel to the teardown, and thus shorten the lead time of the operation. Unlike the other components of the operation, the wait time is not scheduled using a calendar.

Move time
The move time follows the wait time and deals with the time required to move the work piece to the next work center. A normal (**Nor. move time**) and a minimal value (**Min. move time**) are also maintained for the move time; here, the normal value during the reduction is reduced to the minimal value.

Location groups and move time matrix
Instead of maintaining the move times for each operation of the routing, you can determine the move time using a move-time matrix. Here, location groups are assigned to the work centers, and in the move-time matrix the normal and the minimal move times between the location groups are given. The working times maintained in the move time matrix are used for the scheduling of the move times. Figure 10.36 shows the maintenance of the location groups and the move time matrix that is performed with the Customizing Transaction OPJR.

The location groups are assigned to the work center in the **Scheduling** view, as the sample in Figure 10.37 shows.

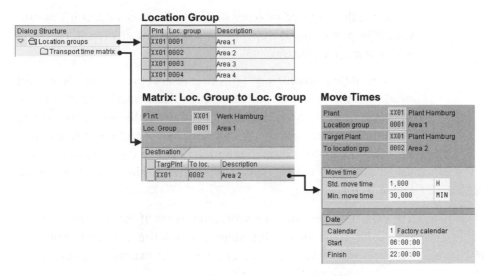

Figure 10.36 Maintaining the Location Groups and the Move Time Matrix

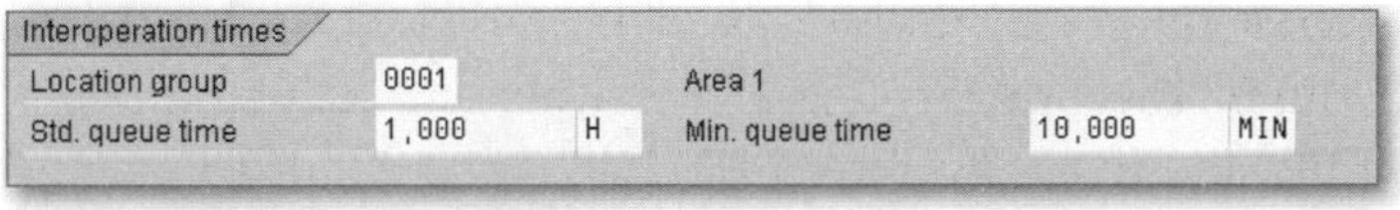

Interoperation times					
Location group	0001		Area 1		
Std. queue time	1,000	H	Min. queue time	10,000	MIN

Figure 10.37 Assigning the Location Group to the Work Center (Section from Scheduling View)

10.5.4 Splitting and Overlapping

Splitting and overlapping are two options for reducing the lead time of operations. Splitting reduces the processing duration of an operation, and overlapping retains the processing duration of the operations, while the lead time of the operation as a whole is reduced. Figure 10.38 illustrates these two possibilities for an order, consisting of the three operations **0010**, **0020** and **0030**.

Through splitting, an operation is split into several sub-operations that can be processed in parallel with each other. This reduces the lead time of the operation.

Splitting

A prerequisite for the splitting is that the capacity must contain several individual capacities; otherwise, a parallel processing is not possible. The number of splits—i.e., the number of parts into which the operation is split—is determined by the split parameter. Figure 10.39 shows the maintenance of the split parameter in the operation of the routing.

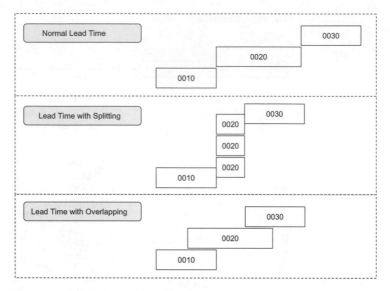

Figure 10.38 Splitting and Overlapping

Figure 10.39 Split Parameter in the Routing

The **Number of splits** specifies the maximum number of splits that may take place for the operation. For a split to be worthwhile, there must be a minimum processing time (**MinProcessngTime**). If this is not reached after the splitting, no splitting will take place.

Splitting will only be performed during the scheduling if the split parameter **Required splitting** is set; otherwise splitting is only used during the reduction (see Section 10.5.5). When a required split is used without specifying the number of splits and the minimum processing time, the system distributes processing equally across the maximum available number of capacities. Figure 10.40 shows the splitting in the operation detail of the production order.

The operation detail of the production order, in addition to the maximum number of splittings from the routing, also specifies the actual number of splittings performed for this operation. The splitting reduces the processing duration, as is shown in the operation's dates.

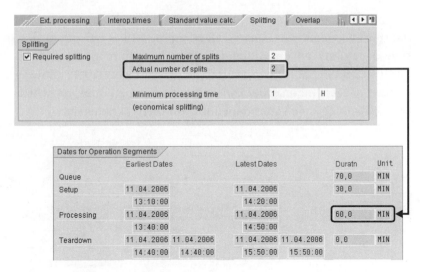

Figure 10.40 Operation Split in the Production Order

The parameters for the *Overlapping*—the minimum send-ahead
quantity and the minimum overlapping time—are also maintained in
the operation data of the routing (see Figure 10.41). These parameters relate to the overlapping with the follow-up operation.

Overlapping

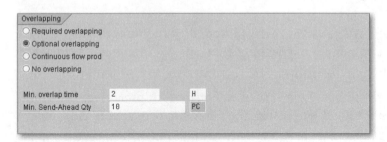

Figure 10.41 Overlapping Parameters in the Routing

Because an overlapping requires extra effort from an organizational
point of view, it may not be worthwhile to perform an overlap for
very short overlapping durations. This threshold value is reflected by
the minimum overlapping time (**MinOverlapTime**). If the overlapping time with the follow-up operation does not at least correspond
to this overlapping time, no overlapping takes place.

The second parameter, the minimum send-ahead quantity (**MinSndAheadQty.**), determines how many plant pieces must already
have been processed in order for you to continue their processing in

the follow-on operation. For example, batch sizes can modeled for transport between work centers. Overlapping will or will not be possible depending on the order quantity, the minimum send-ahead quantity, and the minimum overlapping time. Figure 10.42 shows a number of cases for an order consisting of two operations, for which the overlapping time varies depending on these parameters.

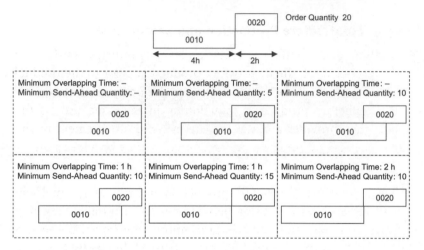

Figure 10.42 Overlapping

The following rules are derived from the conditions that are defined by the minimum overlapping time and the minimum send-ahead quantity.

▸ After the minimum send-ahead quantity is processed, the operation must last longer than the minimum overlapping time.

▸ The follow-on operation must last for at least as long as the minimum overlapping time.

▸ If no minimum send-ahead quantity exists, the operation can begin at the same time as the follow-on operation.

▸ If the minimum overlapping time is not reached (for example because the remaining processing time after the processing of the minimum send-ahead quantity is too small), no overlapping takes place.

The minimum overlapping relates to the processing time. Wait times and move times do not contribute to the minimum overlapping time.

During scheduling, overlapping is either performed during the reduction (**optional overlapping**), always (**required overlapping**) or never (**no overlapping**). Flow manufacturing represents a special case. Here the execution time of all operations that are also flagged with the **Flow manufacturing** parameter is extended to the longest of the processing durations.

10.5.5 Float Before Production and Safety Time

In addition to the buffers at operation level, two further buffers are used at order level: the float before production prior to the production start date, and the safety time after the production start date. The float before production, functioning in the same way as the queue time, provides a buffer for late material procurement or the late processing of previous orders. The safety time provides a buffer for the late processing of this order.

When you set the float before production and the safety time, you must bear in mind that using buffer times has a certain stabilizing effect on the plan and that this can improve the capital tie-up and throughput. However, if the buffer is increased, the reverse happens. Because date buffers are essentially replaced by quantity buffers, which are easier to assess in terms of their effect, this represents an alternative to high date buffers for B and C parts in particular (see Dittrich et al. 2003, p. 171–182).

The float before production and safety time are set down in the scheduling margin key. The Customizing path for this is **Production • Production Scheduling • Operations • Scheduling • Define Scheduling Margin Key** (see Figure 10.43).

Scheduling margin key

Scheduling Margin Key

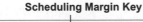

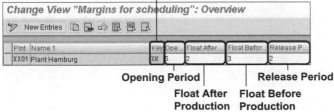

Figure 10.43 Scheduling Margin Key

As well as the order buffer times, the scheduling margin key contains the opening period and the release period. The scheduling margin key is maintained plant-specifically and is assigned to the material master in the view **MRP 1** (see Figure 10.44).

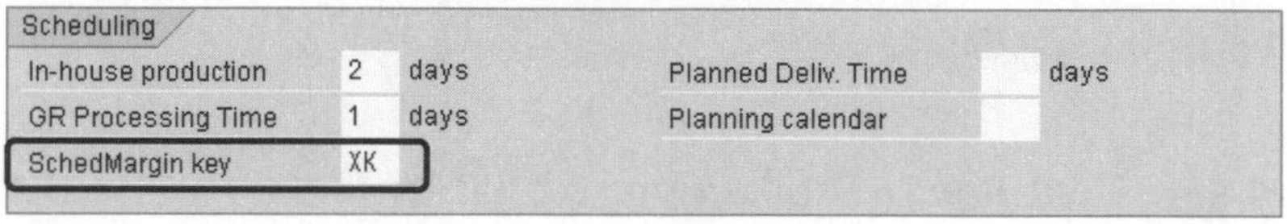

Scheduling					
In-house production	2	days	Planned Deliv. Time		days
GR Processing Time	1	days	Planning calendar		
SchedMargin key	XK				

Figure 10.44 Assigning the Scheduling Margin Key to the Material Master

Opening period and release period

The opening date is a date of the planned order and is used for the collective conversion, as described in Section 10.3. The opening date falls close to the opening period, prior to the basic start date of the planned order. Similarly, the release date is around the release period prior to the production start date of the production order.

10.5.6 Reduction

Buffers can be maintained at various places during the scheduling. These buffers can be canceled if needed. The cancellation is generally performed in several reduction levels. Here, the reduction strategies determine what buffers are reduced, and how far.

Determining the reduction and the production date

Let's examine an example of the use of reduction if the production dates determined by the finite scheduling do not fall within the basic dates. In this case, the system tries to reduce the buffers to the point that the basic dates can be adhered to. Figure 10.45 illustrates this procedure.

The lead time can be reduced at operation level and at order level. The following measures are taken at operation level:

▸ Reduction of the normal queue time up to the minimum queue time

▸ Reduction of the move time up to the minimum move time

▸ Splitting of operations

▸ Overlapping of operations

The float before production and the safety time can be reduced at order level.

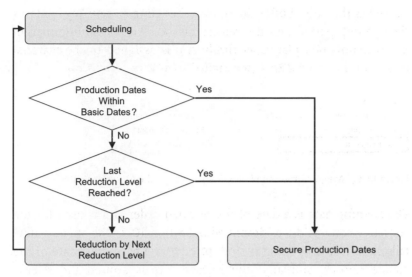

Figure 10.45 Determining Production Dates and Reduction

The **General** view of the production order header specifies whether a production order was reduced (see Figure 10.46).

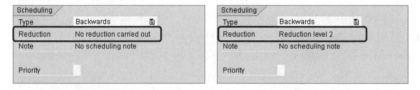

Figure 10.46 Reduction Information in the Production Order

Reduction strategies are maintained plant-specifically with the Customizing Transaction OPJS. One or several reduction levels are defined for each reduction strategy; the reduction levels in ascending sequence increasingly reduce the lead time. Figure 10.47 shows the maintenance of the reduction strategy. **Reduction strategies**

The reduction strategy of the order type-dependent parameters is used if no reduction strategy was maintained in the routing.

The reduction strategy only describes the reduction of the operations by shortening the queue, wait, and move times, as well as through splitting and overlapping. The extent to which the order-related buffers—namely the float before production and safety time—should also be reduced is determined in the order type-dependent scheduling profile using Transaction OPU3 (see Figure 10.48).

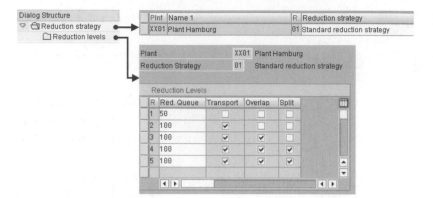

Figure 10.47 Reduction Strategy

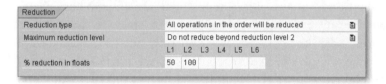

Figure 10.48 Scheduling Profile: Reducing the Safety Times

The percentage reduction of the float before production and the safety time is stored here, depending on the reduction level. In this case, the float before production and safety time are reduced by half in reduction level 1 and completely reduced in reduction level 2 (see the line **% reduction in floats** in Figure 10.48).

10.6 Availability Check

10.6.1 Types of Availability Checks

Availability checks can be called in different ways, either automatically during the creation or the release of the production order, or interactively. The interactive availability check, in turn, can either be performed for the individual production order or as a collective availability check.

There are three different availability checks for the production order.

▶ The *material availability check* checks the availability of the components for the production order, either against actual stocks (and optionally receipts) or against the planning.

▸ The *PRT check*, through a status in the master date, checks whether the required PRT is free.

▸ The *capacity availability check* checks whether sufficient free capacity is available for the order's operations.

The additional significance of the various settings for the material availability check will be explained in the following section. The capacity availability check will be discussed in detail in Section 11.3.

10.6.2 Material Availability Check

The goal of the material availability check is to avoid disruption in the processing of an order at a work center because the required components are not available. The material availability check examines whether the required components are available for the production order. If not, the check creates a missing parts list that the MRP controller or the production scheduler can use for procurement of the specific components required. Depending on the sector and type of the missing part, these efforts will be more or less successful, but at least the planners will be informed in good time of any missing parts and can take measures accordingly. You can consequently set in the check control whether a creation or a release is allowable in the absence of material availability.

The result of the material availability check is reflected in the status of the production order. An unchecked production order has the status NMVP (material availability not checked), while a production order whose component requirements have been checked and confirmed receives the status MABS (material confirmed). If one or several components could not be confirmed, the order receives the status FMAT (missing material), and a missing parts list is created.

Status and material availability check

Figure 10.49 shows this process for the interactive material availability check from the production order.

Interactive material availability check

Where a material is not available, the information is offered in three forms.

The availability check log shows the individual information and warning messages for missing material availability, but it is less appropriate for offering an overview of more complex cases.

Availability check log

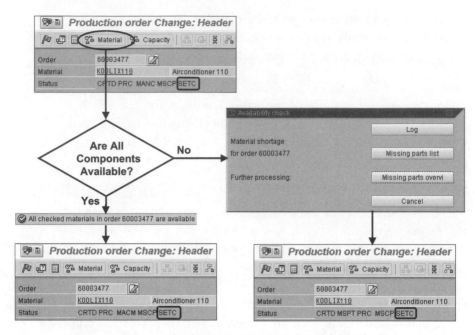

Figure 10.49 Process for the Interactive Material Availability Check

Missing parts list | The missing parts list, on the other hand, shows all the components with missing material availability as well as the number of checked components and any delayed confirmation date (see Figure 10.50).

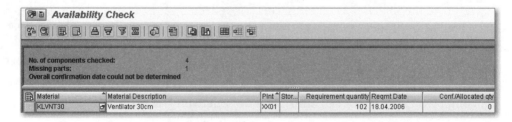

Figure 10.50 Missing Parts List

Missing parts overview | The missing parts overview offers you—in addition to the missing parts list—the option of obtaining more detailed information on the production order, the requirements quantity, and on the component's availability situation (see Figure 10.51).

Missing parts information system | The missing parts list shown in Figure 10.50 and the missing-parts overview from Figure 10.51 are only accessible in the interactive availability check. The missing-parts information system is available with Transaction CO24 for a subsequent evaluation, for example if the availability check is run in the background. Figure 10.52 shows the result of the evaluation for a selection by MRP controller; however, a selection by production scheduler is equally possible.

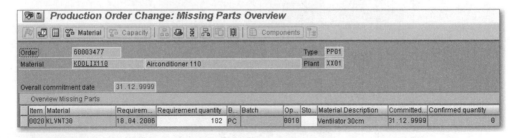

Figure 10.51 Missing Parts Overview

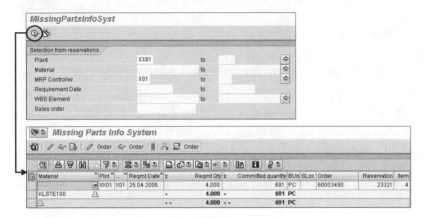

Figure 10.52 Missing Parts Information System

It is also possible to branch directly to the production order from the missing parts information system.

You also can trigger the material availability check interactively for a group of production orders. One application for this would be a repeated check of production orders with missing parts, once you have succeeded in procuring the missing parts. This is done with the collective availability check, which is called with Transaction COMAC. Like the collective release, it is based on the mass processing of production orders. Figure 10.53 shows the procedure for the collective availability check.

Collective availability check

The check control decides whether, and how, the automatic availability check is performed during creation or release. The following section provides more details.

Availability check during creation and release

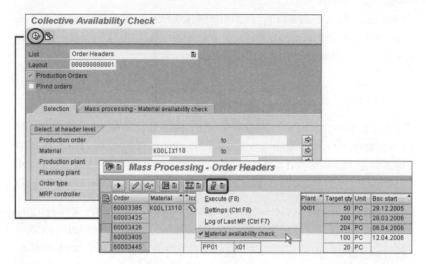

Figure 10.53 Collective Availability Check

10.6.3 Parameters for the Material Availability Check

The way the material availability check is performed—for example whether the stock in quality inspection may be used for the confirmation—is controlled by many parameters. These include the **Availability operation** (creation or release of the production order), the **Checking group** and the **Checking rule**, and others that are contained in the objects **Check control** and **Check scope**. Figure 10.54 provides an overview of the objects involved. The objects with a gray background—all of them except for the material master—are set in Customizing.

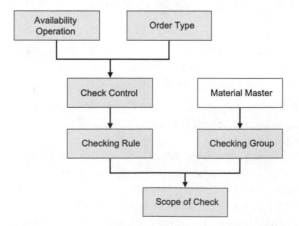

Figure 10.54 Overview of the Objects for the Material Availability Check

The check scope contains most of the settings for performing the material-availability check. It is determined through the checking group from the material master and, through the checking rule.

The checking rule is contained in the check control, which for its part is determined through the order type and the availability operation.

There are two records of check control parameters for the availability check, namely for the creation and the release of production orders. Both the creation and the release represent an *availability operation*, which determines the check control together with the order type.

Availability operation

The *check control* decides, first, whether and how the availability check takes place upon the creation or release of the production order. Second, the check control determines how the availability check runs. The check control is maintained with the Customizing Transaction OPJK and along with the material availability check also controls the availability checks for PRTs and capacities. Figure 10.55 shows the check control for creation production orders of the order type **PP01**.

Check control

In the case shown, when the order is created, a material availability check is performed with the **PP checking rule,** and a capacity availability check is performed with the **OverallProfile SAPSFCG013**.

The check control defines what step should be carried out during the collective conversion in the event of a missing material availability. The result depends on the availability operation for creation the production order for a collective conversion or for the release. The check control addresses the following issues.

▸ Should the production order be created nevertheless?

▸ Should it not be created?

▸ Should it be left to the user to decide on this?

The same control possibilities also exist for the availability check of the PRTs and the capacity.

A prerequisite for performing an availability check is that the parameter **No check** may not be set in the check control. This parameter only relates to the automatic check. An interactive material availability check is nevertheless possible.

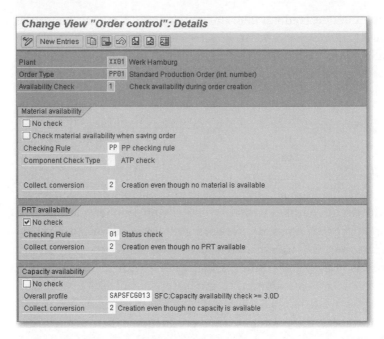

Figure 10.55 Check Control

How the material availability check is performed is decided by the checking rule and by the parameter *Type of component check* (**Type ComponentCheck**). Here you can select between the ATP check against stocks (and optionally, receipts) and the check against planning. Both parameters are also maintained in the check control.

ATP check   During the *Availability check according to ATP logic*, the quantity required for the order of a material component is compared with current stock and with the planned receipts. To this end, an Available to Promise (ATP) quantity is determined for the materials, and this is reduced by the corresponding quantity when the availability is confirmed. This ensures that during another availability check for this material only the reduced ATP quantity will now be drawn.

Check against   The *Check against planning* is a somewhat more simple form of avail-
planning   ability check. Here, the required quantities of the material components are not checked against current stocks or receipts, but rather against the planned independent requirement quantities determined in the planning. Here again, when the availability is confirmed, the planned independent requirements are consumed with the required quantities, so that during later availability checks for this material

only the unconsumed planned independent requirement quantities will be taken into account. The check against planning, which is considerably faster than the checks against ATP logic, can be used if it can be assumed that the actual production will broadly correspond with the planning.

If a material availability check is performed both during the creation and for the release, the check during the release can be shortened with the parameter **Status check** of the check control. Instead of running the check against stocks, receipts or planning, the system ensures that the production order does not contain any missing parts status. Prior to release, we thus only check whether the material availability check was successful during the creation (or interactively afterwards). To this end, there is an additional field in the check control for the release (see Figure 10.56).

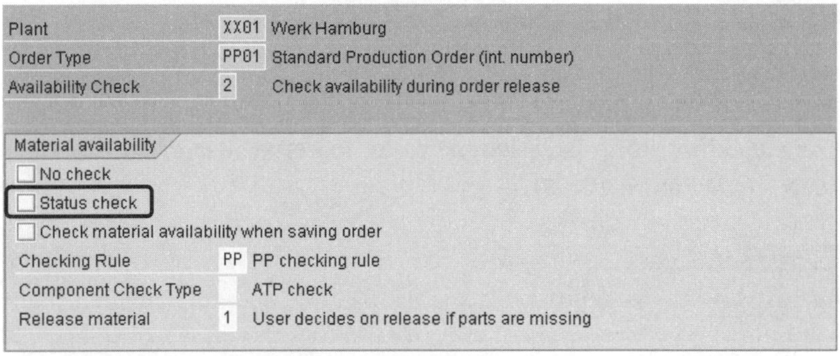

Status check during the material availability check

Plant	XX01	Werk Hamburg
Order Type	PP01	Standard Production Order (int. number)
Availability Check	2	Check availability during order release

Material availability		
☐ No check		
☐ Status check		
☐ Check material availability when saving order		
Checking Rule	PP	PP checking rule
Component Check Type		ATP check
Release material	1	User decides on release if parts are missing

Figure 10.56 Check Control Status Check

The status check offers performance advantages against the normal material availability check.

The *Checking rule* that is stored in the check control is maintained with the Customizing path **Production • Production Scheduling • Operations • Availability Check • Define Checking Rule**. No further information is attached to the checking rule itself. Usually, the PP checking rule is used for the material availability check. The significance of the checking rule is that it determines the check scope together with the checking group. Since the material availability check is not only important for production orders but also in other areas such as in sales or materials management, different check scopes can be defined using checking rules.

Checking rule

Checking group

The *Checking group* is maintained with Customizing Transaction OVZ2 and defines, among other things, whether:

- Individual requirements or total requirements are checked
- The material is locked during the availability check
- The material availability check is switched off
- The system checks against planning

Figure 10.57 shows the definition of the most common checking groups, **01** for daily requirements and **02** for individual requirements.

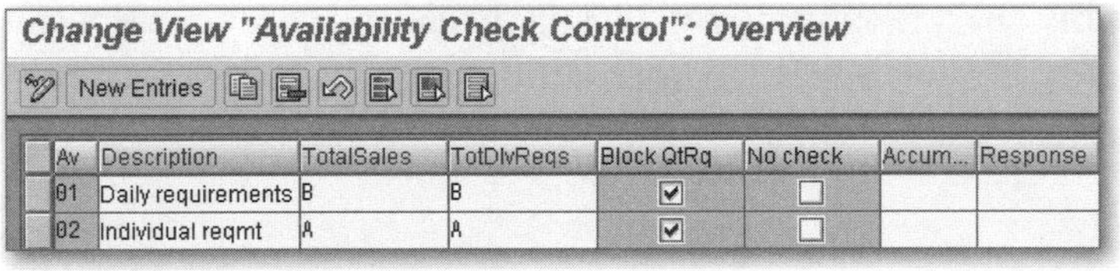

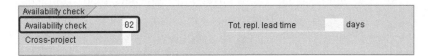

Figure 10.57 Checking Group

The checking group is assigned to the material master in the view **MRP 3** (see Figure 10.58).

Figure 10.58 Assigning the Checking Group to the Material Master

Scope of check

The *check scope* is maintained with Customizing Transaction OPJJ and defines what stock types and what receipts or issues are included in the availability check. When you select the receipts, you should consider such factors as whether the receipt quantity and date are considered sufficiently secure during a purchase requisition for a production order to be subsequently released. Issues are required for the availability check to avoid the multiple issuing of a stock. Figure 10.59 shows the check scope that is used for the PP checking rule and the checking group 02.

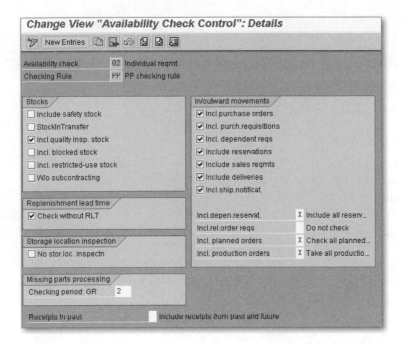

Figure 10.59 Check Scope

Through the definition and assignment of the checking groups, it is possible to define check scopes for various materials. By defining different checking rules, it is also possible to set different check scopes for the creation and release of the production order. For example, you could use planned receipts to confirm creation of the production order, but only to check against stocks during the release.

Capacity requirements planning schedules in detail the worklist, which usually consists of the processes for created or released production orders. Capacity requirements planning delivers a production sequence that is feasible from the capacity viewpoint.

11 Capacity Requirements Planning

11.1 Process Overview

This chapter describes short-term capacity requirements planning that is based on production orders. Other, long-term considerations of capacity have already been described in Chapters 6 and 9.

The goal of capacity requirements planning is to schedule operations with regard to the available capacity as well as to check their feasibility and to create a sequence of operations for production. Figure 11.1 provides a process overview.

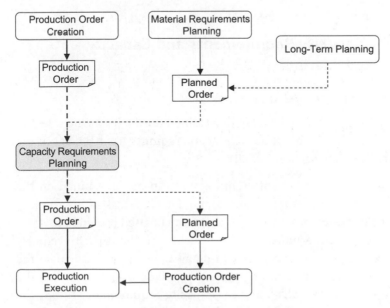

Figure 11.1 Process Overview of Capacity Requirements Planning

In addition to scheduling the operations, capacity requirements planning involves capacity evaluations and a capacity availability check in the production order. The *capacity evaluation* contrasts the available capacity to the capacity requirement, usually in relation to a work center or an order. The *capacity availability check* uses the same information in order to check whether the available capacity is sufficient so that the operations of the production order can be handled in the given period. If that's not the case, the *finite scheduling* function enables you to find a period whose available capacity is sufficient. This may then lead to the rescheduling of an operation, but not to its dispatch. The *dispatch* itself is carried out either in the capacity planning table or in the tabular capacity planning table and consists of the following steps:

▶ Determining the dispatch dates

▶ Creating the dispatching sequence

▶ Finite scheduling of the operation to be dispatched

▶ Midpoint scheduling of non-dispatched operations of the production order

As a result of the dispatching process, the operation is assigned the status DISP which stands for "dispatched" and means that the operation will no longer be rescheduled automatically.

11.2   Capacity Requirements and Capacity Evaluation

11.2.1   Capacity Requirements

The capacity requirements are determined during lead time scheduling provided that the option **Det. Cap. Reqmnts** has been set in the control key (see Section 10.5.2).

Determining the capacity requirement

The volume of the capacity requirement can be determined on the basis of the work center formulas, the default values of the routing, and the order quantity. Order quantity can be used provided that it is included in the formulas used for calculating the capacity requirements. Section 5.4.4 describes in detail how you can calculate the capacity requirement. At this point, we will point out again that the formulas used for calculating the capacity requirement are not the same as the ones used for scheduling.

For each component of an operation, such as setup, processing, and wait times, there is an earliest and a latest date. In contrast to this, the capacity requirement itself is not scheduled in any way. It is rather set to one of the operation dates. In the standard settings, this is the latest setup start date or processing start date, if the operation doesn't provide for any setup time.

Dates of the capacity requirements

An operation can last for several periods. In period-based capacity considerations, as they are used in a capacity evaluation, the *distribution key* determines how the capacity requirement is distributed to the different periods along the operation dates. The distribution key, in turn, contains the distribution strategy and the distribution function (see Figure 11.2).

Distributing capacity requirements

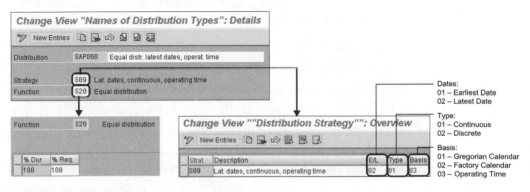

Figure 11.2 Distribution Key

The distribution key defines which operation dates are used and on which basis the distribution process is carried out: operation time, factory calendar, or Gregorian calendar. Moreover, it defines whether a discrete or continuous distribution is used. The function defines basic values for the discrete or continuous distribution. Section 7.2, which deals with the time-based disaggregation of the operations plan, describes the functionality of discrete and continuous distribution, as well as the basic values. You can maintain the distribution key, distribution strategy, and distribution function via the following Customizing path: **Production • Capacity Requirements Planning • Operations • Capacity Requirement • Distribution**.

The capacity requirement is determined during lead time scheduling, and, along with the operation, it has to go through a capacity availability check and the dispatching process. If the operation is con-

Basic load

firmed during the capacity availability check, the capacity requirement is assigned the BSTKZ indicator. The same happens if the operation is dispatched. This way, the capacity requirement is converted into a component of the basic load. The basic load plays an important role in the capacity availability check, given that the available capacity represents the difference between the available capacity and the basic load.

Reducing the capacity requirements

Capacity requirements are reduced by confirming an operation as well as by the technical completion, locking, or setting a deletion flag for the production order. The confirmations update the capacity requirement in correspondence with the remaining operation quantity (the remaining quantity). Accordingly, a partial confirmation only reduces a part of the capacity requirement of the operation.

11.2.2 Standard Evaluations of Capacity Utilization

The SAP ERP system provides several methods of *capacity evaluation*. Some of the standard evaluations have their own transactions, while others are processed as variable evaluations. The following section describes some of the standard evaluations.

Standard evaluations

The standard evaluations that are based on fixed transactions display all capacity requirements, whether or not they are added to the basic load. In general, the capacity requirements are displayed in relation to the work center and are then contrasted to the available capacity. The standard evaluations include the following.

- **Standard overview** (Transaction CM01)
  The load is aggregated by weeks.

- **Detailed capacity list** (Transaction CM02)
  The load is presented per order and week.

- **Pool of orders/operations** (Transaction CM03)
  Only the load of released operations is presented here.

- **Extended selection, work center view** (Transaction CM50)
  Displays an aggregated view of the daily load

- **Extended selection, order view** (Transaction CM52)
  Displays an aggregated view of the weekly load for all work centers that are occupied by the selected orders

Within the evaluations, you can display details about the pegged requirements. Figure 11.3 shows the standard overview called via Transaction CM01 for work center **KLMNTGG05**.

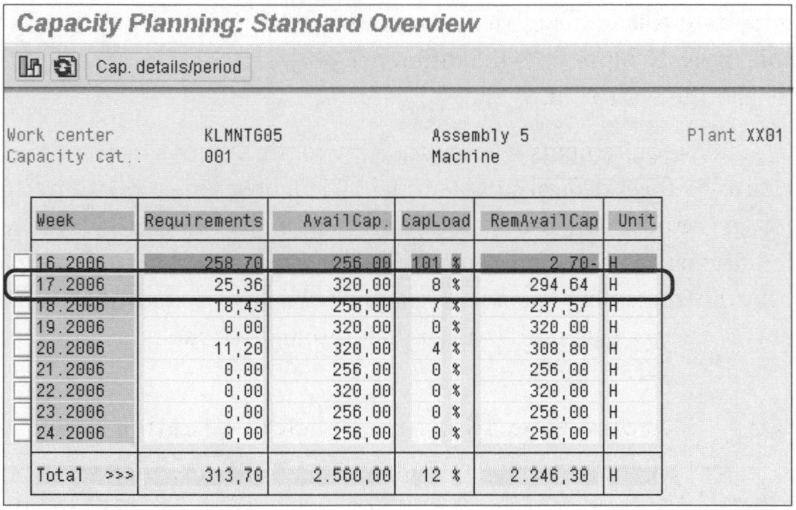

Capacity Planning: Standard Overview					

Work center   KLMNTG05   Assembly 5   Plant XX01
Capacity cat.:   001   Machine

Week	Requirements	AvailCap.	CapLoad	RemAvailCap	Unit
16.2006	258,70	256,00	101 %	2,70-	H
17.2006	25,36	320,00	8 %	294,64	H
18.2006	18,43	256,00	7 %	237,57	H
19.2006	0,00	320,00	0 %	320,00	H
20.2006	11,20	320,00	4 %	308,80	H
21.2006	0,00	256,00	0 %	256,00	H
22.2006	0,00	320,00	0 %	320,00	H
23.2006	0,00	256,00	0 %	256,00	H
24.2006	0,00	256,00	0 %	256,00	H
Total >>>	313,70	2.560,00	12 %	2.246,30	H

Figure 11.3 Standard Evaluation for a Work Center

The figure displays the capacity requirements for each calendar week that result from the production orders. Moreover, the screen shows the available capacity of the work center and the resulting percentage of load a well as the remaining available capacity. For example, in calendar week 17, a capacity requirement of 25.36 hours (H) leads to a utilization of 8 % based on an available capacity of 320 H. As you can see from the data of calendar week 15, periods with an overload are displayed in red color. At this point, we'd like to point out once again that the evaluation does not determine whether or not the capacity requirement was checked or whether it has been dispatched.

From the standard evaluation you can go to the detailed view. Figure 11.4 shows the jump for calendar week 16. In this case we obtain the same display as when we call Transaction CM02 directly.

This evaluation lists the capacity requirement of each operation including the number of the production order, the header material, and the order quantity. The **choose fields...** button enables you to display additional fields of the operation, such as its start time. Moreover, you can directly jump into the production order from here.

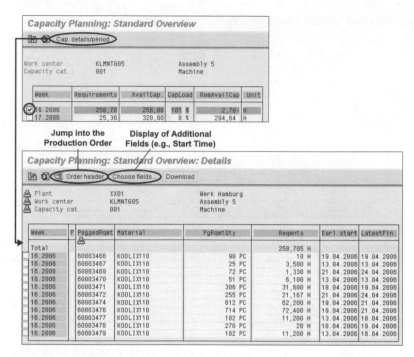

Figure 11.4 Detailed Capacity Evaluation

11.2.3 Variable Evaluations of Capacity Utilization

Variable evaluations enable you to base the capacity evaluation on individual requirements. You can call the variable evaluation using Transaction CM07. The evaluation requires an overall profile that defines the evaluation. Standard profiles are available for this purpose, but you can also define your own profiles. Figure 11.5 shows the variable evaluation using overall profile SAPSFC010. In contrast to the standard overview (Transaction CM01 or overall profile SAPX911), this displays only the requirements of the basic load.

This evaluation is similar to the standard evaluation, but only displays those requirements that affect the basic load (in other words, capacity requirements that have been checked and dispatched). The **Selection list** screen in the bottom right corner of Figure 11.5 displays the restriction to the value **Capacity available**.

Profiles for a variable evaluation
You can define the variable evaluation using profiles. The overall profile is assigned four profiles: the *selection profile*, *option profile*, *list profile*, and *graphic profile*. These profiles, in turn, contain additional profiles. Figure 11.6 provides an overview of the profile structure.

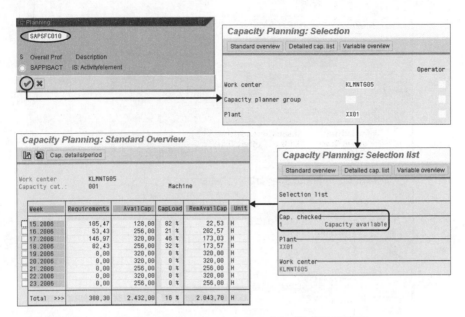

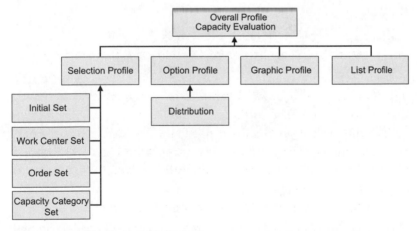

Figure 11.5 Variable Capacity Evaluation Using Overall Profile SAPSFC010

Figure 11.6 Profiles for Variable Evaluation

You can create the *overall profile* using Customizing Transaction OPA6. Figure 11.7 shows the assignment for overall profile SAPSFC010.

Overall profile

The *selection profile* can be created using Customizing Transaction OPA2. It determines which capacity requirements are to be read. Figure 11.8 shows selection profile SAPSFCA010, which is assigned to overall profile SAPSFC010.

Selection profile

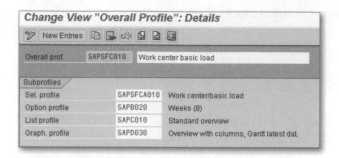

Figure 11.7 Overall Profile for Variable Evaluation

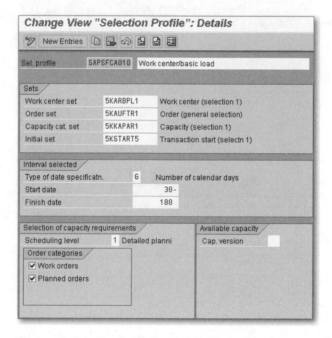

Figure 11.8 Selection Profile for Variable Evaluation

Set combinations   The objects for which capacity requirements are read are determined on the basis of the *set combinations* for the work center, capacity category, and order. They are determined also on the basis of the order categories; that is, whether the order is a production order or a planned order. The initial set determines which restrictions are to be entered during the call. This information is output in the **Selection list** screen (see Figure 11.5). You can create or change the set combinations using Customizing Transaction CMS1 or CMS2 respectively. The sets often use input variables that can be created or changed using Customizing Transaction CMV1 or CMV2 respectively.

The *option profile* (Customizing Transaction OPA3) contains items to Option profile include backlogs, to cumulate the capacity requirements and the available capacity (see next section), and to distribute the capacity requirements. Figure 11.9 shows option profile SAPB020 that is also used for standard evaluation.

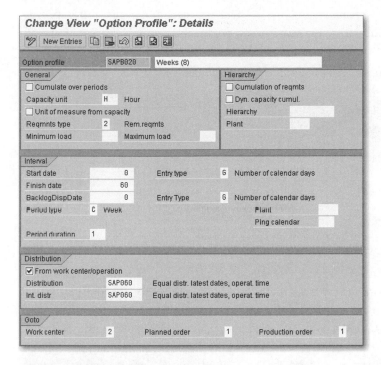

Figure 11.9 Option Profile

The *list profile* (Customizing Transaction OPA4) and the *graphic profile* (Customizing Transaction OPA5) contain additional settings for displaying the evaluation (see SAP Online Documentation).

11.2.4 Cumulating the Capacity Requirements

For a capacity evaluation it is often useful to aggregate groups of similar capacities instead of considering each individual capacity separately. This cumulation of capacities can be carried out statically or dynamically via work-center hierarchies.

The static cumulation is a function of the work center and refers only to the available capacity. To carry out a capacity evaluation in cumulated form—that is, to cumulate both the available capacity and the capacity requirements—you must cumulate the capacity requirements planning dynamically, at least for the capacity requirements. For reasons of system performance, you should use the static cumulation of the available capacity.

Cumulation options in the option profile

The options for dynamic cumulation are defined separately for the capacity requirement and the available capacity in the option profile. The cumulation is always based on a work-center hierarchy that must also be defined in the option profile (see Figure 11.10).

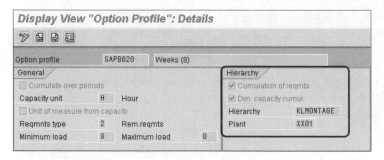

Figure 11.10 Cumulation and Work Center Hierarchy in the Option Profile

You must enter the cumulated capacity evaluation from the work center that represents the hierarchy node. Section 5.4.6 describes the maintenance of hierarchy **KLMONTAGE** that assigns the three work centers **KLMNTG05**, **KLMNTG06**, and **KLMNTG07** to the statistical work center **KLMNTG**. Figure 11.11 displays the evaluation based on these three work centers. The evaluation was entered from the statistical work center **KLMNTG**.

Capacity Planning: Standard Overview

Cap. details/period

Work center   KLMNTG   Plant XX01
Capacity cat.:   001   Machine

Week	Requirements	AvailCap.	CapLoad	RemAvailCap	Unit
16.2006	593,17	768,00	77 %	174,83	H
17.2006	485,40	960,00	51 %	474,60	H
18.2006	89,63	768,00	12 %	678,37	H
19.2006	0,00	960,00	0 %	960,00	H
20.2006	43,80	960,00	5 %	916,20	H
21.2006	0,00	768,00	0 %	768,00	H
22.2006	0,00	960,00	0 %	960,00	H
23.2006	0,00	768,00	0 %	768,00	H
24.2006	0,00	768,00	0 %	768,00	H
Total >>>	1.212,00	7.680,00	16 %	6.468,00	H

Figure 11.11 Cumulated Standard Evaluation

11.3 Checking Capacity Availability

The capacity availability check is carried out for operations of an order before the operations are dispatched. The purpose of the capacity availability check is to find out whether the operations can be dispatched.

This information is obtained on the basis of a period-based consideration. That is to say, the check tries to find out if the available capacity in the period of the operation is bigger than or equal to the capacity requirement of the operation. The length of the period is set in the period profile, which will be described later on in this chapter. The shortest possible period is one day.

Period-based check

Confirmation via the period-based check does not mean that capacity is available on the planned operation date; it only means that capacity is available in the given period.

The available capacity represents the difference between the available capacity of the work center (plus the permitted overload) and the basic load. The basic load does not contain all capacity requirements. By default, only dispatched operations and those for which the capacity has been confirmed affect the basic load. You can display the basic load using the variable evaluation (Transaction CM07) and the profile SAPSFC010.

Available capacity and basic load

If no capacity availability check has been carried out over a longer period of time (for example, if it is being used for the first time), you can create the basic load on the basis of the existing (unchecked) capacity requirements using Transaction CM99. In this case, all capacity requirements will be confirmed.

Because of delays in production, a backlog may be created; that is, there are non-confirmed operations from the past. You can use the parameters **Overall capacity load** in the strategy profile (see Figure 11.22) and the backlog dispatching date (**BacklogDispDate 0**; see Figure 11.26) to define whether you want to include them in the determination of the available capacity. If you do include them, the capacity requirements of the past are temporarily scheduled forward into the current period and, if necessary, into subsequent periods and added to the basic load.

Backlog

Distributing the capacity requirement

An operation can last for several periods. In this case, the distribution key determines the way in which the capacity requirement is distributed to the different periods. The capacity check uses the distribution key that is assigned to the evaluation profile (see next paragraph).

Performing the capacity availability check

The capacity availability check is carried out for each individual order, and all operations are checked one after the other according to their numerical order. A restriction on this capability is that only those operations are checked that exist in work centers relevant to finite scheduling.

The capacity availability check can be carried out at production order creation or release, and interactively.

Interactive capacity availability check

The interactive capacity availability check can be launched from the production order, as shown in Figure 11.12.

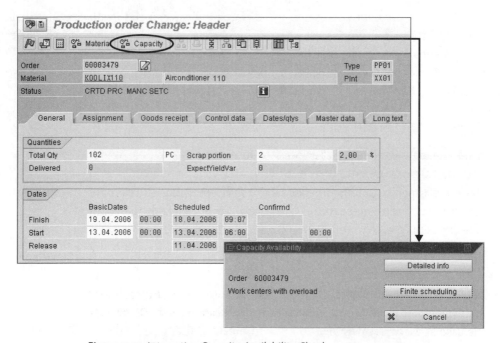

Figure 11.12 Interactive Capacity Availability Check

In the example shown in Figure 11.12, there is at least one operation whose work center does not have sufficient capacity. More detailed information is available as well as the option to use finite scheduling in order to shift the operations into periods with sufficient capacity.

The detailed information for this capacity availability check is shown in Figure 11.13.

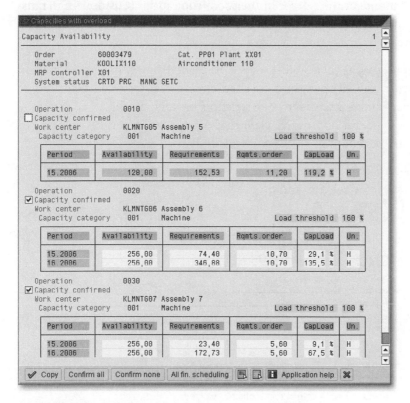

Figure 11.13 Detailed Information for the Capacity Availability Check

Here, the capacity problem exists in the first operation at assembly center 5 because the requirement of 152.53 hours exceeds the available capacity of 128 hours. As this situation leads to a load of 119.2 % and the load threshold is reached at 100 %, the operation with the requirement of 11.2 hours cannot be confirmed.

The load threshold is determined on the basis of the permitted overload specified in the capacity master data and can exceed 100 %, as is the case at **assembly center 6**.

As a result of the capacity availability check, the capacity requirements of operations **0020** and **0030** are confirmed, whereas the capacity requirement of operation **0010** remains unconfirmed. However, it is possible to confirm the capacity requirement interactively by setting the **Capacity confirmed** flag if the planner needs to do that.

The plant and order category-specific check control settings determine whether the capacity availability check is carried out at the creation and/or the release of the production order (Customizing Transaction OPJK). Figure 11.14 displays the check control at order creation.

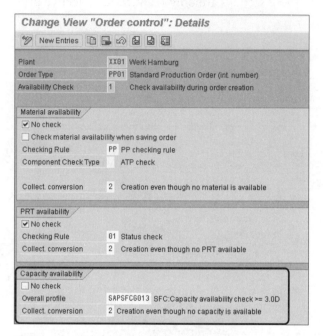

Figure 11.14 Check Control for Capacity Availability Check

The checks during the creation and release represent different availability operations (1 for creation, 2 for release), which is why different sets of parameters exist for the creation and release. Section 10.6 describes the check control in greater detail with regard to a material availability check.

In addition to deciding whether a capacity availability check should be carried out, you must assign the overall profile for the capacity availability check (if no assignment is made here, the system uses the standard profile **SAPSFCG013**). In addition, you must define whether the production order can also be created or released with unconfirmed capacity requirements.

If the capacity requirement of an operation cannot be confirmed, you must make the following definitions in the production scheduling profile (Customizing Transaction OPKP).

▶ Define whether the confirmed capacity requirements are transferred or whether all capacity requirements are discarded

▶ Define whether finite scheduling is to be carried out

Figure 11.15 displays the corresponding fields in the production scheduling profile. These settings are only relevant to collective processing.

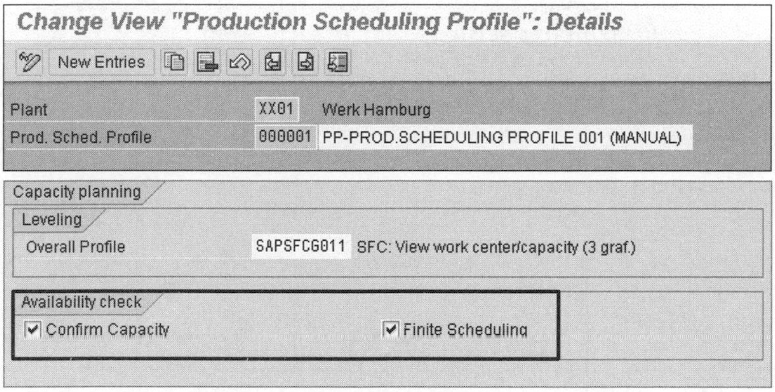

```
Change View "Production Scheduling Profile": Details

   New Entries

Plant                         XX01    Werk Hamburg
Prod. Sched. Profile          000001  PP-PROD.SCHEDULING PROFILE 001 (MANUAL)

Capacity planning
 Leveling
  Overall Profile             SAPSFCG011  SFC: View work center/capacity (3 graf.)

 Availability check
  ☑ Confirm Capacity                     ☑ Finite Scheduling
```

Figure 11.15 Production Scheduling Profile (Section)

The overall profile for capacity leveling is not used for the capacity availability check, but rather for dispatching.

Profiles for the capacity availability check

The overall profile for the capacity availability check has the same structure as the overall profile for dispatching and is maintained with the same Customizing Transaction OPD0. In contrast to dispatching, however, the capacity availability check does not use the overall profile from the production scheduler. Instead it uses the overall profile from check control, or—if there is no profile available there—it uses the overall profile **SAPSFCG013**. Figure 11.16 provides an overview of the profiles involved in the capacity availability check.

As the individual profiles are described in greater detail in Section 11.5 dealing with dispatching, we will only provide a brief description at this point:

▶ The *selection profile* defines the selection of objects for the capacity availability check. Basically, these include the work centers of the selected operations and the capacity requirements of the basic load.

▶ The *control profile* defines the preparation of the data.

▶ The *evaluation profile* is assigned, among other things, the distribution key for distributing the capacity requirements.

▶ The *strategy profile* contains, among other things, the sequence and search direction for finite scheduling.

▶ The *period profile* defines the length of the period for the check.

▶ The *time profile* defines the time fences for the capacity requirements in question.

▶ The *list profile* contains settings for the result output.

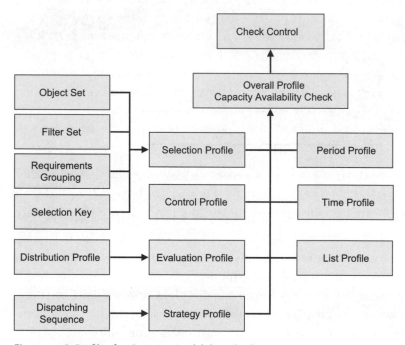

Figure 11.16 Profiles for Capacity Availability Check

Result of the capacity availability check

The result of the capacity availability check is the confirmation of the capacity requirement if the available capacity is sufficient. If the available capacity within the period is not sufficient, you can trigger the finite scheduling process in order to find a period with a sufficient capacity and to confirm the capacity requirement in that new period. The operation is neither dispatched by the capacity availability check nor by finite scheduling.

The capacity availability check gathers information as to whether a sufficient amount of capacity is available for the capacity requirement of the operation in the given period, but it does not dispatch the operation in any way. If the capacity requirement can be confirmed, the flag **Requirement record confirmed** is set for this capacity requirement (field **BSTKZ**). If the check result is negative, you can trigger finite scheduling.

11.4 Finite Scheduling

If the available capacity is not sufficient to meet the capacity requirement of an operation on the requested date, *finite scheduling* can be used to find the next possible date on which the available capacity is sufficient. The scheduling direction that is configured in the strategy profile defines whether the search direction runs from the requested date towards today's date or into the future. A search in the direction of today's date is based on backward scheduling and represents the standard case, while the search into the future is based on forward scheduling. If sufficient capacity can be found in one direction, you can also reverse the search direction.

Finite scheduling can be triggered by both the capacity availability check and the dispatching.

Based on the capacity availability check illustrated in Figures 11.12 and 11.13, Figure 11.17 displays the result of finite scheduling when it is triggered by the capacity availability check.

Result of finite scheduling based on the capacity availability check

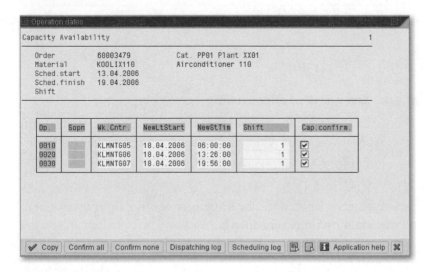

Figure 11.17 Finite Scheduling Result (Triggered by Capacity Availability Check)

353

The figure displays the newly determined latest start dates for all three operations—that's 04/18/2006 for operation 0010—as well as the shift in terms of work days, which in this case is one day. It also displays whether the capacity could be confirmed for this operation. If no capacity was available within the planning period, the capacity requirement of the operation still could not be confirmed even after the finite scheduling process was finished.

Result of finite scheduling based on dispatching When you trigger finite scheduling from the capacity planning table, the finite scheduling result consists of the dates of the dispatched operation. Figure 11.18 shows an example in which finite scheduling has changed the operation dates during the dispatch, due to the capacity commitment.

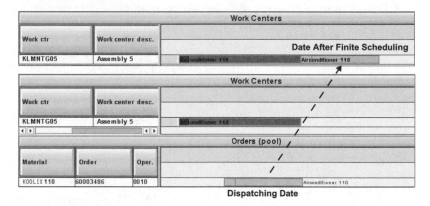

Figure 11.18 Finite Scheduling Result (Triggered by Dispatching)

11.5 Dispatching

11.5.1 Overview of Dispatching

The goal of *dispatching* is to create a feasible production plan; in other words, a plan for which the capacity is available. For this purpose, you must establish a sequence of dates for the individual operations in the work centers.

Non-dispatched operations form the *pool of orders/operations* of the production scheduler. To dispatch operations, the planner selects the operations to be dispatched from the capacity planning table or from the tabular capacity planning table and triggers the dispatching function. The system then carries out the following dispatching steps.

1. **Determine dispatching dates**

   The standard setting uses the operation dates as dispatching dates. However, you can also enter dates interactively or define the dispatching date via drag-and-drop in the capacity planning table.

2. **Create dispatching sequence**

   If you want to dispatch several operations in one step, you must create a dispatching sequence based on specific sorting criteria or on optimal setup times.

3. **Finite scheduling if no capacity is available**

   If no capacity exists on the dispatching date, finite scheduling must be carried out in order to find a feasible dispatching date.

4. **Dispatch operation**

   The operation is dispatched and is assigned the status DISP.

5. **Midpoint scheduling**

   The dates of non-dispatched operations must be adjusted in such a way that a midpoint scheduling process is carried out for them.

You can also base the dispatching process on an unlimited capacity. To do that, you should not select finite scheduling in the strategy profile.

During dispatching you may find that the basic dates of the order cannot be met. Because dispatching is carried out for each operation, it is also possible that the order sequence is violated. You can use the strategy profile to define the extent to which such inconsistencies within the operations of an order can be tolerated. External dependencies—that is, the date-based dependency between orders and customer requirements—must be monitored by the planner.

Basically, each operation is planned separately and therefore does not depend on the sequence within the order. In other words, the painting of a device could be planned prior to its assembly. The **Consider operation sequence in the order** parameter in the strategy profile enables you at least to consider the sequence in the opposite direction of the planning direction.

► If the planning direction is "forward," the parameter makes sure that an operation is not planned prior to its predecessor.

► If the planning direction is "backward," the parameter makes sure that an operation is not planned after its successor.

Planning logs All planning steps are logged. You can call the planning log from the respective application, for instance from the capacity planning table or from finite scheduling in the interactive capacity availability check. Figure 11.19 displays a sample planning log that contains eight information messages and two warnings.

Exce...		Application Area	Msg.no.	Σ N...	Numer.	Order	Seq.	OpAc	Message Text
○△○	W	CY	736	1	1	60003479	0	0020	Order 000060003479 operation 0020 finishes after basic finish date of order
○△○	W	CY	736	1	1	60003479	0	0030	Order 000060003479 operation 0030 finishes after basic finish date of order
○△○				▪ 2					

Figure 11.19 Planning Log

The warnings indicate that the rescheduling in the context of the finite scheduling process causes orations **0020** and **0030** to end after the order finish date.

11.5.2 Profiles for Dispatching

Capacity leveling uses numerous profiles. In order to minimize confusion, this section provides an overview of these profiles and describes the most important settings. Later on in this chapter, we'll mention the respective profiles during the functional descriptions whenever this is necessary.

As is the case for capacity evaluation, the profiles for capacity leveling are cumulated in an overall profile. Figure 11.20 illustrates the profiles of the overall profile as well as other profiles assigned to them.

Overall profile You can create the overall profile using Transaction OPD0. It contains the following profiles:

- ▶ Selection profile
- ▶ Control profile
- ▶ Evaluation profile
- ▶ Strategy profile
- ▶ Time profile
- ▶ Profile for the capacity planning table
- ▶ Tabular planning table profile
- ▶ List profile

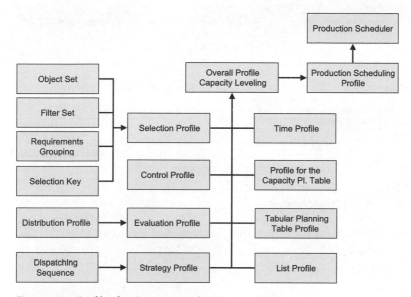

Figure 11.20 Profiles for Capacity Leveling

Figure 11.21 displays the standard overall profile **SAPSFCG011**.

The **Period profile** is not maintained in this case because it is only relevant for a capacity availability check. The following sections describe the individual profiles with the exception of the planning table profiles, which are introduced in Section 11.5.3.

The *strategy profile* is maintained using Customizing Transaction OPDB. It is extremely important for dispatching and rescheduling. Figure 11.22 displays strategy profile **SAP__T001** including its numerous parameters. The most important parameters of the strategy profile control the functions for dispatching, scheduling, and creation of a sequence of operations.

Strategy profile

357

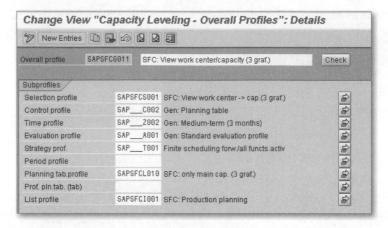

Figure 11.21 Overall Profile for Dispatching

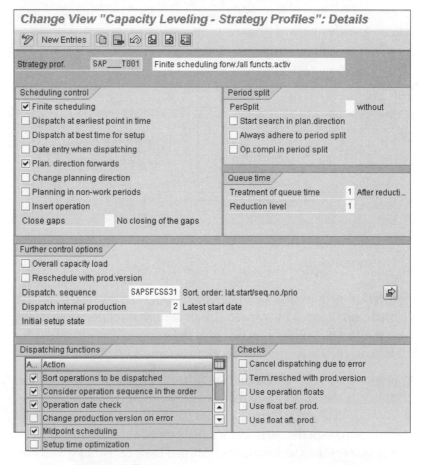

Figure 11.22 Strategy Profile

The parameters of the dispatching function define which options are available for dispatching. These include the following.

▶ **Sort operations to be dispatched** determines that a sequence is created on the basis of the assigned dispatching sequence if several operations need to be dispatched.

▶ **Setup time optimization** creates the dispatching sequence according to the setup time minimization criterion.

▶ You must select a parameter in order to make sure that a **midpoint scheduling process** is immediately carried out for the depending operations. Otherwise, midpoint scheduling will be carried out during the saving process.

▶ **Consider operation sequence in the order** can be used to help prevent the sequence of operations in the production order from being confused. In the case of forward scheduling, the operation cannot be dispatched prior to its predecessor. Likewise, with backward scheduling, the parameter makes sure that the operation is not dispatched after its successor.

The *scheduling control* parameters allow you to make the following settings, among others.

▶ You can set whether you want to carry out **finite scheduling** during dispatching. If this parameter is not set, the dispatch process assumes that unlimited capacity is available.

▶ If you use the **Dispatch at earliest point in time** parameter, the operation is dispatched as early as possible without considering interdependencies with other operations.

▶ The default setting for the planning direction is backward from the point of view of the dispatch date. However, you can change this setting by activating the **Plan. direction forwards** parameter. If no available capacity can be found within the planning horizon, and the **Change planning direction** parameter is set, the search for available capacity continues in the opposite direction.

▶ **Dispatch at best time for setup** chooses the dispatch date on the basis of the existing setup sequence in such a way that the increase in the overall setup time is kept as small as possible. This implies that operations that have already been dispatched must be shifted. For this reason, you must set the **Insert operation** parameter as well. This function is only supported in the capacity planning table and only makes sense if setup matrices for sequence-based setup are used.

▸ The **Planning in non-work periods** parameter overrides the non-work periods in the work center and suggests a 24-hour capacity availability with full rate of capacity utilization to the dispatch process.

▸ The **Close gaps** parameter enables you to automatically close gaps that are caused by de-allocations or rescheduling. This, in turn, implies a rescheduling of operations that have already been dispatched and can only be done in the capacity planning table.

▸ The **Date entry when dispatching** parameter makes sure that, instead of using the operation date during dispatching, a pop-up window opens and prompts the user for an interactive date entry.

Other control options of the strategy profile

The other control options enable you to assign, among other things, the dispatching sequence and the setup group for the initial setup status.

Date check options of the strategy profile

If you use the dispatch function, **Operation date check** you can check whether the new operation dates lie within the floats that can be selected using the following parameters:

▸ Use operation floats (**Use operation floats**)

▸ Use float before production (**Use float bef. prod.**)

▸ Use float after production (**Use float aft. prod.**)

If, in addition, the **Cancel dispatching due to error** parameter is set, no dispatching is carried out outside the floats.

Selection profile

The *selection profile* can be maintained using Customizing transaction OPD1, and it defines which capacity requirements are to be considered for the dispatch. Figure 11.23 displays selection profile **SAPSFCS001**.

The sets (**object set**, **filter set**) are maintained as in the capacity evaluation, see Section 11.2.3.

Control profile

The *control profile* defines how the data is to be presented; whether, for example, it will be presented continuously over time for the capacity planning table or based on periods for the tabular capacity planning table. Another essential parameter of the control profile defines whether the operations can be modified and at which stage locks are to be set. You can maintain the control profile using Customizing Transaction OPDE (see Figure 11.24).

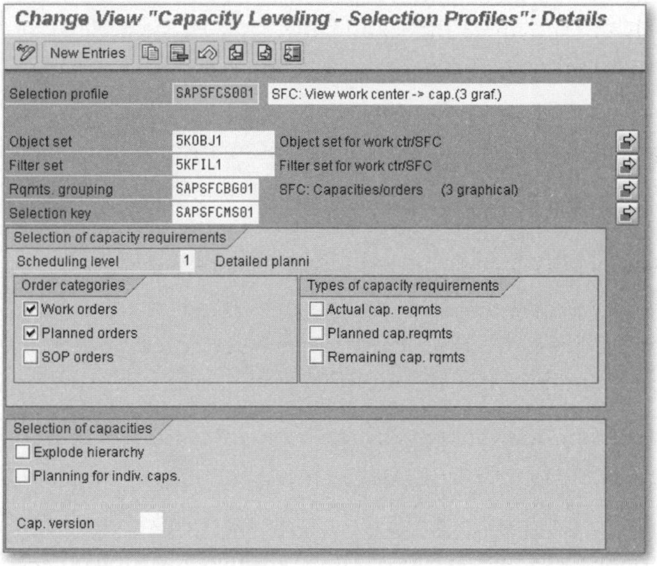

Figure 11.23 Selection Profile for Dispatching

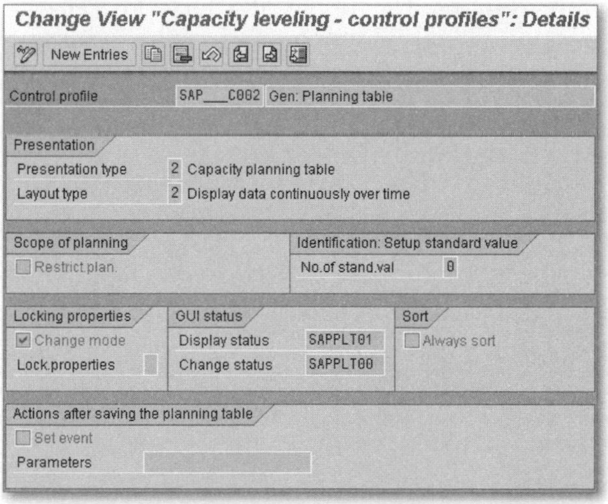

Figure 11.24 Control Profile for Dispatching

The *evaluation profile* is maintained using Customizing Transaction OPD3. It contains the distribution keys for the capacity requirements as well as units of measure and details for the cumulation of capacity

Evaluation profile

requirements and available capacities. Figure 11.25 displays evaluation profile **SAP___A001**.

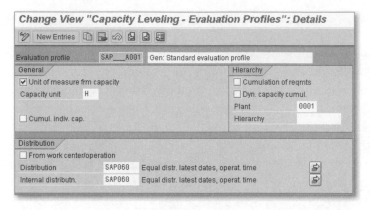

Figure 11.25 Evaluation Profile for Dispatching

Time profile The *time profile* can be maintained using Customizing Transaction OPD2. It contains the time horizons for importing the data records as well as for evaluation and planning. The planning horizon must be smaller than or equal to the evaluation period, which in turn must be smaller than or equal to the database read period. Another entry concerns the date for dispatching backlog on which all backlog capacity requirements are dispatched, provided that the backlog is to be considered. Figure 11.26 displays time profile **SAPPM_Z002**.

Change View "Capacity Leveling - Time Profile": Details

New Entries

| Time profile | SAPPM_Z002 | PM: 2 months + 5 days in the past |

Database read period

| Entry type | J Number of calendar months | Start date | -3 |
| | | Finish date | 3 |

Evaluation period

| Entry type | 6 Number of calendar days | Start date | -5 |
| | | Finish date | 60 |

Planning period

| Entry type | 6 Number of calendar days | Start date | -1 |
| | | Finish date | 60 |

Dispatching of backlog

| Entry Type | 6 Number of calendar days | BacklogDispDate | 0 |

Figure 11.26 Time Profile for Dispatching

The *list profile* defines the presentation of the output lists and can be List profile maintained using Customizing Transaction OPDH.

11.5.3 Dispatching Sequence

For small changes or interactive amendments of a plan, operations are dispatched individually, whereas for a complete redesign of a plan you would want to dispatch several operations together according to specific rules. The simplest rule would be to dispatch operations according to their start dates and times. Rules of this kind can be implemented by means of sorting, while a *layout key* enables you to implement the sorting according to a large number of fields. You can create the layout key using Customizing Transaction CY39 (see Figure 11.27).

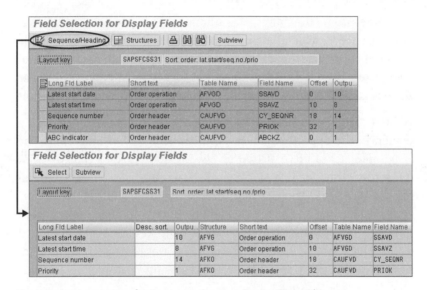

Figure 11.27 Layout Key for Sequence Creation During Dispatching

The field details allow you to select a sorting in ascending or descending order. The layout key is assigned to the strategy profile (see Figure 11.28).

In addition to the layout key, you can also use user exit CYPP0001 to sort the capacity requirements.

The sequence in which the operations are dispatched does not necessarily match the sequence in the work center, because certain conditions of the dispatching process can cause some operations to be dispatched differently. An example of this would be a very long operation that does not fit into any gap that has been created on the basis of operations already dispatched, so that the long operation is dispatched further down the road.

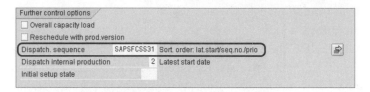

Figure 11.28 Dispatching Sequence in the Strategy Profile

11.5.4 Sequence-Dependent Setup

For some production steps, the amount of setup work depends on the sequence in which the products are to be produced. An example of this is the processing of colored plastics, for which the amount of setup work from light colors to dark colors is small compared to the work involved in the setup from dark colors to light colors.

Setup group category and setup group keys

To model the dependency of the setup work on the processing sequence, the operations in question are assigned *setup groups*. The assignment takes place at two levels: the setup group category and the setup group key. A setup group category can contain several setup group keys. The fact that the assignment occurs at two different levels has the advantage of enabling both a detailed (hence more complex) maintenance between setup group keys and a less detailed maintenance between setup group categories. Setup group categories and setup group keys can be created using Customizing Transaction OP43 (see Figure 11.29).

The setup group categories and keys are assigned to the corresponding operations in the operation details of the routing (see Figure 11.30).

Setup matrix

The setup time between the setup group categories and the setup group key is maintained in a *setup matrix* via Customizing Transaction OPDA. The setup matrix is unique for each plant. Figure 11.31 illustrates an example in which the setup time from a previous operation with setup group category 1 and setup group key 10 to a subsequent operation with setup group category 1 and setup group key

20 is 10 minutes. However, the setup time for the opposite direction, that is, from setup group category 1 and setup group key 20 to setup group category 1 and setup group key 10 amounts to 30 minutes.

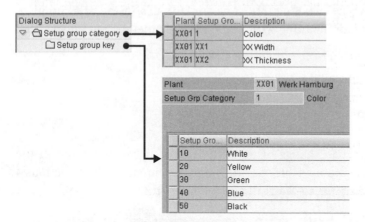

Figure 11.29 Setup Group Category and Setup Group Key

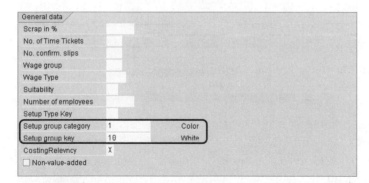

Figure 11.30 Assigning the Setup Group Category and Setup Group Key to the Operation

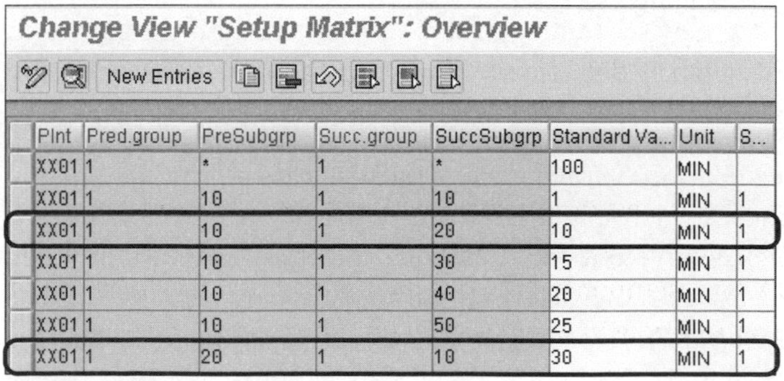

Change View "Setup Matrix": Overview

Plnt	Pred.group	PreSubgrp	Succ.group	SuccSubgrp	Standard Va...	Unit	S...
XX01	1	*	1	*	100	MIN	
XX01	1	10	1	10	1	MIN	1
XX01	1	10	1	20	10	MIN	1
XX01	1	10	1	30	15	MIN	1
XX01	1	10	1	40	20	MIN	1
XX01	1	10	1	50	25	MIN	1
XX01	1	20	1	10	30	MIN	1

Figure 11.31 Setup Matrix

If an operation is not preceded by another operation, the initial setup state from the strategy profile is used if this state exists. Otherwise the default value from the routing is used.

The following planning functions are available in the capacity planning table for planning with sequence-dependent setup times:

- Interactive change of default values
- Automatic adjustment of default values
- Dispatch at best time for setup
- Setup time optimization

Interactive change of default values The interactive change of the setup time can be carried out in the capacity planning table via the following menu path: **Functions • Adjust setup time • Manually** (see Figure 11.32).

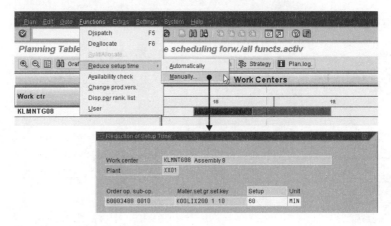

Figure 11.32 Adjusting the Setup Time

You can both reduce and increase the setup time. As a result of the adjustment, a new scheduling process is carried out. If the operation had been previously dispatched, it will be de-allocated after the setup time has been adjusted.

Automatic setup time adjustment The *automatic setup time adjustment* calculates the setup times on the basis of their sequence and reschedules the operations accordingly. To be able to carry out this function, you must first set the **Plan. direction forwards** and **Insert operation** parameters in the strategy profile. In order to close gaps that occur when setup times are reduced, you must also set the **Close gaps** parameter in the strategy profile.

You can carry out the automatic setup time adjustment for the selected work centers from the capacity planning table via the following menu path: **Functions • Adjust setup time • Automatically**. Figure 11.33 shows an example of the automatic setup-time adjustment.

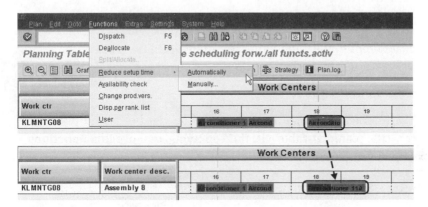

Figure 11.33 Automatic Setup Time Adjustment

With the *Dispatch at best time for setup* function, the system does not try to dispatch the operation at the defined dispatch date, but rather at a point at which the overall setup time for all operations increases as little as possible. To be able to use this function, you must set the **Dispatch at best time for setup** and **Insert operation** parameters in the strategy profile and make sure that the parameter for the **Setup time optimization** dispatch function is *not* set.

Dispatch at best time for setup

To determine the best time for setup, the possible dispatch times are compared with each other. If several best times for setup exist, the system uses the latest of the best times for setup. During the dispatch, the setup time of the operation is not adjusted according to its sequence. Instead it requires an automatic setup-time adjustment in a follow-up step. To dispatch several operations at the same time, the dispatch sequence from the strategy profile is used.

The setup time optimization establishes an optimal setup sequence for a group of operations. This sequence is dispatched in the work center without gaps. In this context, the setup times are automatically adjusted. The setup time optimization is particularly useful for a redesign of the planning because it ensures that the sequence of operations is optimal even after the dispatch. If the dispatch period

Setup time optimization

contains operations that already have been dispatched, the new sequence usually deviates from the previously determined optimal sequence.

For setup-time optimization, you must select the dispatch function, **Setup time optimization**, as well as the **Plan. direction forwards** parameter in the strategy profile. The dispatching sequence of the strategy profile is not taken into account. Figure 11.34 shows an example of dispatching with setup time optimization.

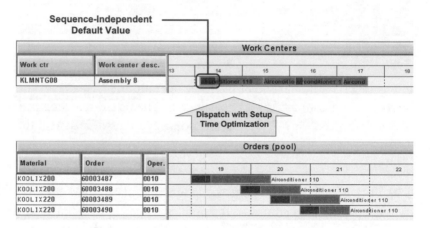

Figure 11.34 Setup Time Optimization

With setup time optimization, the dispatch can occur before the order start date because the dispatch begins on the current date of today. If a work center commitment exists, dispatch can occur after the work center commitment has been done.

11.5.5 Midpoint Scheduling

The dispatch occurs for each individual operation, and during the dispatch of an operation, the dates of the operation can change. In this case, *midpoint scheduling* is used in order to adjust the dates of non-dispatched operations to the changed dates of a dispatched operation.

In a way, midpoint scheduling resembles lead time scheduling, except that it is not based on order start or finish dates. Instead, it starts with a dispatched operation of the order and carries out a backward or forward scheduling process from this operation according to the planning direction defined in the strategy profile. Other dispatched operations of the order are considered as fixed.

Base on a sample order that contains three operations as shown in Figure 11.35, Figures 11.36 and 11.37 illustrate the functionality of midpoint scheduling.

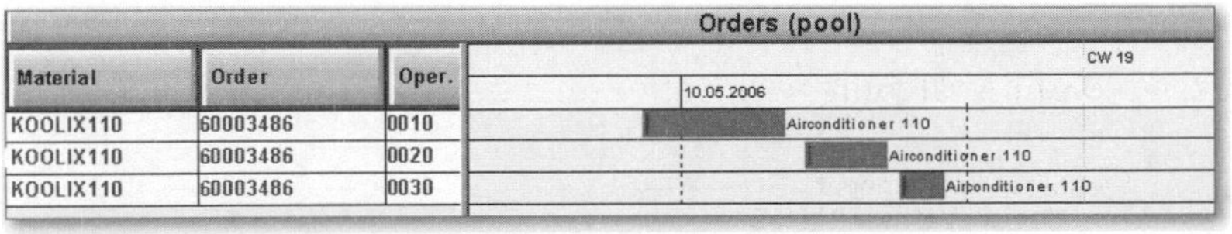

	Orders (pool)				
					CW 19
Material	Order	Oper.	10.05.2006		
KOOLIX110	60003486	0010	Airconditioner 110		
KOOLIX110	60003486	0020		Airconditioner 110	
KOOLIX110	60003486	0030			Airconditioner 110

Figure 11.35 Example: Order Containing Three Operations

In Figure 11.36, the second of the three operations is dispatched and then rescheduled forwards and backwards. The non-dispatched preceding and succeeding operations are adjusted to the new date of the dispatched operation.

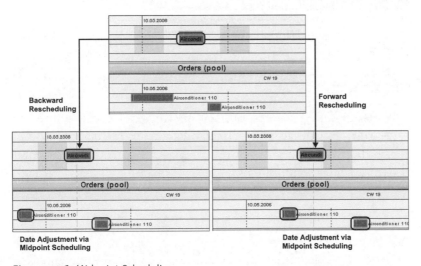

Figure 11.36 Midpoint Scheduling

Figure 11.37 illustrates a situation in which the first operation has already been dispatched and the third operation now is dispatched on a more distant date. Here, midpoint scheduling also adjusts the date of the non-dispatched operation.

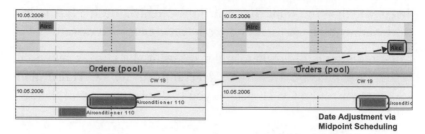

Figure 11.37 Midpoint Scheduling

11.5.6 Mass Processing

The settings for mass leveling can be maintained using Transaction CM40. In this context, you must select the overall profile for capacity leveling, the resources on which processing is to occur, and the action: dispatch, de-allocation, or user exit CY190001. Figure 11.38 displays the definition of the parameters for mass processing.

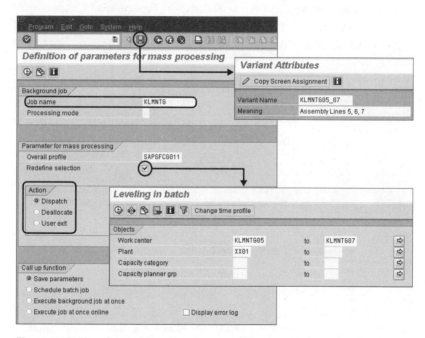

Figure 11.38 Mass Processing

The first time you save the parameters, the system expects you to select the corresponding work centers. If the **Redefine selection** parameter is set, the user is prompted to enter a new selection during the dispatch process. In the **Call up function** section you can define whether you want to dispatch the dispatch job at a later stage (**Save parameters**), dispatch it directly, or to execute it directly.

You can dispatch the job at a later stage using the same transaction. In that case, it is displayed in the general job overview (Transaction SM37). Transaction CM41 enables you to display the logs of the dispatch jobs.

11.6 Capacity Planning Table

The capacity planning table represents a view of the work centers, the sequence of operations dispatched to the work centers, and the pool of non-dispatched operations. This view is continuous over time.

The planning table can, for instance, be called with a reference to the work center or from the production order. Figure 11.39 shows the initial screen after calling the planning table for work centers **KLMNTG05**, **KLMNTG06**, and **KLMNTG07** using Transaction CM21.

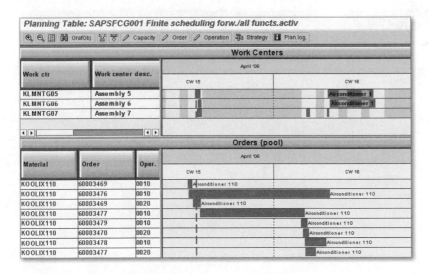

Figure 11.39 Capacity Planning Table

The upper pane displays the work centers including the operations dispatched to them, whereas the lower pane shows the non-dispatched operations as the pool of orders/operations.

The dotted grey line represents the current day. In Figure 11.39, this appears toward the end of calendar week 15.

Sorting

The *sorting* of the pool of orders/operations is defined by the sorting profile of the pane and is carried out after the order start date in the standard setting. De-allocations can disturb this sort sequence because of new objects that are added to the end of the list. In this case, you can use the menu item, **Edit • Sort new** in order to re-establish the previous sort sequence.

Time-based scaling

You can modify the time-based scaling of the planning table via menu path **Settings • Scale**, or by pressing the control key and simultaneously dragging a section of the screen.

Search runs in the planning table

The search function is very useful for navigating through the planning table. As an example, suppose we want to dispatch the first operation of production order 600079. To find this operation, you can call the search window via **Edit • Search** or by pressing the key combination **Ctrl + F**. Then you must enter the production order number in this window (see Figure 11.40).

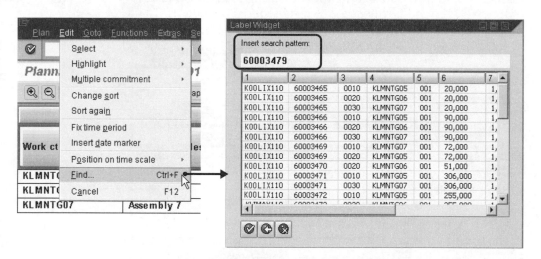

Figure 11.40 Search Window

As a result, the three operations of the production order are listed, the first of which is displayed in first place in the pool of orders/operations pane (see Figure 11.41).

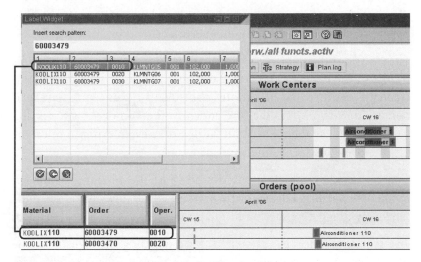

Figure 11.41 Search Result in the Capacity Planning Table

Another means of facilitating the navigation through the capacity planning table is that you can highlight objects that belong together. In our example, we now want to start with the first operation of order **60003479** and highlight the two subsequent operations. To do this, you must first highlight the first operation and then select the menu path **Edit • Highlight • Objects that belong together** in order to highlight the subsequent operations (see Figure 11.42).

Highlighting objects that belong together

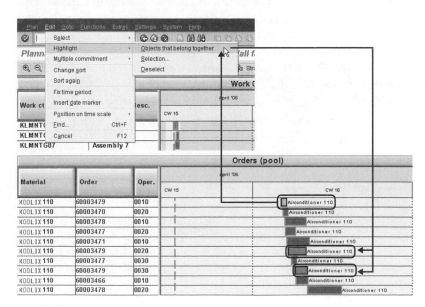

Figure 11.42 Highlighting Objects That Belong Together

Selection key The *selection key* determines which objects are to be considered as belonging together, as it contains the corresponding selection fields. You can change the selection key via the menu path, as shown in Figure 11.43.

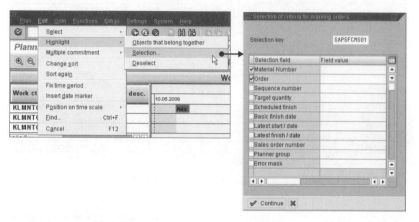

Figure 11.43 Selection Key

Dispatching Basically, there are two ways to dispatch operations using the capacity planning table. You can call the dispatch function by clicking on the relevant button in the menu bar, or you can drag-and-drop the operation using the mouse. In both cases you must first select the operations to be dispatched from the pool of orders/operations. Figure 11.44 displays the dispatch using the dispatch function in the menu bar.

In this case, the dispatch date is the scheduled operation date (by default, the latest start date). Because capacity is available on that date, the operation can be dispatched on the dispatch date. If no capacity was available on the dispatch date, finite scheduling would determine the next possible date on which capacity is available, and the operation would be dispatched on that date.

When you use the drag-and-drop method for dispatching the operation, the "drop" date represents the dispatch date.

De-allocation The de-allocation occurs similarly to the dispatching process: either via the **De-allocation** button in the menu bar (to the right of the **Dispatch** button in Figure 11.44) or via drag-and-drop in the pool of orders/operations pane.

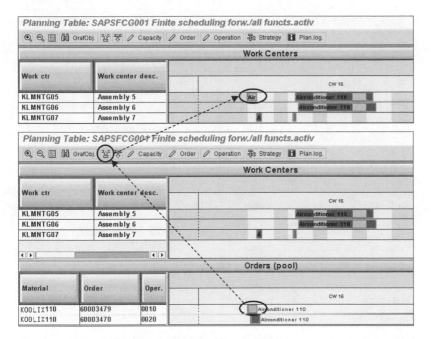

Figure 11.44 Dispatching in the Capacity Planning Table

Based on the settings in the capacity master data, a work center can be occupied by several operations at the same time. In this case, a green line below the operations indicates a multiple commitment. The menu path **Edit • Multiple commitment • Show** enables you to display the multiple commitment of the selected work centers (see Figure 11.45).

Multiple commitment

Because different planning functions require different settings in the strategy profile, particularly when using a sequence-dependent setup, the capacity planning board allows you to change the strategy profile. You also can make temporary changes to the selected strategy profile. These changes then apply to the dispatches that are carried out immediately after that, but they are not stored and will be discarded when you leave the capacity planning table.

Changing the planning strategy

If the available capacity is insufficient, it can be increased, for example by adding another shift. You can adjust the available capacity from the capacity planning table via the following menu path: **Goto • Capacity • Change**.

Capacity increase

375

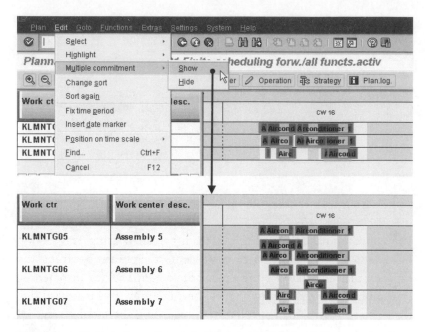

Figure 11.45 Multiple Commitments in the Capacity Planning Table

Displaying the
material stock

Another function of the capacity planning table is that it can display the planned development of the material stock. You can display the material stock pane for selected materials using the following menu path: **Extras • Material stock • Show** (see Figure 11.46).

		Material Stock				
		April '06				
Material	Material description	CW 15	CW 16	CW 17	CW 18	CW 19
KOOLIX 110	Airconditioner 110					

Figure 11.46 Material Stock Pane

Profiles of the
planning table

You can configure the planning table with regard to the number and layout of the panes and objects, and also regarding the scaling. However, a detailed description of the configuration options for the planning table would go beyond the scope of this book.

Tabular capacity
planning table

In addition to the capacity planning table, the system also provides a tabular capacity planning table that contains nearly all functions of the capacity planning table. Exceptions to this are the functions for sequence-dependent setup and the associated settings for the planning strategy. Figure 11.47 displays the initial screen of the tabular capacity planning table.

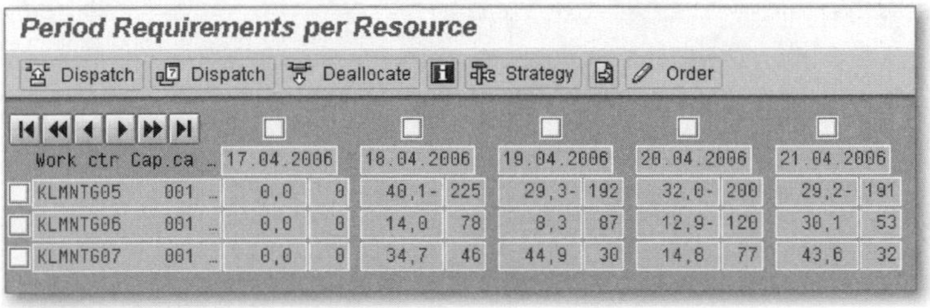

Figure 11.47 Tabular Capacity Planning Table

The tabular capacity planning table can be called using Transaction CM22 during the selection of work centers. Because we think the capacity planning table is the more convenient tool for dispatching and we have already described its the functions in this regard, we won't go into any further detail here regarding the tabular capacity planning table.

The previous chapters have focused on the description of planning, from sales and operations planning to detailed production order creation and capacity requirements planning. In contrast, production execution describes how you can record and control the actual production in the production order from material withdrawal to confirmation to goods receipt and settlement.

12 Production Execution

12.1 Process Overview

Production execution occurs after production order creation or capacity requirements planning. Based on production orders with firm operation dates, the release of the production order represents the system-side "go ahead" for executing the production. Usually, an availability check is carried out along with the release. Also, the order is either printed upon its release or in a separate step later on. The steps to follow after the order is printed are the material withdrawal of components, the confirmation of production steps carried out including yields and scrap, as well as goods receipt (see Figure 12.1).

The production orders remain in the system until they are archived or deleted. Note that you cannot make any changes to completed production orders.

Process control system

Another commonly used procedure is to forward the created and released production orders to a process-control system and carry out the actual production control process, including capacity requirements planning and confirmation of the production orders to SAP PP in that system. With this procedure, the production planning and control function of SAP ERP is mainly used for material requirements planning, days' supply calculation, and costing purposes.

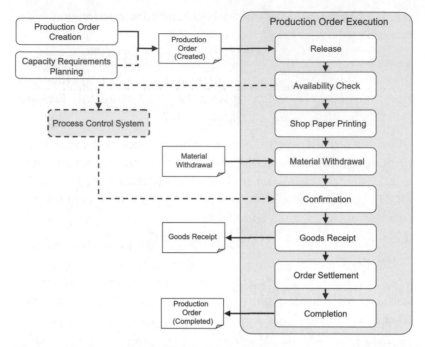

Figure 12.1 Process Overview of Production Execution

12.2 Releasing the Production Order

A newly created production order already contains all the necessary information such as material and capacity requirements and detailed operating dates. Note, however, that you cannot yet start processing it. Only the release of the production order does allow the following operations:

▸ Printing the shop papers

▸ Withdrawing materials

▸ Sending confirmations

▸ Posting goods for the order

You can release the production order directly when creating it, provided this option is set in the production scheduling profile. Alternatively, you can release the order at a later stage in a separate step. You can use the period between the order creation and its release for planning and administration purposes, for example to carry out capacity requirements planning. Depending on the business requirements, the length of the period between order creation and order release can vary.

When you release the production order, it is assigned the status REL (or TREE if only individual operations of the production order have been released). This status replaces the CRTD status that indicates that the production order has been created.

When the order is released, some operations such as the shop paper printing or a new scheduling process can be carried out automatically. In the production scheduling profile (Customizing Transaction OPKP), you can define if you want to carry out actions automatically (see Section 10.2.2 and Figure 10.8).

The release either occurs interactively from the production order or as a collective release. In the production order processing section, you can release the production order via the menu path, **Functions •
Release**, or by clicking on the respective button in the application toolbar (see Figure 12.2).

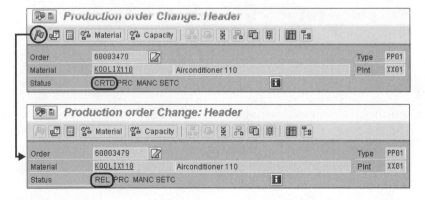

Figure 12.2 Interactive Release of the Production Order

The release of the production order (at header level) automatically causes all operations contained in the production order to be released as well.

You can choose to release only individual operations instead of the entire production order. This is the case, for instance, with production orders that have a very long duration and contain many operations. You can release individual operations in the operation details screen in production order processing via the following menu path:

Operation • Release. Alternatively, you can click on the corresponding button, as shown in Figure 12.3.

When releasing operations, you must pay attention to the sequence of operations. That is to say, to be able to release an operation, its predecessor must also be released.

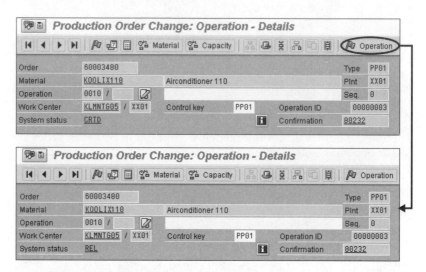

Figure 12.3 Interactive Release of Individual Operations

To avoid having to release every single operation interactively, you can use trigger points (see Section 10.2.4).

The collective release of production orders can be carried out via Transaction CO05N. For this purpose, you can select production orders according to numerous criteria—at header or operation level, for example—by order numbers, materials, data, MRP controllers, production schedulers, and so on. Figure 12.4 shows some of the criteria that can be used to select the production orders to be released.

Based on the selection criteria, a list of the production orders is created from which you must again select those production orders you want to release. The release itself then can be triggered by clicking on the mass processing button (see Figure 12.5).

In correspondence with check control, an availability check can be carried out in the release phase. The availability check has already been described in greater detail in Section 10.6.

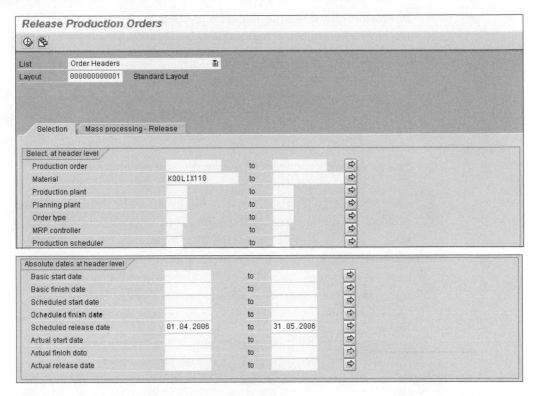

Figure 12.4 Selection for Collective Release (Excerpt)

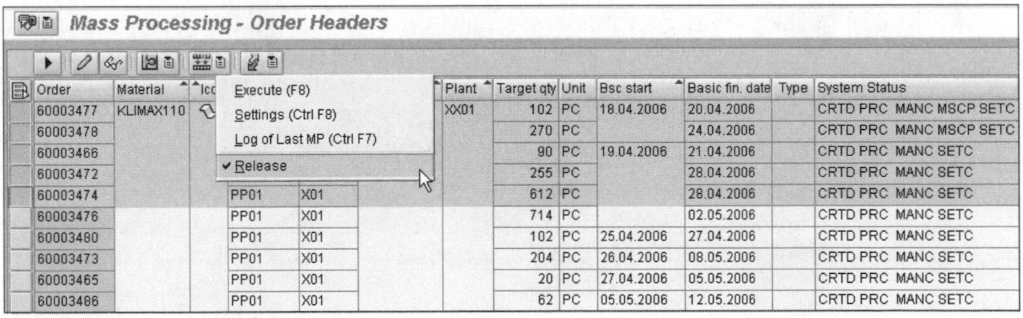

Figure 12.5 Executing the Collective Release

To execute production, it is usually necessary to print out the shop papers that contain the information needed by the workers. This information includes the order number and quantity, the machine, and other information and instructions that can vary from company to company. Shop paper printing occurs either automatically at the time the order is released—provided this has been configured in the

Shop paper printing

production scheduling profile—or by using Transaction CO04N. We won't go into further detail in this book regarding shop paper printing and the layout of the shop papers.

12.3   Material Withdrawal

12.3.1   Goods Issue Posting

Provided the components of the production order are kept in stock, they can be withdrawn from stock. The material withdrawal is mapped via a goods issue posting. Figure 12.6 shows a goods issue posting using Transaction MB1A. This posting can either include a reference to a production order—in our example that's order No. **60003477**—or to a reservation (here, that's reservation **23293**). This example uses movement type **261**. The production order must be released for the goods issue posting to take place.

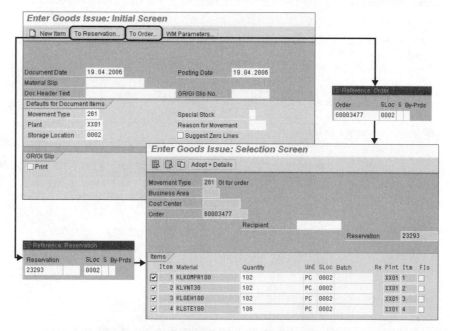

Figure 12.6 Goods Issue for a Reservation and Production Order

Reservations   During the creation of the production order, reservations are created for the component requirements. All components of the production order are assigned the same reservation number but different item numbers. The reservation and item numbers are displayed in the component overview of the production order (here: **Reservation 23293** and **Item 1**; see Figure 12.7).

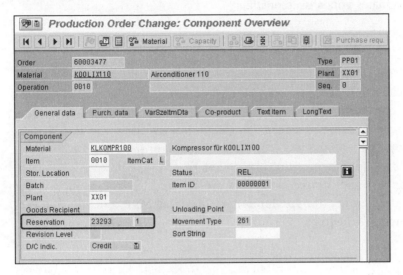

Figure 12.7 Reservation for the Production Order

In addition to the requirement quantity, the component details overview of the production order also displays the committed and withdrawn quantities (see Figure 12.8).

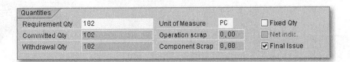

Figure 12.8 Committed and Withdrawn Quantities for the Production Order

The goods issue posting triggers several activities in the background.

▸ The stock quantity of the material is reduced by the withdrawn quantity both at plant and warehouse level.

▸ The consumption statistics are updated because these consumption figures are required for forecasting purposes.

▸ The production order is debited with the actual costs.

▸ The reservation is reduced by the withdrawn quantity.

▸ A material document showing the goods issue is created as well as an accounting document containing all postings in financial accounting (material stock and consumption accounts).

Withdrawn quantities

Effects of goods issue posting

Because the individual goods issue posting represents a special case, we will use the following section to describe the picking process that facilitates goods issue postings.

12.3.2 Picking

Picking enables you to provide the components for each selected production order. As a result of the picking process, you obtain the goods issue posting and the picking list. You can carry out picking using Transaction CO27. This significantly eases the goods issue posting of components for the production order. Figure 12.9 shows the initial screen that displays when you call the picking list. As you can see, the production orders are selected by criteria such as the order number (**Production order**), **Material**, **MRP controller**, or **Production scheduler**.

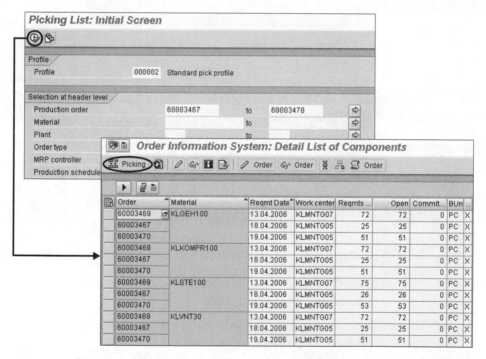

Figure 12.9 Selecting the Pick Part

The first selection generates the list of components for the selected production orders (see Figure 12.9). From this list you must select the parts to be picked. You can select all components by clicking on the respective button.

The **Picking** button enables you to first carry out a stock determination for each component requirement. If the component requirement is available, the stock determination identifies the storage location and any splits that may exist. You can edit or accept the default values (see Figure 12.10).

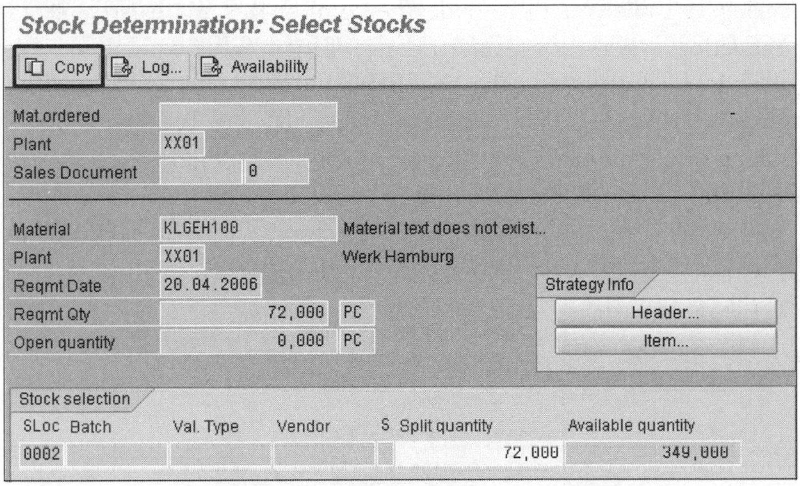

Figure 12.10 Stock Determination During Picking

As a result, you obtain the picking list that contains a line detailing the associated quantity and the identified storage location for each component requirement (see Figure 12.11).

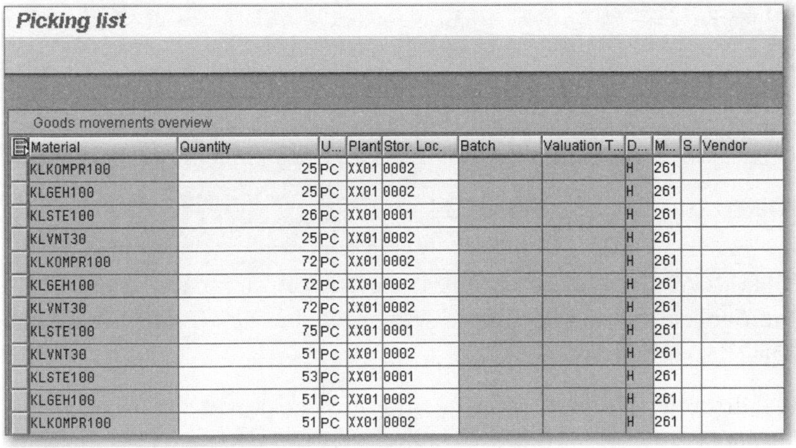

Picking list

Goods movements overview

Material	Quantity	U...	Plant	Stor. Loc.	Batch	Valuation T...	D...	M...	S..	Vendor
KLKOMPR100	25	PC	XX01	0002			H	261		
KLGEH100	25	PC	XX01	0002			H	261		
KLSTE100	26	PC	XX01	0001			H	261		
KLVNT30	25	PC	XX01	0002			H	261		
KLKOMPR100	72	PC	XX01	0002			H	261		
KLGEH100	72	PC	XX01	0002			H	261		
KLVNT30	72	PC	XX01	0002			H	261		
KLSTE100	75	PC	XX01	0001			H	261		
KLVNT30	51	PC	XX01	0002			H	261		
KLSTE100	53	PC	XX01	0001			H	261		
KLGEH100	51	PC	XX01	0002			H	261		
KLKOMPR100	51	PC	XX01	0002			H	261		

Figure 12.11 Picking List

The goods issue postings are carried out as soon as you save the picking list.

Stock determination

The stock determination enables you to identify the special stock, the valuation type, and the storage location of a requirement. In contrast to interactive goods issue postings, the stock determination finds information that has not explicitly been assigned to the component requirement but rather has been determined on the basis of specific rules. You can maintain the **stock determination rule** using Customizing Transaction OSPX. Among other things, the stock determination rule controls the sequence in which the component requirements are to be sorted (see Figure 12.12). The stock determination rule is created and assigned along with a **stock determination group**. Together with the plant, the three objects represent the key for the settings.

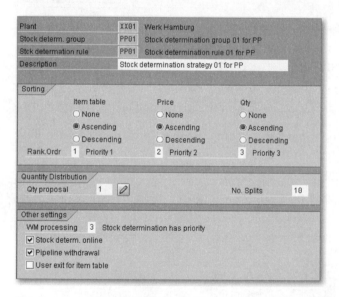

Figure 12.12 Stock Determination Rule

The stock determination group is assigned to the material master in the **General plant parameters** section of the view **Plant Data/Storage 2**, as shown in Figure 12.13.

Finally, you must use Customizing Transaction OPJ2 in order to define the operations for which you want to carry out stock determinations. As shown in Figure 12.14, the stock determination in our example is set for picking and backflushing on the basis of rule **PP01**.

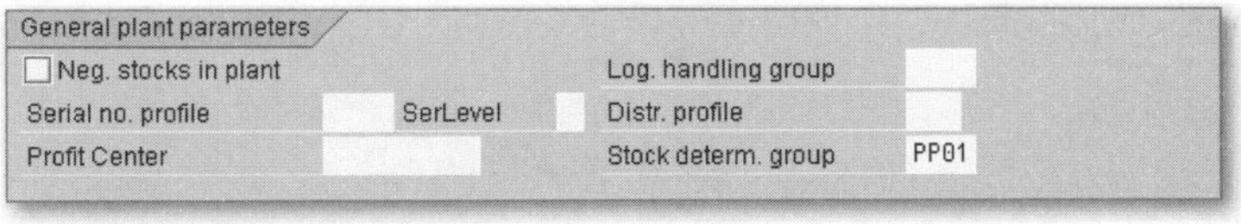

Figure 12.13 Assigning the Stock Determination Group to the Material Master (Excerpt from the Plant Data/Storage 2 View)

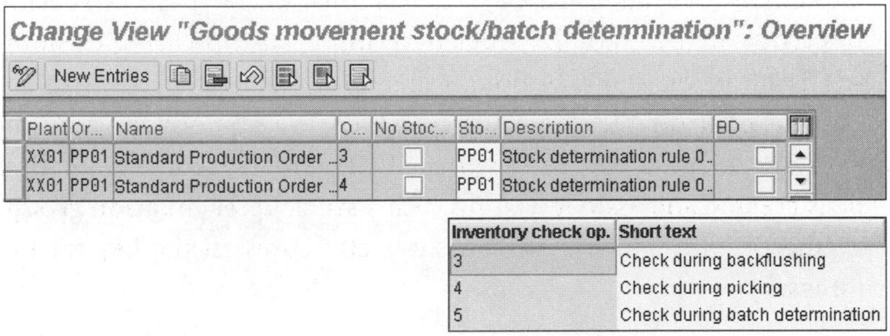

Figure 12.14 Stock Determination

12.3.3 Backflush

In the case of backflushes, the goods issue for the components is not posted until the corresponding operation has been confirmed. This means that the goods issue is posted with a delay caused by the provisioning and operation execution time, which distorts the current stock information. On the other hand, the system-side effort involved in the goods issue posting is reduced to a minimum, and you should consider both aspects when deciding whether a backflush should be carried out. Because the goods issue posting is carried out automatically, backflushed materials are not included in the picking list.

You can set the flag for backflushing in the **MRP 2** view of the material master. This flag allows for the following alternatives: no backflushed materials (no entry), materials can always be backflushed (**1**), or the decision whether materials can be backflushed can be made at the work center (**2**). Figure 12.15 shows this flag in the **MRP 2** view of the material master.

Backflush flag

If you select the **Work center decides whether to backflush** setting, the **Backflush** parameter in the **Basic data** view of the work center controls the backflush (see Figure 12.16).

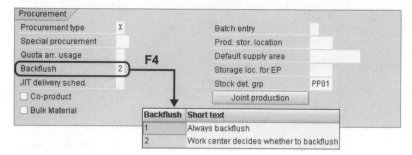

Figure 12.15 Backflush Flag in the Material Master

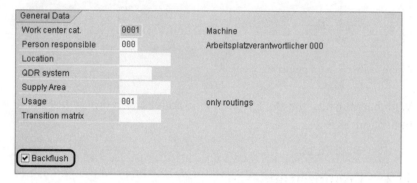

Figure 12.16 Backflush Flag in the Work Center

Moreover, you can also set the backflush parameter as routing-specific in the component overview (see Figure 12.17).

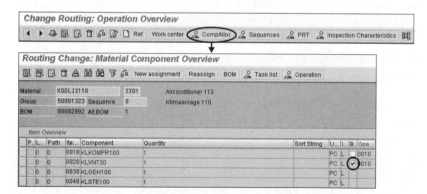

Figure 12.17 Backflush Flag in the Routing

The diagram shown in Figure 12.18 illustrates the decision-making process with regard to whether or not a component should be backflushed.

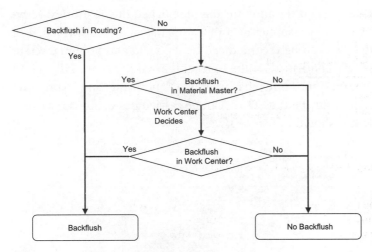

Figure 12.18 Decision on Backflushing

With backflushes, the stock determination is carried out as described in Section 12.3.2.

12.4 Confirmation

The confirmation is used to record and monitor the production process. Only the confirmation makes the production progress transparent to the production scheduler and MRP controller. The following types of data can be confirmed:

▶ Quantities/subsets

▶ Activities (setup time, processing time, and so on)

▶ Dates (start and end dates for setup, processing, and so on)

▶ Personnel data (personnel number, number of employees)

▶ Work centers used

The confirmation automatically triggers other business operations. For example, the actual costs of the order are updated, while the capacity requirements are reduced. If the material components can be backflushed, a goods issue is automatically posted for the production order. Moreover, you also can set that the goods receipt of the produced material must be automatically posted when the confirmation is triggered. Confirmations for the operation can be triggered for the time ticket or for the time event.

Time ticket

In the case of a confirmation for the time ticket, the quantities, activities, dates, and personnel data of an operation are confirmed. The quantities that can be recorded can be the yield and potential scrap. Activities are confirmed on the basis of the activity types assigned to the operation (setup time, machine time, labor time, and so on). The confirmation for the time ticket can be carried out using Transaction CO11N. It is shown in Figure 12.19.

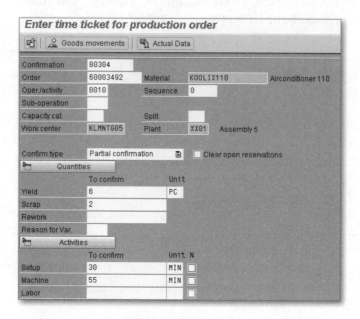

Figure 12.19 Time Ticket for the Operation

Regarding the dates, you can specify the start and end of the execution including time and calendar date. In the personnel data section, you can enter the personnel number of the responsible employee, the wage group, and so on.

Partial confirmation

An operation can also be confirmed if only parts of it have been processed. This can be necessary in order to document an intermediate status of the processing. In this case, the operation is assigned the status PCNF which stands for partially confirmed. A partial confirmation is useful for operations with long lead times. In contrast to that, the final confirmation triggers the status CONF. In case of several partial confirmations, only the newly added quantity is confirmed.

Time event

If you want the confirmations to be based on specific point in time, you can have *time events* to be confirmed. For example, you can specific the date and time of the process start as well as the date and time of the process end. The processing time is then automatically calculated based on this data.

A prerequisite for the confirmation is that the control key (Customizing Transaction OPJ8) allows it. Possible values for the **Confirmation** parameter are as follows: **Confirmation required**, **Confirmation possible but not necessary**, **Confirmation not Possible**, and **Milestone confirmation (not PS/PM)** (see Figure 12.20).

Control key—confirmation-relevant operation properties

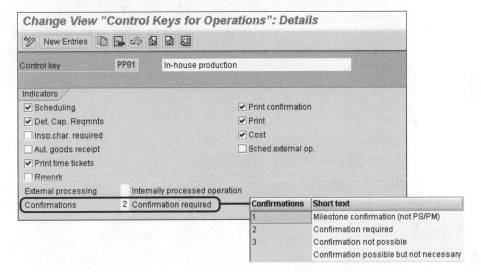

Figure 12.20 Confirmation-Relevant Settings in the Control Key

If an operation is defined as a milestone, the confirmation of the milestone operation includes all previous operations. This can make sense for inspection operations if the scrap quantity can only be determined when the inspection has ended. You can use the confirmation type of the control key to define an operation as a milestone.

Milestone confirmation

Like the milestone confirmation, the *progress confirmation* of an operation automatically includes all previous operations. However, in contrast to the milestone confirmation, the operation in question does not need to be specifically marked. A special characteristic of the progress confirmation is that each confirmation always considers the entire quantity that has been produced until the confirmation is triggered, and not only the newly added quantity. A progress confirmation is useful if several partial confirmations are required and if it is easier to determine the total quantity than only the newly added

Progress confirmation

quantity. You can enter progress confirmations using Transaction CO1F (see Figure 12.21).

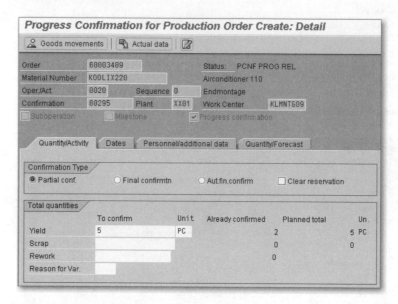

Figure 12.21 Progress Confirmation

Each progress confirmation specifies the total quantity. Let's take a look at an example. For a production order, 100 pieces of a material are produced. The production process is distributed across two days. On the first day, 70 pieces are produced, while the remaining 30 pieces are produced on the second day. If the regular confirmation was used, it would confirm 70 pieces in a partial confirmation on the first day, and include the remaining 30 pieces in the final confirmation on the second day. The progress confirmation confirms 70 pieces on the first day and 100 pieces on the second day.

Confirming an order

Typically, a confirmation refers to an operation in order to provide as much detailed information as possible on the production status. However, you also can use Transaction CO15 to enter a confirmation for the entire order (see Figure 12.22). In this case, the operations are confirmed in relation to the confirmed quantity.

Displaying confirmations

Transaction CO14 provides you with an overview of the confirmations that have actually occurred (see Figure 12.23).

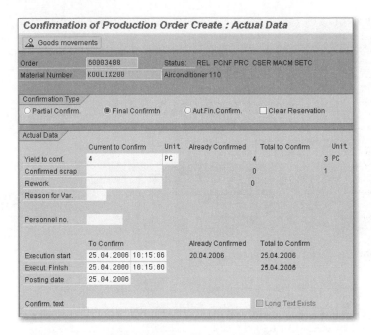

Figure 12.22 Confirmation for a Production Order

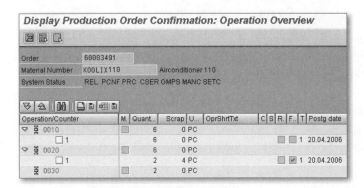

Figure 12.23 Overview of Confirmations

If a confirmation has been entered incorrectly, you can use Transaction CO13 to cancel it. **Cancellation**

The quantity actually produced can deviate in both directions from the planned quantity: It can be higher or lower, depending on whether the planned scrap exceeds or falls below the planned scrap. By default, this deviation is updated as expected yield variation in the production order and thus becomes MRP-relevant (see Figure 12.24). **Deviating confirmation**

395

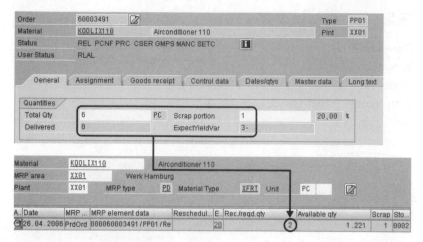

Figure 12.24 Expected Yield Variation

The receipt quantity used for material requirements planning can be calculated from the four quantity fields in the production order according to the following formula:

$$Receipt\ quantity = Total\ quantity - Scrap - Delivered + \\ Expected\ yield\ variation$$

The update of the yield surplus or deficit can be prevented by setting the relevant parameters in the production scheduling profile (Customizing Transaction OPKP; see Figure 12.25).

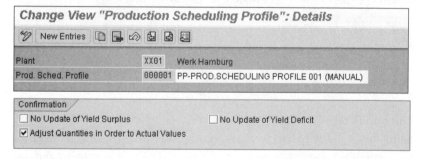

Figure 12.25 Options for Influencing the Effect of the Confirmation in the Production Scheduling Profile

The **Adjust Quantities in Order to Actual Values** parameter can be used to adjust the operation durations and component requirements of subsequent operations on the basis of a scrap-adjusted quantity calculation. In this case, the operations concerned are rescheduled.

12.5 Goods Receipt

Once the production process is finished, the produced material is put in stock. This operation increases the physical inventory and is posted as a goods receipt with reference to the production order via Transaction MB31 (see Figure 12.26).

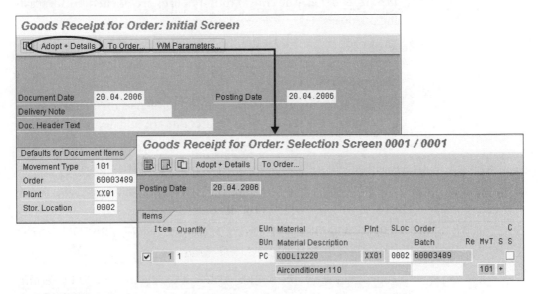

Figure 12.26 Good Receipt Posting for the Production Order

When the material is put in stock, it can be posted into the following three different stock types:

▸ Freely usable stock

▸ Quality inspection stock

▸ Locked stock

The goods receipt posting into the freely usable stock is carried out using movement type 101. You can also post the material directly into consumption, which means that it is directly transferred to another consumer such as a project or a different order. To be able to do that, the recipient must be specified in the production order.

To carry out a goods receipt posting for the production order, a confirmation is not necessarily required.

Effects of the
goods receipt
posting The goods receipt posting triggers several activities in the background:

- If the material is posted to stock, the total stock and the relevant stock type (freely usable stock) increase by the delivered quantity.

- If the material is posted to consumption, the consumption statistics are updated. The consumption figures are needed for forecasting purposes.

- The production order is credited and the stock value increases correspondingly. If the material is posted to consumption, the recipient is debited.

- The G/L accounts in financial accounting such as the material stock account and the factory activity account are updated.

- A material document showing the goods receipt is created as well as an accounting document containing all postings in financial accounting.

Goods receipt
information in the
production order The goods receipt for the production order is updated in the production order and marked as **Delivered** in the quantity information section (see Figure 12.27).

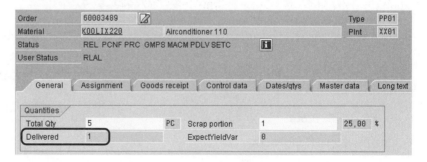

Figure 12.27 Goods Receipt Information in the Production Order

The MRP-relevant receipt quantity is reduced by the delivered quantity on the basis of the relevant formula (see above).

Tolerances Due to the deviating scrap quantity. The order quantity actually produced can also deviate in both directions. If the produced quantity falls below the planned quantity, the system outputs a warning and does not allow the produced quantity to exceed the planned quantity. Tolerances enable you to define which deviations of the goods receipt quantity can be accepted. The tolerances can be maintained in the **Tolerance data** section of the **Work Scheduling** view in the material master (see Figure 12.28).

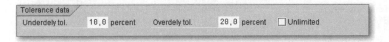

Figure 12.28 Tolerances in the Material Master (Excerpt from the "Work Scheduling" View)

If no entry is made, this means that a tolerance of 0% is used. In order to allow any deviation, you must set the **Unlimited** parameter. The tolerances are copied into the production order and are displayed in the **Goods receipt** view.

In order to reduce the maintenance work, you can have the goods receipt automatically posted when the confirmation for the last order is triggered. For this purpose, you don't need a final confirmation as the automatic goods receipt also works with partially confirmed quantities.

Automatic goods receipt

You can make the automatic goods receipt setting in two different objects: in the control key (see Figure 12.29), and in the production scheduling profile (see Figure 12.30).

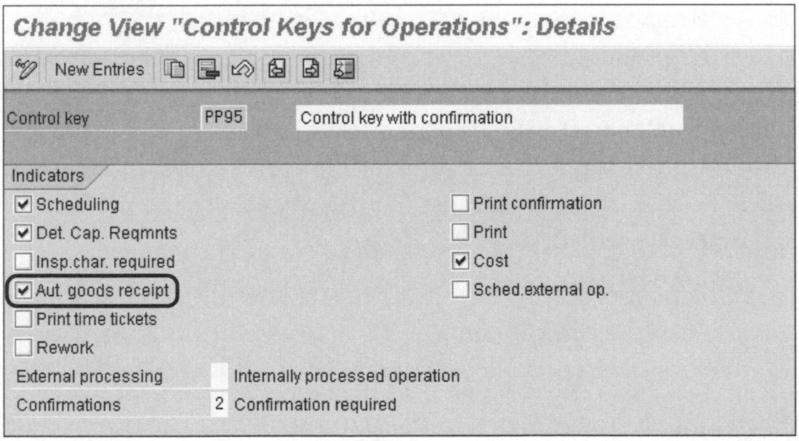

Change View "Control Keys for Operations": Details

New Entries

| Control key | PP95 | Control key with confirmation |

Indicators

☑ Scheduling   ☐ Print confirmation
☑ Det. Cap. Reqmnts   ☐ Print
☐ Insp.char. required   ☑ Cost
☑ Aut. goods receipt   ☐ Sched.external op.
☐ Print time tickets
☐ Rework
External processing   Internally processed operation
Confirmations   2   Confirmation required

Figure 12.29 Automatic Goods Receipt in the Control Key

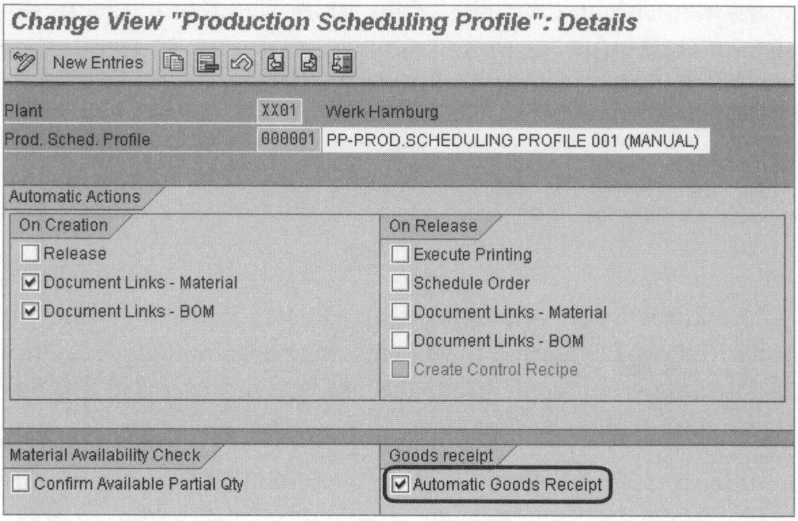

Figure 12.30 Automatic Goods Receipt in the Production Scheduling Profile

12.6 Settlement

During production, costs accrue continuously, including material costs and costs for internal activities. The production order is debited with these actual costs, for example in the case of material withdrawals, confirmations, and goods receipts for external procurement. When the produced material is put in stock, the order is credited accordingly. Crediting occurs in terms of the standard material price, which doesn't necessarily correspond to the actual costs, and for this reason it often happens that some of the costs remain open in the order. Because these costs must also be passed on, the production order must be settled.

The settlement of an order typically occurs after the order has been completed and when all produced materials are in stock. As soon as the order has the status, "delivery completed," it can be settled.

Settlement rule When a production order is created, it is assigned a *settlement rule* that defines the recipient to which the order is to be settled as well as the percentages at which the costs are to be distributed to the various settlement receivers. The settlement receivers can, for instance, be a material, a cost center, a sales order, a project, or a device. By default, the production order is assigned to the account of the material to be produced. In that case, the material is the settlement receiver, and the settlement share is 100%. The distribution rule of the settlement rule can be displayed in production order processing via the following menu path: **Header • Settlement Rule** (see Figure 12.31).

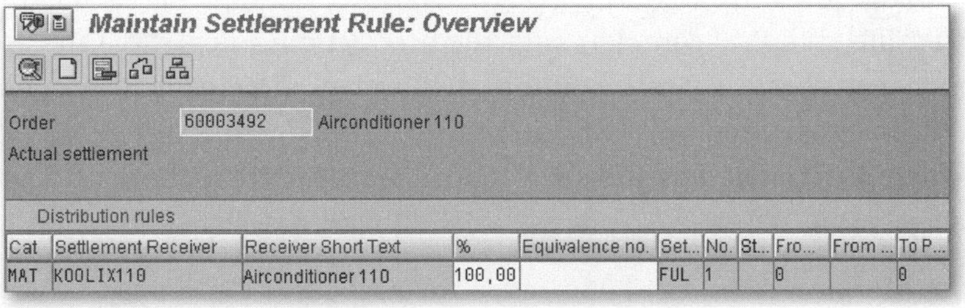

Maintain Settlement Rule: Overview

Order	60003492	Airconditioner 110
Actual settlement		

Distribution rules

Cat	Settlement Receiver	Receiver Short Text	%	Equivalence no.	Set...	No.	St...	Fro...	From ...	To P...
MAT	KOOLIX110	Airconditioner 110	100,00		FUL	1		0		0

Figure 12.31 Settlement Rule in the Production Order

When a finished material is delivered to the warehouse, the production order is credited and the material stock account is debited accordingly. Crediting and debiting occur in terms of a price specified in the material master. The material can be valuated in terms of a standard price or as a moving average price.

If the **Price control** flag is set to **Standard price** in the material master, the material is valuated at the specified price. In the majority of cases, the actual cost contained in the order does not match the stock debiting at the standard price. The difference is then posted to a price difference account when the order is settled.

Standard price

If, for example, a production order provides for the production of 10 units of a specific material whose standard price defined in the material master is US$ 5, the material is debited with an amount of US$ 50 at goods receipt, while the order is credited with US$ 50. If the actual costs for the order amount to US$ 70, the difference of US$ 20 is posted to the price difference account during settlement.

If the **Price control** flag in the material master is set to **V**, the material is not valuated at a standard price, but at a moving average price that is automatically determined by the system. This occurs as follows: The total value of the material stock account is divided by the total quantity of materials that are located in all storage locations pertaining to the plant in question; each valuation-relevant movement then causes the moving average price to be determined anew. Once the order has been settled, the value of the moving average price is 0.

Moving average price

12.7   Completion

The production order remains open and changeable until it is explicitly completed. In this context, a distinction is made between the logistical and the accounting-based completion.

Technical completion

After the technical completion of the production order, the order is no longer logistically relevant; that is, it is marked as being no longer MRP-relevant, and all reservations for components and capacity requirements that may still exist are deleted. The production order is assigned the status TCMP, which stands for technically completed.

A production order can be technically completed at any time. To do that, you must go to production order processing and select the following menu path: **Functions • Limit Processing • Technical Completion**. After that, it is no longer possible to change the production order interactively.

Completion

With the completion of the production order, the order is completed in terms of logistics and accounting. In addition to the restrictions that apply to the technical completion, it is now no longer possible to post any costs to the production order. Moreover, it is no longer possible to trigger any confirmation for the production order.

You can complete the order by selecting the following menu path from the production order processing view: **Functions • Limit Processing • Completion**. The completion is indicated by the status CMPL. To be able to complete a production order, it must have been previously released, and its account balance must have been settled.

Both the completion and the technical completion can be carried out as mass processing steps via Transaction COHV.

Supply chain management represents an approach to improving logistics processes in that it considers the entire supply chain of product groups, as opposed to the non-integrated optimization of individual logistical functions. SAP APO complements the functions of SAP ERP with supply chain management requirements. Because SAP APO focuses solely on planning, the program must be integrated with SAP ERP, which can be done in several different ways.

13 Supply Chain Management and Integration with SAP APO

13.1 Supply Chain Management with SAP APO

The concept of *supply chain management* (SCM) entails the consideration and management of logistical processes along the entire supply chain that includes suppliers, customers, and consumers. The SCM concept thus goes beyond the consideration of material and information flows for an individual operation. The goal is to harmonize and optimize the processes within the supply chain in order to reduce the stocks in the entire supply network and to ensure timely deliveries, among other benefits. In this context, the entire supply chain is integrated across different businesses from sales planning to procurement and production to delivery, and business partners are included in this process. The software support of this concept exceeds the boundaries of your own company as it is extended to the entire supply chain (see Geiger/Kerle, 2001, pp. 69–95).

The four success factors of supply chain management are speed, transparency, virtual supply chain, and added value. Let's examine these in detail.

▶ **Speed**
To a large extent, the Internet is responsible for the increase in the speed of process handling. Companies continuously strive to increase the speed and reduce the costs of production. High com-

munication requirements and the multitude of interfaces involved in internal and external supply chains require closer collaboration between the production and logistics partners. Companies must use the tools and technologies that are necessary to process their business transactions at the speed of the Internet.

▶ **Transparency**
Managing those business processes that are becoming faster requires a growing degree of transparency. The distribution of information within a cross-company supply chain at different points in time and in different systems makes the creation of transparency a big challenge. A high degree of transparency can be attained by using flexible integration technologies for data and process integration.

▶ **Virtual supply chain**
The development of a virtual supply chain increasingly blurs the legal and financial boundaries between companies. For this reason, the coordination of business processes across basic organizational units is constantly gaining in importance. A virtual supply chain makes possible flexibility and mobility, both of which are prerequisites for companies to be able to adapt their networks to the constantly changing market conditions. For the members of a virtual supply chain, the goal is to communicate with each other across company boundaries, collaborate with each other to reach common goals, and exchange information with each other. The virtual supply chain can be implemented on the basis of the currently available Internet technology.

▶ **Added Value**
The added value of a supply chain must be measured as a whole across all business process chains. Instead of using department-specific key figures, you must base your considerations on key figures that are relevant to the entire supply chain, such as the cycle time across the entire chain, overall customer satisfaction, and so on (see Hack, 2001, pp. 325–350). The constantly changing conditions require strategic and tactical supply-chain decisions, resulting in regular revision of the supply chain.

Advanced Planner and Optimizer

With SAP SCM and particularly the *Advanced Planner and Optimizer* (APO) program included therein, SAP provides a solution that extends and complements the functions of SAP ERP by SCM requirements. The range of functions of SAP APO caters for the following logistical processes, partly in conjunction with SAP ERP. SAP APO focuses on planning, while the execution is always based on SAP ERP.

- Demand planning
- Sales order fulfillment (availability check, backorder processing)
- Transportation planning
- Distribution planning and deployment
- Production planning
- Detailed scheduling (sequencing)
- External procurement

The following modules correspond to these processes:

- *Demand Planning (DP)*: demand planning
- *Supply Network Planning (SNP)*: distribution planning and deployment, sales and operations planning, external procurement
- *Production Planning and Detailed Scheduling (PP/DS)*: production planning, detailed scheduling, external procurement
- *Global Available-to-Promise (ATP)*: availability check, backorder processing
- *Transportation Planning and Vehicle Scheduling (TP/VS)*: transportation planning.

You can easily see that the functions of the SAP APO modules overlap to some degree with SAP PP functions. In general, you can say that in those cases the functions provided by SAP APO are more comprehensive than those provided by SAP ERP. However, SAP ERP also contains some functions that are not included in SAP APO, partly because they do not correspond to the integrated planning concept. Table 13.1 compares the process modules described in the previous chapters with those APO modules whose functions could replace the SAP ERP functions of production planning and control in case of integration.

Overlapping functions of ERP and APO

405

Process	APO module
Sales and operations planning	DP (demand planning) SNP (capacity leveling of sales and operations planning)
Demand management	No separate module
Material requirements planning	PP/DS
Long-term planning	PP/DS (detailed) or SNP (rough-cut)—carried out using an inactive planning version
Production order creation	Scheduling using PP/DS
Capacity planning	PP/DS
Production execution	No separate function; only integration from ERP

Table 13.1 Production Planning and Control Processes and APO Modules

13.2   Integration Scenarios

Because of the differences in business requirements, the modular structure of SAP APO, and the overlapping between some of the SAP ERP and SAP APO functions, there is more than one way to integrate SAP APO with SAP ERP. The decisive factors in favor of a specific integration scenario are clearly the specific business requirements. However, if SAP APO is integrated with an existing SAP ERP system that's already being used, the scope of SAP ERP functions that have already been used could also play a role. The following sections therefore describe some possible integration scenarios including their pros and cons.

Advantages of SAP APO over SAP ERP with regard to planning

SAP APO provides numerous advantages over SAP ERP, the most important ones of which—from our point of view—are the following.

▶ *Distribution planning* in SAP APO provides significantly more options than SAP ERP, particularly with regard to deployment; that is, the distribution of available quantities within the network.

▶ *Integrated distribution and production planning* is only possible in SAP APO. The application contains an optimization procedure and another solution process (Capable to Match) for this purpose.

▶ SAP APO provides considerably more functions that are better suited to *detailed scheduling* (sequencing) in order to create a feasible plan in terms of capacity. In contrast to capacity planning in SAP ERP, these functions enable to you account for dependencies between orders. Moreover, you can use optimization procedures that also consider the interdependencies of operations as well as the dependencies of operations to constraints. In addition, the planning algorithms are much more flexible.

▶ If the *availability check* for a sales order reports a non-availability, you can directly create a planned order that triggers production immediately. This is particularly advantageous in make-to-order production scenarios.

▶ The *Alert Monitor* displays exception situations and deviations in a much more transparent manner.

Detailed descriptions of these and other advantages of SAP APO can be found in the relevant literature (see Dickersbach 2005b). Depending on which advantages are decisive for using SAP APO, other integration scenarios can also be of interest to you.

In a simultaneous new implementation of SAP APO and SAP ERP and in companies that largely focus on distribution planning, demand planning often takes place in APO-DP, while distribution and sales and operations planning are carried out in APO-SNP, and production planning and detailed scheduling occur in APO-PP/DS. As a result, planned orders are created that are transferred to SAP ERP. These planned orders are converted into production orders in SAP ERP, where they are then processed. Capacity planning is no longer carried out in SAP ERP. This scenario represents the standard integration scenario.

Standard scenario

In a variant of the standard scenario, you can do without the PP/DS module in SAP APO and either transfer the planned orders created in the APO-SNP module to SAP ERP. Alternatively, you can completely waive production planning in SAP APO and transfer only stock transport requisitions to SAP ERP. Depending on the specific case and the portion of components planned in SAP APO, it may be necessary to carry out material requirements planning in SAP ERP.

Standard scenario—variant

This variant is useful if the level of complexity of production planning processes within the company is medium to low, and as a result the SAP ERP functions are sufficient.

SAP APO for detailed scheduling

If your organization is using SAP APO mainly because APO contains better functions for detailed scheduling, and if you already carry out sales and operations planning in SAP ERP, you do not need to perform demand planning using APO-DP. Instead, the planned independent requirements are transferred from SAP ERP to SAP APO. Based on the requirements, production planning and detailed scheduling are then carried out in the PP/DS module in order to create planned orders. Production order creation and execution are then carried out, as before, in SAP ERP.

Another variant, which is not used very often, is to carry out material requirements planning in SAP ERP as well and to use SAP APO only for detailed scheduling.

Production in case of non-availability

SAP APO provides two functions for the creation of planned orders when the availability check of the sales order reports the non-availability of a product. In this context, you can either check only the material components (*Multilevel ATP*) or both the material components and capacity (*Capable to Promise*). The planned order is then transferred to SAP ERP, where it is executed. This function is particularly useful for make-to-order manufacturers, as the availability check is usually negative in this scenario.

Because different companies have different business requirements and the software is relatively flexible, other integration scenarios are also possible.

13.3   Technical Integration

The integration with SAP APO can be implemented by creating and activating integration models on the part of SAP ERP. In the integration models, you must select the master and transaction data objects that you want to integrate with SAP APO.

Master data

The master data that's required for the PP/DS module is the same as for SAP PP: *plant*, *material*, *work center*, *BOM*, and *routing*. However, note the restriction that both the *BOM* and the *routing* are master data objects in SAP APO Accordingly, the master data object in SAP APO corresponds to the production version in SAP ERP. This involves the requirement that production versions must exist on the side of SAP ERP. SAP APO contains two alternative master data objects that correspond to the production version: the production process model (PPM) and the production data structure (PDS). Table 13.2 provides an overview of the corresponding master data in SAP ERP and SAP APO.

Master data in SAP ERP	Master data in SAP APO
Plant	Location
Material	Product
Work Center	Resource
Production version with BOM and work center	PPM (production process model) or PDS (production data structure)

Table 13.2 Corresponding Master Data in SAP ERP and SAP APO for Production Planning

PPM is the older of the two master data, but it is not being developed further. For this reason, SAP recommends using the production data structure (PDS).

Like SAP ERP, SAP APO contains planned orders, production orders, purchase requisitions, purchase orders, sales orders, planned independent requirements, and so on. However, in contrast to SAP ERP, all those orders have the same structure and only differ by their category. Whereas planned orders, purchase requisitions, and planned independent requirements can be created in SAP APO, production orders, purchase orders, and sales orders must always be created in SAP ERP.

Transaction data

To be able to transfer master data from SAP APO to SAP ERP and transaction data in both directions, you must first create integration models. Integration models also control whether the availability check is carried out in SAP APO.

Integration model

Integration models contain material-dependent and material-independent objects. The material-dependent objects include the majority of master data and almost all transaction data. Material-independent objects include work centers, suppliers, classes, and characteristics. You can create integration models using Transaction CFM1. They are identified by the freely definable model name, the logical system of SAP APO, and the freely definable application. The object types to be transferred must be selected and further restricted using additional criteria. Figure 13.1 shows an integration model in which the following object types are transferred:

▶ Plant **XX01**

▶ All material masters of plant **XX01** that begin with **KL**

▶ All production versions of these materials as PDS objects for SAP PP/DS

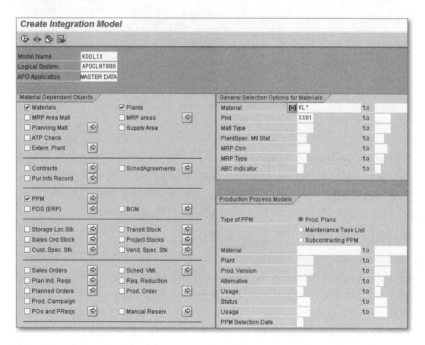

Figure 13.1 Integration Model

Contrary to this example, however, it is recommended that you create a separate integration model for each object in live operations (see Dickersbach, 2005b).

You should store the settings made here as a variant. In the subsequent step, you can generate the model by pressing the **F8** key. This means that those objects that meet the selection criteria at the time the model is generated are included into the model. The number of selected objects is displayed in the screen the displays next. If required, you can further break down this number (see Figure 13.2). Once the integration model has been generated, you must save it.

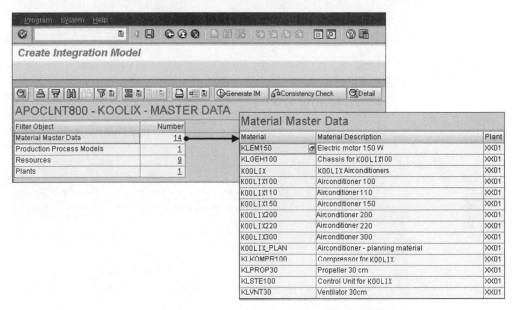

Figure 13.2 Generated Integration Model

The transfer is carried out by activating the model using Transaction CFM2. Figure 13.3 shows the necessary steps. First, the integration models to be activated are displayed on the initial screen.

Once the selection criteria have been entered (1), the integration model to be activated must be selected in the subsequent screen (2). The two columns on the right—**Prev. Status** and **New Status**—are both inactive (indicated by the red cross) because the model hasn't been activated yet. To activate the model, you must first change the **New Status** (3) and then start the activation (4). As a result and indication of the fact that the integration model has been activated, the **Prev. Status** column now is also marked with the green checkmark (5).

Once you have created integration models for all relevant master data, transaction data, and—optionally—the availability check, you can begin setting up the integration scenarios. At this stage, we refer you to the relevant literature that deals with the integration scenarios as well as the settings for the technical integration of SAP ERP and SAP APO (see Dickersbach 2005b).

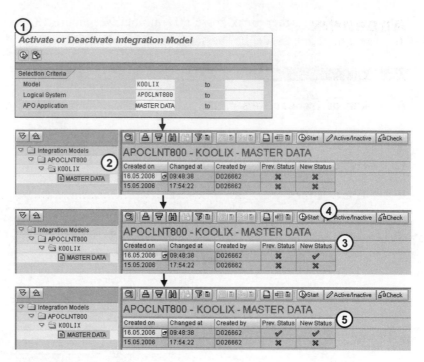

Figure 13.3 Activating the Integration Model

Appendix

A   Glossary

The term definitions used in this Appendix have been taken from the SAP Online Documentation.

Activity type   Unit in a controlling area that classifies the activities performed in a cost center. Examples: machine hours or finished units in production cost centers.

Actual costs   Costs actually incurred.

Alternative BOM   Used to identify one bill of material (BOM) within a BOM group. One product can be represented by several (alternative) BOMs if, e.g., different production processes are used for different lot size ranges. These alternative BOMs are grouped together in a multiple BOM.

Area of validity   Area of the organizational structure in which an object, e.g., bill of material (BOM) or routing, is valid. Example: The area of validity of a BOM is defined in terms of the plant.

Assembly   Group of components of a product that form a technically coherent whole in the production process. A product defined as an assembly can be used again as a component in another assembly.

Assembly order   Request to assemble pre-manufactured parts and assemblies to finished products according to an existing sales order.

Automatic reorder point planning   Special procedure in consumption-based planning. If available stock falls below the reorder point, then an entry is made in the material requirements planning (MRP) file. Then during the next planning run a procurement proposal is created. The reorder point and the safety stock level are automatically determined by the forecast program.

Availability check   This procedure makes sure that there are enough components available for the planned/production orders in production planning and production control.

Available capacity   Output or "ability to execute" a capacity within a specified period. The available capacity is specified by the following values: work start and finish times, duration of breaks, rate of capacity utilization in percent, and the number of individual capacities within one defined capacity.

Backflush   Non-manual posting of an issue of components sometime after their actual physical withdrawal for an order. The goods issue posting for backflushed components is carried out automatically at the time of order completion confirmation.

Backlog   Capacity requirements that have been scheduled, after scheduling or distribution, to periods that lie in the past.

Backorder processing With the backorder processing function, you can process materials for which there are missing quantities. In this process, you can commit requirements up to the amount of the current ATP quantity, or you can reallocate quantities that have already been committed.

Backward scheduling Type of scheduling in which the operations of an order are scheduled backwards starting from the order due date. The scheduled start and scheduled finish of the order are determined via this scheduling type.

Base unit of measure Unit of measure in which the stock of a material is managed. The system converts all quantities entered in other units into the base unit of measure.

Batch Subset of the total quantity of a material held in stock, which is managed separately from other subsets of the same material. Examples: different production lots (such as paints and pharmaceutical products), delivery lots, quality grades of a material.

Batch determination Functionality that can be used for all movements out of the warehouse in order to locate batches in stock using certain selection criteria. Batch determination can be used in: goods movement (inventory management), production orders/process orders, sale orders/deliveries, and transfer orders.

Batch master record Record containing general data on a batch (e.g., shelf life expiration date and date of last goods receipt).

Batch record Record containing all quality-relevant planned and actual data on the production of a batch. A batch record comprises several documents that contain the relevant data of specific SAP ERP objects and archive files from external systems. The layout and contents of the batch record comply with international standards defined in the guidelines on Goods Manufacturing Practices (GMP). Batch records are stored in an optical archive where they cannot be forged. They can be approved using a digital signature.

Batch search strategy The batch search strategy specifies the selection criteria from which batches are selected during batch determination and what further steps are to be taken with them. The batch search strategy record is an application-specific master record.

Batch where-used list Hierarchically structured record of the use or composition of a batch across all production levels. The batch where-used list facilitates both top-down and bottom-up analysis. Top-down analysis indicates the batches of raw materials or semifinished products of which a batch of a finished product is composed. Bottom-up analysis indicates the batches of semifinished products or finished products that contain a certain raw material batch.

Bill of material (BOM) A complete, formally structured list of the components that make up a product or assembly. The list contains the object number of each component, along with the quantity and unit of measure. The components are known as BOM items. You can create the following BOM categories in the SAP ERP system: material BOM, document structure, equipment BOM, functional location BOM, and sales order BOM.

BOM category Classification of bills of material (BOMs) enabling you to represent different objects (such as materials or documents). Specific elements are maintained for the bills of material for the various objects, for example:

▸ Material bill of material (referring to a material master record): materials, documents, and texts

▸ Document bill of material (referring to a document info record): documents and texts

BOM component Part of a bill of material (BOM). If an object (e.g., material) consists of more than one part, you can store these parts as components in a BOM. The following objects can be stored as BOM components: material master record, document info record, or class.

BOM explosion Function for determining all the components of a bill of material (BOM) and listing them. You can explode a BOM to show the structure of the product or to show the total quantity of each component.

BOM explosion number Used to specify a standard explosion date (fixed key date) for all bill of material (BOM) levels.

BOM group Collection of bills of material (BOMs) enabling you to describe a product or a number of similar products. The following bills of material comprise a BOM group: all

the variants of a variant BOM, and all the alternatives of a multiple BOM.

BOM header The part of a bill of material (BOM) containing data that is valid for the whole BOM. Examples: object number/plant/usage, texts, quantity data, effectiveness data, general data, and administrative data.

BOM item Part of a bill of material (BOM) for which information about the quantity and unit of measure are stored. BOM items are separated into various types, and special item data is managed, according to the object reference (e.g., material or document) and other criteria (e.g., inventory management).

BOM usage The bill of material (BOM) usage allows you to maintain BOMs (e.g., for material LAMP) for specific sections of your company. You can maintain a separate BOM for each section in your company (e.g., production), so that each section only processes the items relevant to that section. In customizing functions, you can define which item statuses can be used in which BOM usage. For example, all items in BOMs with a certain usage are relevant to production. The usage is an important selection criterion in the BOM application, which controls automatic explosion of BOMs.

Bottleneck work center A bottleneck work center is defined in capacity requirements planning for purposes of capacity (finite) scheduling. Proceeding from this work center, forward and backward scheduling are carried out.

Bulk material Item in a bill of material (BOM) that is stored loose at the work center, ready for use. This material can be used directly at the work center. Bulk materials are used in small quantities of low value, so these items are not taken into account when costing an order.

Business area Organizational unit of financial accounting that represents a separate area of operations or responsibilities within an organization, and to which value changes recorded in financial accounting can be allocated.

Business partner A natural or legal person or a group of natural or legal persons not part of the business organization but with whom a business interest exists.

CAD Data processing system for Computer Aided Design (CAD) and drawing.

Campaign The uninterrupted execution of process orders of the same kind based on the same master recipe.

Campaign planning The planning of a campaign, comprising the following tasks: scheduling of a campaign, allocation of a campaign to a specific resource (such as a line or a processing unit), and availability check of the resources to which the allocation is made.

Capacity Capacity refers to the ability of a work center to perform a specific task. Capacities are differentiated according to capacity category. They are arranged hierarchically under a work center.

Capacity category A description that classifies a capacity at a work center. A capacity category can only exist once at each work center. However, capacities at different work centers can have the same capacity category.

Capacity leveling Leveling of overloads and underloads at work centers.

Capacity load The capacity load is determined from a comparison of capacity requirements and the capacity available. This value is always specified as a percentage of the available capacity.

Capacity planner group A key for a group of employees who are responsible for capacity planning. You can use this key to select specific capacities.

Capacity requirement Specifies how much capacity output is required for individual orders at a specific time. Capacity categories are assigned to a work center. Capacity requirements can be caused by work orders and planned orders.

Capacity requirements planning A tool for determining available capacity and capacity requirements, and for carrying out capacity leveling. Capacity requirements planning supports long-term rough-cut planning, production rate planning, and short-term detailed planning.

Change master record Data record that contains all the information required for managing a change. A change master record contains descriptive data (such as reason for change) and data with control functions (such as valid-from date and indicators for object types). In addition to this data, which you can maintain directly, there is also data that the system updates automatically (such as administrative data).

Change number Number used to uniquely identify a change master record. All changes made with reference to a change number are controlled and logged by the change master record. Numbers can be assigned both internally and externally.

Checking group The checking group is the criterion that groups together all the checking rules from all application areas for a material. In conjunction with the checking rule, it defines the scope of the availability check for each business event, i.e., which stocks, goods receipts, and goods issues are taken into account in the availability check, and whether replenishment lead time is checked.

Clean-out recipe Recipe that describes the time, resource, and material requirements, as well as the activities that are necessary to clean out a vessel after the productive run of a campaign.

Client In commercial, organizational, and technical terms, a self-contained unit in a SAP ERP system with separate master records and its own set of tables.

Collective order Linking of planned orders or production orders over several production levels.

Company code The smallest organizational unit for which a complete self-contained set of accounts can be drawn up for purposes of external reporting. This includes recording all relevant transactions and generating all supporting documents required for financial statements.

Confirmation A confirmation is a part of order monitoring. It documents the processing status of operations or sub-operations. In the SAP system, a distinction is made between partial and final confirmations. A final confirmation is used to determine at which work center the operation should be carried out, who has carried out the operation, the quantities of yield and scrap quantities that have been produced, and the size of the standard values required for the actual operation.

Consignment Form of business in which the vendor (external supplier) maintains a stock of materials at a customer (purchaser) location. The vendor retains ownership of the materials until they are withdrawn from the consignment stores. Payment for consignment stock is required only when the material is withdrawn. For this reason, the vendor is informed of withdrawals of consignment stock on a regular basis.

Constant model Model for constant consumption flow. A constant consumption applies if consumption values vary very little from a stable mean value. Any individual variations from the average value are caused by random influences that appear on an irregular basis.

Consumable material Material or service that is the subject of procurement and whose value is recorded via the cost element accounts or fixed asset accounts. There are consumable materials without a material master record, with a material master record without inventory management, and with a material master record with inventory management on a quantity basis only.

Consumption Quantity normally updated by the system when a material is withdrawn from the warehouse/stores, which indicates how much of that material has been used or consumed in a given past period.

Consumption-based planning Generic term for the procedure within material requirements planning (MRP) for which stock requirements and past consumption values play a central role. Consumption-based planning is further divided into the following procedures: reorder point planning, recast-based planning, and rhythmic planning.

Container Receptacle in which a material is contained.

Control cycle Controls the replenishment of a specific material via *Kanban*. It determines the replenishment method to be used between the supply and demand source, and the quantity required. Moreover, it determines the number of kanbans and the quantity of each individual kanban, the replenishment strategy used to procure the material, the supply source that is to provide the material, and the production supply area (i.e., the demand source that requires the material).

Controlling area Organizational unit within a company that is used to represent a closed system for cost accounting purposes. A controlling area may include single or multiple company codes that may use different currencies. These company codes must use the same operative chart of accounts. All internal allocations refer exclusively to objects in the same controlling area.

Control recipe A recipe containing all process instructions for the execution of a process order by a process control system or a line operator. Control recipes are created from the process instructions of the process order and sent to the responsible process control instance. One control recipe is generated for each control recipe destination defined in the process order.

Control recipe destination Process control system, process operator, or operating group to which a control recipe is transferred for processing. The control recipe destination specifies the technical address to which a control recipe is transferred, and how the transfer takes place (e.g., initiated by SAP ERP or by process control).

Control station The link between production control and the production process itself. It has interfaces for plant and machine data collection and can be used to control lead time parallel to production and to monitor released orders. The control station is easy to use (with the mouse), has a graphical user interface (for planning tables and statistics), and is constantly available.

Cost center Organizational unit within a controlling area that represents a defined location of cost incurrence. The definition can be based on functional requirements, allocation criteria, physical location, or responsibility for costs.

Costing Process that calculates the cost of goods manufactured or the cost of goods sold of a product or cost object. The costing process is based on the order quantity or the costing lot size in the material master record.

Costing object Reference object for a cost estimate. Examples of reference objects that can be costed are materials, cost object IDs, production orders, Sales document items (inquiry, quotation, sales order), projects (WBS elements), internal orders, and primary cost elements.

Customer Business partner with whom a business relationship exists involving the issue of goods and/or services.

Customer requirements Requirements for non-combinable finished products and for combinable finished products and assemblies, created on the basis of a sales order.

Dangerous goods Substances or objects to be transported that pose a risk to public safety, to the life and health of humans and animals, and to property, due to their nature, properties, or state.

Demand program Container for the requirement quantities and dates for finished products and main assemblies in the form of planned independent requirements.

Dependent requirement Planned product requirement that is caused by the production of higher-level assemblies. During the planning of product requirements, dependent requirements are automatically created for the components that are necessary for the production of a planned order.

Detailed planning Used within capacity planning for short-term planning of individual capacities or people. Detailed planning uses exact times and dates and is based on a routing.

Digital signature Equivalent to a handwritten signature for the processing of digital data. A digital signature ensures that the signed transaction can only be carried out by users with a special authorization, that the signatory identification is unique and forgery-proof, and that the signatory name is documented along with the signed transaction and the date and time, and cannot be falsified. Depending on the application in which the signature is used, you can or must also enter a comment for the digital signature. If a transaction must be signed by several different persons, you can combine individual signatures of different authorization groups into application-specific signature strategies.

Direct procurement Procurement without stockholding. Components are produced directly for the higher-level assembly and consumed. The aim of direct production is to deal with both scheduling and costing procedures for finished products, assemblies, and components in a bill of material (BOM) structure. The components that are produced directly are connected with each other in a multilevel collective order by entering the respective higher-level and leading planned order or production order. The collective order can be scheduled together, and the costs incurred for the collective order can be processed together.

Disaggregation Process in Sales & Operations Planning (SOP) by which the data of a planning hierarchy level is broken down into the data of its respective members.

Dispatching period The planning period is the period of time in which the system takes all the planned orders and plans their sequence according to the selected planning procedure. This term is used in sequencing.

Document management system A set of integrated functions that allows you to manage different types of documents. Some examples of the document management functions supported in the system are: version management, status network, link to objects (such as material masters), classification, engineering change management, and archiving.

Engineering change management Component that allows you to change objects with history (with date validity) or depending on certain criteria (with parameter effectiveness). The different processing statuses of the object are saved. All changes are made with reference to a change master record. In the SAP system, you can change, e.g., the following object types with reference to a change number: bills of material, task lists, documents, and materials.

Engineer-to-order Manufacturing environment in which complex production activities under essentially one-off conditions are undertaken for a specific customer. The production structures are managed using a work breakdown structure. At this level, the following planning steps for the project are carried out: budget management, revenue planning, finance planning, and cost planning. The production processes are managed using a network. The dates, resources, and associated costs are planned at this level.

Exception message Information on any peculiarities or exceptional situations that occurred during the planning run.

Ex-post forecast Forecast for past periods. The ex-post forecast is used for the evaluation of forecast quality, for model selection, for parameter optimization, and for forecasting missing periods in retrospect.

External processing Operations that are carried out at a different company. Within work order processing, the system creates purchase requisitions for externally processed operations. The purchasing department converts these purchase requisitions into purchase orders.

External procurement Procurement of raw materials, operating supplies (MRO items), trading goods/merchandise, or services from an external supplier for the organizational units within a firm that need such items.

Factory calendar Calendar in which working days are numbered sequentially. The factory calendar is defined on the basis of a public holiday calendar. The validity period of a factory calendar must be within the validity period of the public holiday calendar. The weekdays that are working days must also be specified in this calendar.

FIFO principal A stock removal method whereby the materials first transferred to a bin are the first to be removed from the bin (first in, first out).

Final confirmation The confirmation of an operation after it has been completed.

Final issue Last goods issue for a certain material with reference to a reservation item. No further goods issues with reference to this reservation item are expected. The reservation item is regarded as closed.

Final issue indicator Indicator used by the system to denote that a reservation item is closed. The final issue indicator is set automatically when a goods issue is posted if the total reserved quantity is withdrawn. As a result, the reservation item is no longer included in the list of open reservations.

Finite scheduling Scheduling type within capacity planning that takes account of the capacity loads that already exist. Finite scheduling calcu-

lates the start and finish dates for operations in the order.

Float after production Number of working days between the scheduled finish date and the order finish date; used as a float in production scheduling.

Float before production Number of working days between the order start date and the scheduled start date; used as a float in production scheduling.

Flow manufacturing A manufacturing type within the PP system, in which operations are completely overlapped. Operations with short execution times are stretched to match the longest operation. The longest operation sets the pace. Queue times occur in the operations that have been stretched.

Forecast Estimation of the future values in a time series. In the SAP system, the forecast can be carried out using a number of different procedures, such as first-order and second-order exponential smoothing or simple average models.

Forecast-based planning Special procedure in consumption-based planning that is based on future requirements predictions calculated using the forecast. Forecast values for future requirements are determined by the integrated forecasting program. These values then form the basis of the net requirements calculation in the planning run. In the case of a shortage for a forecast requirement, the system creates a procurement proposal.

Forecast error   The difference between the actual consumption values and the forecast values in the last period.

Forecast model   States the structure prevalent in a time series. The following forecast models exist: constant model, trend model, seasonal model, and seasonal trend model.

Forecast parameter   Generic term for all forecast-related data. A distinction is made between forecast parameters that are independent of the forecast model and forecast parameters that depend on the forecast model.

Forecast requirements   Requirements recorded in the system that have resulted from a forecast run.

Forecast value   Value that is usually determined by the system during the forecast and that indicates future consumption for a material within a certain period. The forecast value is updated in the material master record.

Formula (CAP)   A formula represents a mathematical description of a calculation that is used to determine default values by using the CAP module. Formulas consist of characteristics that are linked by mathematical operators and functions. A formula can be used to calculate both final and intermediate results.

Goods issue   Term used in inventory management to describe a reduction in warehouse stock due to a withdrawal of stock or the delivery of goods to a customer.

Goods movement   Physical or logical movement of materials leading to a change in stock levels or resulting in the direct consumption of the material.

Goods receipt   Term from the field of inventory management denoting a physical inward movement of goods or materials. The SAP ERP system differentiates between the following kinds of goods receipt:

▶ Goods receipt with reference to a purchase order

▶ Goods receipt with reference to a production order

▶ Other goods receipts (without reference)

Gross requirements planning Special deterministic procedure within material requirements planning (MRP). In gross requirements planning, no comparison is made between the warehouse stock and the (gross) requirements. This means that these requirements will always be covered by order proposals.

Group counter   A group counter identifies a task list within a task list group. Group counters can, e.g., be used to differentiate between task lists that belong to the same group, but that describe different processing sequences. A group counter in combination with the group key identifies a task list.

Individual capacity   To achieve more detailed planning of resources and commitments, you can subdivide capacities into individual capacities (e.g., individual machines) for which you can maintain available capacities. You can allocate or dispatch capacity requirements to these individual capacities in the graphical or tabular planning table.

Individual customer requirement
Material requirement in a plant that is created by a sales order and transferred separately to material requirements planning (MRP). The system creates a new line in the requirements/stock overview of the material for each document item.

In-house production time The time that is required to produce the material in your own plant. You can enter the in-house production time so that is dependent on the order quantity or independent of the order quantity. It is calculated by adding together the lead times of all operations plus the *float before production* and the *float after production*.

Inspection characteristic Characteristic on the basis of which an inspection is performed. For inspection characteristics, a distinction is made between qualitative and quantitative characteristics (characteristic types). Inspection characteristics are often quality characteristics, but that does not necessarily have to be the case.

Inspection lot Request to a plant to carry out a quality inspection for a specific quantity of material.

Inspection method Describes the procedure for inspecting a characteristic. You create inspection methods as master records and assign them to master inspection characteristics or inspection plans. You can assign several inspection methods to a master inspection characteristic.

Inspection operation Comprises all activities for the inspection or one or more inspection characteristics with specific test equipment at a specific work center. In the SAP ERP system, data for the scheduling, workload assignment, and capacity planning can be assigned to the inspection operation.

Inspection plan Description of the inspection process for materials in a plant.

Inspection point Record of clearly identifiable inspection results that are assigned to an inspection operation. The inspection points are identified by the user by a combination of fields whose meaning is defined based on their usage.

Interoperation time Time containing the following elements:
- Move time from one operation to the next
- Wait time after the execution of an operation
- Floats of the operation/work order
- Queue time
- Float before production
- Float after production

Issue storage location Storage location from which components are withdrawn for production.

Item category Defines items in a bill of material (BOM) according to certain criteria, such as the object type of the component (e.g., material master record or document info record). The item category controls the following: screen sequence, field selection, default values, material entry, inventory management, and sub-items. Examples of item categories are: stock item, non-stock item, and document item.

Kanban A procedure for controlling production and material flow based on a chain of operations in production and procurement. The replenishment or the production of a material is not triggered until a certain production level actually requires the material. The signal for replenishment is issued by a card (kanban) that is sent by a consumer to the supplier.

LIFO principle Stock removal strategy whereby the goods last transferred to a storage type are the first to be transferred out of the storage type (last in, first out).

Line balancing In line design you can create line balances for a line hierarchy. In line balancing you regularly adapt the line hierarchy to a planned production rate by changing the number of takts (processing stations) and individual capacities (persons), and if necessary you can move operations to other line segments.

Line design Integral part of process manufacturing for flow and process manufacturers. Using line design, operations and sub-operations are defined, and their sequence is determined in the form of a rate routing. Line design is also used to structure the production line, i.e., to divide it into segments and takts. In addition, you can optimize the work load in the individual takts or line segments by creating a line balance for the production line.

Line hierarchy Map of the structure of a production line. The pro-

duction line can be split into as many line segments as desired. These line segments can then be split up into individual sub-elements. You can carry out the split over as many levels as you want. The lowest levels of the line hierarchy are the individual takt areas. These takt areas are the smallest physical units of a line. The production line, the line segments, and the sub-elements are created in the system as work centers and grouped in the line hierarchy using a graphic.

Line segment Work center on a production line. You can create line segments in line design by inserting work centers in a line hierarchy. Then you can define the number of takts and the number of individual capacities for the line segments.

Logistics Information System (LIS) The Logistics Information System is made up of the following information systems: Sales Information System, Purchasing Information System, Inventory Controlling, Shop Floor Information System, Plant Maintenance Information System, and Quality Management Information System. The information systems that belong to the LIS have a modular structure, yet they have a variety of techniques in common that allow you to analyze data. This type of structure also allows the individual information systems to retain their special features. The information systems in LIS can be used to plan, control, and monitor business events at different stages in the decision-making process. They are flexible tools for collecting, aggregating, and analyzing data from the operative applications. The information systems provide various views of all information from the live application. The level of detail in which information is displayed is freely definable. Informative key figures enable you to continually control target criteria and to react in time to exceptional situations. Data can be analyzed using either standard analyses or flexible analyses. Flexible planning, the Early Warning System, and the Logistics Information Library are also integrated in the information systems. Tools are available in Customizing that enable you to create a self-defined information system and tailor it to specific requirements.

Long-term planning   Simulation of the future stock and requirements situation.

Lot size   Quantity to be produced or to be procured. The lot size is used as a criterion for selecting alternatives within a multiple bill of material (BOM), selecting a routing as a basis for a production order, selecting an operation within alternative operations, and pricing during the sale and/or the purchasing of goods.

Lot sizing procedure   Procedure in material requirements planning (MRP) that is used to calculate the order and production quantities (lot sizes). The lot sizing procedures are divided into three groups: static lot sizing procedures, period lot sizing procedures, and optimum lot sizing procedures.

Low-level code   The lowest level in which a material appears in any product structure.

Low-level coding   The low-level code defines the sequence in which all materials included in the planning run are to be planned. The procedure of low-level coding takes into account that a material may appear in several products and in more than one explosion level of a bill of material (BOM). This procedure groups together the total requirements for a material at the lowest explosion level in which the material appears, i.e., the low-level code.

Make-to-order production   Type of production in which a product is manufactured specially for a particular customer. Make-to-order production includes both sales-order-related production and engineer-to-order.

Manual reorder point planning   Special procedure in consumption-based planning. If the available stock level falls below the reorder point, then an entry is made in the planning file. The system then creates a procurement proposal in the next planning run. The reorder point and the safety stock level must be defined manually and are saved in the material master record.

Manufacture of co-products   Production of several materials in one process. Unlike with byproducts, some of the production costs are assigned to the joint product in the order settlement. The settlement rule, according to which the production costs are distributed, can be configured individually for each production process.

Manufacturing order   Request asking production to manufacture a specific quantity of a material or perform a specific service on a specific date. A manufacturing order defines which work center or resource is used to manufacture a material and which material components are required.

Master production scheduling In master production scheduling, those parts or products that greatly influence company profits or that take up critical resources are planned with special attention. Master schedule items are marked with the material requirements planning (MRP) procedure for master production scheduling.

Master recipe Description of an enterprise-specific process in the process industry that does not relate to a specific order. The master recipe is used for the production of materials or for rendering of services.

Master schedule item Master schedule items are finished products or important assemblies that play a major part in total turnover, or which dominate the production process due to the production techniques. Special planning tools exist for the particularly careful planning of master schedule items.

Material Good that is the subject of business activity. A material can be traded, used in manufacture, consumed, or produced.

Material availability check Automatic check that is carried out to find out whether there are enough materials to cover a proposed withdrawal from stock.

Material BOM Bill of material (BOM) that is created with reference to a material master. The BOM can contain items of different item categories (such as stock items, non-stock items, document items, and text items).

Material costs Consist of direct material costs and material overhead costs. They are part of production costs.

Material master record Data record containing all the basic information required to manage a material. This data is sorted according to various criteria. A material master record contains data of a descriptive nature (such as size, dimension, and weight) and data with a control function (such as material type and industry sector). In addition to this data, which can be directly maintained by the user, it also contains data that is automatically updated by the system (such as stock levels).

Material overhead costs Costs that are not assigned directly to individual materials, such as procurement costs and storage costs for inventories in which different materials are stored.

Material requirements planning (MRP) Generic term for the activities involved in creating a master production schedule or an external procurement plan for all the materials in a plant or company. Material requirements planning is also referred to as materials planning.

Material shortage This occurs when the requirements quantity is greater than the receipt and stock quantity. The shortage quantity is calculated in material requirements planning (MRP) by the net requirements calculation.

Material stock Part of current assets. Material stock is managed at the plant or storage location level.

Material type Groups together materials with the same basic attributes, e.g., raw materials, semifinished products, or finished products. When creating a material master record, you must assign the material to a material type. The material type you choose determines whether the material is intended for a specific purpose, e.g., as a configurable material or process material, whether the material number can be assigned internally or externally, the number range from which the material number is drawn, which user department data you may enter, and what procurement type the material has, i.e., whether it is manufactured in-house or procured externally, or both. Along with the plant, the material type determines the material's inventory management requirement—i.e., whether changes in quantity are updated in the material master record and whether changes in value are also updated in the stock accounts in financial accounting.

Material valuation Determination of the value of a stock of materials.

Material variant Product variant of a configurable material. The material master record of a material variant contains assigned characteristic values.

Material where-used list Bill of material (BOM) reporting function that determines which BOMs a material is used in, along with the quantity. We distinguish between the following lists: direct where-used list and multilevel where-used list.

Materials planning Generic term for the activities involved in creating a master production schedule or an external procurement plan for all the materials in a plant or company. Materials planning is also referred to as material requirements planning (MRP).

Midpoint scheduling Scheduling type where an order is rescheduled on the basis of changes to dates. Starting from the start time of the operation, all the previous operations are scheduled backwards. Starting from the finish time of the operation, all the previous operations are scheduled forwards. This type of scheduling is used, e.g., in production planning and control when the operation dates are changed during capacity leveling (e.g., bottleneck planning).

Milestone confirmation A type of completion confirmation in which several operations in a processing sequence are automatically confirmed. An operation is marked as a milestone operation using its control key. If you confirm an operation that is marked as a milestone, the system automatically confirms all preceding operations.

Minimum lot size Minimum quantity that must be reached during procurement. The minimum lot size can be taken into account in lot size calculation.

Minimum range of coverage Minimum number of days that the dynamic safety stock should cover requirements. The minimum range of coverage is defined in the range of coverage profile.

Minimum stock level Lower limit for the dynamic safety stock. The minimum stock level is calculated using the formula *minimum range of coverage * average daily requirement*.

MRP area Organizational unit for which you can carry out material requirements planning (MRP) separately. An MRP area can include one or several storage locations of a plant or a subcontractor. You can define MRP areas within a plant. By defining MRP areas, you can carry out MRP specifically for each area. This enables the right quantity of materials to be provided on time for each individual area, such as a particular production line or a storage location for spare parts or subcontractor stock.

MRP controller The person responsible for a group of materials within material requirements planning (MRP) in a plant or company. Any material that takes part in MRP must be assigned to an MRP controller.

MRP element Generic term for all objects that are displayed as items in the material requirements planning (MRP) list or in the stock/requirements list. Such objects include planned orders, purchase orders, reservations, and sales orders.

MRP group Groups certain materials together from a material requirements planning (MRP) standpoint to allocate them special control parameters for planning. These control parameters include the strategy group, the planning horizon, and the creation indicator for the planning run.

MRP list Overview of the results of the material requirements planning (MRP) run.

MRP lot size A key that defines which lot sizing procedure the system uses for calculating the quantity to be procured in the material requirements planning (MRP) run.

MRP procedure Procedure that specifies how planning is carried out for a material. Material requirements planning (MRP) procedures are subdivided into two main groups: MRP and consumption-based planning (reorder point). MRP is based on future requirements. Assembly and component requirements for finished products produced in-house are calculated by exploding the bill of material. Consumption-based planning (reorder point) is based on historical data. Requirements are calculated using past consumption values.

MRP run Implements material requirements planning (MRP) for all materials or assemblies for which a planning file entry has been created.

MRP type Key that controls the material requirements planning (MRP) procedure (MRP or reorder point) to be used for planning a material. It contains additional control parameters, e.g., for using the forecast for the materials planning, for firming procurement proposals, and so on.

Net requirements calculation Check carried out by the system to determine whether the requirements are covered by available warehouse stock and planned receipts from the purchasing department or from production. If the forecast requirements are not covered, then the system will generate a procurement proposal.

Network Object containing instructions on how to carry out tasks in a specific way, in a specific order, and in a specific time period.

Non-stock item The item category "non-stock item" is used if you enter a material as a component in a bill of material (BOM) and the material is not kept in stock. A purchase requisition is created for non-stock items.

Object dependencies Knowledge that describes the mutual interdependencies between objects. For example, you can define dependencies between characteristics and characteristic values such that 21-speed gears are only allowed for racing bicycles. You can also use object dependencies to ensure that the correct bill of material (BOM) items and operations are selected when an object is configured. You describe object dependencies in a dependency editor using a special syntax. There are different types of object dependencies for different purposes.

Opening period for planned order Number of working days between the date that the order is created and the planned start date. This time is available for the material requirements planning (MRP) controller to convert a planned order into a purchase requisition or a production order.

Operating facilities All facilities necessary during production, such as: means of production (machines, plants), further production resources, such as tools or inspection equipment, means of transport, warehousing facilities, organizational resources, property and buildings, and energy and waste disposal facilities.

Operation Describes an activity in a work step in a plan or work order. Examples: production operations, inspection operations, and network activities.

Operation lead time The lead time of an operation is made up of its queue time, setup time, processing time, teardown time, and wait time.

Operation number All operations in a routing are assigned a continuous number (operation number). This number allows you to identify an operation and to distinguish one operation from another.

Operation segment An operation is subdivided into the following segments: queue, setup, processing, teardown, and wait. Capacity requirements can be calculated for the following operation segments: setup, processing, and teardown.

Operative production rate Control parameter for takt-based scheduling in sequencing. Just like the planned rate, the operative rate specifies the quantity per time unit that you can produce on a production line. With the operative rate you can overwrite the planned rate in order to react to short-term changes in supply or requirements.

Operative takt time Takt times are control parameters for the takt-based scheduling of sequencing and are defined for a production line. Just like the planned takt time, the operative takt time is the time interval in which a material enters the production line and a processed material leaves the line. With the operative takt time, you can overwrite the planned takt time, in order to react to short-term changes in requirements and supply.

Order Describes a task that is to be carried out within a company. The order specifies which task is to be carried out, when the task is to be carried out, what is needed to carry out the task, and how the order costs are to be settled.

Order BOM Single-level bill of material (BOM) that you generate for a sales order from a material BOM, and that you modify specific to the order so that the material BOM remains unchanged. An order BOM is uniquely identified by the sales order number, the sales order item, and the material number. Order BOMs can be created for both configurable and non-configurable materials.

Order lead time The lead time of an order is the time between the basic order dates minus the order floats.

Order record Record containing all quality-relevant planned and actual data for a process order.

Order-related production Type of production in which the manufactured products are delivered to inventory without reference to a sales order. The order costs are collected on production orders and settled to inventory.

Order settlement Complete or partial crediting of an order. The costs that have accrued to an order are debited to one or more allocation receivers belonging to financial or management accounting.

Order split Function in Shop Floor Control with which an existing production order is divided into two production orders that, from a logistical standpoint, are separate from each other. During order split, part of the order quantity (split quantity) of a production order (parent order) is split off at a particular operation (split operation) in the standard sequence. The quantity that is split off is produced in a separate production order (child order).

Order type Order types categorize orders according to their purpose. The order type contains numerous pieces of information that are necessary for managing the orders. Order types are client-specific. This means that the same order type can be used in all controlling areas in one client. Examples: order type for production orders, order type for maintenance orders, order type for capital investment orders, order type for marketing orders.

Organizational structure An organizational plan that sorts the tasks in an enterprise into task areas and determines the jobs and departments that are to process those tasks.

Original plan First version that is saved of a planned independent requirement (demand management).

Overhead cost order Internal order used to monitor overhead costs incurred for a restricted period when executing a job, or for long-term monitoring of portions of overhead costs. Regardless of the cost center structure and the business processes of the organization, overhead cost orders collect the plan and actual costs incurred. This allows costs to be controlled continuously. The overhead costs assigned to the overhead cost orders are settled (in full) as costs to cost centers, orders, WBS elements, or profitability segments.

Overlapping A means of reducing the lead time by starting the next operation before the current operation is finished. The system calculates the operation start and finish dates in such a way that the overlapped operations can be processed without interruption. This is done taking into account the minimum send-ahead quantity and the minimum overlap time.

Partial confirmation A partial confirmation is the confirmation of an operation that is still being processed.

Pegged order Function for determining the requirements quantities and dates of intermediate products and finished products that are the source of a fixed and planned receipt at a specific production level. The pegged order is used to determine which assemblies and planned or customer-independent requirements are not covered if delivery or production is delayed or incomplete.

Pegged requirement In the evaluations for material requirements planning (MRP), the pegged requirement shows the order from the next higher level of the bill of material (BOM) that is the source of the requirement in a lower level.

Pegging Evaluation that displays the source requirements or the source procurement proposal of a chosen material requirements planning (MRP) element. This evaluation is used to check which planned independent requirements are endangered if certain procurement proposals are cancelled or if dates or quantities in the procurement proposal are changed.

Period indicator This indicator specifies the period of time that consumption values and forecast values are to be stored in the system.

Period lot sizing procedure
Procedure that groups together requirement quantities from one or several periods to form a lot size. Costs incurred from storage, from setup procedures, or from purchasing operations are not taken into account. The number of periods that are grouped together into a procurement proposal can be defined as desired. Lot sizes can be daily, weekly, monthly, or according to flexible period length (accounting periods).

Phase   A subdivision of an operation in the process industry. Phases can be arranged in sequential or parallel order. A phase can have materials from the material list allocated to it. Phases have the same primary resource as the operation.

Picking   The process of issuing and grouping certain partial quantities (materials) from the warehouse on the basis of goods requirements from the sales or the production department. Picking can be done using transfer orders or picking lists.

Planned costs   Costs anticipated for a particular undertaking (such as an order).

Planned delivery time   Number of days required to procure the material via external procurement.

Planned independent requirement   Planned requirement quantity for a finished product over a given period of time. It is not based on sales orders.

Planned lot size   Lot size value that the system uses as a default during costing. The non-proportional costs refer to this value.

Planned order   Request created in the planning run for a plant to trigger the procurement of a plant material for a certain quantity for a specific date.

Planned order date   The creation date, planned order date, and order finish date of order proposals are called "basic dates." They are calculated in material requirements planning (MRP).

Planned withdrawal   Issue of a material with reference to a reservation. A planned withdrawal is carried out on the basis of a reservation list and, as a rule, results in the updating of the total consumption (usage) statistics for the material.

Planning file entry   Material entry in the planning file. The system creates the entry automatically when a material has been changed in a way that is relevant to materials planning. The material is entered in the planning file as soon as it has been created with a valid material requirements planning (MRP) type.

Planning hierarchy   A user-defined combination of characteristics from an information structure that is used in Sales & Operations Planning (SOP). It allows both top-down and bottom-up planning, and therefore the integration of centralized and decentralized planning functions.

Planning horizon   The planning horizon is the period that is set for the "net change planning in the planning horizon." For this type of net change planning, the only materials planned in the planning run are those that have a change relevant to material requirements planning (MRP) within the period (in work days). At a minimum, the planning horizon should include the following: period in which customer orders enter, delivery times, and complete material processing time.

Planning ID   A planning identification (ID) is a key that makes possible a grouping of different materials in terms of time and location for planning and evaluation purposes. For example, you can assign a planning identification to all materials that are manufactured on a particular production line.

Planning material A planning material is required in the *planning with planning material* planning strategy. Non-variable parts for similar finished products can be planned using this strategy. The planning material is then assigned to the material master record of the finished products to be planned. Planned independent requirements are created for the planning material. Incoming sales orders consume the planned independent requirements of the planning material.

Planning plant Plant in which, after order execution, the goods receipt takes place for the material produced. The planning plant can be used, e.g., if Sales and Distribution is to be organized as an independent plant.

Planning run Execution of materials planning for all materials or assemblies that have the necessary entries in the planning file. The planning run is divided into four main work steps: net requirement calculation, lot size calculation, procurement element/type determination, and scheduling.

Planning run type There are three different types of planning runs: regenerative planning, net change planning, and net change planning in the short-term planning horizon.

Planning segment Line segment that controls the display of the order quantity in the planning table. The planning table displays a line for the planning segment in the

screen area Material data. In this line you can test the planned orders scheduled in the line segment, and if necessary change them. You define the planning segment in the line hierarchy. You can change the planning segment from the planning table.

Planning table profile Contains sub-profiles for controlling the structure, appearance, and behavior of the graphic planning table as well as the graphic objects that it also contains.

Planning table The planning table in repetitive manufacturing assists the planner in planning production quantities by lines. The planning table makes it possible to check production quantities at a glance and to determine the actual capacity load utilization of production lines, as well as check the availability situation of materials.

Planning time fence Defined period in which no automatic changes are carried out to the master plan during material requirements planning (MRP). Within the planning time fence, no new planned orders are created automatically, and already existing planned orders are not changed automatically.

Planning version In Sales & Operations Planning (SOP), one or more versions of the planning data in an information structure can exist. This allows you to maintain multiple plans of the same information structure in parallel. For example, you might plan your data several times using different forecasting techniques, or with the inclusion and then exclusion of events you expect to happen in the future. The active version is A00. The active version normally acts as the definitive version. All other versions are inactive.

Plant data collection   Collection and display of operational plant data and any related information on its processing, preparation, evaluation, and transfer. This information is used to accumulate required data on machine use, order status, quality, and so on. Plant data collection information is basically either person- and machine-related messages (clock-in/clock-out times, off-site work, setup, and processing times, quantities, and malfunctions) or statistics (machine use, scrap, and malfunction data).

Plant maintenance   Measures taken to maintain operational systems in working order (e.g., machines, production installations). According to DIN 31051, maintenance comprises the following activities: inspection (all measures that determine the actual condition of an operational system), maintenance (all measures that maintain the target condition of an operational system), and repair (all measures that restore the target condition of an operational system).

PPC planning calendar   The definition of flexible period lengths at a plat level. In Production Planning (PP), the PPC planning calendars can be used to define procurement dates for determining period sizes. In the stock and requirements list, and in the material requirements planning (MRP) list, MRP elements can be grouped into period totals according to the specifications in the PPC planning calendar. The planning calendar can also be used for creating periodicity and aggregating scheduling agreement releases (MM).

Preliminary costing   Process that determines the planned costs for objects such as orders.

Primary costs   Costs that arise through the consumption of goods and services that originate from outside the company.

Primary resource   The primary resource is the processing unit or reaction vessel at which an operation is carried out. It is committed for the duration of the operation, which means that all the phases of this operation are automatically carried out at this primary resource.

Process control   All the activities of measuring, controlling, and regulating processes, regardless of whether or not they are carried out manually or automatically.

Process data documentation
A component of PP-PI used to generate lists of quality-relevant production data and store them in an optical archive. In process data documentation, you can archive batch records and order records.

Process data request   Process instruction that specifies that process control is to send a process message with actual process data to the SAP ERP system. A process data request contains the following information: the process message category to be used for the process message and the information to be provided by process control.

Process instruction   Structure used to transfer data or instructions from PP-PI to process control. Process instructions are allocated to the phases of the master recipe and the process order. They are combined in a control recipe and transferred to process control for execution. Depending on the type of information sent, there are the following types of process instructions: process parameters, process data requests, process message subscriptions, process data calculation formulas, inspection data requests, dynamic function calls, and sequence definitions.

Process instruction characteristic
A characteristic of a characteristics group released for use in process instructions. Process instruction characteristics are allocated to process instructions either directly or via the instruction category. Along with the corresponding characteristic values, they determine the information transferred or requested in a process instruction (e.g., the status of a control recipe) and how the requested data is to be processed (e.g., the message category to be used to report the data).

Process management   A component of PP-PI that represents the interface to process control. Process management comprises the following functions: receiving released process orders from process planning, creating control recipes from process order data, passing on control recipes to the line operator or process control system involved, receiving, checking, and distributing process messages, and manual entry of process messages.

Process manufacturing   The processing of gases, granular materials, or liquids. The manufacturing processes involved can be continuous or discontinuous.

Process material   Material type that is designed particularly to represent the manufacture of co-products. A process material is not a physical entity. It merely represents a production process. When manufacturing co-products, you can use process materials as the header material in the bill of material (BOM) and master recipe. This is useful if production is not initiated by material requirements planning (MRP), e.g., but by the availability of ingredients and capacities. You can create process orders both for the process material and co-product. Values and quantities are updated at the co-product level.

Process message   A structure used to send actual data on a process from process control to one or several destinations of the following types: other SAP ERP components, user-defined ABAP/4 tables, users of the SAPoffice Mail system, and external function modules. Process messages are used to update existing data records, as well as to generate batch and production records. The content of process messages is determined by the process message characteristics as well as by the characteristic values assigned to them.

Process message destination
A user or component to which process messages are sent for processing. The SAP ERP system supports the following types of message destinations: SAP ERP function mod-

ules, user-defined ABAP/4 tables, users of the SAPoffice Mail system, and external function modules.

Process order Manufacturing order used in process industries.

Process planning Detailed planning of process orders. This involves the scheduling of operations, the checking of material availability, and the release of process orders for production.

Process structure The task of the process structure is the design of process flows in an enterprise. Process flows are procedures for completing business tasks that may be processed sequentially or in parallel.

Procurement proposal Material requirements planning (MRP) element that is generated if a material shortage occurs. Procurement proposals are saved in the system in the form of planned orders, purchase requisitions, or delivery schedules.

Procurement type Classification determining whether a material is produced in-house, externally, or both.

Product costing Tool for planning costs and establishing prices. Product costing calculates the cost of goods manufactured and the cost of goods sold per product unit. Products are costed automatically using the bills of material (BOMs) and routings in Production Planning (PP).

Product group Groups together products (materials). The criteria by which this grouping takes place can

be defined individually by each user. For example, the products may be similar to each other in some way, or they may be finished products that were produced on the same machine. A product group can be multilevel or single-level. A product group is multilevel if its members are other product groups. However, the lowest product group in the hierarchy must contain materials.

Production campaign Grouping of planned orders and process orders to produce a certain amount of a material over a certain period of time. This is done in an uninterrupted sequence on one production line.

Production cost collector Object in cost accounting used in repetitive manufacturing and kanban production control. A separate production cost collector can be created for each production version or material. The collected costs are settled to inventory at the end of the period. Actual costs result from the following business transactions: final backflush, reporting point backflush, internal activity allocation, revaluation of activities at actual prices, and overhead calculation. The functions performed for production cost collectors during the period-end closing process include: work in process (WIP) calculation, variance calculation, and settlement.

Production costs Portion of the cost of goods manufactured that consists of the following costs: direct cost of production (direct labor), production overhead costs, and special direct costs of production.

Production line Combination of several processing stations or an individual processing station. A production line is used in flow and repetitive manufacturing as a work station. Production lines represent the processing stations in flow and repetitive manufacturing. Therefore, you can combine individual processing stations in a purely logical fashion through a production line by creating it as a work center. However, for every processing station, you can also create separate work centers or production lines and represent this structure using a line hierarchy.

Production lot Particular production quantity of an assembly (finished product or semi-finished part) that is planned and produced along with reference to a number. Using this number, you can determine the costs for the production of a production lot. The number of the production lot is, from a technical standpoint, a WBS element that the system creates when the user creates the number.

Production order Production document used for discrete manufacturing.

Production overhead Costs incurred in production that are not or cannot be assigned to particular cost objects.

Production plan Production plans are created in the planning table of Sales & Operations Planning (SOP). Production targets can be set for materials, product groups, and/or

characteristic values from an information structure and derived from sales targets or using self-defined or standard macros.

Production rate Control parameters for takt-based and rate-based scheduling in sequencing. Rates are defined for a production line. The following types exist:
- Maximum rate: The maximum quantity you can produce on a production line per time unit.
- Planned rate: Quantity that you want to produce per time unit in a specific period.
- Operative rate: Overrides the planned rate in order to react to short-term changes in supply or requirements.

Production resource/tool Moveable operating resource used in production or plant maintenance.

Production series A group of materials of limited duration that share similar characteristics.

Production storage location Default storage location for component withdrawal for final processing as well as the goods receipt of the product. The production storage location is determined, e.g., in the material master for a material.

Production type Method of production, such as order-related production or repetitive manufacturing.

Production version Determines the various production techniques that can be used to produce a material. The production version specifies the bill of material (BOM) alternative for a BOM explosion, the task list type, the task list group, and the group counter for the allocation to task lists, lot size restrictions, and area of validity.

Pull list Helps determine which components a production line needs and when and where these components should be made available. The quantities given in the list are the result of a comparison between requirements and the stock available at a production storage location. The pull list can be used to pull the required quantities from the distribution center.

Purchase order Request or instruction from a purchasing organization to a vendor (external supplier) or a plant to deliver a certain quantity of material or to perform certain services at a certain point in time.

Purchase requisition Request or instruction for purchasing to procure a certain quantity of a product or a service so that it is available at a certain point in time.

Purchasing info record Source of information on the procurement of a certain material from a certain vendor.

Purchasing organization Organizational unit within Logistics that subdivides an enterprise according to purchasing requirements. A purchasing organization procures materials and services, negotiates purchase conditions with vendors, and bears responsibility for such transactions.

Quality management Broad term for quality-related activities and objectives. Activities for quality planning, quality inspection, quality control, and QM representation.

Quality notification Description of nonconformance of a business object, with a quality requirement. In addition, the quality notification includes a request to take appropriate action.

Queue time A float that can be used to compensate for delays in the production process. It can be maintained in the work center or in the operation.

Quota arrangement Mechanism enabling the system to compute which source of supply is to be assigned to a requirement that has arisen for a material. The quota arrangement facilitates determination of the applicable sources of supply for a purchase requisition at a certain point in time. The setting of quotas permits the automatic apportionment of a total material requirement over a period to different sources. A quota arrangement consists of quota arrangement records identifying the source (vendor, internal plant, etc.), the validity period, and the quota.

Range of coverage Number of days you plan for a material to be available to prepare for fluctuations in requirements. The work scheduler defines the range of coverage as a number of days for which a material has to be available, and the system creates corresponding order proposals, if necessary. The system also calculates the range of coverage in material requirements planning (MRP) evaluations, in order to enable the work scheduler to see how many days' requirements are covered by the material available. This applies to the days' supply, the receipt days' supply, and the statistical range of coverage.

Rate-based planning Rate-based planning operates under the capacity- planning planning type to prevent bottlenecks in resources for production-rate-related production. Rate-based planning generally takes place via rate routings.

Rate of capacity utilization The percentage difference between actual capacity and the capacity that is theoretically available.

Rate routing A routing that can be used in repetitive manufacturing for planning production quantities/volumes. You can define the production quantity and a fixed reference point for each operation in a rate routing and therefore determine the production rate.

Recipe The general instructions for the use of a production process. There are manufacturing recipes describing a production process as well as non-manufacturing recipes, which check to see that all functions of a resource are working perfectly, or which carry out the clearing or changeover of a line. Master recipes and control recipes are manufacturing recipes, while changeover recipes, setup recipes, and clean-out recipes are non-manufacturing recipes.

Recipe counter Key that uniquely identifies a recipe in a recipe group.

Recipe group Grouping of recipes that describe alternative production processes. Together with a recipe

counter, a recipe group uniquely identifies a recipe.

Recipe material list A list containing all materials required to execute a process order as well as their quantity specifications.

Reorder point If the amount of stock on hand of a material falls below this quantity, an entry is automatically set in the material requirements planning (MRP) file for the material.

Reference operation set Routing type that defines a sequence of operations that is repeated regularly. A reference operation set is created to reduce the effort of entering data in a routing.

Reference rate routing Task list type that defines a sequence of operations that is repeated regularly. A reference rate routing is used to reduce the effort of entering data in rate routings.

Release period Number of workdays between the planned start date of the production order and the date for releasing the order. If the order release indicator is set, the production order is released by a background program that takes all dates into account.

Remaining capacity requirements Capacity requirements in a work order or planned order that have not yet been reduced.

Reorder point planning Special procedure in material requirements planning (MRP). If the reorder point is greater than warehouse stock, a procurement proposal is created by

MRP. A distinction is made between automatic reorder point planning and manual reorder point planning.

Repetitive manufacturing A component in the SAP system for the planning and control of repetitive manufacturing and flow manufacturing. It enables the period-dependent and quantity-dependent planning of production lines, reduces the work involved in production control, and simplifies backflushing (confirmation and goods receipt posting).

Repetitive manufacturing profile A collection of data that determines which variant of repetitive manufacturing should be used for a certain material (repetitive manufacturing with production cost collector or with production orders).

Replenishment lead time Total time for the in-house production or for the external procurement of a product. With in-house production, the replenishment lead time covers all bill of material (BOM) levels.

Reporting point An operation in repetitive manufacturing that is flagged as a milestone in the routing. When carrying out a reporting point backflush, the system backflushes all the materials that have been withdrawn and consumed between two reporting points.

Reporting point backflush Type of backflush in repetitive manufacturing in which several operations in the processing sequence can be backflushed automatically. Using the reporting point backflush procedure, you can backflush components close to actual consumption.

From the Controlling view, it is possible to display work in process for assemblies that have not completely been backflushed. The repetitive manufacturing profile determines whether the reporting point backflush can be carried out for a material; you use the control key to determine whether an operation is a reporting point operation (milestone). If an operation is a reporting point operation, all previous operations are backflushed automatically together. If several operations are marked as reporting points, the system should backflush components according to the processing sequence of the reporting point operations. The system backflushes up to the previous reporting point.

Requirement Quantity of material that is required in a plant at a certain point in time.

Requirements grouping Grouping together of the material requirements of different project stock owners (WBS elements) under one WBS element in order to carry out joint requirements planning.

Requirements planning Method of guaranteeing material availability both internally and externally. Requirements planning involves the procurement of goods on time, the monitoring of stock levels, and the automatic generation of order proposals. Requirements planning can be both consumption-driven or requirements driven. Stocks can be planned for all the plants in a company.

Requirements type Classification of the various independent requirements into customer requirements, planned independent requirements, or warehouse requirements, for example.

Reservation   Request to the warehouse or stores to keep a material ready for issue at a future date for a certain purpose. The purpose of a reservation is to ensure that a material is available when required. A material can be reserved for a cost center, an asset, or an order, for example.

Reserved stock   Sum of all quantities of a material reserved for withdrawal from stock.

Resource   Means of production and persons involved in a production process that have capacities assigned to them. Resources are subdivided into resource categories, such as production line, labor, and storage.

Resource category   A grouping of resources of the same kind. A resource category is user-defined via Customizing. You can, e.g., define the following resource categories: line, processing unit, team, labor, transport, storage, and service.

Resource network   Description of the physical links between resources, such as processing units (reactors, vessels, etc.) in a plant. A resource network describes the flow of materials through a plant.

Routing   Description of the production process used to manufacture plant materials or provide services in the production industry. Routing type that defines one or more sequences of operations for the production of a material. To re-

duce the effort of entering data in a routing, you can reference or copy reference operation sets as many times as required and in any sequence.

Routing header   Part of the routing that contains data that is valid for the entire routing. For example, the following data is stored in the header: (task list) group, group counter, plant, short description, status, usage, header unit of measure, lot size interval, planner group.

Run schedule header   Determination of a valid production version to be used when producing a plant material in repetitive manufacturing and of a time period for collecting the costs.

Run schedule quantity   A quantity that is to be manufactured in a certain period. Technically speaking, run schedule quantities are created as planned orders. Unlike the other planned orders, run schedule quantities do not have to be released and converted into production orders.

Safety stock   Quantity of stock held to satisfy unexpectedly high requirements in the stocking-up period. The purpose of the safety stock is to prevent a material shortage from occurring. In order to determine the safety stock level, you must first specify the risk of a material shortage and also the desired service level. Usually the safety stock will not be used in production.

Sales & Operations Planning (SOP)
A forecasting and planning tool with which sales, production, and

other supply chain targets can be set on the basis of historical, existing, and/or estimated future data. Resource planning can also be carried out to determine the amount of work center capacities and other resources required to meet these targets.

Sales and operations plan Sales quantities and the resulting production quantities for a material/plant (SKU) or product group in a specific planning horizon. The difference between the production quantity and the sales quantity in any month is the closing stock for that month.

Sales order A customer request to a company for the delivery of goods or services at a certain time. The request is received by a sales area, which is then responsible for fulfilling the contract.

Sales order costing Method of costing that costs the items in a sales order. You can also cost the items in inquiries and quotations.

Sales order stock Defined quantity of a product that is held in stock and required for the execution of a sales order. The sales order stock is committed to a particular sales order. Components can only be used to produce the product ordered by the customer, and the product produced can only be delivered to the customer with reference to the relevant order.

Sample One or several units taken from the inspection lot (population) to gain information about the quality of the inspection lot. The word "sample" is used to describe distinguishable (discrete) units, e.g., piece goods that are subject to a sampling procedure.

Scheduling In scheduling, the system calculates the start and finish dates of orders or of operations within an order. Scheduling is carried out in material requirements planning (MRP). The in-house production times and the delivery times specified in the material master record are taken into account. In capacity planning, scheduling is carried out using routings. A distinction is made between lead time scheduling, in which capacity loads are not taken into account, and finite scheduling, in which capacity loads are taken into account. In networks scheduling calculates the earliest and latest dates for the execution of the activities as well as the capacity requirements and the floats. The following scheduling types exist:

▸ Forward scheduling (scheduling starting from the start date)
▸ Backward scheduling (scheduling starting from the finish date)
▸ Midpoint scheduling (combined forward and backward scheduling, starting from any midpoint activity in an order)
▸ "Today" scheduling (a scheduling type that can be used to reschedule an order if the start date is in the past)
▸ Scheduling to current date (scheduling starting from the current date)

Scheduling work center Work center that is used for scheduling and capacity planning in flow manufacturing and repetitive manufacturing. If you have not defined a line hierarchy, the production line is the scheduling work center. If you have maintained a line hierarchy for a production line, you define a work center in the line hierarchy as a scheduling work center. This term is used in line design.

Scrap Percentage of a material that does not meet quality requirements.

Seasonal trend model Model used for a seasonal trend consumption pattern. A seasonal trend consumption flow is characterized by a continual increase or decrease of the mean value.

Secondary resource Resource that is required in addition to the primary resource and can be assigned to an operation or a phase (such as an operator or a transportation container). Secondary resources can be assigned a start/finish time that is relative to the start/finish time of the operation or phase (time offset).

Semi-finished product Unfinished product. Describes the material type.

Sequence Sequence of operations that are sorted according to operation number. By defining various sequences in routings or inspection plans, you can create structures that are similar to networks but less complex. The following sequence categories are distinguished in routings: standard sequence, alternative sequence, and parallel sequence.

Sequence definition Process instruction that you use at the start of a phase to specify that this phase can only be processed in the PI sheet after you have finished processing another phase. By generating sequence definitions automatically, you can copy the phase relationships maintained in the process order to the PI sheet. In the PI sheet, the process instructions of the phase containing the sequence definition remain inactive until all message data has been reported for the predecessor phases. The system only recognizes phases that belong to the same PI sheet.

Sequence schedule Product of sequencing. The system presents the sequence of planned orders graphically in the sequence schedule.

Sequencing Determines the sequence in which planned orders are produced. The order sequence of the finished products for a line is represented graphically in the sequence schedule. The sequence schedule displays the exact schedule, which is time-dependent, per line or per line segment. Therefore, sequencing is a tool for sequence plan scheduling in flow and repetitive manufacturing.

Serial number Number that you give to an individual item of material in addition to the material number, in order to differentiate that individual item from all the other items of the material. Each serial number is unique.

Service Intangible good that is the subject of business and that can be performed internally or procured externally (outsourced). Services are regarded as being consumed at the time of their performance. They cannot be stored or transported. Examples of services include construction work, janitorial/cleaning services, and legal services.

Settlement Full or partial allocation of calculated costs from one object to another. The following objects can be settlement senders: internal orders, maintenance orders, CO production orders, production orders, process orders, service orders, general cost objects, sales order items, networks, and projects. The following objects can be settlement receivers: assets, internal orders, profitability segments, cost centers, sales order items, materials, networks, projects, and general ledger accounts.

Setup The act of preparing a work center for the operation to perform there.

Setup group category Groups together the setup group keys. For example, you can combine lathes with different setup group keys to form a setup group category called "Turning."

Setup group key Key used in routings to group operations with the same or similar setup conditions. The setup group key can be used in capacity leveling to optimize the setup time. This is done by determining the setup sequence with the shortest setup times.

Setup time The time needed to prepare the work center for the operations to be carried out there. The setup time is part of the lead time.

Shift definition The start, finish, and break times of a shift are determined in the shift definition. Shift definitions reduce the work involved in determining available capacity when working hours change because they are maintained centrally.

Shift sequence A sequence of shifts defined for several work centers for a period of time. Updating shift sequences centrally reduces the work of changing the order of shift definitions.

Shop floor papers Documents required for carrying out a work order, including operation control tickets, job tickets, pick lists, time tickets, and confirmation slips.

Single-level BOM Represents all components that are used to map one or more assemblies. The single-level bill of material (BOM) contains the immediate components of an assembly. Components that represent assemblies by themselves are not further exploded.

Special stock Stocks of materials that have to be managed separately for reasons of ownership or factors involving the location at which they are kept (e.g., consignment stocks from vendors).

Standard available capacity The standard available capacity refers to the available capacity of a certain capacity category. It is valid if no interval of available capacity has been defined. The standard available capacity is specified by entering work start time, work finish time, breaks, and rate of capacity utilization.

Standard BOM Bill of material (BOM) that is used internally only in the following areas: plant maintenance and standard networks. The components of a standard BOM represent frequently occurring structures that are not object-dependent and can be allocated to the activities in a project-independent standard network.

Standard cost estimate The most important type of cost estimate in material costing. Forms the basis for profit planning or product costing where the emphasis is on determining the variances. A standard cost estimate for each product is usually created once at the beginning of the fiscal year or new season. Standard cost estimates calculate the standard prices for semi-finished products and finished products. The costs calculated in standard cost estimates are used to valuate materials with standard price control.

Standard costing Type of product costing. Standard costing allows for considering obvious variations to the planned costs of goods manufactured by using MRP-based changes to the valuation approaches without creating a new standard cost estimate.

Standard plan A plan in which employees are automatically enrolled.

Standard sequence Sequence of operations that describes a production process, and from which parallel and alternative sequences can branch. The first sequence of operations maintained in a routing is automatically stored as the standard sequence.

Standard trigger point A standard trigger point is a reference object used to create trigger points. By using standard trigger points, you can minimize the effort involved in creating trigger points.

Static lot sizing procedure Procedure in which the lot size is calculated using the entered quantities in the material's material master record. Costs incurred from storage, from setup procedures, or from purchasing operations are not taken into account. There are three different criterions according to which the lot size can be calculated: lot-for-lot order quantity (exact lot size), fixed lot size, and replenishment up to maximum stock level.

Stock Materials management term for part of a company's current assets. It refers to the quantities of raw materials, operating supplies, semi-finished products, finished products, and trading goods or merchandise on hand in a company's storage facilities.

Stock determination Cross-application function allowing you to determine the stock from which material is to be withdrawn in the course of stock removal, order picking, and staging operations.

Stock in quality inspection Portion of total valuated stock that is currently undergoing quality inspection. The stock in quality inspection is not freely available.

Stock in transfer Quantity of a material that (in a physical stock transfer using the two-step procedure) has already been taken out of stock at the point of issue but has not yet arrived at the point of receipt. Stock in transfer is part of valuated stock at the point of receipt but cannot yet be labeled "unrestricted-use." Stock in transfer comprises the quantity transferred through transfer postings within Inventory Management but does not include the quantity transferred on the basis of stock transport orders. The latter type of stock is termed "stock in transit."

Stockkeeping unit Unit of measure in which stocks of a material are managed. The system converts all quantities that have been created with a different unit of measure into the stockkeeping unit. The term "stockkeeping unit" is exclusively an SAP Inventory Management term and is synonymous with the term "base unit of measure" used in other applications.

Stock material Material that is constantly kept in stock (e.g., a raw material). A stock material has a material master record and is managed on a value basis in a material stock account.

Stock/requirements list Up-to-date overview of a material's stock situation, which is generated using a function that draws together all the current and relevant data (production orders, sales orders, and so on). Therefore, it always shows the most up-to-date availability situation for a material, as opposed to the material requirements planning (MRP) list, which reflects the stock/requirements situation at the time of the last planning run.

Stock transport order Purchase order used to request or instruct a plant to transport material from one plant to another within the same enterprise. The stock transport order allows delivery costs incurred as a result of the stock transfer to be debited to the material that was transported.

Stock type Means of subdividing storage location stock or special stock. The stock type indicates the usability of a material. The storage location stock and special stocks on a company's own premises are subdivided into three different types: unrestricted-use stock, stock in quality inspection, and blocked stock.

Storage costs Costs incurred from the storage of a material. They are recorded in the material master record as a percentage of the valuation price and are referred to by optimizing lot sizing procedures during the lot size calculation.

Storage location An organizational unit facilitating differentiation between the various stocks of a material within a plant.

Storage location MRP In storage location material requirements planning (MRP), the planning run is carried out at the storage location level. The storage location stock is not contained in the available stock at the plant level. Instead, it is planned separately. The following possibilities are available:

▸ The storage location is excluded from the planning run. If the storage location is excluded from materials planning, then the storage location stock is neither included in the available stock, nor is materials planning carried out for it. The storage location stock is available for stock withdrawal without limitations.

▸ The storage location is planned separately. If you have defined a reorder point and a replenishment level for storage location MRP, the system can monitor the storage location stock automatically. When the stock level falls below the reorder point, the system creates a procurement proposal for the replenishment quantity. The net requirements calculation is, however, limited to the storage location.

Subcontracting   The processing (by an external supplier) of materials provided by a customer. The result of this processing is the manufacture by the supplier (subcontractor) of an ordered material or product, or the performance by the supplier of an ordered service.

Subcontracting component
Material made available by a customer to a subcontractor to enable the latter to execute an order placed with them by the customer.

Sub-item   Subdivision of a bill of material (BOM) item. The difference between one sub-item and others is the installation point. A sub-item has no control functions in the BOM. It can be used to help create company-specific automatic assembly programs.

Supply area   Area in the shop floor where a material is provided that can be directly used for production. The supply area is used in Kanban production control and for material staging using Warehouse Management (WM), for example.

Takt   Physical areas of a production line where work takes place. A material passes through one takt of the production line in the minimum takt time, where it is processed. In line design you can define the number of takts for the individual line

segments of a line hierarchy. The total number of takts therefore determines the length of a production line.

Takt area   Physical area in which a material is processed within the takt time. Each processing center on the lowest level of the line hierarchy corresponds to one takt area. The system totals the number of takt areas on the lowest level to display the amount of takt areas covered by the upper levels. This term is used in Line Design.

Takt-based scheduling   Contrary to lead time scheduling using the routing, takt-based scheduling takes place depending on the length of the production line (which is defined by the number of takts) and/or the takt times or rates. You determine how long a material remains in a takt and the time interval in which a material enters or leaves the line.

Takt time   Control parameters for takt-based scheduling in sequencing. Takt times are defined for a production line. The following three types of takt times exist:

▶ Minimum takt time: Time for which a material remains in one takt of the production line for processing.

▶ Planned takt time: Interval of time in which a product enters the production line and a processed product leaves the production line.

▶ Operative takt time: Overwrites the planned takt time in order to react to short-term changes in requirements and supply.

Task list Describes the non-order-related process for implementing an activity. The main objects of a task list are: task list headers, operations, material assignments, production resources/tools, and inspection characteristics. If the task list objects have deadlines and quantities, an order is created. Examples: routings, reference operation sets, rate routings, maintenance task lists, inspection plans, standard networks, and master recipes.

Task list group A task list group combines task lists that describe similar production processes or that are used to produce similar materials. A task list group can be used, e.g., to group task lists with different lot size ranges. In conjunction with the group counter, the task list group uniquely identifies a task list.

Task list header Part of a task list that contains data that is valid for the entire task list. Typical data in the task list includes: usage, planner group, status, lot size range, and header unit of measure.

Task list type Classifies task lists according to their functionality. In PP, the following task list types are used: routing, reference operation set, rate routing, and standard rate routing

Teardown time The time needed to restore a work center to its normal state after the operations have been processed. The teardown time is part of the execution time.

Test equipment Measurement equipment that is used during quality inspections. Generally speaking, test equipment denotes equipment, instruments, papers, and materials required during the quality inspection (inspection tools). Test equipment can be fixed pieces of equipment at a work center or moveable instruments and objects. Test equipment can be defined in various degrees of detail in the inspection plan using different types of master records: material master records, production resource/tool (PRT) master records, document master records, and equipment master records.

Time-phased materials planning Type of materials planning in which the materials are planned according to a specific cycle. If a vendor always delivers a material on a certain day of the week, it makes sense to carry out the planning run according to the same cycle and displaced by the delivery time.

Trend model Model for a consumption flow that represents a trend. You have a trend if consumption values fall or rise constantly over a long period of time, with only occasional deviations.

Trend value Part of the forecast model displaying the past level of the forecast model during forecasting. For trend models and seasonal trend models, the system determines the increase in value with the trend value and updates the increase with it. The trend value is first calculated by means of the past values of the system, but it can also be entered manually. After this, the system updates the trend value after processing every period using the beta factor.

Trigger point Trigger points are used to trigger certain functions when the status of an operation changes. A trigger point can be assigned to an operation in a routing or an order. The user specifies conditions in a trigger point via parameters. The specified function is only carried out if these conditions are met.

Trigger point group A combination of standard trigger points. When you assign a trigger point group to an operation, you automatically assign all the standard trigger points in the group. By using trigger point groups, you can minimize the effort involved in creating trigger points.

Unit costing Method of costing that does not use bills of material (BOMs) or routings. Unit costing calculates planned costs for base planning objects and also supports detailed cost planning for objects such as material cost estimates without a quantity structure, additive costs, orders, cost objects, projects, and sales document items.

Unplanned consumption Difference between total consumption and planned consumption. Unplanned consumption is updated if goods are withdrawn from stock without a reservation. On the other hand, planned consumption is updated if goods are withdrawn on the basis of a reservation.

Unplanned withdrawal Issue of a material without reference to a reservation. As a rule, unplanned withdrawals result in the updating of the figures for total and unplanned consumption in the consumption (usage) statistics for the material.

Valuated stock Stock of a material belonging to a firm that is part of the firm's current assets. Various procedures can be applied to valuate stock. The valuated stock of a material at a plant is the sum of unrestricted-use stock held at all storage locations, stock in quality inspection at all storage locations, and stock in transfer at the storage location and plant levels.

Valuation area Organizational unit in Logistics subdividing a company for the purpose of valuating material stocks in a uniform and consistent manner.

Variable cost Portion of the total cost that varies with the operating rate and the lot size.

Variant BOM Combination of a number of bills of material (BOMs) that enables you to describe a product or several products that have a large proportion of identical parts. The variant BOM describes each object (e.g., the product "lamp") completely. Each variant BOM contains all the components. This type of BOM is not configurable.

Variant configuration Description of complex products that are manufactured in many variants (e.g., cars). All variants are defined as one variant product. The variant product has a super bill of material (BOM), containing all the components that can be used the product, and a super task list, containing all the operations that can be used to manufacture the product. By assigning the variant product to a class, you assign characteristics to the variant product. You use these characteristics to describe an individual variant. Object dependencies ensure that the correct components are selected from the super BOM and the correct operations are selected from the super task list.

Vendor Business partner from whom materials or services can be procured.

Wait time Time between the end of the execution time and the start of move time. The SAP system distinguishes between maximum wait time and minimum wait time. In scheduling, only the minimum wait time is taken into account. The maximum wait time is only used for informational purposes.

Warehouse stock A quantity of material in a storage bin differentiated according to various stock criteria. Warehouse stock can also be recorded for different batches or for different movement types separately (if materials are valuated separately). Stock that belongs to business partners and order-specific stock is classified as special stock in storage bins.

Work center An organizational unit that defines where and when an operation should be carried out. The work center has a particular available capacity. The activities performed at or by the work center are valuated by charge rates, which are determined by cost centers and activity types. Work centers can be: machines, people, production lines, or groups of craftsmen.

Work center hierarchy The representation of a structure in which work centers and their relationships to each other are displayed in levels. Work center hierarchies are used within capacity planning to cumulate available capacities or capacity requirements. The hierarchy can also be used to locate work centers.

Work in process (WIP) Unfinished products whose costs are calculated in one of two ways:
▸ By calculating the difference between the actual costs charged to an order and the actual costs credited to an order
▸ By valuating the "yield confirmed to" date for each milestone or reporting point, less the relevant scrap.

Work order An order that specifies a task to be carried out within the company. The term "work order" is a generic term for the following order types: production orders, process orders, inspection orders, maintenance orders, and networks.

Work scheduler group Key used to differentiate between the departments responsible for planning (work scheduling, inspection planning, and so on). For example, these groups may be responsible for processing specific materials, orders, or routings.

B   List of Transactions

For quick reference, the transactions described in the individual chapters are summarized in the following tables.

B.1   Organizational Structure and Master Data

Transaction	Description	Customizing
EC01	Company code	x
EC02	Plant	x
OX18	Assignment Plant – Company Code	x
OX09	Storage Location	x
OPJ9	Production Scheduler	x
MM01/MM02	Create/Change Material Master	
CS01/CS02	Create/Change BOM	
OS13	Item Category for BOM	x
OS23	BOM Status	x
OS20	BOM Usage	x
CS11	Multilevel BOM Explosion	
CS15	Where-Used BOM	
CR01/CR02	Create/Change Work Center	
OP40	Work Center Category	x
OP45	Task List Usage	x
OP4A	Shift Sequence	x
CR11/CR12	Create/Change Capacity or Pooled Capacity	
OPCX/OP7B	Parameter for Standard Value	x
OPCM	Standard Value Key	x
OP21	Formula	x
CR21/CR22	Create/Change Work Center Hierarchy	

Table B.1 Transactions for Organizational Structure and Master Data

Transaction	Description	Customizing
CA01/CA02	Create/Change Routing	
OPJ8	Control Key	x
CF01/CF02	Create/Change Production Resource/Tool with Master Record	

Table B.1 Transactions for Organizational Structure and Master Data (cont.)

B.2 Sales and Operations Planning

Transaction	Description	Customizing
MC21/MC22	Create/Change Information Structure	x
MC7F	Planning Parameters of the Information Structure	x
MC84/MC85	Create/Change Product Groups	
MC91	Graphical Presentation of Product Groups	
MC61	Create Planning Hierarchy	
MC62	Planning Hierarchy – Edit Proportional Factors	
MC9A	Generate Master Data for Flexible Planning	
MC8U	Calculate Proportional Factors based on Actual Data (consistent planning)	
MC9B	Calculate Proportional Factors based on Planning Hierarchy (consistent planning)	
MC8A/MC8B	Create/Change Planning Type	
MC87/MC88	Create/Change Standard SOP (material)	
MC81/MC82	Create/Change Standard SOP (product group)	
MC8M	Determine Opening Stock in the Background	
MC76/MC77	Create/Change Two-Level Planning Table for Aggregation and Disaggregation (Standard SOP)	
MC93/MC94	Create/Change Flexible Planning	
MC96	Forecast Profile	x
MC64/MC65	Create/Change Event	

Table B.2 Transactions for Sales and Operations Planning

Transaction	Description	Customizing
MC35/MC36	Create/Change Rough-Cut Planning Profile	
MC74	Transfer Standard SOP to Demand Management (material)	
MC75	Transfer Standard SOP to Demand Management (product group)	
MC90	Transfer Flexible Planning to Demand Management	
MC7A	Plant Distribution	x
MC8T	Mass Processing Activity	
MC8S	Transfer Profile	
MC8Z	Copy Profile	
MC8D/MC8E	Create/Change Mass Processing Job	
MC8F	Delete Mass Processing Job	
MC8G	Schedule Mass Processing Job	
SM37	Job Overview	
MC8I	Mass Processing Job Status	

Table B.2 Transactions for Sales and Operations Planning (cont.)

B.3 Demand Management

Transaction	Description	Customizing
OMPO	Requirements Class for Planned Independent Requirements	x
OMP1	Requirements Type for Planned Independent Requirements	x
MD61/MD62	Create/Change Planned Independent Requirements	
OMJJ	Transaction Types	x
MD74	Reorganization of Planned Independent Requirements	

Table B.3 Transactions for Demand Management

B.4 Material Requirements Planning

Transaction	Description	Customizing
OMI4	MRP Lot Size, Storage Costs Indicator	x
OWD1	Rounding Profiles	x
CS01/CS02	Create/Change BOM	
CA01/CA02	Create/Change Routing	
OPPP	Alternative BOM Selection	x
MP30/MP31	Create/Change Individual Forecast	
MP38	Overall Forecast	
MMBE	Stock Overview	
MD21	Planning File	
MD43	Interactive Material Requirements Planning	
MD02	Multilevel MRP	
MD03	Single-Level MRP	
MD11/MD12	Create/Change Planned Order	
ME51N/ME52N	Create/Change Purchase Requisition	
MD04	Requirements/Stock List	
MD05	MRP List	
OPPQ	Plant Parameters	x
OPPR	MRP Group	x

Table B.4 Transactions for Material Requirements Planning

B.5 Long-Term Planning

Transaction	Description	Customizing
MS31/MS32	Planning Scenario	
MS29	Determine Average Plant Stock	
OS31	BOM Usage Priority Order	x
MS21	Planning File Entries for Planning Scenario	

Table B.5 Transactions for Long-Term Planning

Transaction	Description	Customizing
MS01	Online MRP Run (Planning Scenario)	
MSBT	Background MRP Run (Planning Scenario)	
MS02	Single-Item Planning, Single-Level (Planning Scenario)	
MS03	Single-Item Planning, Multilevel (Planning Scenario)	
MS65	Change Planned Independent Requirement (Planning Scenario)	
MS11	Create Simulative Planned Order	
MS04	Requirements/Stock List (Planning Scenario)	
MS05	MRP List (Planning Scenario)	
MS44	Material Planning Situation (Planning Scenario)	
MS47	Product Group Planning Situation (Planning Scenario)	
CM38	Capacity Requirements Work Centers (Planning Scenario)	
MFS0	Graphical Planning Table (Planning Scenario)	
MCB&/MCB)	Inventory Controlling Analysis (Planning Scenario)	
MCEC	Purchasing – Material Analysis (Planning Scenario)	
MCEA	Purchasing – Supplier Analysis (Planning Scenario)	
MCEB	Purchasing – Material Group Analysis (Planning Scenario)	
MS70	Build Data in Purchasing Information System (Planning Scenario)	
MS64	Copy Planned Independent Requirement Version	
MD62	Activate Planned Independent Requirement Version	

Table B.5 Transactions for Long-Term Planning (cont.)

B.6 Production Order Creation

Transaction	Description	Customizing
CO01/CO02	Create/Change Production Order	
OPJH	Order Type	x
OPJK	Check Control	x
OPU3	Scheduling Profile	x
OPL8	Order Type-Dependent Parameters	x
OPJF	Automatic Selection of Alternative Plan	x
OPJI	BOM Selection ID	x
OPJM	Assign Selection ID to BOM Usage	x
OS32	BOM Selection by Due Date	x
CO31/CO32	Create/Change Standard Trigger Point	
CO40	Individual Conversion of Planned Order	
CO41	Collective Conversion of Planned Order	
CO07	Production Order Creation Without Material Reference	
SCAL	Maintain Factory Calendar	x
OPJN	Maintain Scheduling Types	x
OP67	Control Key	x
OPJR	Location Groups and Move Time Matrix	x
OPJS	Reduction Strategy	x

Table B.6 Transactions for Production Order Creation

B.7 Capacity Planning

Transaction	Description	Customizing
CM01	Capacity Evaluation – Standard Overview	
CM02	Capacity Evaluation – Detailed Capacity List	
CM03	Capacity Evaluation – Pool of Orders/ Operations	

Table B.7 Transactions for Capacity Planning

Transaction	Description	Customizing
CM50	Capacity Evaluation – Extended Selection Work Center View	
CM52	Capacity Evaluation – Extended Selection Order View	
CM07	Capacity Evaluation – Variable View	
OPA6	Capacity Evaluation – Overall Profile	x
OPA2	Selection Profile	x
CMS1/CMS2	Create/Change Selection Sets	x
OPA3	Option Profile	x
OPA4	List Profile	x
OPA5	Graphics Profile	x
OPJK	Check Control	x
OPKP	Production Control Profile	x
OPD0	Overall Profile of Capacity Availability Check and Scheduling	x
OPDB	Strategy Profile	x
OPD1	Selection Profile	x
OPDE	Control Profile	x
OPD3	Evaluation Profile	x
OPD2	Time Profile	x
OPDH	List Profile	x
CY39	Layout Key	x
OP43	Setup Group Categories and Setup Group Keys	x
OPDA	Setup Matrix	x
CM40	Mass Planning for Capacity Leveling	
SM37	Job Overview	
CM41	Scheduling Job Logs	

Table B.7 Transactions for Capacity Planning (cont.)

Transaction	Description	Customizing
CM21	Graphical Planning Table (Entry via Work Center)	
CM22	Tabular Capacity Planning Table (Entry via Work Center)	

Table B.7 Transactions for Capacity Planning (cont.)

B.8 Production Execution

Transaction	Description	Customizing
CO05N	Collective Release for Production Orders	
CO04N	Shop Paper Printing	
MB1A	Material Withdrawal for Production Order	
CO27	Picking	
OSPX	Stock Determination Rule	x
OPJ2	Assign Stock Determination Rule to Business Transaction	x
CO11N	Time Ticket Confirmation	
OPJ8	Control Key	x
CO1F	Progress Confirmation	
CO15	Order Confirmation	
CO14	Display Confirmations	
CO13	Cancel Confirmation	
OPKP	Production Scheduler Profile	x
MB31	Goods Receipt for Production Order	
COHV	Production Order Mass Processing	

Table B.8 Transactions for Production Execution

B.9 Integration with SAP APO

Transaction	Description	Customizing
CFM1	Generate Integration Models	
CFM2	Activate Integration Models	

Table B.9 Transactions for the Integration with SAP APO

C   List of Abbreviations

APO	Advanced Planner and Optimizer
ATP	Available to Promise
CAD	Computer Aided Design
CIM	Computer Integrated Manufacturing
CO-PA	Controlling, Profitability Analysis
DP	Demand Planning
EDP	Electronic Data Processing
ERP	Enterprise Resource Planning
GMP	Good Manufacturing Practices
HR	Human Resources
LIS	Logistics Information System
MM	Materials Management
MRP	Material Requirements Planning
NC	Numeric Control
PDC	Plant Data Collection
PDS	Production Data Structure
PM	Plant Maintenance
PP	Production Planning
PPM	Production Process Model
PPS	Production Planning System
PRT	Production Resource/Tool
PS	Project System
PSA	Production Supply Area
QM	Quality Management
SD	Sales and Distribution
SIS	Sales Information System
SNP	Supply Network Planning
SOP	Sales and Operations Planning
TP/VS	Transportation Planning and Vehicle Scheduling
WBS	Work Breakdown Structure

D   Literature

Arnolds, H.; Heege, F.; Tussing, W.: Materialwirtschaft und Einkauf. 9th edition. Wiesbaden 1996.

AWF—Ausschuß für wirtschaftliche Fertigung e. V. (Eds.): AWF-Empfehlung – Integrierter EDV-Einsatz in der Produktion – CIM (Computer Integrated Manufacturing). Eschborn 1985.

Bäck, H.: Erfolgsstrategie Logistik. München 1984.

Bartels, H.-G.: Logistik. In: Albers, W. (Eds.): Handwörterbuch der Wirtschaftswissenschaft. Stuttgart et al. 1980, pp. 54–73.

Bloech, J.: Problembereiche der Logistik. In: Schriften zur Unternehmensführung. Issue 32. Wiesbaden 1984, pp. 5–30.

Bowersox, D.-J.: Logistical Management. New York, London 1974.

Bullinger, H.-J.; Niemeyer, J.; Huber, H.: Computer Integrated Business (CIB)-Systeme. In: CIM Management. 2 (1987) 3, pp. 12–19.

Datta; S.: mySAP High Tech – Branchenlösung für die Elektronikindustrie. In: Kagermann, H.; Keller, G. (Eds.): SAP-Branchenlösungen – Business Units erfolgreich managen. Bonn 2001, pp. 145–172.

Dickersbach, J. T.: Characteristic Based Planning with mySAP SCM. Berlin, Heidelberg 2005a.

Dickersbach, J. T.: Supply Chain Management with APO. 2n edition. Berlin, Heidelberg 2005b.

Diedenhoven, H.: Für die NC-Programmierung nutzbarer Gehalt von CAD-Daten. In: CAE-Journal. (1985) 5, pp. 58–65.

DIN – Deutsches Institut für Normung (Eds.): Normung von Schnittstellen für die rechnerintegrierte Produktion (CIM). Fachbericht 15. Berlin, Köln 1987.

Dittrich, J.; Mertens, P.; Hau, M.; Hufgard, A.: Dispositionsparameter von SAP R/3-PP. 3rd edition. Wiesbaden 2003.

Eversheim, W.: Organisation in der Produktionstechnik – Arbeitsvorbereitung. 2n edition. Düsseldorf 1989.

Geiger, K.; Kerle, M.: mySAP Automotive – Branchenlösung für die Automobilindustrie. In: Kagermann, H.; Keller, G. (Eds.): SAP-Branchenlösungen – Business Units erfolgreich managen. Bonn 2001, pp. 69–95.

Glaser, H.: Material- und Produktionswirtschaft. Düsseldorf 1986.

Glaser, H.; Geiger, W.; Rohde, V.: PPS – Produktionsplanung und -steuerung. Wiesbaden 1991.

Grabowski, H.: CAD/CAM-Grundlagen und Stand der Technik. In: Fortschrittliche Betriebsführung und Industrial Engineering. 32 (1983) 4, pp. 224–233.

Grochla, E.: Grundlagen der Materialwirtschaft. 3rd edition. Wiesbaden 1978.

Hack, S.: Collaborative Business Maps – Prozessintegration über Unternehmensgrenzen hinweg. In: Kagermann, H.; Keller, G. (Eds.): SAP-Branchenlösungen – Business Units erfolgreich managen. Bonn 2001, pp. 325–350.

Hackstein, R.: Produktionsplanung und -steuerung (PPS). 2nd edition. Düsseldorf 1989.

Harrington, J.: Computer Integrated Manufacturing. New York 1973.

Hoitsch, H. J.: Produktionswirtschaft – Grundlagen einer industriellen Betriebswirtschaftslehre. München 1985.

Hüllenkremer, M.: Rechnerunterstützte Arbeitsplanerstellung im CIM-Konzept. In: Krallmann, H. (Eds.): CIM – Expertenwissen für die Praxis. München, Wien 1990, pp. 48–57.

Keller, G.: Informationsmanagement in objektorientierten Organisationsstrukturen. Wiesbaden 1993.

Keller, G.; Curran, T.: SAP R/3 – Prozesse analysieren und anwenden. Sonderdruck der DEKRA Akademie. Bonn 1999.

Keller, G. & Partner: SAP R/3 prozeßorientiert anwenden. 3rd edition. Bonn 1999.

Kief, H. B.: NC/CNC-Handbuch. Michelstadt 1989.

Kilger, W.: Industriebetriebslehre. Wiesbaden 1986.

Kilger, W.: Flexible Plankostenrechnung und Deckungsbeitragsrechnung. 9th edition. Wiesbaden 1988.

Kirsch, W.: Betriebswirtschaftliche Logistik. In: Zeitschrift für Betriebswirtschaft. 41 (1971), pp. 221–234.

Kosiol, E.: Organisation der Unternehmung. Wiesbaden 1962.

Kühn, M.: CAD und Arbeitssituation – Untersuchungen zu den Auswirkungen von CAD sowie zur menschengerechten Gestaltung von CAD-Systemen. Berlin et al. 1980.

Lederer, K. G.: EDV-gestützte Kommunikationssysteme in der Automobilindustrie. In: Fortschrittliche Betriebsführung und Industrial Engineering. 33 (1984) 1, pp. 23–29.

Maier-Rothe, C.; Busse, K.; Thiel, R.: Computerverbundsysteme planen, steuern und kontrollieren den Produktionsprozeß. In: Maschinenmarkt. 89 (1983) 8, pp. 106–109.

Meffert, H.: Marketing – Grundzüge der Absatzpolitik. 7th edition. Wiesbaden 1986.

Nordsieck, F.: Betriebsorganisation. 4th edition. Stuttgart 1972.

Pahl, G.; Beitz, W.: Konstruktionslehre. 2nd edition. Berlin et al. 1986.

Pfohl, H.-C.: Logistiksysteme – Betriebswirtschaftliche Grundlagen. 5th edition. Berlin et al. 1996.

Rembold, U. et al.: CAM-Handbuch. Berlin et al. 1990.

SAP AG (Eds.): Funktionen im Detail – Ergebnis- und Vertriebs-Controlling. Walldorf 1996.

SAP AG (Eds.): Funktionen im Detail – Produktionsplanung. Walldorf 1996.

Schäfer, E.: Der Industriebetrieb – Betriebswirtschaftslehre der Industrie auf typologischer Grundlage. Volume 1. Köln, Opladen 1969.

Scheer, A.-W.: Factory of the Future – Vorträge im Fachausschuß "Informatik in Produktion und Materialwirtschaft" der Gesellschaft für Informatik e. V. In: Scheer, A.-W. (Eds.): Veröffentlichungen des Instituts für Wirtschaftsinformatik. Issue 42. Saarbrücken 1983.

Scheer, A.-W.: CIM – Der computergesteuerte Industriebetrieb. 4th edition. Berlin et al. 1990.

Scheer, A.-W.: Wirtschaftsinformatik – Informationssysteme im Industriebetrieb. 3rd edition. Berlin et al. 1990.

Schomburg, E: Entwicklung eines betriebstypologischen Instrumentariums zur systematischen Ermittlung der Anforderungen an EDV-gestützte Produktionsplanungs- und -steuerungssysteme. Aachen 1980.

Schneeweiß, C.: Einführung in die Produktionswirtschaft. 5th edition. Berlin et al. 1993.

Spur, G.: Die Roboter verschwinden in der automatischen Fabrik. In: VDI-Nachrichten. 38 (1984) 52, pp. 6.

VDI VEREIN DEUTSCHER INGENIEURE (Eds.): VDI 2210 Entwurf: Datenverarbeitung in der Konstruktion – Analyse des Konstruktionsprozesses im Hinblick auf den EDV-Einsatz. Düsseldorf 1975.

Venitz, U.: CIM-Rahmenplanung. Berlin et al. 1990.

Wöhe, G. Einführung in die Allgemeine Betriebswirtschaftslehre. 19th edition. München 1996.

E   The Authors

Dr. Jörg Thomas Dickersbach works as a Solution Architect for supply chain management at SAP AG. His work focuses on project reviews, critical implementation projects, and workshops on specific SCM-related subjects. Since 1998, he has been engaged in modeling and implementing logistical processes in the industries of discrete manufacturing, high-technology, consumer goods, chemicals, and pharmaceuticals using SAP programs. He worked as a consultant for five years at SAP Deutschland AG & Co. KG and IMG AG.
E-mail: *dickersbach@gmx.de*

Having been awarded a doctor's degree by Prof. Dr. August-Wilhelm Scheer, **Dr. Dipl.-Kfm. Dipl.-Ing. Gerhard Keller** was responsible for method development and the structuring of reference processes for the SAP ERP system (formerly R/3 system) at SAP AG. Gerhard Keller is a shareholder and partner of Bonpago GmbH, Germany (*www.bonpago.de*), where he is responsible for value-based consulting and advanced development of concepts and new approaches in the areas of strategy, processes, and IT for industrial enterprises and financial service providers. In addition, he is an associate lecturer for process management and architectures in the information management section of the Central European Master of Business Administration (CeMBA) program at the European School of Management (ESCP-EAP).
E-mail: *keller@bonpago.de*

Klaus Weihrauch joined SAP in 1990 where his work focuses on the Production Planning and Control solution (PP). Among other things, he created the data and process model for the R/3 PP component and was responsible for the production planning area in AcceleratedSAP. Klaus Weihrauch currently manages projects in the area of best practices for SAP SCM, in which preconfigured solutions for supply chain management are created.

Index

Understanding the SAP Logistics Information System

www.sap-press.com

Martin Murray

Understanding the SAP Logistics Information System

Gain a holistic understanding of LIS and how you can use it effectively in your own company. From standard to flexible analyses and hierarchies and from the Purchasing Information System to Inventory Controlling, this book is full of crucial information and advice.
Learn how to fully use this flexible SAP tool that allows you to collect, consolidate, and utilize data. Learn how to run reports without any ABAP experience thus saving your clients both time and money.